Margit V. Wunsch Gaarmann

The War in Our Backyard
The Bosnia and Kosovo Wars through the Lens of the German Print Media

Margit V. Wunsch Gaarmann completed her PhD in International History at the London School of Economics and Political Science (LSE) in 2013. Currently, Wunsch Gaarmann is the project coordinator for a research project on the First World War at the Freie Universität Berlin.

Margit V. Wunsch Gaarmann

The War in Our Backyard

The Bosnia and Kosovo Wars through the Lens of the German Print Media

Neofelis Verlag

The work on this PhD-thesis was kindly supported
by the Konrad Adenauer Stiftung.

German National Library Cataloguing in Publication Data
A catalogue record for this book is available from the German National Library:
http://dnb.d-nb.de

Cover Design: Marija Skara
Printed by PRESSEL Digitaler Produktionsdruck, Remshalden
Printed on FSC-certified paper.
ISBN (Print): 978-3-95808-011-9
ISBN (PDF): 978-3-95808-056-0

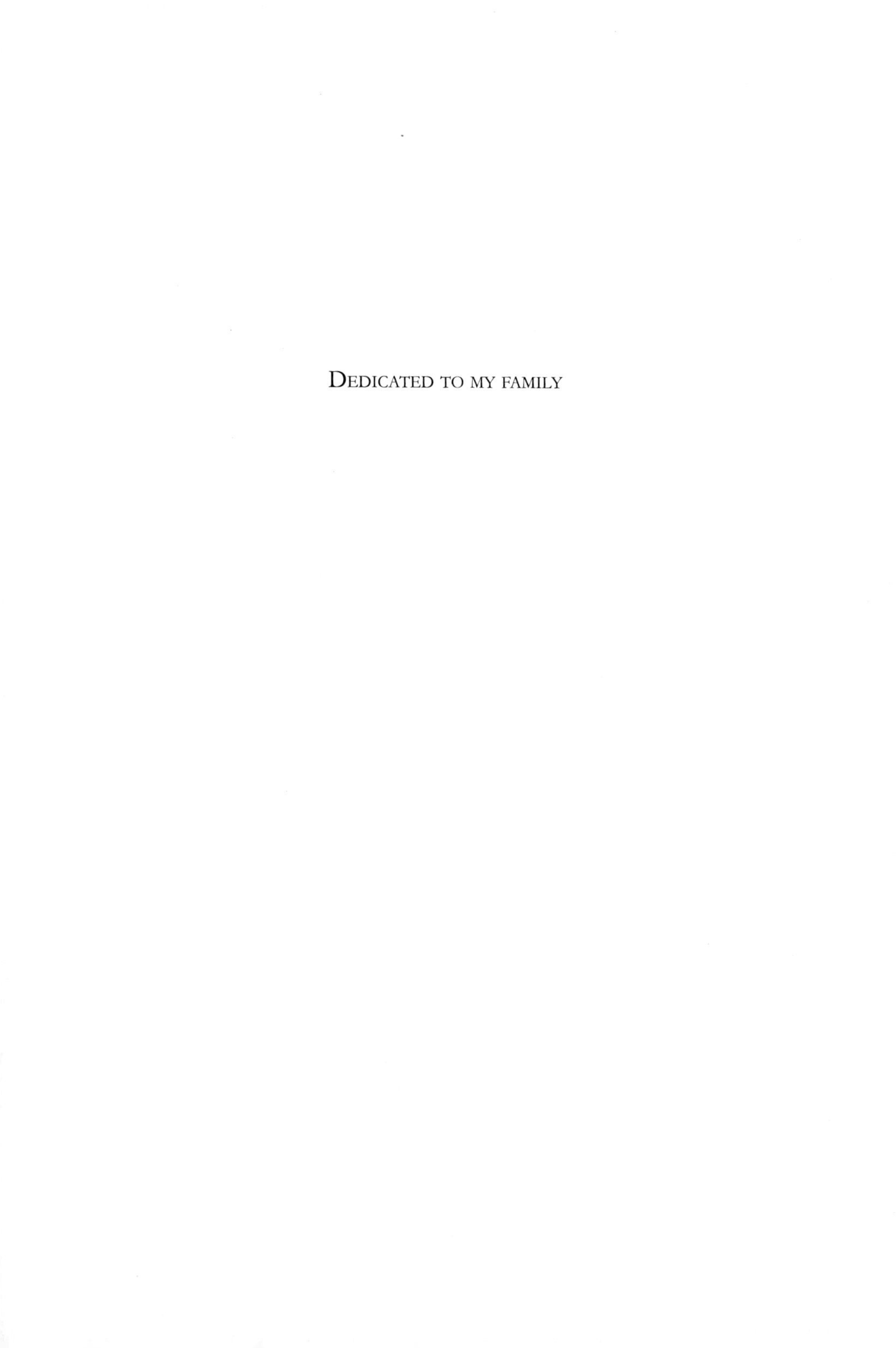

DEDICATED TO MY FAMILY

Contents

Acknowledgements

I would like to express my sincere gratitude to my former PhD supervisor, Professor Mia Rodriguez-Salgado whose guidance and scrutinising feedback significantly shaped my research and this manuscript. A big thank you to Dr. Kristina Spohr and Professor Brendan Simms for their helpful comments and insights on a previous draft. The PhD scholarship from the Konrad-Adenauer-Foundation generously funded my research for this book, for which I am very grateful.

I would also like to thank Burkhard Mohr, Renate Behrendt-Müller, Walter Hanel, Horst Haitzinger, Christian Jungeblodt, Thomas Körner, Felix Mussil's family, Livio Senigalliesi and Klaus Stuttmann for allowing me to use their photos and cartoons in this book.

A big thank you to Mathias Gaarmann, Edith Wunsch, Thalia Gigerenzer, Kyle Chan, Claudia Bacon, Julien Bacon and Zhong Zhong Chen for their helpful advice on various chapters of this book. Lastly, I would like to thank my parents, Udo and Hertha Wunsch who have supported and encouraged me for so many years.

Remarks

When writing about the diverse and war-torn Balkan region, the mere reference to a locality in its Bosnian, Serbo-Croatian or Albanian form can indicate allegiance to one national narrative. I have chosen the form most common in the English language, which happens to be Serbo-Croatian in most cases. Consequently I refer to Kosovo rather than Kosova or Kosovë; Račak instead of Reçak and Priština in the place of Prishtinë or Prishtina, to name a few examples. The only exception is in direct citations from primary sources and secondary literature. This does not reflect any partisanship with a particular national narrative or interpretation of history. Accordingly, terms such as Chetnik and Ustasha will be used in its anglicised form. Direct citations may use different spellings, such as Četnik or Ustaša.
For ease of reading I have translated the German sources to English. All translations are my own, unless stated. None of the material, including images, can be reproduced without permission from the original copyright holder.

Introduction

"...They are herding them to the concentration camp" ("...Sie treiben sie ins KZ") was the headline chosen by the German tabloid *BILD* on their front page on 1 April 1999. A picture of a long refugee trek, with hundreds of desolate Kosovo-Albanians carrying their few remaining belongings following the Serbian ethnic cleansing that had unfolded in Kosovo since 1998, accompanied this headline.[1] The context for this story was a statement made by the German Minister of Defence, Rudolf Scharping (SPD), who had claimed that 'genocide' was unfolding and that concentration camps existed in Kosovo. Scharping had used this argumentation to justify the first German engagement in active combat since the Second World War, which had begun mere days earlier, on 24 March 1999.

Aside from *BILD*, a number of German broadsheets including *Frankfurter Allgemeine Zeitung*, *Die Welt*, *die tageszeitung* and *Frankfurter Rundschau* reported Scharping's claim of 'genocide' occurring in Kosovo.[2] Notably, the headlines and articles were less sensational, though the message conveyed was the same: "Scharping: Strong Indication of Concentration Camps existing in Kosovo" (*Welt*)[3] or "[...]Scharping is also speaking of genocide" (*FR*)[4].

1 Anonymous: ...Sie treiben sie ins KZ. In: *BILD*, 01.04.1999, p. 1.

2 Martin S. Lambeck / Martina Fietz: Scharping: Starke Hinweise auf Existenz von Konzentrationslagern im Kosovo. In: *Die Welt*, 01.04.1999, p. 1; Alfred Dregger: Den Krieg beenden. In: *Frankfurter Allgemeine Zeitung* [henceforth *FAZ*], 06.04.1999, p. 16; Markus Franz: Fischer: „Jetzt nicht wackeln". In: *die tageszeitung* [henceforth *taz*], 01.04.1999, p. 1; dpa/rtr/ap: Albanien prangert „barbarische" Gewalt an. In: *Frankfurter Rundschau* [henceforth *FR*], 29.03.1999, p. 1; ap/afp/rtr/dpa: Nato bombt an Ostern weiter. In: *FR*, 01.04.1999, p. 3.

3 Lambeck und Fietz: Scharping: Starke Hinweise auf Existenz von Konzentrationslagern im Kosovo. In: *Die Welt* [Henceforth *Welt*], 01.04.1999, p. 1.

4 Monika Kappus: Die leicht geneigte Haltung eines Lastenträgers. In: *FR*, 01.04.1999, p. 1.

However one week later, these claims could not be substantiated and indeed were disproven by photographic evidence of the alleged concentration camp site taken by *Bundeswehr*-drones. Significantly, none of the papers that had quoted Scharping, rectified the error, leaving the German public with the lasting impression that concentration camps existed in Kosovo and that elements of the Holocaust were re-occurring in Europe over fifty years after the Second World War had ended.[5]
Was this a singular example of bad journalism or do more examples corroborate this impression of fragmentary research, poor reporting and hysterical headlines? Were allusions to the Second World War concertedly used by politicians and newspapers to present their argument regarding German involvement in the wars in Bosnia and Kosovo? These questions form the crux of this book, which analyses the German print media coverage of the wars in Bosnia and Kosovo in the 1990s.

In the early 1990s, Europe found itself in a whirlwind of political changes: the 1989 revolutions in Eastern Europe, the fall of the Berlin Wall in the same year, Germany's unification in 1990, as well as the collapse of the Soviet Union in 1991. In this larger context, right in Europe's backyard, Yugoslavia descended into a decade of violence that enveloped Slovenia (1991), Croatia (1991–1995), Bosnia (1992–1995) and later Kosovo (1998–1999), all with a varying degree of intensity. This book examines the last two wars in detail. Bosnia had a pre-war population of approximately 4.3 million. The bitter four-year war was marked by war crimes and displaced more than 2.2 million people according to the UN Refugee Agency (UNHCR).[6] The death toll of the war remains disputed, ranging between the more recent estimate of 102,000[7] and initial approximations of 200,000[8]. Several years after Bosnia had been pacified, violent conflict intensified in Kosovo. Until the cessation of violence in June 1999, there had been approximately 10,000 fatalities (an

5 For a detailed discussion of this topic, see p. 241.

6 *Scott Pohl / Naveed Hussain:* Jolie Highlights the Continuing Suffering of the Displaced in Bosnia. http://www.unhcr.org/print/4bbb422512.html (accessed 20.08.2014), and Mark Cutts: The Humanitarian Operation in Bosnia, 1992–95: Dilemmas of Negotiating Humanitarian Access. UNHCR Policy Research Unit, Working Paper No. 8. http://www.unhcr.org/3ae6a0c58.pdf (accessed 20.08.2014).

7 Ewa Tabeau / Jakub Bijak: War-related Deaths in the 1992–1995 Armed Conflicts in Bosnia and Herzegovina. A Critique of Previous Estimates and Recent Results. In: *European Journal of Population* 21,2 (2010), pp. 187–215, here p. 207.

8 Nedim Dervišbegovic: Revised Death Toll for Bosnian War.. http://www.bosnia.org.uk/news/news_body.cfm?newsid=1985 (accessed 20.08.2014).

upper estimate) and 90% of Kosovo's population of 2 million people had been forced to leave their homes.[9]

Meanwhile, back in Germany, the average citizen was trying to make sense of the Balkan conflicts, turning to the national media as a main source of information. Why had violence erupted? What armed forces were engaged in conflict? Who were the victims and who the perpetrators? Was Germany getting involved? If so, why? The international coverage of the wars in Bosnia and Kosovo is frequently associated with the famous quote "the first casualty when war comes, is truth" which is attributed to the American Senator Hiram Johnson, though the Greek philosopher Aeschylus has also been credited. The common perception reinforced by this quotation is that rather than reporting 'the truth', 'the media' manipulated public opinion to support the controversial international interventions in Bosnia and Kosovo.[10]

However, none of these claims are substantiated by elaborations how 'the media' manipulated, to what extent its impact on public opinion is measurable, what important information was concealed and to what effect. Phillip Knightley's monograph *The First Casualty: The War Correspondent as Hero and Myth-Maker from the Crimea to Kosovo* is one such example. Knightley – an avid opponent of the NATO-intervention in Kosovo – claims that the alliance had a monopoly of information, which he argues NATO used to manipulate the media in its favour. However, most of his claims remain unsupported. For example he posits that NATO-members had a "[…] meticulously prepared system of propaganda and media control […which] swung into action […]" as the bombardment of Serbia and Kosovo commenced in March 1999. Thus Knightley suggests that all media outlets in the 19 member-states, ranging from Turkey to Canada, acted in coordination without explaining how this was done or who may have spearheaded such an endeavour. Without

9 Mark Webber: The Kosovo War: A Recapitulation. In: *International Affairs* 85,3 (2009), pp. 447–459, here p. 451, and U.S. State Department: Erasing History: Ethnic Cleansing in Kosovo, May 1999. http://balkanwitness.glypx.com/erasing-history.pdf (accessed 20.08.2014).

10 Some literature that proportes this claim include: Thomas Deichmann: From "Never Again War" to "Never Again Auschwitz": Dilemmas of German Media Policy in the War against Yugoslavia. In: Philip Hammond / Edward Herman (eds): *Degraded Capability: The Media and the Kosovo Crisis*. London: Pluto 2000, pp. 153–163; Barry Lituchy: Media Deception and the Yugoslav Civil War. In: Clark Ramsey (ed.): *NATO in the Balkans: Voices of Opposition*. New York: International Action Center 1998; Heather Cottin / Alvin Dorman: War Propaganda Aimed at Jewish Opinion. In: Ramsey Clark (ed.): *NATO in the Balkans: Voices of Opposition*. New York: International Action Center 1998, pp. 210–219; Michel Collon: *Media Lies and the Conquest of Kosovo: NATO's Prototype for the Next Wars of Globalization*. New York: Unwritten History 2007; Jürgen Elsässer: *Nie wieder Krieg ohne uns: Das Kosovo und die neue deutsche Geopolitik*. Hamburg: Konkret 1999.

giving sources for his claims, he vaguely stated that pressure was exerted "…in NATO-countries to publish atrocity stories from Kosovo…"[11] While Knightley's claims could be plausible, his unsubstantiated assertions render his work unreliable. Nonetheless, it must be noted that no research has been produced disproving these wide-spread allegations of NATO manipulating information during the Kosovo War. Consequently, such charges suggesting intrigue call for an in-depth examination of this coverage, which this book offers by examining a wide range of examples of the German press.

Analysing the textual and visual coverage of the violence in Bosnia and Kosovo in nine German national publications – namely *Die Welt*, *Frankfurter Allgemeine Zeitung* (*FAZ*), *Frankfurter Rundschau* (*FR*), *die tageszeitung* (*taz*), *BILD-Zeitung*, *Der Spiegel*, *Junge Freiheit* (*JF*), *Konkret* and *Allgemeine Jüdische Wochenzeitung* (*AJW*) – forms the basis of this book. These newspapers reflect the political spectrum from far-right *(JF)* to far-left *(Konkret)*, while simultaneously including broadsheets *(Welt, FAZ, FR, taz)*, a tabloid *(BILD)*, a newsmagazine *(Spiegel)*, and a weekly newspaper targeting Germany's Jewish population *(AJW)*. This selection encapsulates the plurality of views present in German society. Consequently, rather than referring to the blanket term of the 'German media', the analysis of various distinct publications enables a differentiated interpretation. *AJW*, a weekly, later bi-weekly cultural newspaper published by the Central Council of Jews in Germany (*Zentralrat der deutschen Juden)*, did not aim to report on daily political events. Rather it picked up on certain topics when they impacted Jewish life around the world. Consequently, *AJW* did not always report on the wars in Bosnia and Kosovo with much detail, or at all. Nonetheless, the coverage is an important perspective for the analysis conducted in this book and will therefore be drawn upon in chapters 3 and 8.

In the course of this analysis, it is not my intention to test the content of the German press coverage according to veracity or against a universally accepted narrative of events – which rarely exists in any case. Rather, I present and analyse what the publications reported and how certain interpretations and viewpoints were communicated. In addition, analysing the German press' visual content – in the form of pictures and cartoons – proves to be a valuable facet of the German press' reporting. Both types of visual material offer a distinctive medium that can express more subtle viewpoints which are at times left unsaid in texts. Moreover, cartoons feature a format in which

11 Phillip Knightley: *The First Casualty: The War Correspondent as Hero and Myth-Maker from the Crimea to Kosovo.* Baltimore: Johns Hopkins University Press 2002, p. 508.

opinion can be expressed much more bluntly than in text. The nature of caricatures demands the condensation of complex subject matters to effectively communicate a desired message. The reliance on stereotypes in this process reveals important nuances regarding a publication's views of a conflict as well as the actors involved, and is therefore also a crucial element of an in-depth media analysis.

The examination of the wars in Bosnia and Kosovo through the prism of selected German publications offers a unique narrative of recent events that differs distinctly from the more common diplomatic history. A press analysis exposes the interpretations presented to the broad public as the conflicts unfolded, which were tailored to a non-specialist, yet often targeted readership and written without the benefit of hindsight. While of course television was an omnipresent factor in the news cycle of the 1990s, the print media nevertheless played a crucial role in informing the public, as well as initiating and reporting on important debates. Studying the coverage of this near decade of violence and warfare in nine publications demands a condensation of the period. Consequently this book focuses on three key timeframes from each war. The first part – consisting of three chapters – examines the Bosnian War, studying the initial phase of the conflict, the Srebrenica Massacre, and lastly the international involvement which ended the immediate violence, namely the diplomatic negotiations in Dayton, USA. The second part of the book analyses the Kosovo War and also consists of three chapters. Again, the early phase of the conflict is studied first, followed by a chapter on an incident of mass violence in Račak. The last chapter scrutinises the international involvement in the region that ended the violence, namely the early period of NATO's bombardment of Serbia and Kosovo.

The German press is a particularly interesting case study for two reasons. Firstly, as will be elaborated momentarily, both conflicts in Bosnia and Kosovo were instrumental in shaping Germany's post-unification foreign policy. Having accomplished the unification of East and West Germany in 1990, the country which had become the demographically largest in Western Europe faced questions regarding its role within the European Community (EC)/European Union (EU), the North Atlantic Treaty Organisation (NATO) and the world in general. While Chancellor Helmut Kohl had assured the world that Germany's post-unification future would be inextricably linked to Europe,[12] it

12 Kristina Spohr: German Unification: Between Official History, Academic Scholarship, and Political Memoirs. In: *The Historical Journal* 43,3 (2000), pp. 869–888, here p. 878.

remained unclear how this would reflect in the realities of the country's foreign policy when confronted with war in Europe. Secondly, the violence in Bosnia, which some observers termed 'genocidal', raised questions about the extent to which collective memory of the Holocaust should influence Germany's foreign policy towards the Balkans. How would Germany negotiate the politics of collective memory and the duties of membership in a military alliance when faced with the deployment of soldiers into active combat, as was the case in Kosovo? Such matters naturally consumed the country's policymakers. However, analysing how they were conveyed to the German public in the national press and to what extent these larger discourses coloured the print media's coverage of the violence in Bosnia and Kosovo offers a new understanding regarding the debates that engaged the broad public and what arguments they were presented with.

Politics of Memory: Collective Memory of the Holocaust

The emergence, evolution and transformation of collective memory in post-war West-Germany has been widely covered, both in German and English language literature.[13] A general consensus exists in the literature that 'generational memory' dominated the collective memory of the Holocaust, which is exposed most clearly in the dichotomy between the adults of the 'Adenauer Era' (1949–1963) and their children who belonged to the '1968-generation'. The latter are often linked to the student movement at German universities in the late 1960s, from where the generation derives its name, though the student movement was not an exclusively German phenomenon. A third generational shift occurred in the early 1990s, when an 'internationalisation' of the responsibility for the Holocaust developed.

The 'Adenauer era', named after Germany's first post-war Chancellor, Konrad Adenauer, was marked by two distinct attitudes: "[…]'to put this chapter behind us', [paralleled with…] an awareness of responsibility […]"[14] Jeffrey Herf elaborates the argument by claiming that a '*Schlussstrichmentalität*'

13 Wolfgang Bergem (ed.): *Die NS-Diktatur im deutschen Erinnerungsdiskurs*. Opladen: VS Verlag für Sozialwissenschaften 2003; Jeffrey Alexander et al.: *Cultural Trauma and Collective Identity*. Berkeley: University of California Press 2004; Sabine Bode: *Die deutsche Krankheit – German Angst*. Stuttgart: Klett-Cotta 2006; Hans-Joachim Hahn: *Repräsentationen des Holocaust: Zur westdeutschen Erinnerungskultur seit 1979*. Heidelberg: Winter 2005; Dan Michman: *Remembering the Holocaust in Germany, 1945–2000: German Strategies and Jewish Responses*. New York: Peter Lang 2002; Charles Maier: *The Unmasterable Past: History, Holocaust and German National Identity*. Cambridge, Mass.: Harvard University Press 1997.

14 Michman: *Remembering the Holocaust in Germany*, p. 1.

dominated the immediate post-war years and that the German people urgently desired to 'draw a line' and forget about the past.[15] Bernhard Giesen largely agrees with this conclusion, claiming that the Adenauer era was dominated by a 'coalition of silence' during which German society was overshadowed by a 'moral numbness' regarding the recent past. He contends that Germans were aware of their responsibility for the Holocaust, but were unable to face both the resulting trauma as well as the victims so shortly after the Second World War.[16]

This changed with the next generation, the colloquially-named '1968-generation,' which called for – amongst other demands – a more public awareness of Nazi crimes.[17] In his book *Utopia or Auschwitz: Germany's 1968 Generation and the Holocaust*, Hans Kundnani elaborates that the slogan "*Nie wieder Krieg*", or "never again war" became the utmost paradigm and the most important lesson from the National-Socialist past for the 1968-generation. Many individuals later found their political home in the pacifist Green Party, which was founded in 1980. Amongst them were two prominent "68-ers", Joschka Fischer, Germany's Foreign Minister between 1998 and 2005, and Daniel Cohn-Bendit, a German and French politician and Member of the European Parliament since 1994.[18]

This shift in generational memory implicated a gradually increasing public responsibility for the Holocaust. Historians have regarded the '*Betroffenheitsdiskurs*' or 'discourse of dismay' which dominated the memory culture of the 1980s and early 1990s as the climax of German collective memory. A deep, all-encompassing shame defined Germany's interpretation of its recent past, which had not existed thus far.[19] The centrality of the victims in this new discourse relegated Germany to be the 'country of perpetrators',

15 Jeffrey Herf: Remembering the Holocaust in Germany. In: Dan Michman (ed.): *Remembering the Holocaust in Germany, 1945–2000*. New York: Peter Lang 2002, pp. 9–30, here p. 11.

16 Bernhard Giesen: The Trauma of Perpetrators: The Holocaust as the Traumatic Reference of German National Identity. In: Jeffrey Alexander et al. (eds): *Cultural Trauma and Collective Identity*. Berkeley: University of California Press 2004, pp. 112–154, here pp. 116–117.

17 Bode: *Die deutsche Krankheit*, p. 135; Ludger Volmer: *Die Grünen und die Außenpolitik – ein schwieriges Verhältnis: Eine Ideen- Programm- und Ereignisgeschichte grüner Außenpolitik*. Münster: Westfälisches Dampfboot 1998; Hans Kundnani: *Utopia or Auschwitz: Germany's Generation and the Holocaust*. London: Hurst & Company 2009, pp. 1–5.

18 Kundnani: *Utopia or Auschwitz*.

19 Darius Zifonun: *Gedenken und Identität: Der deutsche Erinnerungsdiskurs*. Frankfurt am Main: Campus 2004, p. 152; Hahn, *Repräsentationen des Holocaust*, pp. 67–68; Julia Kölsch: Politik und Gedächtnis: Die Gegenwart der NS-Vergangenheit als politisches Sinnstiftungspotenzial. In: Bergem (ed.): *Die NS-Diktatur im deutschen Erinnerungsdiskurs*. Opladen: VS Verlag für Sozialwissenschaften, pp. 137–150, here p. 147.

causing communal guilt and shame to transcend the collective memory of the Holocaust.[20]

After this peak, various authors have argued that an internationalisation of the Holocaust memory and Nazi crimes in general occurred starting in the early 1990s. Lothar Probst traces this tendency in historical research, which he argues increasingly considered the role of Swiss banks, the French Vichy Regime and the analysis of various countries which had supported the persecution of the Jews and other enemies of the Nazis. Moreover, the refusal of certain European neighbours to admit Jewish refugees from Nazi-Germany was a prominent theme.[21] Here a shift occurred from blaming solely Germany to including other international actors without diminishing Germany's responsibility. Bernhard Giesen identifies this progression as a 'metaphysical guilt', which applies to all human beings, not just Germans.[22] As a result, the historical burden stemming from the Holocaust began to shape and influence global discourse on international human rights and international tribunals as well as humanitarian-motivated military interventions.[23] As the Holocaust historian Yehunda Bauer summarises, "the Holocaust has […] become the symbol for genocide, for racism, for hatred of foreigners, and of course for anti-Semitism […]"[24] This in turn has led to repeated comparisons between the Holocaust and other international crimes against humanity.

As this short excursion has demonstrated, the collective memory of the Holocaust in West-Germany evolved in various stages. Consequently, the conclusion that the Second World War and collective memory thereof influenced the German media coverage of the wars in Bosnia and Kosovo, as other media studies have deduced, must be considered with more discernment. While various other studies have concluded that the Holocaust influenced the language and interpretation of various international publications in their coverage of the violence in Bosnia and Kosovo,[25] the discourse of collective

20 Zifonun: *Gedenken und Identität*, p. 152; Hahn: *Repräsentationen des Holocaust*, p. 68.

21 Lothar Probst: Der Holocaust – eine neue Zivilreligion für Europa? In: Bergem (ed.): *Die NS-Diktatur im deutschen Erinnerungsdiskurs*, pp. 227–238, here p. 230.

22 Giesen: The Trauma of Perpetrators, pp. 144–145.

23 Wolfgang Bergem: Barbarei als Sinnstiftung? Das NS-Regime in Vergangenheitspolitik und Erinnerungskultur der Bundesrepublik. In: Id. (ed.): *Die NS-Diktatur im deutschen Erinnerungsdiskurs*, pp. 81–104, here p. 99.

24 Yehuda Bauer: *Rethinking the Holocaust.* New Haven: Yale University Press 2001, p. xi.

25 Rossella Savarese: 'Infosuasion' in European Newspapers: A Case Study on the War in Kosovo. In: *European Journal of Communication* 15,3 (2000), pp. 363–381; Reiner Grundmann / Dennis Smith / Sue Wright: National Elites and Transnational Discourses in the Balkan

memory has never been systematically applied to the international media coverage of the violence in Bosnia and Kosovo.

German Foreign Policy

Parallel to the progression of collective memory in Germany, the changing nature of post-1945 German foreign policy must be considered at this point.[26] A number of academics have argued that West-German foreign policy after the Second World War was marked by a sense of responsibility evoked by the country's previous militarism as well as the Holocaust, which resulted in an unwillingness to assert military power to attain national interests.[27] Labels such as 'tamed power' [Peter Katzenstein] or 'civilian power' [Hanns Maull] to describe Germany encapsulate this foreign policy.[28] Defining the latter term as " [...] a particular foreign-policy identity which promoted multilateralism, institution-building and supranational integration [...],"[29] Maull postulates

War: A Comparison between the French, German and British Establishment Press. In: *European Journal of Communication* 15,3 (2000), pp. 299–320; Christiane Eilders / Albrecht Lüter: Germany at War: Competing Framing Strategies in German Public Discourse. In: *European Journal of Communication* 15,3 (2000), pp. 415–428.

26 Arnulf Baring: *Germany's New Position in Europe: Problems and Perspectives.* Oxford: Berg 1994; Anja Dalgaard-Nielsen: *Germany, Pacifism and Peace Enforcement.* Manchester: Manchester University Press 2006; Scott Erb: *German Foreign Policy: Navigating a New Era.* Boulder: Lynne Rienner Publishers 2003; Adrian Hyde-Price: Germany and the Kosovo War: Still a Civilian Power? In: Douglas Webber (ed.): *New Europe, New Germany, Old Foreign Policy? German Foreign Policy since Unification.* London: Routledge 2001; Josef Janning: A German Europe – a European Germany? On the Debate over Germany's Foreign Policy. In: *International Affairs* 72,1 (1996), pp. 33–41; Rainer Lepsius: Das Erbe des Nationalsozialismus und die politische Kultur der Nachfolgestaaten des „Großdeutschen Reiches". In: Max Haller / Hans-Jürgen Hoffmann-Nowottny / Wolfgang Zapf (eds): *Kultur und Gesellschaft: Verhandlungen des 24. deutschen Soziologentages, des 11. österreichischen Soziologentags und des 8. Kongresses der schweizerischen Gesellschaft für Soziologie in Zürich 1988.* Frankfurt am Main: Campus 1989; Hanns Maull: Germany in the Yugoslav Crisis. In: *Survival* 37,4 (1995), pp. 99–130; Hanns Maull: Germany and the Use of Force: Still a "Civilian Power"? In: *Survival* 42,2 (2000), pp. 56–80

27 Including: Hyde-Price: Germany and the Kosovo War; Ronald Asmus: *German Strategy and Opinion after the Wall: 1990–1992.* Santa Monica: RAND 1994, p. 12; Janning: A German Europe – a European Germany?; Michael Schwab-Trapp: Der Nationalsozialismus im öffentlichen Diskurs über militärische Gewalt: Überlegungen zum Bedeutungswandel der deutschen Vergangenheit. In: Bergem (ed.): *Die NS-Diktatur im deutschen Erinnerungsdiskurs*, pp. 171–185, here p. 173; Jonathan Bach: *Between Sovereignty and Integration: German Foreign Policy and National Identity after 1989.* Hamburg: LIT 1999, pp. 120–121.

28 Maull: Germany and the Use of Force; Maull: Germany in the Yugoslav Crisis; Hanns W. Maull: German Foreign Policy, Post-Kosovo: Still a "Civilian Power"? In: *German Politics* 9,2 (2000), pp. 1–24; Peter Katzenstein: United Germany in an Integrating Europe. In: Id. (ed.): *Tamed Power: Germany in Europe.* Ithaca: Cornell University Press 1997, pp. 1–48, here pp. 2–3.

29 Maull: Germany and the Use of Force, p. 56.

with this seminal theory that Germany's militaristic past created a hesitance to step outside multilateral bodies in terms of foreign policy. Indeed, Germany refused military involvement, even within its multilateral alliance structures. Simultaneously this meant that post-war West-Germany was largely reliant on the "guaranteed protection" from America and NATO, Nina Philippi asserts.[30] In this context, Germany's Minister of Defence between 1992 and 1998, Volker Rühe (CDU), coined the term 'culture of reticence.'[31]
However, the unification of East and West Germany in 1990 was a significant turning point, after which the country had to reposition itself in the global context. Amongst other issues, its foreign political stance had to be redefined, which included the discussion whether German forces should and would participate in "collective security actions", as Ronald Asmus calls them.[32] From the vantage point of a strong, unified Germany, retaining Rühe's concept of 'culture of reticence' as a continuing foreign and defence policy approach was viewed by some as continuing proof that the country had learned from its past by limiting its militaristic possibilities. Opponents saw it as an 'easy way out' with regard to collective security – benefitting from multilateral structures while not contributing enough.[33] Germany faced this dilemma debating various UN and NATO-missions of the early 1990s such as Iraq, Cambodia, Somalia and later Bosnia, to which Germany was asked to contribute forces by its alliance-partners.[34]

Against this backdrop of finding a new and comfortable foreign policy for a unified Germany while simultaneously adhering to the demands of its allies, a noteworthy milestone occurred in 1994. On 12 July, Germany's Constitutional Court (*Bundesverfassungsgericht*) ruled that the *Grundgesetz* enabled the participation of the *Bundeswehr* in out-of-area operations with a majority approval in the *Bundestag*.[35] While the constitutional framework of multilateral

30 Nina Philippi: *Bundeswehr-Auslandseinsätze als außen- und sicherheitspolitisches Problem des geeinten Deutschland.* Frankfurt am Main: Peter Lang 1997, p. 203.

31 Asmus: *German Strategy*, pp. xv and 5.

32 Ibid., p. 55; also in Michael Schwab-Trapp: *Kriegsdiskurse: Die politische Kultur des Krieges im Wandel 1991–1999.* Opladen: VS Verlag für Sozialwissenschaften 2002, p. 119; Alexander Siedschlag: *Die aktive Beteiligung Deutschlands an militärischen Aktionen zur Verwirklichung kollektiver Sicherheit.* Frankfurt am Main: Peter Lang 1995, p. 50.

33 Asmus: *German Strategy*, p. 55; Gregor Schöllgen: *Die Außenpolitik der Bundesrepublik Deutschland: Von den Anfängen bis zur Gegenwart.* Munich: C. H. Beck 2004, p. 210.

34 Explored in Schöllgen: *Die Außenpolitik der Bundesrepublik Deutschland*, p. 211; Philippi: *Bundeswehr-Auslandseinsätze*, pp. 156–161; Siedschlag: *Die aktive Beteiligung Deutschlands*, pp. 43–44.

35 Schöllgen: *Die Außenpolitik der Bundesrepublik Deutschland*, p. 216; Thomas Banchoff: *The*

peacekeeping operations had been subject to debate since the early 1990s, it was the "high emotions surrounding the war in former Yugoslavia [that] finally pushed the out-of-area debate towards its [...] resolution" Jonathan Bach writes.[36] Consequently, future involvement in collective security missions which included UN, NATO and WEU[37]-deployments outside of the alliance's territory was legally possible.[38]

In spite of this ground-breaking shift in the country's legal framework, Germany's past and the lessons to be learned from it remained a prominent issue. Bach asserts that the 1994 court ruling was more than a judicial decision. Rather it reinforced the political questions of 'normalcy' and 'historical responsibility' in relation to German foreign policy.[39] Accepting on the one hand that the country held a particular obligation to deliberate employing militaristic means to implement its foreign policy, various politicians (especially from CDU[40] and FDP[41]) argued that Germany could not continue to restrain itself from combat while its allies shoulder the burden of international security. Consequently, a 'discourse of normalcy' could be detected in political speeches of the 1990s, as Bach postulates. The 'normalcy' arguments maintained that in light of Germany's size, economic strength and geographical location, it had to assume a more prominent position in collective security. "This role is nothing less than what is 'normal' for a country with Germany's characteristics," as Bach paraphrased Klaus Kinkel (FDP), Germany's Foreign Minister between 1992 and 1998.[42] Moreover this allowed the country to meet its allies' expectations regarding Germany's contribution to 'global peacekeeping tasks.'[43] The opposition parties, Social Democratic Party of Germany (*Sozialdemokratische Partei Deutschlands,* or SPD, the Green Party and the Party of Democratic Socialism *(Partei des Demokratischen Sozialismus*, or PDS initially

German Problem Transformed: Institutions, Politics, and Foreign Policy, 1945–1995. Ann Arbor: The University of Michigan Press 1999, p. 136; Bach: *Between Sovereignty and Integration*, p. 119; Anthony Glees: *Reinventing Germany: German Political Development since 1945*. Oxford: Bloomsbury Academic 1996, p. 273; Philippi: *Bundeswehr-Auslandseinsätze*, pp. 48–58.

36 Bach: *Between Sovereignty and Integration*, p. 126; also discussed in Philippi: *Bundeswehr-Auslandseinsätze*, pp. 143–146, and Schwab-Trapp: *Kriegsdiskurse*, p. 115.

37 Western European Union, a forum for matters of European security and defence.

38 Philippi: *Bundeswehr-Auslandseinsätze*, p. 53.

39 Bach: *Between Sovereignty and Integration*, pp. 121, 130–136; Schwab-Trapp: *Kriegsdiskurse*, pp. 115–119.

40 Christian Democratic Union of Germany (*Christlich Demokratische Union Deutschlands*).

41 Free Democratic Party (*Freie Demokratische Partei*).

42 Bach: *Between Sovereignty and Integration*, p. 140.

43 Ibid., pp. 141–142.

objected to this interpretation of Germany's historical responsibility leading to 'normality,' arguing that the lesson to be drawn from the country's past was never to engage in combat again, even as part of a peacekeeping-mission.[44] However, as Nina Philippi demonstrates, from 1992 onwards, various opposition politicians also called for military intervention in Bosnia to stop the on-going violence.[45]

Indeed, the violence in former Yugoslavia proved instrumental in solidifying a post-unification foreign policy in Germany.[46] Josef Janning contends that for many observers, the Yugoslav wars eroded the legitimacy of pacifism and argues that Germany should discard any illusionary pacifism and no longer seek special excuses for free-riding in terms of foreign policy.[47] Similarly, Adrian Hyde-Price argues that in Bosnia one was " […] confronted by mass murder and ethnic cleansing, [and thus] traditional pacifist ideas proved inadequate," allowing room for political transformation.[48] Michael Schwab-Trapp asserts that while previously Germany's past did not allow German soldiers to engage in active combat, a new argumentation developed that Germans had a particular duty *because* of their past. Consequently they were responsible, even obliged, to prevent or combat comparable crimes elsewhere in the world, which echoes Bernhard Giesen's concept of 'meta-physical guilt'.[49] Hence, it was during the Balkan violence in the early 1990s that for the first time, the German past was used to legitimise a military intervention rather than a non-intervention.[50]

However, as the violence spread to Kosovo in the late-1990s, the foreign political predisposition in Germany changed.[51] By the time violence erupted

44 Bach: *Between Sovereignty and Integration*, p. 145.

45 Philippi: *Bundeswehr-Auslandseinsätze*, pp. 147–148.

46 Klaus Becher: Nationalitätenkonflikte auf dem Balkan. In: Karl Kaiser / Hanns Maull (eds): *Deutschlands neue Außenpolitik*, vol. 2: Herausforderungen. Oldenburg: Forschungsinstitut der Deutschen Gesellschaft für Auswärtige Politik 1995, pp. 137–155; Karl Kaiser / Joachim Krause: Deutsche Politik gegenüber dem Balkan. In: Iid. (eds): *Deutschlands neue Außenpolitik*, vol. 3: Interessen und Strategien. Oldenburg: Forschungsinstitut der Deutschen Gesellschaft für Auswärtige Politik 1996, pp. 175–188.

47 Janning: A German Europe – a European Germany?

48 Hyde-Price: Germany and the Kosovo War, pp. 19–21.

49 Schwab-Trapp: Der Nationalsozialismus im öffentlichen Diskurs über militärische Gewalt, pp. 173–174.

50 Schwab-Trapp: Der Nationalsozialismus im öffentlichen Diskurs über militärische Gewalt, p. 183; Brendan Simms: From the Kohl to the Fischer Doctrine. In: *German History* 21,3 (2003), pp. 393–414, here p. 404.

51 Much of the most important literature on the topic has been summarised and condensed in Brendan Simms' review article: From the Kohl to the Fischer Doctrine, pp. 393–414.

in Kosovo, Kohl's government had been replaced by a red-green coalition which had been elected in October 1998. Chancellor Gerhard Schröder (SPD) and Foreign Minister Joseph – more widely known as Joschka – Fischer of the Green Party (Bündnis 90/Die Grünen) governed Germany. Both parties were traditionally sceptical of war; the Green Party had even been founded on the principle of pacifism. Nonetheless, it was this government that decided to contribute *Bundeswehr*-soldiers to the 1999 NATO-intervention in Kosovo, initiating the first deployment of German soldiers into active combat since the Second World War. This decision was explained by drawing on the previously mentioned paradigm 'Never again war' which was associated with 'Never again Auschwitz'. Accordingly, Fischer along with other politicians of the red-green coalition argued that in the case of Kosovo, military means were necessary to ensure that genocide would not ensue and international human rights were protected.[52] This will be discussed further in the chapter discussing the German press coverage of the Račak incident and the NATO-intervention.[53] However, for now it is important to note the changing perceptions and interpretations of German foreign policy, which permeated the 1990s and thus influenced the country's stance on the violence in Bosnia and later Kosovo. The extent to which Germany's past still played a role in the German press' debates about the country's involvement in the region will be traced in this book.

Note on Terminology

Before proceeding, a brief note on terminology is necessary. Two controversial terms will re-appear throughout this media analysis of the wars in Bosnia and Kosovo, namely 'genocide' and 'ethnic cleansing.' According to Daniel Chirot and Clark McCauley, in some cases the two are difficult to distinguish, as there can be an overlap.[54] The term 'genocide,' a compilation of the Greek word '*genos*' meaning race or tribe and the Latin '*cide*', which means killing,[55] was more commonly used than 'ethnic cleansing,' until the Yugoslav Wars in the 1990s.[56] The former was coined in 1944 by the Polish-Jewish jurist

52 Volmer: *Die Grünen und die Außenpolitik*, pp. 464–467, 563.

53 See pp. 225–228 and pp. 254–256.

54 Daniel Chirot / Clark McCauley: *Why Not Kill Them All: The Logic and Prevention of Mass Political Murder*. Princeton: Princeton University Press 2006, p. 11.

55 Raphael Lemkin: *Axis Rule in Occupied Europe*. Clark: The Lawbook Exchange 2005, p. 79.

56 Chirot / McCauley: *Why Not Kill Them All*, p. 11.

Raphael Lemkin, who, in the context of the National-Socialist Holocaust, defined genocide as

> a coordinated plan [...with the objective of disintegrating] the political and social institutions of culture, language, national feelings, religion, and the economic existence of national groups and the destruction of the personal security, liberty, health, dignity and even the lives of the individuals belonging to such groups. Genocide is directed against the national group as an entity, and the actions involved are directed against individuals, not in their individual capacity, but as members of the national group.[57]

Lemkin's rather narrow definition foresaw the complete destruction of a national group and was the basis for the broader "United Nations Convention on the Prevention and Punishment of the Crime of Genocide," which was passed in 1948. Articles I and II stated that all contracting parties would "[...] undertake to prevent and punish" genocide, which was defined as " [...] acts committed with intent to destroy, in whole or in part, a national, ethnical, racial or religious group [...]"[58] The Convention listed these acts in five bullet points:

> (a) Killing members of the group;
> (b) Causing serious bodily or mental harm to members of the group;
> (c) Deliberately inflicting on the group conditions of life calculated to bring about its physical destruction in whole or in part;
> (d) Imposing measures intended to prevent births within the group;
> (e) Forcibly transferring children of the group to another group.[59]

This definition of genocide with its focus on ethnic and national groups has since been criticised as too limiting, as it disregards the systematic killing of political enemies, for example, as practiced by Joseph Stalin.[60] Nevertheless, it continues to form the crux of the UN Genocide Convention. The legal obligation of the contracting parties to stop genocide when it occurs anywhere in the world is the most important statement of the document and is the central difference for the international community between genocide

57 Lemkin: *Axis Rule in Occupied Europe*, p. 79.

58 United Nations: Convention on the Prevention and Punishment of the Crime of Genocide. Adopted by the General Assembly of the United Nations on 9 December 1948. http://treaties.un.org/doc/Publication/UNTS/Volume%2078/volume-78-I-1021-English.pdf (accessed 25.08.2014), p. 3.

59 Ibid.

60 Chirot / McCauley: *Why Not Kill Them All*, p. 16; Adam Jones: *Genocide: A Comprehensive Introduction*. London: Routledge 2011, p. 11.

and 'ethnic cleansing,' which does not demand such a binding international reaction.[61]

The term 'ethnic cleansing' was formally defined by the UN in 1994 as "[…] rendering an area ethnically homogenous by using force or intimidation to remove from a given area persons from another ethnic or religious group,"[62] which seems to reflect the way it was used and understood prior to 1994. However, this is often difficult to demarcate from other forms of mass violence, as Andrew Bell-Fialkoff explained. "At one end it is virtually indistinguishable from forced emigration and population exchange while at the other it merges with deportation and genocide."[63] According to the historian Norman Naimark, the first peoples to use the term 'ethnic cleansing' to describe their experiences was the Serbian minority population living in Kosovo, who in the 1980s felt discriminated against by the dominant Kosovo-Albanian population.[64] However, it became more widely known during the Yugoslav Wars of the 1990s and was generally associated with the Serbian policy towards Bosnian Muslims and later Kosovo-Albanians. As Bell-Fialkoff stated, "the central aim of the Serbian campaign [was] to eliminate a population from the 'homeland' in order to create a more secure, ethnically homogeneous state […]"[65]

The utilisation of the two terms 'genocide' and 'ethnic cleansing' is not merely a matter of semantics and will be traced throughout the German print media coverage. The distinction between these terms was imperative to the formation of Germany's foreign policy and the press' interpretation of the violence in Bosnia and Kosovo. Thus, I will pay special attention to the manner in which these terms were employed in the German press and with what intention. For example, did publications use 'genocide' to suggest an international intervention to stop it, as the UN Genocide Convention stipulates? Were there instances where the term was rather used as a hyperbole to shock the reader of the gruesome violence? Considering these significant repercussions, I will refrain from using both terms on my own accord throughout this book. Instead I will draw on vocabulary such as "violence" or "killings". While at

61 UN: Convention on the Prevention and Punishment of the Crime of Genocide.

62 United Nations: The Policy of Ethnic Cleansing, 28.12.1994. http://ess.uwe.ac.uk/comexpert/ANX/IV.htm (accessed 25.09.2012).

63 Andrew Bell-Fialkoff: A Brief History of Ethnic Cleansing. In: *Foreign Affairs* 72,3 (1993), pp. 110–122.

64 Norman Naimark: Ethnic Cleansing. In: *Online Encyclopedia of Mass Violence*. http://www.massviolence.org/IMG/article_PDF/Ethnic-Cleansing.pdf (accessed 25.08.2014).

65 Bell-Fialkoff: A Brief History of Ethnic Cleansing, pp. 110–122.

times such vague terminology may appear forced or disparaging to the reader, this ensures that I do not superimpose the conflictive terms where they were not initially utilised. This in turn allows a more distinct linguistic analysis: when they appear in this book, the terms will either be paraphrased or in quotation. In both cases a reference will indicate the source. These deliberations regarding the terms 'genocide' and the potential political ramifications of its utilisation introduce a central theme throughout this press analysis, namely the prevalence of the Holocaust in arguing both for and against a potential German involvement in any wars. The only exception is the Srebrenica Massacre, which I analyse in chapter four. The International Criminal Tribunal for former Yugoslavia (ICTY) has designated Srebrenica to have been genocide. As the word is part of the legal understanding of the massacre, I deem it acceptable to utilise it without restrictions.

Chapter 1
Historical Background: Important Milestones of Balkan History

While each chapter entails an overview of the historical context pertinent to that particular timeframe, at this point it is worth considering the broader context regarding the wars in Bosnia and Kosovo. Considering the complexities of Bosnia, Serbia and Kosovo as individual countries, as well as the region as a whole, a comprehensive historical background of the region goes beyond the scope of this book. A wide range of sound academic studies is available on the history of the Balkans,[1] however, for our purposes, certain key periods will be discussed that introduced factors which later became relevant during the disintegration of Yugoslavia in the 1990s and were thus repeatedly referenced in the course of the German press coverage. These pertinent

1 To name a few: Mark Mazower: *The Balkans*. London: Modern Library 2000; Nevill Forbes / Arnold J. Toynbee / D. Mitrany / D.G. Hogarth: *The Balkans: A History of Bulgaria, Serbia, Greece, Rumania, Turkey*. Oxford: Clarendon 1915; Slobodan Stankovic: *Titos Erbe*. Munich: R. Oldenbourg 1981; Vladimir Dedijer / Ivan Bozic / Sima Cirkovic / Milorad Ekmecic: *History of Yugoslavia*. New York: McGraw Hill 1974; Robert Kaplan: *Balkan Ghosts: A Journey through History*. New York: Picador 2005; Noel Malcolm: *Bosnia: A Short History*. London: Macmillan 1994; Noel Malcolm: *Kosovo: A Short History*. London: Harper Perenniel 1998; Marie-Janine Calic: *Geschichte Jugoslawiens im 20. Jahrhundert*. Munich: C.H. Beck 2010; Julie Mertus: *Kosovo: How Myths and Truths Started a War*. Berkeley: University of California Press 1999; Dennison Rusinow: *Yugoslavia: Oblique Insights and Observations*. Pittsburgh: University of Pittsburgh Press 2008; Tim Judah: *The Serbs: History, Myth and the Destruction of Yugoslavia*. New Haven: Yale University Press 1997; Tim Judah: *Kosovo: War and Revenge*. New Haven: Yale University Press 2002; Christopher Bennett: *Yugoslavia's Bloody Collapse: Causes, Courses and Consequences*. London: Hurst & Company 1995; Miranda Vickers: *Between Serb and Albanian: A History of Kosovo*. London: Hurst & Company 1998; Norman Naimark / Holly Case (eds): *Yugoslavia and Its Historians: Understanding the Balkan Wars of the 1990s*. Stanford: Stanford University Press 2003.

historical milestones are: the region's medieval history, specifically the 1389 Battle of Kosovo and the advent of three major religions, as well as World War Two.

Medieval Balkans

Beginning with the first époque, the medieval history of the Balkans is a dense narrative of varying powers dominating the region in turn. Particularly the Hungarian, Serbian and Ottoman Empires were important influences to the religious and cultural composition of the region.[2] During the Middle Ages, three main religions – namely Christian Orthodoxy, Catholicism and Islam – took root in the region which split the Balkans into an "Eastern and Western cultural zone", as Vladimir Dedijer and his co-authors termed it.[3] While Serbia and Macedonia were strongly influenced by the Byzantine Empire and hence the Orthodox Church, the Western Balkans were dominated by Charlemagne's Roman-Catholic Franks.[4] Further religious and political influences were introduced to the Balkans in the course of the Ottoman conquest in late 14th century. By the 1380s, the Ottoman armies had reached Serbian territory and without strong regional defences from the deeply divided and competing local rulers, they quickly took over the land, reaching Bosnia in 1388.[5] Throughout the different cultural zones, various competing cultures, religions and alphabets established themselves. The effects are still visible in the present day: in Serbia, the Serbian-Orthodox Church is dominant and a Cyrillic alphabet is used; in Croatia Roman-Catholicism is the primary religion and the Latin alphabet is used. Bosnia is more diverse: though Islam is the dominant religion, Latin letters are used here as well.

1389: Battle of Kosovo and Serbia's National Myth

One particular battle, which occurred during the 1380s Ottoman conquest of Serbia and Bosnia stands out. In 1389, the Serbian Prince Lazar attempted to

2 Dedijer / Bozic / Cirkovic / Ekmecic: *History of Yugoslavia*; Malcolm: *Bosnia: A Short History*; Fred Singleton: *A Short History of the Yugoslav Peoples*. Cambridge: Cambridge University Press 1985; Ivo Banac: *The National Questions in Yugoslavia: Origins, History, Politics*. Ithaca: Cornell University Press 1984; Vickers: *Between Serb and Albanian.*

3 Dedijer / Bozic / Cirkovic / Ekmecic: *History of Yugoslavi,* pp. 98–99.

4 Ibid., pp. 98–99; also in Malcolm: *Bosnia*, p. 9.

5 Malcolm: *Bosnia*, p. 20; also in Vickers: *Between Serb and Albanian*, pp. 10–12.

halt the Ottoman advance at Kosovo Polje, the field of the blackbirds.[6] Sultan Murad triumphed over his Serbian counterpart, who was captured and executed. During the following five centuries of Muslim rule, Islam was solidified in the region. While this battle could have been overlooked as one of many battles in the Medieval Balkans, it became a watershed milestone in the Serbian national narrative, and with the rise of nationalism in the 19th century was transformed into a national myth.

Michael Sells systematically reconstructs the creation of this Serbian national myth surrounding the 1389 battle in his monograph.[7] He argues that amidst the epoch of 19th century literary romanticism, the battle became a central theme in Serbian epic poetry and immortalised Prince Lazar as a hero.[8] He explains:

> Lazar's death represents the death of the Serb nation, which will not be resurrected until Lazar is raised from the dead and the descendants of Lazar's killers [Muslims] are purged from the Serbian people.[9]

With quotes from various political speeches, excerpts from plays and poems as well as visual material, Sells elaborates the centrality of the 1389 battle in the Serbian national conscience. Taking a purely historical perspective, the British historian Noel Malcolm argued that "[…] the truth is a little less dramatic" and that this single battle did not lead to the demise of the Serbian nation.[10] Instead Malcolm attributes Serbia's eventual downfall to the dominant strength of the Ottoman forces over a number of years. Comparing the myth's content with the proven historical facts goes beyond the scope of this book. However, more important for our purposes is that the 1389 battle became a turning point for the region and that the Serbian interpretation and mythologized memory of the battle lay the foundation of divisive nationalism. Both the myth and the resulting nationalism remained central to the Serbian national narrative during the disintegration of Yugoslavia in the 1990s.

6 Vickers: *Between Serb and Albanian*, pp. 12–16; Malcolm: *Bosnia*, p. 20; Dedijer / Bozic / Cirkovic / Ekmecic: *History of Yugoslavia*, pp. 115–116.

7 Michael Sells: *The Bridge Betrayed: Religion and Genocide in Bosnia*. Berkeley: University of California Press 1998, pp. 29–52.

8 Ibid., p. 37.

9 Ibid., p. 31; also discussed in Michael Sells: The Construction of Islam in Serbian Religious Mythology and Its Consequences. In: Maya Shatzmiller (ed.): *Islam and Bosnia: Conflict Resolution and Foreign Policy in Multi-Ethnic States*. Montreal: McGill-Queen's University Press 2002, pp. 56–85, here pp. 62–63.

10 Malcolm: *Bosnia*, p. 20.

The Role of Religion

One important product of Balkan medieval history was the presence of three strong religious spheres in the Balkan region: Catholicism, Islam and Serbian Orthodoxy. Consequently, the role of religion must briefly be considered. Judaism had been introduced to the Balkan region during the Roman rule of Yugoslavia, though the Jewish population was insignificant in number when compared to the other three denominations.[11] Many key works on Balkan history identify the coexistence of various religions as a distinguishing, but not truly dividing factor for the Bosniaks,[12] Serbians and Croats.[13] As Malcolm explains, "[…] it was not state policy [in Bosnia] to convert people to Islam or make them behave like Muslims […]"[14] Due to the absence of forced conversions by Muslim rulers, along with a large measure of political and cultural autonomy for non-Muslims, the subsequent centuries were not marked by religious persecutions or conflicts but rather peaceful coexistence.[15]

According to various scholars, religious differences only gained prominence when they were combined with nationalism in the late 19th century, though many reiterate that this was a pan-European phenomenon and not singular to the Balkans.[16] For example, Mark Mazower postulates that "if there was no ethnic conflict [during the Ottoman rule of the Balkans], it was not because of 'tolerance' but because there was no concept of nationality among the Sultan's subjects […]"[17] Maya Shatzmiller expands on the interpretation that 19th century nationalism fomented religious tensions, asserting that "Islam […] only became the divisive and decisive factor in the conflict [of the 1990s] when it was combined with ethnic nationalism."[18] Summarily, by the dawn of the 20th century, the region was entrenched in religious and national differences.[19]

11 Malcolm: *Bosnia*, pp. 107–114.

12 Most scholarly and journalistic works refer to Bosniaks as Bosnian Muslims or simply Muslims. Henceforth I will do the same.

13 Banac: *The National Questions in Yugoslavia*; Bennett: *Yugoslavia's Bloody Collapse*; Misha Glenny: *The Fall of Yugoslavia: The Third Balkan War*. London: Penguin 1996; Judah: *The Serbs*; Malcolm: *Bosnia*; Mazower: *Balkans*; Singleton: *A Short History*.

14 Malcolm: *Bosnia*, p. 49.

15 Mazower: *The Balkans*, p. 8, 54; Banac: *National Question in Yugoslavia*, pp. 69, 410; Singleton: *A Short History*, p. 21.

16 Mazower: *Balkans*, pp. 6–7; Singleton: *A Short History*, p. 21.

17 Mazower: *Balkans*, pp. 15–16.

18 Maya Shatzmiller: Introduction. In: Ead. (ed.): *Islam and Bosnia*, pp. xi–xxiv, here p. xii.

19 Mazower: *Balkans*, pp. 6–7; Singleton: *A Short History*, p. 21; Shatzmiller: Introduction, p. xii.

World War Two

Departing from the medieval Balkans, the second historic milestone relevant to this book lies several centuries ahead. On the 6 April 1941, Nazi-Germany and its allies attacked Yugoslavia and occupied the region until 1945. Serbia came under direct German administration. Other parts of Yugoslavia were distributed amongst Hitler's allies that had also launched the attack, namely Italy, Bulgaria and Hungary.[20] In addition, a fascist "Independent State of Croatia" was created, which consisted of Croatia, Slavonia[21] as well as Bosnia-Herzegovina and was known by its Serbo-Croatian initials, NDH.[22] Ante Pavelić, the leader of the Croatian fascist movement, Ustasha,[23] became the head of this puppet-state. Noel Malcolm summarises the history of Yugoslavia during the Second World War as "[…] the story of many wars piled […] on top of another […]"[24] In the first instance, there was the most obvious war between Nazi-Germany and Yugoslavia. Another conflict was that between the fascist occupiers and their Croatian allies, the Ustasha, against the local resistance movements, but there was also a war between the two main resistance formations themselves: the Royalist Serbian Chetniks[25] and communist Partisans. While the latter pursued the goal of creating a communist Yugoslav state, the Royalists aimed to reinstate the Kingdom of Yugoslavia under Serbian command. Amongst them were 'rabid Serb nationalists,' as Malcolm labelled them, whose aim was to achieve a homogenous Serbian land.[26]

As in other countries, the deportation of the local Jewish population ensued shortly after the Nazi-occupation.[27] However, as Malcolm writes, "anti-Semitism was of only secondary concern to Ustaša ideologists […]" Their primary goal was to eliminate the considerable Serbian minority – 1.9 million out of a population of 6.3 million – from NDH-territory.[28] Fred Singleton holds Croatia's fascist leader Ante Pavelić, whom he labels a 'Puppet-*Führer*', responsible for the persecution of the Serbian civilians. Basing his research

20 Dedijer / Bozic / Cirkovic / Ekmecic: *History of Yugoslavia*, pp. 566–574; Malcolm: *Bosnia*, pp. 174–175.

21 A region in Eastern Croatia, not to be confused with Slovenia.

22 Which stands of Nezavisna Država Hratska.

23 Sometimes spelled Usatša.

24 Malcolm: *Bosnia*, p. 174.

25 Sometimes spelled Četnik.

26 Malcolm: *Bosnia*, p. 178.

27 Dedijer/Bozic/Cirkovic/Ekmecic: *History of Yugoslavia*, pp. 577–581.

28 Malcolm: *Bosnia*, p. 176; also in Dedijer et al.: *History of Yugoslavia*, pp. 574–582; Singleton: *A Short History*, pp. 175–206.

on an extensive selection of both Yugoslav and English secondary literature and memoirs, he claims: "the [NDH-]regime declared that one of its chief objectives was to 'purify' Croatia of alien elements, especially the Serbs."[29] Vladimir Dedijer, a former Yugoslav Partisan fighter and later historian, as well as Josip Tito's official biographer, also portrayed Pavelić to have followed Hitler's example. "Taking the Nurnberg laws as a model, [...Pavelić] passed a legal decree on April 30, 1941, on the protection of Aryan blood and the honour of the Croatian people [...]"[30]

The epitome of the NDH's elimination of 'alien elements' was the concentration camp Jasenovac, where thousands of Serbians died along with other persecuted minorities including Jews and Roma.[31] Various works have explored this topic in detail,[32] though Dedijer's detailed account of the Ustasha-camp and the killing methods used against its prisoners is the most comprehensive.[33] Particularly important for our purposes is the argument in David Bruce Macdonald's monograph, who states that Jasenovac remained distinctly dominant in the Serbian collective memory of the 1990s and was frequently drawn on to reiterate the crimes the Serbian people had been subjected to.[34] Though Malcolm's seminal work only mentions Jasenovac once as a side-note, significantly he terms NDH's policies towards the Serbs as 'genocidal'.[35] This is important to keep in mind during the disintegration of Yugoslavia in the 1990s when Serbians argued that they had been victims of 'ethnic cleansing' and even 'genocide' by Croatians. Moreover, it was used to explain the Serbian treatment of distinctive, or as some nationalist politicians perceived it, hostile identities including Croats and Bosnian Muslims.

The last 'layer' of war Malcolm had spoken about in his monograph was the conflict between the fascists and the communist Partisans, who were led by Josip Broz Tito. These partisans belonged to the Yugoslav Communist Party,

29 Singleton: *A Short History*, p. 177.

30 Dedijer/Bozic/Cirkovic/Ekmecic: *History of Yugoslavia*, pp. 581–82.

31 Mark Biondich: *The Balkans: Revolution, War & Political Violence since 1878*. Oxford: Oxford University Press 2011, p. 140.

32 For example Vladimir Dedijer: *Jasenovac. Das jugoslawische Auschwitz und der Vatikan*. Freiburg: Ahriman 2011; David Bruce Macdonald: *Balkan Holocausts? Serbian and Croatian Victim-Centred Propaganda and the War in Yugoslavia*. Manchester: Manchester University Press 2002; Jovan Byford: When I Say "the Holocaust", I Mean "Jasenovac": Remembrance of the Holocaust in Contemporary Serbia. In: *East European Jewish Affairs* 37,1 (2007), pp. 51–74.

33 Dedijer: *Jasenovac*, pp. 145–161.

34 Macdonald: *Balkan Holocausts?*, p. 160.

35 Malcolm: *Bosnia*, p. 192.

which consisted of approximately 6,000 members by 1940.[36] Their ultimate victory over the fascists and the Chetniks led to the creation of a communist Yugoslav state in 1945, which consisted of six republics (Croatia, Slovenia, Bosnia-Herzegovina, Serbia, Macedonia and Montenegro), as well as two autonomous provinces (Vojvodina and Kosovo). Tito ruled this Socialist Federal Republic of Yugoslavia under the mantra 'Unity and Brotherhood.' By superimposing Communism on the diverse republics, which in some cases were at enmity with one another, academics generally agree that tensions stemming from various historical eras ranging from the Middle Ages to the Second World War, subsided.[37] However, after Tito's death in 1980, a decade of political instability and conflict ensued, which escalated in the 1990s. In this decade of renewed violence, the Croatian Ustasha and Serbian Chetnik movements were revived as associations. This transported decade-old conflicts from the 1940s – and the inextricably linked memory of war crimes perpetrated by both sides – to the 1990s.

36 Ibid., p. 177.

37 For example Malcolm: *Bosnia*; Biondich: *The Balkans*, and Rusinow: *Yugoslavia: Oblique Insights.*

Chapter 2
The Eruption of War in the 1990s

In the late 1980s and early 1990s, Yugoslavia began to crumble due to a number of political and economic reasons. Slobodan Milošević (1941–2006), a communist apparatchik, became President of the Serbian Republic within Yugoslavia in 1989. In this position, Milošević's foremost political goal was to uphold Serbia's position as the strongest and most dominant republic in Yugoslavia.[1] Consequently, mere months after becoming the Serbian President, he introduced constitutional reforms. Citing inefficiencies of Tito's 1974 constitution, Milošević weakened the federal authority in favour of a stronger centralised state ruled from Belgrade.[2] As a result, "most non-Serb nationalities believed that they were handicapped by a system in which Serbs were proportionally overrepresented in federal institutions [...]", such as the Yugoslav Peoples' Army (JNA).[3] Opposing the Serbian dominance in Yugoslavia, Slovenia led by Lojze Peterle and Croatia with Franjo Tudjman as President declared their independence in June and October 1991, respectively.

Mere months after Croatia and Slovenia had gained international recognition of their independence, the same political desire engulfed Bosnia. However, Bosnia's population was much more diverse, comprising of roughly 43% Muslims, 32% Serbs and 18% Croats. This constellation proved onerous for the pursuit of independence, as the 32% Bosnian Serbs demanded

1 Josip Glaurdić: *The Hour of Europe: Western Powers and the Breakup of Yugoslavia.* New Haven: Yale University Press 2011, p. 7.

2 Adam LeBor: *Milošević. A Biography.* London: A&C Black 2003, p. 125; Mertus: *Kosovo*, pp. 175–179; Klejda Mulaj: Resisting an Oppressive Regime: The Case of the Kosovo Liberation Army. In: *Studies in Conflict and Terrorism* 31,12 (2008), pp. 1103–1119, here p. 1104.

3 Biondich: *The Balkans*, p. 198.

that Bosnia remain a part of the Serbian dominated Yugoslavia. Due to this internal divergence, the EC made its recognition of Bosnia's independence contingent on a referendum, which was held from 29 February to 1 March 1992. As the report submitted by the international election monitors summarised, approximately 63% of Bosnia's population voted, of which 99% were in favour of Bosnia's independence.[4] The missing percentage predominantly constituted the Serbs living in Bosnia who had largely boycotted the referendum, as they felt it did not represent their views, but that simultaneously they did not have a strong enough voice to make their concerns heard.[5] Regardless, as the majority of Bosnia's population had voted in favour of the country's seperation from Yugoslavia, Bosnia declared its independence on 1 March 1992 with Alija Izetbegović as its President and was officially and unanimously recognised by the EC on 6 April. In response to Bosnia's declaration of independence, what was left of Yugoslavia declared war on 3 March 1992, as had been the case when the EC had recognised Croatia's and Slovenia's independence several months earlier. In all cases these wars were led by the JNA and spearheaded by Yugoslavia's strongest republic, Serbia. While the war in Slovenia lasted mere ten days, ending with Slovenia's victory on 7 July 1991, the violence in Bosnia and Croatia lasted nearly four years.

During the Bosnian war, Sarajevo's armed forces, various paramilitary formations as well as the JNA and the Bosnian-Serb army engaged in a bitter war. This was marked by grave war crimes, including 'ethnic cleansing.'[6] A 1994 UN-report entitled *The Policy of Ethnic Cleansing* stated that all parties committed 'grave breaches' of the Geneva Conventions, a manifest of international law about the humanitarian treatment of victims of war. "These violations include the killing of civilians, rape, torture, and the deliberate destruction of civilian property, including cultural and religious property, such as churches and mosques."[7] The report continues that the majority of these crimes were committed by Serbians against Bosnian Muslims and that "Bosnian Muslim

4 Commission on Security and Cooperation in Europe: The Referendum on Independence in Bosnia-Herzegovina February 29–March 1, 1992. http://csce.gov/index.cfm?FuseAction=UserGroups.Home&ContentRecord_id=250&ContentType=G&ContentRecordType=G&UserGroup_id=5&Subaction=ByDate (accessed 25.08.2014), p. 19.

5 Francine Friedman: *Bosnia and Herzegovina: A Polity on the Brink*. London: Routledge 2004, p. 43.

6 Biondich: *The Balkans*, p. 215; Jones: *Genocide*, pp. 317–339.

7 M. Cherif Bassiouni: The Policy of Ethnic Cleansing: Final Report of the United Nations Commission of Experts Established Pursuant to Security Resolution 780 (1992), 28.12.1994. http://ess.uwe.ac.uk/comexpert/ANX/IV.htm (accessed 27.10.2012), p. 3.

forces" – as the report labelled them – did not engage in 'ethnic cleansing.'[8] Men of fighting age were the primary targets and were either eliminated in mass killings or confined in large detention centres, or concentration camps, as they were widely known.[9] Moreover, women became victims of sexual violence perpetrated by police, army and paramilitary forces.[10]

The most well-known incident of mass violence during the Bosnian War, and what has since become known as the worst war crime in Europe since the Second World War, was the Srebrenica Massacre. In merely eight days, between 6 and 13 July 1995, the Bosnian-Serb army captured the town of Srebrenica in eastern Bosnia, expelling thousands of women and children and killing approximately 8,000 civilians (mainly boys and men). This massacre, which has been termed 'genocide' by the International Criminal Tribunal for Former Yugoslavia (ICTY), occurred in spite of the presence of Dutch UN-soldiers in the area, whose mandate did not allow them to intervene militarily.[11] The genocidal dimension of the Srebrenica Massacre as well as the disbelief that the UN had watched it unfold without intervening compelled the international community to intervene in the Bosnian War more decidedly than in previous years.

Consequently, the international community increased diplomatic pressure, which combined with NATO's airstrikes against Serbian forces in Bosnia, eventually lead to a peace conference under the auspices of the USA, Great Britain, France and Germany. Held in Dayton, Ohio, this conference aimed not only to bring peace to the region, but also to devise a concrete plan regarding Bosnia's political future together with the Yugoslav President Milošević, Bosnia's President Izetbegović and the Croatian President Tudjman.[12] While the wars in Bosnia and Croatia ended in 1995 with this peace treaty, which had been brokered by the United States of America and its European allies, violent conflict returned to the region in 1998, this time in Kosovo.

8 Bassiouni: The Policy of Ethnic Cleansing, pp. 3–4; also in Roger Cohen: C.I.A. Report on Bosnia Blames Serbs for 90% of the War Crimes. In: *New York Times*, 09.03.1995. http://www.nytimes.com/1995/03/09/world/cia-report-on-bosnia-blames-serbs-for-90-of-the-war-crimes.html (accessed 25.08.2014).

9 Biondich: *The Balkans*, pp. 215, 218–221; also in Roy Gutman: *A Witness to Genocide: The First Inside Account of the Horrors of 'Ethnic Cleansing' in Bosnia.* Shaftesbury: Element 1993.

10 Biondich: *The Balkans*, p. 215; Bassiouni: The Policy of Ethnic Cleansing, pp. 4–7.

11 See chapter 4 for a detailed discussion of the Srebrenica Massacre.

12 See chapter 5 for more details on the Dayton Conference.

Three main causes are seen as catalytic in Kosovo's path to violence: Milošević's aggressive rhetoric of the late 1980s,[13] which culminated in the revocation of Kosovo's autonomy in 1989,[14] as well as the birth of the Kosovo Liberation Army (KLA).[15] The Kosovo-Albanian majority had sought more autonomy from Serbia for several decades. However, while Muslim Albanians had settled in Kosovo for centuries, the region had also been the "heartland of [... the Serbian] medieval empire and the site of the patriarchate of the Serbian Orthodox Church."[16] Indeed, Kosovo was "[...] the centre of many of Serbia's greatest works of religious art and architecture [...]"[17] Due to the cultural centrality of the region to Serbia, any movement of the Kosovo-Albanians towards independence was repressed. Yugoslavia's communist leader, Josip Tito, had sought to reduce these tensions by constitutionally granting Kosovo the status of an autonomous province within the Republic of Serbia in 1974.[18] This promised the Kosovo-Albanians "[...] equality, schools in the mother tongue of its children, a full freedom for cultural expression and development as an ethnic group."[19] Moreover, being an autonomous region gave Kosovo the legal right to secede.[20] As Tim Judah summarised, "after 1974 the province became a republic in all but name [...]"[21] With these constitutional rights in place, the tensions were reduced significantly.

However, during the previously mentioned constitutional reforms introduced by Milošević in 1989, Yugoslavia's two autonomous provinces, Kosovo and Vojvodina, lost all sovereignty.[22] These changes granted Serbia "[...] more

13 Sells: *Bridge Betrayed*, p. 67; Judah: *The Serbs*, p. 29; Judah: *Kosovo*, p. 33; Milošević's 1989 Speech in Gazimestan, the Field of Black Birds (or Kosovo Polje). http://www.hirhome.com/yugo/bbc_milosevic.htm (accessed 25.08.2014).

14 Amnesty International: *Kosovo: The Evidence*. London: Amnesty International 1998, p. 8.

15 Malcolm: *Kosovo*; Rusinow: *Yugoslavia*; Mertus: *Kosovo*; Sells: *Bridge Betrayed*; Judah: *The Serbs*; Judah: *Kosovo*; Tim Judah: Growing Pains of the Kosovo Liberation Army. In Michael Waller / Kyril Drezov / Bülent Gökay (eds): *Kosovo: The Politics of Delusion*. New York: Frank Cass Publishers 2001, pp. 25–29; Matthew Bennett: The Kosovo Liberation Army. In: Matthew Bennett / Paul Latawski (eds): *Exile Armies*. London: Routledge 2005, pp. 159–170; Mulaj: Resisting an Oppressive Regime, pp. 1103–1119; Chris Hedges: In Yugoslavia, the Consequences of Not Reporting the Truth. In: *Nieman Reports* 53,2 (Summer 1999), pp. 15–16.

16 Rusinow: *Yugoslavia*, p. 237; Sells: *Bridge Betrayed*, p. 53.

17 Sells: *Bridge Betrayed*, p. 53.

18 Rusinow: *Yugoslavia*, pp. 250–251; Judah: *Kosovo*, pp. 34–38.

19 Rusinow: *Yugoslavia*, p. 238.

20 Independent International Commission on Kosovo: *The Kosovo Report: Conflict, International Response, Lessons Learned*. Oxford: Oxford University Press 2000, p. 36.

21 Judah: *The Serbs*, p. 151.

22 LeBor: *Milošević*, p. 126; Judah: *Kosovo*, pp. 55–56; Mertus: *Kosovo*, pp. 175–179; Mulaj: Resisting an Oppressive Regime, p. 1104.

direct control over Kosovo's security, judiciary, finance and social planning."[23] Immediately, Albanian schools and media outlets were closed and the Serbian police increasingly harassed the civilian population.[24] According to Amnesty International, "most ethnic Albanians working in the state sector lost their jobs […]" Moreover, the Serbian military presence in Kosovo increased significantly, fuelling the mutual distrust between Serbians and Kosovo-Albanians.[25] These inequalities caused a more distinct striving for Kosovo's independence on behalf of the Kosovo-Albanians. Consequently, unilateral parliamentary elections were carried out in May 1992, which were won by the Democratic League of Kosovo (LDK). The only candidate, Dr. Ibrahim Rugova, who was LDK's leader, became the President of Kosovo.[26] Rugova was a professor of literature at the University of Priština and had been the party's leader since its founding in 1989.[27] Rugova's victory led to the establishment of "'parallel' institutions, including a parliament, a president, taxation and their own education and health systems."[28] This shadow-state was 'sheer make-believe', as Malcolm labelled it, but pursued the long-term goal that

> […] foreign governments might eventually feel obliged to admit that they were the ones who were engaging in fiction when they continued to treat Kosovo as a mere region of the Serbian state.[29]

However, Rugova's pacifist policies were challenged by the creation of the 'Kosovo Liberation Army' in 1996.[30] The army's declared goal was to attain Kosovo's independence, resorting to military force against Serbians in the region. The KLA's violence against Serbian police forces, Serbian civilians and suspected Kosovo-Albanian collaborators, intensified the violent reprisals of the Serbian police units against Kosovo-Albanian civilians as well as the KLA. The latter, at times also referred to as UÇK, which stands for its Albanian name, *Ushtria Çlirimtare e Kosovës*,[31] has thus been identified by

23 Mertus: *Kosovo*, p. 179; Judah: *Kosovo*, pp. 55–56.

24 Commission on Kosovo: *The Kosovo Report*, p. 41.

25 Vickers: *Between Serb and Albanian*, p. 259.

26 Ibid., pp. 259–260.

27 Malcolm: *Kosovo*, p. 348.

28 Amnesty International: *Kosovo: The Evidence*, p. 30; also in: Judah: *The Serbs*, p. 305; Malcolm: *Kosovo*, p. 348.

29 Malcolm: *Kosovo*, pp. 348–349.

30 Ibid., p. 355; Bennett: The Kosovo Liberation Army, p. 162; Wolfgang Petritsch / Robert Pichler: *Kosovo/Kosova: Der lange Weg zum Frieden.* Klagenfurt: Wieser 2004, pp. 100–102.

31 Bennett: The Kosovo Liberation Army, pp. 159–170; Judah: Growing Pains of the Kosovo Liberation Army, pp. 20–29; James Pettifer: The Kosovo Liberation Army: The Myth of

various academics as the driving force in transforming the conflict into a war.[32] Particularly the exclusion of Kosovo in the peace talks at Dayton has been seen as a catalyst amongst Kosovo's leading figures to realise that their problems had found no international interest and that this propelled the KLA into action.[33]

The reasons for omitting Kosovo in the Dayton negotiations were manifold. The political status of Kosovo was that of an autonomous province within Yugoslavia and was thus deemed an internal Yugoslav affair. The diplomats in Dayton, who feared that insisting on including Kosovo in the negotiations would prevent a peace agreement for Bosnia and Croatia, dismissed the topic as too contentious. In an interview with Wolfgang Ischinger, the leader of the German delegation at Dayton, he recalled broaching the topic of Kosovo with Milošević. The latter 'exploded' at the mere mention of the province, insisting this was Yugoslavia's internal problem in which the international community should not get involved.[34] Interestingly, the academic literature does not represent the non-inclusion of Kosovo at Dayton as a short-coming of 'the West'. This suggests a comprehension of how difficult it had been to broker peace in Bosnia and Croatia and acknowledged that including Kosovo into these negotiations would have jeopardised the entire undertaking.

It is generally agreed that the KLA was approximately 30,000 men strong by mid-1999 and was predominantly funded by Kosovo-Albanian *Gastarbeiter* in Germany and Albanian ex-patriots elsewhere.[35] The army had obtained most of its weapons in the spring of 1997 when the Albanian government collapsed. During the political chaos that ensued, circa one million Kalashnikovs were released onto the Black Market for approximately $16 each.[36] The details of KLA's leadership were secret, though Bujar Bukoshi, the Prime Minister of the Kosovo-Albanian shadow-state, who was exiled in Switzerland, was

Origin. In: Michael Waller / Kyril Drezov / Bülent Gökay (eds): *The Politics of Delusion*. New York: Frank Cass 2001, pp. 25–29; Mulaj: Resisting an Oppressive Regime, pp. 1103–1119; Hedges: In Yugoslavia, the Consequences of Not Reporting the Truth, pp. 15–16; Judah: *Kosovo*, pp. 131–133.

32 Judah: Growing Pains of the Kosovo Liberation Army, p. 20.

33 Ibid., pp. 21–22; Pettifer: The Kosovo Liberation Army: The Myth of Origin, p. 26; Mulaj: Resisting an Oppressive Regime, p. 1109; Amnesty International: *Kosovo: The Evidence*, p. 12; Commission on Kosovo: *The Kosovo Report*, p. 1.

34 Roland Friedrich: *Die deutsche Außenpolitik im Kosovo-Konflikt*. Wiesbaden: VS Verlag für Sozialwissenschaften 2005, pp. 29–30.

35 Mulaj: Resisting an Oppressive Regime, p. 1111; Bennett: The Kosovo Liberation Army, p. 162; Judah: *Kosovo*, p. 135.

36 Judah: Growing Pains of the Kosovo Liberation Army, p. 22.

considered a key figure.[37] The secondary literature is also largely unanimous in seeing Serbian atrocities against Kosovo-Albanian civilians as one of KLA's primary motivations. While its militarised activities were contextualised and even justified in light of these atrocities, the army's existence and activities were nonetheless portrayed to be a central reason for the Kosovo Conflict of the late 1990s.

While the KLA has been subject to extensive research, comparably little concrete information is available about its Serbian counterpart: the police forces active in Kosovo, which had been trained specifically to fight terrorism. These units were armed with tanks, artillery, helicopters and machine guns and thus resembled an army more than a police unit.[38] According to German press coverage, Milošević was adamant about deploying police units rather than the army, as the unrest in Kosovo was an internal matter. This was also Belgrade's central argument why the international community should not get involved in Kosovo.[39] No academic or journalistic sources cite any numbers, making it difficult to quantify KLA's opponents.

During the early phase of the violence in Kosovo (beginning of 1998), the Serbian police engaged in low-scale attacks on Kosovo-Albanian villages in the Drenica region; frequently the inhabitants were expelled or killed.[40] As the region was a KLA-stronghold, Milošević was determined to obliterate the Kosovo-Albanian army in a campaign that was initiated in March 1998. Targeting Adem Jashari, a KLA-leader, who lived in Drenica, Serbian forces shelled and bombed "[…] Jashari's compound for three consecutive days [starting on 5 March 1998], killing fifty-eight people […] including eighteen women and ten children."[41] This attack initiated a wave of violence by Serbian police forces, which aimed to find and eradicate all KLA-members in the villages of the Drenica region. However, this went hand-in-hand with expelling or killing Kosovo-Albanian civilians – a process both academics and journalists termed 'ethnic cleansing.'[42] Responding to the intensified violence, the

37 Bennett: The Kosovo Liberation Army, p. 162; Vickers: *Between Serb and Albanian*, p. 259.

38 Petritsch / Pichler: *Kosovo-Kosova*, pp. 105–106; LeBor: *Milosevic*, p. 280.

39 For example afp/dpa/rtr/kann: Nato schickt Kampfbeobachter auf den Weg. In: *FR*, 25.03.1999, p. 1; Gerhard Quast: 'Unsere Geduld ist am Ende'. In: *Junge Freiheit* [henceforth *JF*], 13.03.1998, p. 2; also mentioned in LeBor: *Milosevic*, p. 281.

40 OSCE: Kosovo/Kosova: As Seen, As Told: An Analysis of the Human Rights Findings of the OSCE Kosovo Verification Mission October 1998 to June 1999, 05.11.1999. http://www.osce.org/odihr/17772 (accessed 27.08.2014), pp. 272–282.

41 Mulaj: Resisting an Oppressive Regime, p. 1110.

42 See Introduction, fn. 63.

Kosovo-Albanian army increased its militarised activities, attacking Serbian police units, Serbian civilians and suspected Kosovo-Albanian collaborators.[43] As Wolfgang Ischinger evaluated in retrospect, the Kosovo Conflict cannot be understood without the violence that unfolded in Drenica at the time.[44]
Amidst the on-going violence in Kosovo, which was marked by massacres on both sides and ethnic cleansing perpetrated by Serbian forces against Kosovo-Albanian civilians, one parcularly incident – in Račak – has gained much attention. Račak is a Kosovo-Albanian town where 45 people were killed in January 1999, though it remains disputed if they were massacred civilians or Kosovo-Albanian combatants. Importantly, until today there is no generally accepted narrative of the incident. Following the initial surge of violence in 1998, a ceasefire known as the Holbrooke-Milošević-Agreement was negotiated on 13 October, 1998. This stipulated amongst other points that 2,000 unarmed OSCE-observers headed by the American diplomat William Walker would monitor Kosovo and ensure that the ceasefire was adhered to.[45] Nevertheless, both Serbian and Kosovo-Albanian combatants continued their military endeavours on a small yet persistent scale, consolidating their strength.[46] Soon, conflict escalated "[…] around the country, with Račak being one of the 'hot spots'" where 45 people were killed.[47] Previously, on 8 and 10 January, two Serbian soldiers had been ambushed and killed by KLA-fighters from Račak, a KLA stronghold.[48] In retaliation, Serbian forces moved towards Račak, where fighting broke out between Serbian and Kosovo-Albanian combatants during the morning of the 15 January. Serbian soldiers pushed back the KLA and took over the village. According to Judah,

> twenty-three men were […] taken away. Shooting was heard at 3.00 pm […] The villagers thought that the 23 had been taken to Štimlje police station, but […] at 4.00 a.m., according to the testimonies given to Human Rights Watch, the villagers discovered the bodies.[49]

43 OSCE: Kosovo/Kosova: As Seen, As Told.

44 Günter Hofmann: Wie Deutschland in den Krieg geriet. In: *Die Zeit*, 12.05.1999. http://www.zeit.de/1999/20/199920.krieg_.xml, p. 2 (accessed 27.08.2014).

45 Petritsch / Pichler: *Kosovo-Kosova*, pp. 136–138, 141.

46 Mark Wolfgram: Democracy and Propaganda: NATO's War in Kosovo. In: *European Journal of Communication* 23,153 (2008), pp. 153–171, here p. 156.

47 Chris Bird: Kosovo Slides back into War. In: *The Guardian*, 17.01.2001. http://www.guardian.co.uk/world/2001/jan/17/warcrimes.balkans (accessed 27.08.2014).

48 Wolfgram: Democracy and Propaganda, p. 159; Petritsch / Pichler: *Kosovo-Kosova*, p. 159; Heinz Loquai: *Der Kosovo-Konflikt*. Baden-Baden: Nomos 2000, pp. 45–46.

49 Judah: *War and Revenge*, p. 193.

These bodies were found in a ditch while other fatalities were detected in various locations in the village. When the bodies were discovered on 16 January 1999, Walker immediately labelled the incident a 'massacre' and 'grave crime against humanity' in a press conference and blamed the Serbian forces for the atrocities.[50] Although these were his personal conclusions and lacked judicial or forensic evidence, his accusation was widely echoed in the international media.

Based on this sequence of events, the killings in Račak could accurately be termed a 'massacre.' However, sceptical voices within the OSCE itself as well as in the international media, for example *The Guardian* and *Le Monde,* expressed their reservations, deeming Walker's assessment too unreflected and one-sided.[51] The Serbian government vehemently contested this version and maintained that all the fatalities were KLA-soldiers who had fallen in combat and had later been changed into civilian clothing by the KLA to make the incident appear as a 'massacre' of innocent victims.[52] Due to these competing perceptions of the events in Račak and the remaining ambiguities surrounding the incident, the term 'massacre' will only be used in this book when in direct citations, or else placed in quotation marks. Regardless, the international community perceived the incident as an indisputable breach of the cease-fire by Serbian forces and as a sign that the violence in Kosovo would persist unless diplomatic and military pressure was applied.

In 1999 alone, one million Kosovo-Albanians had been forced to leave their homes – a significant increase from the previous year, when 300,000 people had been forced to flee. Eye-witness reports of "summary executions" and rape were frequent.[53] The humanitarian urgency of the situation was cited by international politicians – including Germany's Chancellor Gerhard Schröder and his Foreign Minister, Joschka Fischer – to intervene in Kosovo militarily and to stop Milošević after a decade of mass violence in the Balkans. Proponents of such an international intervention feared a Russian veto in the UN Security Council. Consequently, this forum of international diplomacy was avoided and instead NATO launched air-strikes against Serbia and Kosovo in April 1999. By contributing to the bombardment of Serbian troops in Kosovo

50 Petritsch / Pichler: *Kosovo-Kosova*, p. 159; Loquai: *Der Kosovo-Konflikt*, p. 45.

51 Petritsch / Pichler: *Kosovo-Kosova*, pp. 159–160.

52 Loquai: *Der Kosovo-Konflikt*, p. 46.

53 Ivo Daalder / Michael E. O'Hanlon: *Winning Ugly: NATO's War to Save Kosovo*. Washington, D. C.: Brookings Institution Press 2000, p. 108–110.

as well as major Serbian cities including Belgrade and Novi Sad, German soldiers participated in active combat for the first time since the Second World War; significantly without a UN-mandate.[54]

The following chapters will analyse the various timeframes of the wars in Bosnia and Kosovo through the prism of the German print media coverage. In the next chapter we will commence with the eruption of violence in Bosnia in 1991/1992.

54 For more details on the Kosovo War and German involvement in it, see chapter 8.

Chapter 3
1991–1992:
The Descent into War – Early German Press Coverage

The disintegration of Yugoslavia in the early 1990s heralded a decade of war and atrocities. The region's geographical proximity to Western Europe and that it was the first war in Europe since the Second World War awoke the international community's interest.

Historical Background

Following Slovenia's and Croatia's previously mentioned declarations of independence in 1991, Germany, led by a conservative-liberal coalition of the Christian-Democrats (CDU) and the Free Liberal Party (FDP), readily supported both countries and was willing to recognise their self-government. Chancellor Helmut Kohl (CDU) and Foreign Minister Hans-Dietrich Genscher (FDP), who was replaced by Klaus Kinkel (FDP) in 1992, were the most important German actors with regard to the country's policy towards the Balkans. Widely known as the "father of German unity", Kohl had spearheaded the successful unification of East and West Germany in 1990 after the fall of the Berlin Wall in 1989.[1] This process of unification had been strongly influenced by the notion of the peoples' right to self-determination,[2] which in turn coined the Kohl government's foreign policy in the Balkans.

1 Heribert Prantl: Ikone mit löchrigem Mantel. In: *Süddeutsche Zeitung*, 26.09.2012. http://www.sueddeutsche.de/politik/altkanzler-helmut-kohl-ikone-mit-loechrigem-mantel-1.1478853 (accessed 25.08.2014).

2 Spohr: German Unification, p. 877.

Thus, both Kohl and his respective foreign ministers supported the republics' striving for independence.

The EC-members had initially been divided in their reactions to these declarations. While Great Britain and France feared that a disintegrated Yugoslavia would cause severe geo-political instability in the region, Germany insisted on the right to self-determination and endorsed both as independent republics on 23 December 1991.[3] The remaining EC-members followed on 15 January 1992.[4] Germany's hasty recognition, often referred to as an *Alleingang*,[5] caused considerable discord in the EC. Fearing an exceedingly confident and assertive Germany so soon after unification, particularly British politicians accused Germany of pursuing a 'Fourth Reich', which Daniele Conversi terms 'German-bashing'.[6] The author further argues that contrary to EC-allegations, Germany's policies did not accelerate the Yugoslav Wars.

The reasons for Germany's hasty and unilateral recognition have puzzled many scholars and have been attributed to various factors. Among them range disillusionment of the EC's disparate and previously ineffective policies and the aim to allow other countries the right of self-determination, which had been granted to Germany in the course of its recent unification.[7] Furthermore, Marie-Janine Calic alludes to Germany's historical experiences as a further component that influenced the country's foreign policy in Yugoslavia. "Many Germans believed that inherited guilt obliged the Federal Republic to assume responsibility for the people in the former Yugoslavia."[8]

When Bosnia declared its independence on 1 March 1992, the EC's response was more uniform and the new country was recognised by all EC-members. However, following previous policy decisions, what was left of Yugoslavia

3 Daniele Conversi: German-Bashing and the Breakup of Yugoslavia. In: Sabrina Ramet (ed.): *The Donald W. Treadgold Papers*. Seattle: Henry M. Jackson School of International Studies, University of Washington 1998, pp. 12–13; Maull: Germany in the Yugoslav Crisis, p. 102; see also Marc Weller: The International Response to the Dissolution of the Socialist Federal Republic of Yugoslavia. In: *The American Journal of International Law* 86,3 (1992), pp. 569–607; Hanns Maull: Germany in the Yugoslav Crisis. In: *Survival* 37,4 (1995–96), pp. 99–130.

4 Michael Libal: *Limits of Persuasion: Germany and the Yugoslav Crisis, 1991–1992*. Westport: Praenger 1997, p. 86.

5 German term for unilateral policies, literally meaning 'going-it-alone.'

6 Conversi: German-Bashing, pp. 8–9, 21.

7 Weller: The International Response to the Dissolution of the Socialist Federal Republic of Yugoslavia; Lawrence Freedman: Why the West Failed. In: *Foreign Policy* 97 (Winter 1994–95), pp. 53–69; Jonathan Eyal: *Europe and Yugoslavia: Lessons from a Failure*. London: Royal United Services Institute for Defence Studies 1993; Maull: Germany in the Yugoslav Crisis, pp. 104.

8 Marie-Janine Calic: German Perspectives. In: Alex Danchev / Thomas Halverson (eds): *International Perspectives on the Yugoslav Conflict*. Houndmills: Palgrave Macmillan 1996, p. 72.

declared war on Bosnia two days later, on 3 March 1992. Due to the EC's previous recogntion of Bosnia's independence, Western Europe – and with it Germany – were drawn into this war.

This chapter will examine the German print media coverage between 1 December 1991 and 9 May 1992, which encompasses the months leading up to and the initial weeks of the Bosnian War. Themes explored in this chapter include the German press' explanations for the violence, the role of the Yugoslav Peoples' Army (JNA) in the coverage, while also examining issues such as language and authorship. In this period, the far-left magazine *Konkret* only published one article pertaining to the Balkans.[9] Its content did not cover any of the issues analysed in this chapter, but will be included where fitting. Lastly, it must be noted that as this lead-up to the Bosnian War overlapped with the on-going war in Croatia, some of the articles drew on the Croatian case-study to underline their arguments. However, due to largley the same actors and connected relevant themes, the German press coverage is very relevant to the Bosnian case-study.

Explaining the Violence

With tensions increasing in Bosnia, the first questions explored by the German press inevitably addressed the reasons for this violence. *BILD* only published 47 articles on the Balkans in total – a mere fraction compared to 190 *taz*-articles and 258 in *FAZ* – of which none addressed the historic background of the violence or why the conflict ignited. This can be attributed the tabloid's general style. Articles were very short – no longer than 30 to 50 words – and thus only covered the bare minimum of current events, if that. In contrast, most other publications contextualised their day-to-day coverage with references to specific historical events. These partly mirror those mentioned in the previous chapter on the historical background, namely: the Ottoman rule of the Balkans;[10] the 1914 assassination of the Austrian Archduke Franz Ferdinand in Sarajevo that sparked World War One;[11] the Second

9 Due to the magazine's monthly editorial cycle, the June 1992 edition will also be analysed in this chapter.

10 Karl Grobe: Die vergiftete nationale Frage. In: *FR*, 24.01.1992, p. 3; Peter Sturm: Großmächte, Rivalitäten, Völkervielfalt. In: *FAZ*, 13.02.1992, p. 6; Anonymous: Wir sind des Wahnsinns müde. In: *Der Spiegel* [henceforth *Spiegel*], 03.02.1992, p. 174; Gerd Schumann: Die bosnische Zwickmühle. In: *taz*, 09.12.1991, p. 11; Carl Gustaf Ströhm: Der bosnische Topf. In: *Welt*, 27.02.1992, p. 2.

11 yr: Prüfstein Bosnien. In: *FR*, 27.01.1992, p. 3; Anonymous: Serben, Kroaten,

World War[12] – which will be discussed in more detail in a moment – and Tito's Communist Yugoslavia.[13] The common conclusion was that hatred between Serbs, Croats and Muslims had existed throughout all of these periods, explaining the disintegration of Yugoslavia with these rivalries. As can be expected from day-to-day press coverage, none of the publications provided coherent historical narratives, and when offering a historical context at all, articles frequently alluded to it superficially in a single sentence or paragraph at most while concentrating primarily on current affairs.[14] This may have resulted from the complexity of Balkan history or the limited space available in the articles. However, this could also result from the nature of news, which "[…] is not about long-term processes but about short-term events […] Reporters tend to be more interested in events than causes."[15]

These references to ancient rivalries were phrased in very general terms. For example a *Spiegel*-article mentioned almost casually that "the Serbs, who are still aspiring a *Großreich* […]" were waging a war for territory.[16] Similarly an article in *FR* stated that "briefly one can say that in the entire Balkan-peninsula, the idea of national identity has constantly been misused as an instrument by

Moslems – worum geht es in diesem Krieg? In: *BILD*, 22.04.1992, p. 2; Peter Sturm: Großmächte, Rivalitäten, Völkervielfalt. In: *FAZ*, 13.02.1992, p. 6; Erich Rathfelder: Serbien oder Klein-Jugoslawien? In: *taz*, 28.01.1992, p. 11; Carl Gustaf Ströhm: Heraus aus dem Konvoi. In: *Welt*, 17.12.1991, p. 2.

12 Harry Schleicher: Prüfstein für Frieden. In: *FR*, 27.01.1992, p. 2; Hermann Baumann: Ein konzeptloses Vorpreschen. In: *Allgemeine Jüdische Wochenzeitung* [henceforth *AJW*], 09.01.1992, p. 2; Johann Georg Reißmüller: Kroatien und Slowenien die Opfer. In: *FAZ*, 18.02.1992, p. 1; Anonymous: Operation Tintenklecks. In: *Spiegel*, 02.12.1991, pp. 178–179; dpa/afp/ap: Altstadt von Dubrovnik verwüstet. In: *taz*, 09.12.1991, p. 8; Ströhm: Heraus aus dem Konvoi. In: *Welt*, 17.12.1991, p. 2.

13 Nicole Janigro: „Mit den anderen zu sprechen wird immer schwieriger." In: *FR*, 04.01.1992, p. 18; Paul Lendvai: Das Gespenst der Balkanisierung. In: *FAZ*, 29.02.1992, p. 51; thos: „Relative" Mehrheiten im Dreivölkerstaat. In: *taz*, 06.04.1992, p. 3; Walter Mayr: In den Köpfen ist Krieg. In: *Spiegel*, 20.01.1992, pp. 152–158; Carl Gustaf Ströhm: „Moslems, lauft nicht weg, das ist euer Land." In: *Welt*, 09.05.1992, p. 3.

14 The only exceptions are Olaf Ihlau: Krakeel auf dem Balkan. In: *Spiegel*, 23.12.1991, p. 137; Schumann: Die bosnische Zwickmühle. In: *taz*, 09.12.1991, p. 11; Karl Grobe: Die vergiftete nationale Frage. In: *FR*, 24.01.1992, p. 3; Harry Schleicher: Wir werden keinen Fussbreit unseres Bodens hergeben. In: *FR*, 29.01.1992, p. 5; Wolfgang Günter Lerch: Wieder Schüsse in Sarajevo. In: *FAZ*, 03.03.1992, p. 12; Stefan Dietrich: Ferner Balkan, naher Krieg. In: *FAZ*, 18.02.1992, p. 5.

15 Nel Ruigrok / Jan A. de Ridder / Otto Scholten: News Coverage of the Bosnian War in Dutch Newspapers: Impact and Implication. In: Philip Seib (ed.): *Media and Conflict in the Twenty-First Century*. New York: Palgrave Macmillan 2005, pp. 157–184, here p. 159.

16 Anonymous: Im Maul des Krokodils. In: *Spiegel*, 09.12.1991, p. 171; also in Olaf Ihlau: Krakeel auf dem Balkan. In: *Spiegel*, 23.12.1991, p. 137.

great powers […]"[17] Lastly, a *taz*-article asserted in equally general terms that Balkan "politicians like nothing more than to talk about the past […] Polemics replace arguments. Abrasiveness eliminates reason."[18] This vague word-choice left the reader with the impression that Yugoslavia was a powder-keg, threatening to explode at any time. However, the reader actually gained very little insight where this antagonism came from and how century-old conflicts could fuel discontent in the 1990s. It must be noted that this missing depth did not necessarily result from the correspondents' ignorance regarding the complexities of Balkan history. Rather, the 'ancient hatreds' theory was the common interpretation found in the literature produced before the 1990s which would have informed a journalist at that time.[19]

FAZ and *taz* also portrayed the abstruse hatreds in cartoons. Both conveyed disbelief that 20th century politics could be marked by seemingly out-dated concepts such as historical hatreds.[20]

Figure 1: Fritz Behrendt; printed in *FAZ*, 30 March 1992, p. 3.

Figure 2: Fritz Behrendt; printed in *FAZ*, 4 May 1992, p. 3.

Both cartoons portrayed the Serbian character in the same way: as a man dressed in traditional clothing, with a rugged beard and Chetnik insignia on his hat. In both cases the Chetnik is the sole initiator of violence. While

17 Karl Grobe: Die vergiftete nationale Frage. In: *FR*, 24.01.1992, p. 3; also in Peter Sturm: Großmächte, Rivalitäten, Völkervielfalt. In: *FAZ*, 13.02.1992, p. 6.

18 Gerd Schumann: Die bosnische Zwickmühle. In: *taz*, 09.12.1991, p. 11.

19 For example Forbes / Toynbee / Mitrany / Hogarth: *The Balkans: A History of Bulgaria, Serbia, Greece, Rumania, Turkey*; Singleton: *A Short History*; Robert Kaplan: *Balkan Ghosts: A Journey through History*. New York: Picador 2005; Ivo Banac: *The National Questions in Yugoslavia*. Ithaca: Cornell University Press 1984.

20 For example taz/ap/dpa / dora: Carringtons schwierige Mission. In: *taz*, 19.12.1991, p. 12.

figure 2 also criticises the EC's inability to stop the violence, the central message of *FAZ's* two visual representations was that the Serbian protagonist, but also his Bosnian victim in figure 2, were stuck in their backward, out-dated ways. This condescension created a stark dichotomy between 'the Balkans,' which appeared barbaric and uncivilised, and 'the West' depicted by formally-dressed bureaucrats. The vague yet judgemental representation of Yugoslavia as a backward powder-keg may have coloured the broad public's understanding of the evolving conflict and prohibited a deeper engagement with the region, its history and the sources of its problems.

World War Two

Amidst this vague yet threatening notion of ancient hatreds, the Second World War was particularly relevant in the German press coverage. As detailed in chapter one, two opposing extremist actors during the Second World War were Croatia's fascist Ustasha and the Serbian Chetniks. Both had perpetrated war crimes against their enemy, specifically targeting civilians. The radical formations in Croatia and Serbia that were forming in the 1990s used the Ustasha or Chetniks as role models, adopting their predecessors' names and insignia. All publications except *BILD* saw the antagonism stemming from these two opposing extremist formations and their echo as pivotal to explain the violence of the 1990s, though they interpreted this nexus very differently. While *FR*, *Spiegel* and *AJW* primarily focused their blame on the fascist Ustasha, *FAZ*, *Welt* and *taz* concentrated on the Chetniks' culpability. *JF* lay in the middle of these two factions.

Starting with the first category, Daniel Riegger's *FR*-article argued that the Ustasha-crimes had never been processed or reconciled sufficiently and were therefore resurfacing in the 1990s.[21] Without offering any further details, the reader was left with self-constructed images of fascist war crimes, which implicitly blamed Croatia in the 1990s for reviving their fascist tendencies. A similarly vague yet accusatory tone could be found in two *Spiegel*-articles published in January and March 1992, which presented the Ustasha as the primary perpetrators of atrocities during the Second World War. In January, Walter Mayr reported that in one case "during the Second World War" – without offering a date or location – Serbian civilians had been massacred by the Nazis' elite troops, the *Schutzstaffel* (SS), along with collaborating Ustasha

21 Daniel Riegger: Versöhnung nicht notwendig. In: *FR*, 24.02.1992, p. 2; also mentioned in Harry Schleicher: Angst vor der „Nacht der langen Messer". In: *taz*, 07.12.1991, p. 6.

and Muslims. By reminding the reader that the Ustasha had collaborated with the Nazis, they were immediately discredited in most readers' minds, though the article gave no concrete information, nor specific evidence.[22] In March, *Spiegel* featured an interview with the main Serbian opposition leader against Milošević, Vuk Drašković. While Drašković also blamed Serbian nationalism for the violence in the 1990s, he primarily accused the Ustasha. He argued that "for 45 years the Croats imputed the Ustasha-crimes to the Germans. But now it has been historically proven that the Germans [themselves] were horror-stricken over the gruesome Croatian methods."[23] Again the reader did not gain any knowledge about the details of the horrific cruelty. However by presenting them as so extreme that even the Nazis were shocked by them, the reader was left with a vague yet appalling view of the Ustasha's brutality.

AJW's articles also focused exclusively on Ustasha's culpability, but introduced a novel aspect by concentrating on its anti-Semitism, arguing that Tudjman aimed to revive these sentiments amongst Croats in the 1990s.[24] Wolf Oschlies' article reiterated that Tudjman's movement resembled the Croatian Ustasha, or as the author called them 'Croatian Jew-butchers.' Oschlies corroborated his accusations of Tudjman being anti-Semitic by drawing on his autobiography, where Tudjman wrote that 'only' 30,000–40,000 people had been killed in the Ustasha concentration camp Jasenovac. The author continued that a more accurate estimate was 300,000, most of whom had been Jews.[25] By focusing primarily on Tudjman's anti-Semitism, *AJW's* articles placed the Jewish victimhood in the centre of their narrative. Consequently, they did not explain the historical antagonism between Ustasha and the Serbian Chetnik; the latter was not even mentioned by name. These articles could have led the reader to believe that the ancient tensions, which were now being revived, had existed between fascist Croatians and Jews.

An article in the far-right *JF* did focus on the Serbian-Croatian nexus, while simultaneously presenting many of the issues from *AJW's* articles very differently. In a June article by Michael Paulwitz, the author defended Tudjman and his association with the Ustasha, praising him for valuing the Ustasha-state, which had broken a taboo. The author postulated that its previous 'demonisation' had been a part of Tito's Yugoslav 'reason of state' and had merely been utilised to hinder Croatia's striving for independence. The article then

22 Walter Mayr: In den Köpfen ist Krieg. In: *Spiegel*, 20.01.1992, p. 154.

23 Anonymous: Wir sind des Wahnsinns müde. In: *Spiegel*, 03.02.1992, p. 174.

24 Hermann Baumann: Ein konzeptloses Vorpreschen. In: *AJW*, 09.01.1992, p. 2.

25 Wolf Oschlies: Tudjman und sein trauriges Juden-Bild. In: *AJW*, 06.02.1992, p. 2.

continued that Tudjman had rightfully corrected the frequently cited number estimating that 700,000 Serbians had been killed in the Jasenovac concentration camp, positing that 60,000 people had been killed in all Croatian camps combined.[26] The different numbers cited in *JF* and *AJW* suggests the level of disagreement amongst various parties regarding historical facts. While *JF* did not extrapolate the antagonism from the Second World War to the violence of the 1990s, its praise for Tudjman's historical revisionism proves the paper's positive disposition towards Croatia.

In contrast to the previous publications, *FAZ*, *Welt* and *taz* drew on the antagonism between Croats and Serbs during World War Two to blame the Serbs for the on-going violence. For example on 24 April 1992, *FAZ*-editor Johann Georg Reißmüller wrote that the hatred between Croats and Serbs during the Second World War resulted in gruesome massacres on both sides. However, at the end of the war, Reißmüller continued, the Serbian Chetniks "[...] carried the murder to a genocidal climax [...]" The author continued that the Croatian people had continually searched for a peaceful pan-Slavic solution, but all efforts failed because of perpetual Serbian offensives. "Only the Serbian war of aggression in this past year [...had] finally disposed the Croats of this idea,"[27] he argued. The author's complete disregard for Ustasha war crimes combined with his utilisation of the loaded term 'genocide' to describe the Chetniks' atrocities underlined his one-sided comprehension of past events. According to him, Croatia had always been a peace-seeking country suffering under its brutal Serbian neighbour. Reißmüller's pro-Croatian interpretation appeared in numerous articles,[28] which merited the scornful title of being a 'Croat-protector' as stated by *Spiegel*-founder Rudolf Augstein.[29]

The single *Konkret*-article published about the Balkans in this time-period discussed precisely this matter. In the magazine's January edition, Wolfgang Pohrt cited various pieces by Reißmüller which displayed particular anti-Serbian tendencies. In one example Pohrt quoted, Reißmüller had recently stated that 'the Serbs' had assaulted the Croatian population. Pohrt contested

26 Michael Paulwitz: Kroatiens Ustasha. In: *JF*, June 1992, p. 8.

27 Johann Georg Reißmüller: Manchmal verbündet, manchmal entzweit. In: *FAZ*, 24.04.1992, p. 14; also in Reißmüller: Kroatien und Slowenien die Opfer. In: *FAZ*, 18.02.1992, p. 1.

28 The collection of his articles published in Johann Georg Reißmüller: *Der Krieg vor unserer Haustür*. Stuttgart: DVA 1992, offers some evidence, for example: Der Terror der „Volksarmee": Ein Abend in der Landstadt Virovitica, 19.02.1991; Hoffnung auf eine friedliche Trennung, 23.02.1991; Die drohende Vernichtung, 04.10.1991; Ein verwüstetes Land: Folgen des serbischen Angriffskrieges, 31.10.1991.

29 Rudolf Augstein: ... sondern auch Wut und Haß. In: *Spiegel*, 06.01.1992, p. 23.

that "whether the Serbs are as Reißmüller portrays them – which is hard to imagine – or if one can say at all what the Serbs are like, is completely insignificant […]" to Reißmüller.[30] This very good point begs a more differentiated analysis that avoids blanket-terminology such as 'the Serbs'. While this could undoubtedly be applied to other publications aside from *FAZ*, what must be recorded at this point is *FAZ's* interpretation of the antagonism during the Second World War in a manner which favoured the Croatian Ustasha.

Surprisingly the left-leaning *taz* took a similar approach, discrediting Serbian politics and arguing that Serbia distorted history to serve its agenda and reignite old tensions. For example, in a January-article Erich Rathfelder accused the country of making the co-existence of Serbs and Croats difficult by insisting on apologies from Croatia for murdering Serbs and Jews during the Second World War.[31] Interestingly, the article did not describe the atrocities committed by the Ustasha and instead focused only on Serbia's allegedly unjust claims of victimhood, which he claimed perpetuated the conflict. Another *taz*-article reported that some Serbian politicians were insisting that Serbia had fallen victim to 'genocide' perpetrated by the fascist Ustasha during the Second World War.[32] Readers at the time may have interpreted this use of the term 'genocide' as inflated and may consequently have challenged such claims.

The portrayal of the exaggerated Serbian claims was further corroborated by a *taz*-interview with Tudjman, in which he dismissed the linkages between the fascist Ustasha and the contemporary violence. At this point it is worth noting that *taz* was the only publication at the time to report Tudjman's response to these allegations. In the interview, which he gave during a state-visit in Bonn,[33] he stated that while 'extremist elements' such as Croatian militias wearing old Ustasha-uniforms certainly existed, these were very few in number. Moreover the Croatian President reiterated that he had distanced himself from the Ustasha many years ago and insisted on democratic developments.[34] Significantly, the interview is also marked by lacking discernment. For example, even though Tudjman insisted that he had distanced himself from the Ustasha, the

30 Wolfgang Pohrt: Tödliche Liebschaften. In: *Konkret*, January 1992, p. 42.

31 Erich Rathfelder: Sarajevo wird zur geteilten Stadt. In: *taz*, 22.01.1992, p. 9.

32 Roland Hofwiler: Bosnien als neuer Kriegsherd. In: *taz*, 11.01.1992, p. 2; also in Joszef Bata: Mobilisierung gegen Milosevic. In: *taz*, 09.03.1992, p. 8.

33 Reported in G. H.: Belgrad will Großserbien um jeden Preis: Präsident Tudjman vor der Deutschen Gesellschaft für Auslandskunde. In: *FAZ*, 07.12.1991, p. 2.

34 Hasso Suliak: Tudjman: Frühere Anerkennung Kroatiens hätte Opfer verhindert. In: *taz*, 07.12.1991, p. 1.

article does not remind the reader – or follow-up with Tudjman in the interview – that the fascist formation's insignia, songs and legends had been reintroduced by Tudjman, showing a clear affiliation between his contemporary movement and the fascist party.[35]

Just as *FAZ* and *taz*, the conservative broadsheet *Welt* also focused on the Serbians as the main perpetrators of war crimes during the Second World War. However, *Welt*'s East-Europe correspondent Carl Gustaf Ströhm took a different approach by placing Bosnia within the historical antagonism. Ströhm concentrated on the massacres perpetrated by Serbians against Bosnia's Muslim population and consequently never mentioned their Croatian counterparts.[36] He argued that the Serbians' 'bloody butchery' of the 1940s resulted in a paralysing fear which still dominated the politics of the Bosnian President Alija Izetbegović, whom critics had deemed 'weak' due to his keen interest to preserve peace, even if this meant conceding to Serbia diplomatically.[37] Shortly after the Bosnian War commenced in April 1992, Ströhm mirrored the victimhood of Bosnians to the contemporary conflict: "airstrikes [...were] launched, Muslims praying in a mosque [...were] gunned down [...]"[38] This focus on the Serbian atrocities against Bosnia's defenceless population both during the Second World War and in the 1990s gave *Welt's* readership the perception that the Bosnian Muslims had been victimised for several decades – to the extent that in the 1990s they were too paralysed by fear to counteract the Serbian aggression.

The centrality of the Second World War and hostile paramilitary formations stemming from that period to explain the historical context to the readers is unmissable in the German coverage. However the divergent interpretations offered by the press regarding the Serbian-Croatian antagonism during the Second World War underlines how differently historical narratives can be constructed. Moreover it is striking how little the uninformed reader actually learned about this historic background of the region. None of the articles cited concrete numbers of Croatian and Serbian victims during World War Two, or specific war crimes which may have fuelled the antagonism. Rather

35 Carl Jacobsen: War Crimes in the Balkans: Media Manipulation, Historical Amnesia and Subjective Morality. In: *Coexistence* 4 (1993), pp. 313–325, here p. 313.

36 Carl Gustaf Ströhm: Vor einem Glaubenskrieg? In: *Welt*, 23.12.1991, p. 2; also in id.: Bosnien droht ein noch schlimmeres Blutbad. In: *Welt*, 27.12.1991, p. 5.

37 Carl Gustaf Ströhm: Moslemisches Dilemma. In: *Welt*, 04.03.1992, p. 2; Ströhm: „Moslems, lauft nicht weg, das ist euer Land". In: *Welt*, 09.05.1992, p. 3.

38 Carl Gustaf Ströhm: Barbarei in Bosnien. In: *Welt*, 09.04.1992, p. 2.

the articles gave a sense of general, barbaric violence seeping into the 1990s from the dark age of fascism.

The Jewish Dimension

The interpretation that fascist elements were returning to the Balkans can also be traced in selected articles in *AJW*, *FR* and *taz*. These three publications singled out the theme of Jews living in Former Yugoslavia in the 1990s, introducing a unique perspective to interpret the violence. Starting with *AJW's* articles, these are remarkable, as they presented Yugoslavia's Jewish population as the primary victims of the violence in the 1990s.[39] None of them framed the on-going violence in former Yugoslavia as a conflict between Croats, Serbs and Muslims. For example on 16 April 1992, an *AJW*-article reported that Israel was planning the evacuation of all Jews living in Bosnia. It elaborated that since the beginning of the violence in the Balkans last year, 210 of the 5,000 members of Yugoslavia's Jewish communities had already left for Israel.[40] In a second article, published one week later, the author Wolf Bruer reported that with war breaking out in Bosnia, "thousands of civilians had to flee, including many belonging to the local Jewish communities." The author continued that 160 Jews had already left Sarajevo for Belgrade, where they felt safe, though another 1,200 Bosnian Jews were still in the fought-over territories.[41] The sole focus on the Jewish victims of the war is jarring and disregards the basic framework of the conflict. One could argue that *AJW* is a special-interest newspaper that primarily reports on Jewish cultural life around the world and can be seen merely as a weekly supplement to other daily newspapers. Nonetheless, the complete omittance of the on-going war in *AJW*'s coverage, which arguably could have enriched and explained its articles, underlines the one-dimensional interpretation offered by this Jewish cultural publication.

In addition to *AJW's* coverage, the theme of the Jewish identity as a noteworthy factor also influenced the interpretation of the on-going violence in the left-leaning *FR* and *taz*. The former featured an interview with the

39 Wolf Oschlies: Tudjman und sein trauriges Juden-Bild. In: *AJW*, 06.02.1992, p. 2; Anonymous: Israel plant Evakuierung der Juden aus jugoslawischen Kriegsgebieten. In: *AJW*, 16.04.1992, p. 2; Wolf Bruer: Gespalten in einem zerbrochenen Land. In: *AJW*, 23.04.1992, p. 1.

40 Anonymous: Israel plant Evakuierung der Juden aus jugoslawischen Kriegsgebieten. In: *AJW*, 16.04.1992, p. 2.

41 Wolf Bruer: Gespalten in einem zerbrochenen Land. In: *AJW*, 23.04.1992, p. 1.

Serbian theatre scholar Dragan Klaić which focused on his Jewish heritage. With questions such as "you lived as a Jew amongst Serbs?" the interviewer led the conversation into the same direction as *AJW's* articles, in which the Jewish community in former Yugoslavia was studied. Klaić explained that he had never been exposed to anti-Semitism and had always seen himself as a Yugoslav more than a Jew. However, with the break-up of Yugoslavia, this identity no longer existed, leaving him with an indeterminable status.[42] While his struggle to construct an identity other than Yugoslav is crucial in light of the country's disintegration, the reader is left in the dark why the journalist assumed that Serbians would have demonstrated anti-Semitic tendencies. A *taz*-interview with the French philosopher Alain Finkielkraut introduced the same theme equally clumsily. The opening question – "does your Jewish heritage play a role in your decision to side with Croatia in the current conflict?" – deflected from the intended content of the interview, namely the international community's role in the conflict.[43] Similar to the *FR*-article, the larger context of the centrality of Jewish heritage in this conflict was not explained. Moreover, both interviews portrayed Serbia as a particular threat to the Jewish population in the Balkans while contradictorily *AJW's* article had reported that 160 Jews from Sarajevo had sought refuge in Belgrade. This adds to the assessment that *taz's* and *FR's* pieces were arbitrary and could have benefitted from more explanatory context. Perhaps the intended effect was to encourage German readers to associate anti-Semitism with Serbia.

The Role of Religion

As discussed previously, various historians identified religion as a cause for tensions when combined with nationalism in the 19th century.[44] With the resurgence of nationalism in the wake of the disintegration of Yugoslavia in the 1990s, religion returned as a divisive factor. Noel Malcolm postulates that parallel to the rise of Serbian and Croatian nationalism fortified by the policies of Slobodan Milošević and Franjo Tudjman, the Bosniaks strengthened their Muslim identity through a nationalist movement. Its conduit was the party of the Bosnian President, Alija Izetbegović, the SDA,[45] which expressed its

42 Heinz Klunker: „Auch Intellektuelle sind mitschuldig an diesem Bürgerkrieg". In: *FR*, Christmas 1991 [24.12.–26.12.1991], p. 11.

43 Ivo Glaser: Bürgerkrieg oder serbische Aggression? In: t*az*, 13.01.1992, p. 19.

44 See p. 32.

45 Stands for Stranka Demokratske Akcije, or Party of Democratic Action.

religious component through symbols such as the green crescent.[46] In addition, "[…] Islamic symbols and quotations from the Koran started to show up among [Bosnian] army units […]"[47] Moreover, the party emphasised its policy of Muslim nationalism in its "Statement of Programmatic Principles", which was published in March 1990. This declared that the SDA would "[…] revitalise this national consciousness of BH [Bosnia-Herzegovinian] Muslims and insist on respect for the fact of their national distinctness […]"[48]

Izetbegović was an appropriate leader for this cause, as his person was strongly associated with Islam. He had been jailed in 1983 for "alleged anti-state activities."[49] These charges arose from Izetbegović's publication *Islamic Declaration*, which "[…] the former communist authorities in Yugoslavia interpreted as a call for the introduction of fundamentalist Sharia law in Bosnia-Hercegovina […]"[50] Malcolm dismisses this interpretation as 'propaganda,' countering that

> this treatise, written in the late 1960s, is a general treatise on politics and Islam, addressed to the whole Muslim world; it is not about Bosnia and does not even mention Bosnia.[51]

Ivo Banac agrees that although Izetbegović "[…] champion[ed] a new Islamic order, he underscore[d] its commitment to the freedom of conscience [and] women's rights […]"[52] Nonetheless, in the 1990s, as Yugoslavia disintegrated and Bosnia defined an independent identity, Izetbegović's party drew heavily on Muslim characteristics to define their identity. This in turn was exclusionary towards other religious groups – the largely Catholic Croats and predominantly Orthodox Serbians – who also lived in Bosnia.

In spite of this presence of religious divisions, the German press barely referred to religion as a reason for the Bosnian conflict between December 1991 and early May 1992, which is puzzling as all publications adopted

46 Malcolm: *Bosnia*, pp. 218–219.

47 John Fine: The Various Faiths in the History of Bosnia: Middle Ages to the Present. In: Shatzmiller (ed.): *Islam and Bosnia*. Montreal: McGill-Queen's University Press 2002, pp. 3–23, here p. 19.

48 Gerard Toal / Carl Dahlman: *Bosnia Remade: Ethnic Cleansing and its Reversal*. Oxford: Oxford University Press 2011, p. 89.

49 Biondich: *The Balkans*, p. 203.

50 Anonymous: Obituary: Alija Izetbegovic. In: *BBC*, 19.10.2003. http://news.bbc.co.uk/2/hi/europe/3133038.stm (accessed 27.08.2014).

51 Malcolm: *Bosnia*, p. 219.

52 Ivo Banac: Bosnian Muslims: From Religious Community to Socialist Nationhood and Post-Communist Statehood, 1918–1992. In: Mark Pinson (ed.): *The Muslims of Bosnia-Herzegovina: Their Historic Development from the Middle Ages to the Dissolution of Yugoslavia*. Cambridge, Mass.: Harvard CMES 1996, pp. 129–154, here p. 148; also in Biondich: *The Balkans*, p. 203.

the common term 'Muslims' for Bosniaks.[53] Indeed, an uninformed reader may not even have realised that Serbs were predominantly Orthodox and Croats mostly Catholic. The topic of religion as an important factor in fuelling the conflict was only alluded to in isolated cases and primarily in *Spiegel*.[54] For example, Walter Mayr wrote a detailed exposé on the war, in which he described an Imam he met at a mosque in Sarajevo, who carried a loaded pistol under his robe and organised armed training for members of his congregation five times per week in the event of a Serbian ambush.[55] This portrayal of the Muslim territorial defence as a violent paramilitary formation with religious overtones alluded to a religious dimension in the conflict, which no other publication expressed so blatantly. A single *Welt*-article mentioned a religious dimension to the conflict. Carl Gustaf Ströhm reported that Izetbegović had been imprisoned by the communists for his religious publication.[56] After giving details of the increasing violence, the author concluded that Izetbegović had two options: "[...] either subservience to Serbia and the army or open conflict. That could lead Bosnia to a religious war between Muslims and Orthodox [Christians...]"[57] These isolated cases which mentioned religion did not see it as a cause for the conflict, but rather a symptom of it and a way in which the violence would develop.

The Role of the Yugoslav Peoples' Army

In addition to this historical context or lack thereof, the publications took more contemporary factors into account when designating the responsibility for the on-going violence, namely Milošević and the Yugoslav Peoples' Army (JNA).[58] Starting with the latter, the JNA was one of the main military actors in the Bosnian and Croatian Wars. After their declaration of independence, Milošević used the army as a vessel to re-establish a Serbian-dominated Yugoslavia and inclusive of the secessionist republics. Due to this centrality of the army, all publications except *JF* focused primarily on the JNA to explain the violence. Interestingly, *FAZ* consistently placed the army's name in quotation

53 In isolated cases the religious dimension was alluded to, e.g. Walter Mayr: In den Köpfen ist Krieg. In: *Spiegel*, 20.01.1992, p. 152, or Carl Gustaf Ströhm: Vor einem Glaubenskrieg. In: *Welt*, 23.12.1991, p. 2.

54 Anonymous: Wir sind des Wahnsinns müde. In: *Spiegel*, 03.02.1992, p. 174.

55 Walter Mayr: In den Köpfen ist Krieg. In: *Spiegel*, 20.01.1992, p. 152.

56 Carl Gustaf Ströhm: Vor einem Glaubenskrieg. In: *Welt*, 23.12.1991, p. 2; also in Anonymous: Grüne Fahnen. In: *Spiegel*, 23.12.1991, p. 145.

57 Carl Gustaf Ströhm: Vor einem Glaubenskrieg. In: *Welt*, 23.12.1991, p. 2.

58 This acronym is derived from the army's Yugoslav name "Jugoslovenska Narodna Armija".

marks when referring to it, perhaps to underline the fact that it did not represent the entire Yugoslav population, but rather the dominant Serbian section of it.

Before studying each publication individually, the coverage of one specific EC-report is worth noting, as four publications – *Welt*, *FAZ*, *FR* and *Spiegel* – all picked up on it in early December 1991. As the articles stated, the confidential report had been leaked to the press, though no other information was given regarding its framework, for example why it had been compiled or who its authors were.[59] It called JNA 'cowardly and immoral' and claimed that the army purposefully and preferably targeted schools, museums and hospitals and also massacred civilians, as *FAZ*, *Welt* and *Spiegel* reported.[60] *FR* was the only newspaper to elaborate that the report had also accused Croatian forces of "brutal and deliberate violence."[61] This selective coverage indicated that *FR* was much more inclined to report both viewpoints than the other publications. Considering *Spiegel's* previous reporting about the antagonism between Croats and Serbs during World War Two, which took a pro-Serbian stance, it is surprising that *Spiegel* did not follow *FR's* example, reminding the reader of Croatian war crimes. This discrepancy could be explained with the larger context of the *Spiegel*-article, which elaborated that the Croatian city of Osijek had been bombarded even after a cease-fire – the fourteenth – had been negotiated. This disregard for diplomatic endeavours and Serbian aggression may have fuelled *Spiegel's* selective coverage of the EC-report focusing on JNA's war crimes.

Apart from covering this EC-report, *Welt* did not pay much attention to JNA. Only two other articles stated that the army was responsible for "[…] the bloody disregard of minorities and human rights […]"[62] and that the army's attacks on Bosnia were unprovoked.[63] *FAZ* and *BILD* on the other hand focused much more on JNA. One *FAZ*-article for example portrayed the army as the crux of the violence, quoting EC-diplomat Lord Carrington

59 DW: EG-Beobachter für Gegenschläge. In: *Welt*, 04.12.1991, p. 10; AP: EG-Beobachter: „Volksarmee ist feige". In: *FAZ*, 04.12.1991, p. 1; AP/Reuters/AFP: EG-Beobachter klagen Armee der Serben an. In: *FR*, 04.12.1991, p. 1; Anonymous: Im Maul des Krokodils. In: *Spiegel*, 09.12.1991, pp. 170–172.

60 DW: EG-Beobachter für Gegenschläge. In: *Welt*, 04.12.1991, p. 10; AP: EG-Beobachter: „Volksarmee ist feige". In: *FAZ*, 04.12.1991, p. 1; Anonymous: Im Maul des Krokodils. In: *Spiegel*, 09.12.1991, p. 171.

61 AP/Reuters/AFP: EG-Beobachter klagen Armee der Serben an. In: *FR*, 04.12.1991, p. 1.

62 Lothar Rübel: Perez hilft Belgrad. In: *Welt*, 09.12.1991, p. 2.

63 Carl Gustaf Ströhm: „Moslems, lauft nicht weg, das ist euer Land". In: *Welt*, 09.05.1992, p. 3.

who had stated "[…] that the 'Peoples' Army' […was] the true evil in all this confusion.'"[64] Other articles conjured the vision of an uncontrollable force, which was the main perpetrator of war crimes.[65] For example, *FAZ's* Balkan-correspondent Viktor Meier asserted in one article that "[…] the ghosts which Milošević awoke, especially the army, […were] now autonomous […]"[66] Similarly, *BILD* singled out the 'Serbian-dominated' Yugoslav army to be breaking cease-fires, rendering it solely responsible for the violence and consequently encouraging a one-sided interpretation of the subject-matter.[67] In a further article, the tabloid referred to the '*Kommunistenarmee*', a polemical and slightly derogatory form of 'Communist army', as one of the main actors in the war.[68] There was no cross-reference to JNA or explanation why it was deemed a communist army. Consequently this term seemed to be a deliberate attempt on behalf of *BILD* to denigrate the Yugoslav army by associating it with communism.

Rather than creating the sense of general calamity caused by JNA, articles in *taz*, *FR* and *Spiegel* were more concrete, reporting on specific atrocities. One such *taz*-article drew on a piece from the British broadsheet *The Guardian*, which reported of a 92-year-old Croatian farmer who had been brutally mowed down by a JNA-tank.[69] *taz's* Roland Hofwiler reprocessed this part in

64 Viktor Meier: Das eigentliche Übel ist die „Jugoslawische Volksarmee". In: *FAZ*, 13.04.1992, p. 7.

65 V.M.: Mehrere hundert Tote bei Kämpfen in Bosnien-Herzegovina. In: *FAZ*, 06.04.1992, p. 2; Ho.: Aufhebung der Sanktionen gegen Serbien? In: *FAZ* , 08.04.1992, p. 2.

66 Viktor Meier: Eine Zukunft ohne Jugoslawien. In: *FAZ*, 18.12.1991, p. 12.

67 Vollrath von Heintze: Der verlogene Waffenstillstand. In: *BILD*, 08.01.1992, p. 2; Peter Meyer-Ranke: Serben schießen gegen UNO. In: *BILD*, 31.01.1992, p. 2; Anonymous: Die 3 Brennpunke der Welt: Jugoslawien, Libyen, Afghanistan; B-H: Soforthilfe von der EG. In: *BILD*, 18.04.1992, p. 2.

68 Von Heintze: Der verlogene Waffenstillstand. In: *BILD*, 08.01.1992, p. 2.

69 Roland Hofwiler: Serbien beansprucht kroatisches Gebiet. In: *taz*, 18.01.1992, p. 8; Ian Traynor: Yugoslav Army "Guilty of Atrocity Campaign". In: *The Guardian*, 17.01.1992, p. 1; other examples: Anonymous: Tudjman: Frühere Anerkennung Kroatiens hätte Opfer verhindert. In: *taz*, ; 07.12.1991, p. 1; Roland Hofwiler: Serben gegen das „Diktat aus Brüssel". In: t*az*, 20.12.1991, p. 2; Erich Rathfelder: Warten auf den Waffenstillstand. In: *taz*, 06.01.1992, p. 3; dpa/ap: Serbiens Haltung verhärtet sich. In: *taz*, 24.01.1992, p. 8; Mirna Lincir: Todesschwadronen in Osijek. In: *taz*, 09.03.1992, p. 8; thos: In Sarajevos Altstadt wird geschossen. In: *taz*, 07.04.1992, p. 8; wps/taz/dpa/ap/thos: Baker will Serbien unter Druck setzen. In: *taz*, 16.04.1992, p. 8; Dunja Melcic: Sanktionen ohne Wenn und Aber! In: *taz*, 25.04.1992, p. 12; Erich Rathfelder: Wo endet Europa? Bosnische Flüchtlinge werden an der deutschen Grenze zurückgewiesen. In: *taz*, 05.05.1992, p. 12; afp/ap/dpa: Serben in Bosnien auf dem Vormarsch. In: *taz*, 22.04.1992, p. 10.

an article,[70] though interestingly he left out other excruciating details of Ian Traynor's original account. The latter had also reported that Croatian civilians had their throats slit by Yugoslav soldiers and were then laid beside dead pigs to symbolise that the Croatians were swine.[71] *FR* also referred to and summarised the same *Guardian*-article, though it equally avoided the graphic details Traynor had reported.[72] Rather, the more abstract assessment made by a JNA-reservist was emphasised: "'they loot, rape, even butcher.'"[73]

In addition to its articles, *taz* also published a memorable cartoon treating JNA's crimes.

Figure 3: Thomas Körner; printed in *taz*, 9 January 1992, p. 12.
"In order to prevent a further regrettable disruption of the cease-fire, the leadership of the Peoples' National Army has decreed the order…
…to exclusively use silencers from now on!"

70 Roland Hofwiler: Serbien beansprucht kroatisches Gebiet. In: *taz*, 18.01.1992, p. 8.

71 Ian Traynor: Yugoslav Army "Guilty of Atrocity Campaign". In: *The Guardian*, 17.01.1992, p. 1.

72 Reuter/dpa: Serbien meldet Ansprüche an. In: *FR*, 18.01.1992, p. 1; Traynor: Yugoslav Army "Guilty of Atrocity Campaign". In: *The Guardian*, 17.01.1992, p. 1. Other articles on the topic include Reuter: Lord Carrington erwägt Aufgabe. In: *FR*, 02.01.1992, p. 2; Reuter/dpa: Serbien meldet Ansprüche an. In: *FR*, 18.01.1992, p. 1; AP/Reuter/dpa/AFP: Kriegsverbrechen angeprangert. In: *FR*, 24.01.1992, p. 2; Reuter/AFP/dpa/AP/FR: USA drohen Serben Isolierung an. In: *FR*, 16.04.1992, p. 1.

73 Reuter/AP/dpa/AFP: Mesic gibt Amt offiziell auf. In: *FR*, 06.12.1991, p. 2.

While such coverage may have caused anti-Serbian sentiments amongst the readers, various articles in *FR* and *taz* created a balance by simultaneously reporting on atrocities committed by Croatian forces.[74] Reports about massacred Serbian civilians offered by these two publications indicate a differentiated portrayal of the matter. Similarly, *Spiegel* questioned Serbia's sole responsibility for the violence in general. The matter was first addressed casually in a December article, in which the author referred to the civil war, "[…] for which supposedly Serbia alone […was] responsible […]"[75] The piece did not further explore the theme of culpability and an inattentive reader may have even read over the significant word '*angeblich*', or 'supposedly'. However, this balanced portrayal that JNA-soldiers were not the only armed forces involved was largely lost amidst the graphic and thus more memorable articles about JNA's atrocities.

Milošević – The Main Culprit?

While JNA was deemed the primary source of the violence by the German press, none of the publications mentioned the names of specific generals who controlled this vague entity. Neither was Milošević as an individual allocated much responsibility by the German press at this time. Indeed, *JF*, *BILD* and *AJW* did not mention him by name throughout this entire five-month period and *FR* did so only in passing.[76] The conservative *Welt* was the only publication at this time that identified Milošević as responsible for the on-going violence. He was referred to as the '*großserbischer*'[77] Milošević' who "[…] unleashed the first bloody war in Europe since 1945."[78] Moreover *Welt* reported that the Serbian leadership "[…] display[ed] a downright obsession for territorial conquest […]"[79] and that Milošević personally was

74 dpa: Bonn sichert Kroatien Hilfe zu. In: *FR*, 20.12.1991, p. 2; Reuter/AFP/dpa/AP: Druck auf Serben-Führer. In: *FR*, 01.02.1992, p. 2; AFP/AP/dpa/Reuter: Blauhelme für zunächst ein Jahr. In: *FR*, 19.02.1992, p. 2; AFP/AP/Reuter/dpa: Zahlreiche Tote bei Kämpfen in Bosnien. In: *FR*, 04.04.1992, pp. 1–2; dpa/aft/ap/taz: Serbiens KSZE-Stuhl wackelt. In: t*az*, 21.04.1992, p. 2; afp/dpa/taz: Sarajevo steht in Flammen. In: *taz*, 06.05.1992, p. 8.

75 Anonymous: Besser hier Sterben. In: *Spiegel*, 02.12.1991, p. 68.

76 Nicole Janigro: „Mit den anderen zu sprechen wird immer schwieriger". In: *FR*, 04.01.1992, p. 18; Harry Schleicher: Serbiens politische Opposition wird selbstbewusst. In: *FR*, New Years Eve 1991 [31.12.1991], p. 3.

77 German: striving for a Greater Serbia.

78 Carl Gustaf Ströhm: Sog der Anerkennung. In: *Welt*, 15.01.1992, p. 2.

79 Carl Gustaf Ströhm: Sog der Anerkennung. In: *Welt*, 15.01.1992, p. 2; id.: Neo-Jugo-Titoslawien. In: *Welt*, 14.03.1992, p. 2.

responsible for disseminating propaganda.[80] *Welt* explained all failing diplomatic efforts with Milošević's unwillingness "[…] to conform to a European peace settlement."[81] Indeed, in spite of the EC-negotiated cease-fires, "[…] Milošević and his generals […were] happily marching on […]", upsetting these brief moments of peace.[82]

This remarkable interpretation found solely in *Welt* departs from the state-of-knowledge found in the secondary literature at the time. While much of the secondary literature produced towards the end of and after the Bosnian War points to Milošević's culpability to explain the violence[83] – indeed Norman Cigar argues that the Bosnian genocide was part of a concerted Serbian war strategy[84] – this interpretation could not be found in secondary literature available in 1991/92. This pioneering analysis can be partially explained by the biography of the broadsheet's Balkan-correspondent, who authored most of these articles. Dr. Carl Gustaf Ströhm, a historian, was a starkly anti-communist conservative who also wrote a column for the far-right *Junge Freiheit* until his death in 2004. As his obituary in *Welt* stated, Ströhm took pride in not interviewing high-ranking Communist officials while he was the broadsheet's East-Europe correspondent.[85] This anti-communist stance may also have coloured Ströhm's perception of Milošević, who commenced his career in the Yugoslav Communist Party. A further explanation for his staunch anti-Milošević standpoint could be his role as adviser to the Croatian President Tudjman, as one of his obituaries in *JF* reveals.[86]

FAZ, *taz* and *Spiegel* explored the Serbian leader's role in the ever-increasing violence, though unlike *Welt*, all three publications dismissed the notion that Milošević as an individual held much responsibility. The general consensus

80 Michael Stössinger: Von Rollkommandos und dem stillen Protest der Serben. In: *Welt*, 06.12.1991, p. 3.

81 DW: Friedensprozess wird fortgesetzt. In: *Welt*, 09.01.1992, p. 2.

82 Carl Gustaf Ströhm: Die Armee entwaffnet. In: *Welt*, 18.04.1992, p. 2.

83 Such as Norman Cigar: *Genocide in Bosnia: The Policy of 'Ethnic Cleansing'*. College Station: Texas A&M University Press 1995; James Gow: *Triumph of the Lack of Will: International Diplomacy and the Yugoslav War*. London: Hurst 1997; Allan Little / Laura Silber: *The Death of Yugoslavia*. London: Penguin 1996; Glaurdić: *The Hour of Europe*; Ivo Banac: Sorting out the Balkans: Three New Looks at a Troubled Region. In: *Foreign Affairs* 79,3 (2000), pp. 152–157, here p. 152.

84 Cigar: *Genocide in Bosnia*, p. 4.

85 Fac: Ein Herz für kleine Nationen. In: *Welt*, 18.04.2004. http://www.welt.de/print-welt/article314465/Ein-Herz-fuer-die-kleinen-Nationen-Zum-Tode-von-Carl-Gustaf-Stroehm.html (accessed 27.08.2014).

86 Nachrufe auf Carl Gustaf Ströhm. In: *JF*, 21.05.2004. http://www.jf-archiv.de/archiv04/224yy29.htm (accessed 27.08.2014).

was that he was a man whose powers were declining. For example, *taz's* Erich Rathfelder stated in January that with Milošević's steadily dwindling popularity, it was only a matter of time before Serbian leaders outside of Serbia, namely Milan Babić in Croatia and Radovan Karadžić in Bosnia would become more powerful.[87] By March, another *taz*-article predicted that the opposition would overthrow Milošević.[88] The conservative *FAZ* presented a similar interpretation, though significantly this can be found predominantly in the broadsheet's political cartoons.[89]

Figure 4:
Fritz Behrendt;
printed in *FAZ*,
4 January 1992, p. 3.

Figure 5:
Fritz Behrendt;
printed in *FAZ*,
9 January 1992, p. 3.

87 Erich Rathfelder: Serbien oder Klein-Jugoslawien? In: *taz*, 28.01.1992, p. 11.

88 Jozsef Bata: Mobilisierung gegen Milošević. In: *taz*, 09.03.1992, p. 8.

89 For example Cartoons in *FAZ*, 04.01.1992, p. 3; *FAZ*, 09.01.1992, p. 3; *FAZ*, 18.01.1992, p. 3; *FAZ*, 01.02.1992, p. 6; *FAZ*, 08.02.1992, p. 3; *FAZ*, 25.02.1992, p. 3; *FAZ*, 05.03.1992, p. 3.

The two examples shown above delineated a powerless Milošević, though both expressed very different subliminal messages. The first portrayed him as having no power or control over the Yugoslav constituent republics, even though he was armed. This underlined that Milošević was not taken seriously or perceived as a threat by any republics or regions except Montenegro and Kosovo, which were shaking with fear. Figure 5 showed the Serbian President Milošević as one individual amongst many. Veljko Kadijević, a JNA-General, Blagoje Adžić, Yugoslavia's Minister of Defence, and Vojislav Šešelj, President of the Serbian Radical Party (depicted as a Chetnik), were shown marching next to Milošević, implying that he had to share power with them. The three military individuals were portrayed as more threatening and powerful than Milošević, who was wearing a statesman's black suit. Together, all four individuals ignored the insignificant EC and UN, which are armed with only an umbrella to emphasise its impotence.

Spiegel painted a similar picture, reporting that independent paramilitary formations were 'lurking around', which Milošević was unable to control.[90] Another article portrayed Milošević as powerless, his hand forced by the army, identifying the 'Belgrade ultra [radicals]' and 'warlords' as being in control.[91] The most dismissive conclusion asserted that "though Milošević desire[d] peace, he no longer [...had] the power to broker it."[92] Surprisingly this interpretation of Milošević's declining powers and marginal role was corroborated in a *Spiegel*-interview with the Bosnian leader Alija Izetbegović. In one question Izetbegović was asked if Milošević had finally given up his idea of a 'Greater Serbia', to which the Bosnian President responded that "surely [...Milošević] had lowered his territorial ambitions." Unfortunately the reader is not provided with an explanation for this presumed change of Milošević's war aims. Instead the focus shifts to Bosnian forces. When asked about the source of weapons belonging to the heavily armed Bosnian population, Izetbegović replied: "the Serbian population [...had] been armed by the army. The rest has been armed by fear."[93] Evidently the Bosnian President did not answer the question about the source of the weapons and instead used a seemingly well-prepared phrase to underline the Bosnians' victimhood, even when speaking about armed violence.

90 Anonymous: Ein Kriegsherr unter Feuer. In: *Spiegel*, 09.03.1992, p. 187.

91 Olaf Ihlau: Amok auf dem Balkan. In: *Spiegel*, 11.05.1992, p. 162.

92 Anonymous: Sklave seiner Schüler: In Belgrad wächst der Widerstand gegen den Uno-Friedensplan. Präsident Milošević wankt. In: *Spiegel*, 27.01.1992, p. 129.

93 Anonymous: Einfach erschöpft: SPIEGEL-Interview mit dem bosnischen Präsidenten Alija Izetbegović. In: *Spiegel*, 13.01.1992, p. 124.

This interview is very interesting, as it does not give the perspective one would expect from the Bosnian President. Rather than focusing on his country's victimhood and corresponding culpability of Milošević, the armed Bosnian population was emphasised. This gives the reader the sense of a civil war developing rather than one-sided Serbian aggression. Simultaneously, however, it is striking that the interviewer did not press Izetbegović for more details for example how this Bosnian militia was funded, where its weapons came from and whether it had political support. This in turn indicates that Izetbegović was perceived as less dangerous and responsible for violence than his Serbian counterpart.

The lacking interest in Milošević in all publications except for *Welt* stands in harsh contrast to the post-1995 secondary literature which focuses almost exclusively on Milošević and his nationalist policies to explain the violence.[94] Here the nature of the primary sources which did not have the benefit of hindsight is crucial. In the early 1990s, the German press nearly completely dismissed Milošević as a fading influence. Perhaps external observers could not yet discern whether Milošević, who at the time was President of Serbia – an office he created – would stay in power, especially in light of these secessionist movements. This interpretation is fortified by Josip Glaurdić, who remembers that "very few aspects of Milošević's political career [...] suggested that he could become the political leader of the brewing nationalist movement."[95]

Representing the Victims Visually

In addition to the interpretations offered by the different publications regarding the causes for the violence, it is worth considering how the victims of this violence were portrayed pictorially. All publications except for *AJW*, which did not publish any pictures in this timeframe, used the visual medium to depict the victims of the violence.

One image, which resurfaced in *BILD*, *Welt* and *FR* is particularly striking. It depicts an elderly woman standing next to her packed bags, armed with a rifle.[96] The notion of an old woman feeling so vulnerable and exposed to the

94 Such as Norman Naimark: Introduction. In: Naimark / Case (eds): *Yugoslavia and its Historians*, pp. i–xix, here p. xvi; Daniel Goldhagen: If You Rebuild It…A New Serbia. In: *The New Republic* 220,20 (17.05.1999), p. 16; Bennett: *Yugoslavia's Bloody Collapse*, p. 6; see footnote 240 for further sources.

95 Glaurdić: *The Hour of Europe*, p. 18.

96 Anonymous: Die alte Frau, die Heimat und das Gewehr. In: *BILD*, 09.12.1991, p. 2; dpa:

Figure 6: "Bosnia-War in former Yugoslavia; "Operation Storm" (liberation of the Krajina region); near the city of Banja Luka – after the displacement of the Serbs from Krajina…Serbian Cross; 28.08.1995." Photographer: Christian Jungeblodt[97]

violence around her that she travelled with a large rifle is very moving, but simultaneously suggests how widely armed the civilian population was. It is remarkable that *FR* published this image four months after *BILD* and *Welt*. This proves that the pictures a newspaper chose to publish at a specific time did not necessarily record a recent event. *taz* also presented the theme of an elderly woman with a rifle in one of its images, again depicting how exposed the civilian population was to violence.[98] In this second image, the state of emergency was further underlined by a young boy following the armed elderly woman, wearing ill-fitting clothing. While neither image showed violence directly being perpetrated or armed forces engaged in battle, the viewer discerned a stifling feeling of omnipresent terror from which even elderly civilians and young children could not escape. Equally both images convey the sense of a general war in which even the blatantly civilian population was

Geheimdienstchef sieht Kroatien besiegt. In: *Welt*, 09.12.1991, p. 8; Elmar Altvater: Die Festung Europa muss ihre Zugbruecken herunterlassen. In: *FR*, 3 April 1992, p. 15.

97 While this precise image was not published by any of the newspapers considered in this book, it is an example of the few images published at the time portraying Serbian victims. The photographer contributed a number of images to *taz*.

98 Anonymous: Bürgerkrieg in Bosnien weitet sich aus. In: *taz*, 21.04.1992, p. 1.

armed. Both images included captions which revealed that the civilian victims were Croatian. With the absence of balancing pictures, the reader was left with an overwhelming perception of Serbian culpability.
Indeed, in the five months analysed in this timeframe, only four images portrayed Serbian civilians suffering from the war.[99] While the pictures showing Serbian civilians were quantitatively insignificant, qualitatively, they were very meaningful, as they portrayed genuine suffering and thus aroused deep sympathy. This was underlined by the focus on elderly women and children. Nonetheless, the reduced interest is striking and congruent with the previously mentioned focus of the German publications on the Serbian-dominated JNA. Aligning the primary perpetrator of the violence with victims from the same 'side' was perhaps too complex. Another explanation for this imbalance could be that as the war was carried out on Bosnian and Croatian territory, there were simply fewer Serbian victims. Nonetheless, a one-sided pictorial selection of the victims of the on-going violence was clearly evident in the coverage.

Germany's Role in the Balkans

Turning to a very different topic, it is worth exploring how the national press presented Germany's foreign policy towards the Balkans in the 1990s. Particularly, Germany's early recognition of Croatia and Slovenia was covered with heightened interest in the national press and was treated largely positively. *FR* and *Spiegel* were the only publications to express careful scepticism regarding an active foreign policy in the Balkans, though they did not specifically criticise the country's recognition policy towards Croatia and Slovenia.[100]

99 Images published in *BILD*, 30.12.1991, p. 2; *taz*, 06.01.1992, p. 9; *FR*, 07.05.1992, p. 2; *FR*, 04.01.1992, p. 18.

100 Some include fy: Deutschland will Kroatien und Slowenien anerkennen. In: *FAZ*, 06.12.1991, p. 1; fy: Kroatische Städte unter schwerem Beschuss. Rauchwolken über der Altstadt von Dubrovnik. In: *FAZ*, 07.12.1991, pp. 1–2; Sto.: Gespräche „von großem Ernst" zwischen Bonn und Belgrad. In: *FAZ*, 24.04.1992, p. 7; C. G.: Keine Anerkennung durch Bonn. In: *FAZ*, 29.04.1992, p. 2; DW: Schutz fuer serbische Minderheiten. In: *Welt*, 05.12.1991, p. 10; DW: Bonn wird Donnerstag Kroatien anerkennen. In: *Welt*, 16.12.1991, p. 1; DW: Das Kabinett beschliesst Kroatiens Anerkennung. In: *Welt*, 20.12.1991, p. 1; DW: EG-Partner kritisieren Kroatien. In: *Welt*, 21.02.1992, p. 6; DW: Bonn Startet Jugoslawien-Sanktionen. In: *taz*, 10.12.1991, p. 2; Thomas Schmid: Kompromiss mit faulem Geruch. In: *taz*, 18.12.1991, p. 12; dpa/ap/taz / BZ: 166.000 flüchten aus Bosnien. In: *taz*, 15.04.1992, p. 8; ap/taz: Genscher ist gegen Anerkennung. In: *taz*, 29.04.1992, p. 8; AFP/dpa/Reuter: Kohl macht Tudjman Zusage. In: *FR*, 06.12.1991, pp. 1–2; Reuter/dpa/AP/AFP/yr: Perez bringt Bonn nicht von Anerkennungskurs ab. In: *FR*, 14.12.1991, pp. 1–2; Erich Hauser: Bonn in EG wegen Kroatien isoliert. In: *FR*, 17.12.1991, pp. 1–2; Erich Hauser: Bonn will Besetzung des UN-Postens durch Belgrad anfechten. In: *FR*, 13.03.1992, p. 2 .

Both saw Germany's National-Socialist past as a reason to 'tread lightly.' For example, two *FR*-articles reported that some Serbian and European diplomats found it problematic to recognise Bosnia's independence on 6 April, as Hitler had begun his air strikes against Belgrade on 6 April 1941, which could evoke unwanted inferences amongst the local population.[101] With these cautions, *FR's* articles demonstrated a degree of knowledge and sensitivity regarding Germany's past and how the country's foreign policy could be perceived, which is not present in other papers.

Spiegel was much more explicit about its view that Germany should not act in the region due to its historical baggage. A December-article stated that even if the war continued, German troop deployment to the Balkans was out of the question, simply because the Nazis had occupied Yugoslavia.[102] This point of view was further underlined in an interview with Vuk Drašković, the main Serbian opposition leader against Milošević. In it he stated that "for historic reasons, Germany should not have been the driving force in Croatia's secession."[103] However, while *Spiegel's* articles asserted that Germany's past should prevent military intervention, its pioneering diplomacy was deemed necessary *because* of its past, which had given the country particular diplomatic insights. An opinion piece, in which the author Olaf Ihlau referred to the 'Greater Serbian chauvinists,' sarcastically stated that in postponing the recognition of Croatia and Slovenia, the EC-countries must have been waiting for a miracle, implying that Germany had identified the correct diplomatic path in the Balkans. This sentiment was fortified by the preceding paragraph which outlined Germany's long-standing ties and extensive experience with the region.[104] However, neither this article nor any other explored the notion that Germany and the international community could have prolonged or intensified the war through a hasty and ill-considered recognition. Rather, *Spiegel* portrayed German politicians as experts in the field, who had triumphed in convincing their international allies of their course of action. This combined argumentation is interesting because it applied Germany's historical baggage in two different, almost contradicting ways. With regard to military engagement, Germany's fascist past was used as a reason not to get involved in the Balkans, while a pioneering diplomatic role was necessary

101 Daniel Riegger: Streit um die Landkarte. In: *FR*, 31.03.1992, p. 2; AFP/Reuter: Schwere Luftangriffe in Bosnien. In: *FR*, 06.04.1992, p. 1.

102 Anonymous: Operation Tintenklecks. In: *Spiegel*, 02.12.1991, pp. 178–179.

103 Anonymous: Wir sind des Wahnsinns müde. In: *Spiegel*, 03.02.1992, p. 174.

104 Olaf Ihlau: Krakeel auf dem Balkan. In: *Spiegel*, 23.12.1991, p. 137.

because of Germany's history. This suggests that the weight of history – which could be interpreted in both ways – was utilised by *Spiegel* in whatever manner was deemed useful.

In contrast, the conservative newspapers *Welt*, *FAZ* and *BILD*, but also the left-wing *taz* did not include any restraints in their portrayal of Germany's role in the Balkans, but rather whole-heartedly supported Germany's foreign policy.[105] *Welt* and *FAZ* explained that a unified Yugoslavia had become an impossible illusion. Thus Germany's foreign policy had been realistic and pragmatic, as a *Welt*-article stated, continuing that Foreign Minister Genscher had rightfully proclaimed that non-recognition would intensify the conflict.[106] Numerous other *Welt*-articles reiterated that Germany insisted on respecting human rights, which was so important that it would be worth stepping out of European line in foreign policy for the first time since the Second World War.[107] *FAZ* portrayed Germany to have become the 'number one scapegoat' amongst its Western partners and Serbia for insisting on this righteous principle.[108] With such articles, both conservative broadsheets presented Germany as a country acting with the highest sense of morals and commitment to international law while the international community failed to appreciate or value this dedication. Two *FAZ*-cartoons further underlined this interpretation of Germany's recognition policy as a genuinely good approach.

Figure 7 portrayed Germany's '*Anerkennung*' or recognition of Croatia and Slovenia as the two countries' only hope in a sea of darkness. Metaphorically this cartoon expressed that due to Germany's recognition policy, Croatia and Slovenia now had the basic means for survival, namely light, warmth and hope. Figure 8 depicted Chancellor Kohl dressed up as Father Christmas, bringing the gift of recognition to a burning city. Both, therefore, praise German foreign policy as positive and beneficial to Croatia and Slovenia.

105 Erich Rathfelder: Franjo Tudjmans Popularität schwindet dahin. In: *taz*, 02.12.1991, p. 9; taz/dpa / thos/rola: Offener Streit um die Anerkennung Kroatiens. In: *taz*, 16.12.1991, p. 9; dora: EG-Partner lassen Bonn hängen. In: *taz*, 17.12.1991, p. 2; taz/dpa/aft / dora: Bonn erleichtert über EG-Kompromiss. In: *taz*, 18.12.1991, p. 9; Thomas Schmid: Kompromiss mit faulem Geruch. In: *taz*, 18.12.1991, p. 12; fy: Deutschland will Kroatien und Slowenien anerkennen. In: *FAZ*, 06.12.1991, p. 1; Leo Wieland: Eine amerikanische Stimme für Kroatien. In: *FAZ*, 19.12.1991, p. 10; DW: Vance sondiert in Belgrad. In: *Welt*, 02.12.1991, p. 8; Co.: Kohl verspricht Anerkennung. In: *FAZ*, 04.12.1991, p. 10; Anonymous: Deutschland zu mächtig? In: *BILD*, 08.01.1992, p. 6.

106 Carl Gustaf Ströhm: Seltsames von Perez. In: *Welt*, 16.12.1991, p. 2.

107 Carl Gustaf Ströhm: Heraus aus dem Konvoi. In: *Welt*, 17.12.1991, p. 2; Enno von Löwenstern: Politik des Gewissens. In: *Welt*, 13.01.1992, p. 2.

108 Viktor Meier: Eine Zukunft ohne Jugoslawien. In: *FAZ*, 18.12.1992, p. 5.

Figure 7: Fritz Behrendt; printed in *FAZ*, 20 December 1991, p. 3.

Figure 8: Fritz Behrendt; printed in *FAZ*, 21 December 1991, p. 3.

Various articles underlined this positive estimation of Germany's foreign policy by repeatedly covering Croatia's gratitude towards Germany.[109] *taz* and *BILD* reported that after the EC-recognition of Croatia, a 'Café Genscher' had been opened in Zagreb to acknowledge the support of Germany's Foreign Minister Hans-Dietrich Genscher, who had been a strong advocate for the international recognition.[110] Moreover, as *taz*, *BILD* and *Welt* reported, a pop-song entitled 'Thank you, Germany' became very popular, to which *Welt* published the lyrics.[111] *taz* underpinned the Croatian gratitude visually, showing the celebrations in Zagreb after Croatia had been granted recognition. The caption explained that the jubilant Croatians were 'tearing up' the Yugoslav flag.[112] The desecration of a state flag by protesting youth could also have been perceived as destructive and dangerous. However, the accompanying article text did not allow room for such interpretation, which underlines how versatile pictures can be when they stand alone.

Other articles in *taz* even went so far as to accuse Germany's partners of having betrayed their ally, as the title of one piece summarised: "EC-Partners leave Bonn in the lurch".[113] A *taz*-interview with the Croatian President

109 Carl Gustaf Ströhm: Seltsames von Perez. In: *Welt*, 16.12.1991, p. 2; F.A.Z.: Wieder Kämpfe in Kroatien. In: *FAZ*, 07.12.1991, p. 2.

110 dora: Geburtshelfer für einen neuen Balkan. In: *taz*, 16.01.1992, p. 3; Anonymous: „Café Genscher". In: *BILD*, 04.01.1992, p. 6.

111 dora: Geburtshelfer für einen neuen Balkan. In: *taz*, 16.01.1992, p. 3; Anonymous: Kroatien anerkannt. In: *BILD*, 16.01.1992, p. 1; Carl Gustaf Ströhm: Heraus aus dem Konvoi. In: *Welt*, 17.12.1991, p. 3.

112 Photo caption: *Die Innenstadt von Zagreb vorgestern Nacht: Die jugoslawische Fahne wird zerfetzt.* In: *taz*, 17.01.1992, p. 10.

113 dora: EG-Partner lassen Bonn hängen. In: *taz*, 17.12.1991, p. 2.

Franjo Tudjman reinforced the interpretation that Germany's diplomatic *Alleingang* had been correct. Tudjman stated that an even earlier international recognition of Croatia's independence could have prevented many victims of violence. In the interview Tudjman further insisted on the urgency of international recognition, mentioning that his people were suffering under the 'barbaric war' that was being forced upon the country by Serbia.[114] The timing of the interview is very important. Published in early December 1991, while heated debates about Germany's *Alleingang* ensued, such an interview could have convinced the potentially sceptical German readership of the urgency to recognise Croatia in spite of international resistance. By implication, this justified Germany's policies and criticised the international community's lack of support. The possible contrary perception – that Germany was acting selfishly and was thus harming the international cause – was not considered.

The representation of Germany in the national press largely mirrored the dilemma faced by German politicians in the early 1990s who were aiming to find a path towards 'normalcy' while retaining the lessons learned from Germany's past.[115] As a result, the country's National-Socialist past did not influence the publications' evaluation of German foreign policy aside from a few exceptions in *FR* and *Spiegel*. This near complete omission both in the media, but presumably also in the general political discourse, sparked an angry reaction in *AJW*, expressing the only criticism of Germany's recognition policy. Hermann Baumann stated in one article that it was "[…] unfathomable why Germany […had] taken on this pioneering role" in recognising Croatia and Slovenia.[116] He continued with historical references to the Third Reich and Hitler's 1941 occupation of Yugoslavia, which Baumann considered ample reason for Germany not to play such a prominent role in the region. Though this argument was never further explained, it implied that Germany's assertion of an independent foreign policy could awaken the feeling that the country would relapse into hegemonic strivings. The article went on to argue that 'the Germans' had a "tendency to suppress" their history, asserting that only this repression could explain why the country would pursue such an active Balkan policy.[117] A second *AJW*-article reported that Germany's Federal Criminal Agency (*Bundeskriminalamt)* had confirmed that German right-wing

114 Anonymous: Tudjman: Frühere Anerkennung Kroatiens hätte Opfer verhindert. In: *taz*, 07.12.1991, p. 1.

115 See pp. 21–22.

116 Hermann Baumann: Ein konzeptloses Vorpreschen. In: *AJW*, 09.01.1992, p. 2.

117 Ibid.

nationalists supplied weapons and fighters to the Croatian forces – some of which closely associated themselves with the Ustasha.[118] Significantly, the article was a word-by-word *dpa*-dispatch,[119] which while widely available, was not printed or used by any other publication.

This portrayal of a country which continuously repressed its history, while simultaneously witnessing a renewed rise of a right-wing movement that was prone to violence, stands in direct opposition to the secondary literature discussed previously about Germany's collective memory of the Holocaust. This asserts that since the 1980s a public shame and a sense of collective guilt amongst the Germans dominated the country's collective memory of its past.[120] While scholars such as Bernhard Giesen gradually saw a more 'meta-physical' guilt take the place of the exclusively German shame of the *Betroffenheitsdiskurs*,[121] none have suggested that the country had returned to repressing its history as it largely did in the Adenauer-era immediately after the war. The almost unanimous euphoric evaluation of Germany's *Alleingang* without mentioning the country's past, could substantiate *AJW's* assertions and indicates a departure from the *Betroffenheitsdiskurs* of the 1980s. However, this could be explained with a desire in Germany to show strength having been recently unified, which was clearly condoned by the country's press.

The Press' Language

The language utilised in the German print media coverage must also be considered, as this enables the identification of subtle undercurrents that coloured the coverage. Firstly, various articles in *FAZ*, *taz* and *BILD* used the blunt generalisation of 'the Serbs' to allocate responsibility for the violence and aggression emanating specifically from the Serbian leadership or armed forces. For example, one *BILD*-article stated that "the Serbs [...were] destroying Croatia's churches, cultural monuments, Croatia's economy and tourism."[122] This undifferentiated allocation of guilt can be found in various articles[123] and by April *BILD* reported with deliberate provocation that "the

118 dpa: Neonazis mit eigener Truppe im jugoslawischen Bürgerkrieg. In: *AJW*, 12.03.1992, p. 2.

119 el: Neonazis im jugoslawischen Bürgerkrieg? In: *dpa*, 08.03.1992, 09:48 a. m.

120 See p. 19.

121 See p. 19.

122 Corinna Zell: Serben und Kroaten in Berlin. In: *BILD*, 17.12.1991, p. 3.

123 Peter Meyer-Ranke: Kroatien: Noch 10 Tage. In: *BILD*, 14.12.1991, p. 2; Zell: Serben und Kroaten in Berlin. In: *BILD*, 17.12.1991, p. 3; Anonymous: Serben, Kroaten, Moslems – worum geht es in diesem Krieg? In: *BILD*, 22.04.1992, p. 2.

Serbs […] want[ed] a Greater Serbian Reich […]"[124] Using an equally undistinguished terminology, *FAZ*-articles reported that "the arguments the Serbs […were] voicing […were] fanatical and irrational."[125]

taz-articles used the term 'the Serbs' most frequently, however usually did so casually when talking about the Serbian people as a whole, simultaneously referring to 'the Croats'. While this was equally undifferentiated, mostly it was not as polemical. Nonetheless, various *taz*-articles utilised the generalisation to categorise and blame the entire Serbian peoples.[126] For example, one article quoted Mehmed Bahic, a Muslim journalist who stated that "'[…] they do not even shrink back from genocide. Already the Serbs are dominating everything here.'"[127] The most drastic and thus memorable reference to 'the Serbs' was in an article written by Dunja Melčić, a Croatian guest contributor, in which she referred to "[…] the cannibals in Belgrade […]"[128] waging war. This expression unquestionably went beyond any 'normal' coverage and calls attention to the severe anti-Serbian stance that must be noted at this point.

While generic terms are not unusual for the press coverage of a complex conflict, which demands clear categorisations, importantly, only three publications resorted to this alignment and they range from right to left and from broadsheet to tabloid. Interestingly almost all of the articles referring to 'the Serbs', were written by a correspondent from the respective newspaper. Therefore its utilisation cannot be explained with a common source such as press-agency articles but rather seems to be an interpretation particular to individual journalists and their deliberate choice of words.

A second device used throughout the articles analysed in this section is the subtle integration of terminology that either originated from Nazi-Germany's propaganda or was heavily associated with what the regime represented. Phrases such as a Serbian desire for more '*Lebensraum*',[129] the never-ending Balkan violence becoming a 'total war',[130] and that Serbian forces were

124 Anonymous: Serben, Kroaten, Moslems – worum geht es in diesem Krieg? In: *BILD*, 22.04.1992, p. 2.

125 V. M.: Der Weg zur Konsolidierung wird dornenreich. In: *FAZ*, 05.03.1992, p. 3.

126 afp/taz: Putschgerüchte im Verteidigungsministerium. In: *taz*, 11.01.1992, p. 2; taz: EG soll Sicherheitsrat wegen Bosnien anrufen. In: *taz*, 22.04.1992, p. 1.

127 Roland Hofwiler: Bosniaken gehen getrennte Wege. In: *taz*, 02.03.1992, p. 8.

128 Dunja Melcic: Europa steht im Wort. In: t*az*, 17.12.1991, p. 12.

129 Dunja Melcic: Sanktionen ohne Wenn und Aber! In: *taz*, 25.04.1992, p. 12; Stefan Dietrich: Ferner Balkan, naher Krieg. In: *FAZ*, 18.02.1992, p. 5

130 AP: No Title. In: *FR*, 18.12.1991, p. 2; Anonymous: Wir sind des Wahnsinns müde. In: *Spiegel*, 03.02.1992, p. 174.

conducting 'pogroms'[131] were interspersed in the coverage. This last term – while also used in different historical eras – would have been particularly meaningful to a German reader, as '*Reichs***pogrom***nacht*' is the German term for 'The Night of Broken Glass,' on 9 November 1938. *taz* also referred to Serbian '*Blitzkrieg*'-tactics[132] and repeatedly reported that Serbia perceived international attempts to ensure peace as a '*Diktat*'.[133] Meanwhile *FAZ* reported that Serbians saw themselves as the region's '*Herrenvolk*' or 'master race', creating references to Nazi-Germany's strivings for a superior Aryan race. All these terms were so heavily loaded with Nazi-ideology that through the mere placement of such key words, a German reader would very likely have associated Serbian politics with the darkest age of German history. The only publications with no such terminology were *BILD* and *AJW*. It is comprehensible that the latter avoided such language, as arguably the casual (mis) use of terms derived from or associated with Nazi-Germany would trivialise a topic to which *AJW*-readers would be particularly sensitive. However, it must be noted that the tabloid *BILD* did not resort to such polemical semantic connections, which perhaps could have been expected from its reporting-style. As mentioned previously, *BILD*-articles about the Balkans were approximately 30–50 words long. Consequently such linguistic connections between Nazi-Germany and Serbia of the 1990s could have been an effective way of communicating a certain bias without many words.

In a *Spiegel*-article published in December 1991, the anonymous author criticised an attack launched by *Politika*, a Belgrade newspaper that had likened German Balkan policy to the striving for a 'Fourth Reich'.[134] While *Welt*, *FAZ* and *taz* also reported that Serbian propaganda had made such accusations,[135] *Spiegel* chose to counter these allegations with language equally reminiscent of the Nazi-regime. In the heated defence of Germany's policies, the

131 DW: Serbische Offensive in Bosnien. In: *Welt*, 11./12.04.1992, p. 8; F.A.Z.: Serben auf dem Vormarsch in Bosnien. In: *FAZ*, 11.04.1992, p. 7.

132 Roland Hofwiler: Ultraradikale beugen sich Milošević. In: *taz*, 09.01.1992, p. 8.

133 Roland Hofwiler: Serben gegen das „Diktat aus Brüssel". In: *taz*, 20.12.1991, p. 2; Hofwiler: Serbische Oppositionelle unter Druck. In: *taz*, 27.04.1992, p. 10; Hofwiler: „Drittes Jugoslawien" gegründet. In: *taz*, 28.04.1992, p. 8; Hofwiler: Bosnien will Waffenhilfe der KSZE. In: *taz*, 08.05.1992, p. 8.

134 Anonymous: Kampf dem Vierten Reich: Die serbische Kampagne gegen die Jugoslawien-Politik der Deutschen. In: *Spiegel*, 09.12.1991, p. 26.

135 Carl Gustaf Ströhm: Heraus aus dem Konvoi. In: *Welt*, 17.12.1991, p. 2; Ströhm: Serben fordern neuen Dialog mit Deutschland. In: *Welt*, 13.03.1992, p. 6; dpa: „Das dritte Jugoslawien entsteht". In: *FAZ*, 17.01.1992, p. 5; Hofwiler: Serben gegen das „Diktat aus Brüssel". In: *taz*, 20.12.1991, p. 2; Erich Rathfelder: Serbien oder Klein-Jugoslawien? In: *taz*, 28.01.1992, p. 11.

anonymous *Spiegel*-author denigrated *Politika* as being on the same level of the Nazi propaganda-organ *Stürmer*, which seemed to immediately dismiss these charges.[136] It is worth noting that an April-article cited *Politika* again without noting its function as Milošević's mouthpiece, even though one could assume that *Spiegel* would hesitate to rely on a publication it had likened with the *Stürmer* just four months earlier.[137] This could indicate that the analogy to fascism had been deliberately utilised to dismiss *Politika's* claims and not because the publication was deemed inherently unreliable.

Interestingly, allusions to communism appeared in the coverage, though to a much lesser extent than the fascist terminology. All publications except for *FR* and *AJW* deliberately associated Serbia with communism. The two conservative broadsheets *Welt* and *FAZ*, but also the left-leaning publications *Spiegel* and *taz* included anti-communist language in their articles.[138] For example *Welt's* articles casually referred to 'communist Serbs' and warned the reader of the *großserbisch*-communist Generals' megalomania.[139] Similarly, *Spiegel's* articles resorted to the terms 'Bolshevik' and 'national-Bolshevik' to describe the Serbian leadership.[140] One *FAZ*-article in particular is worth noting, as it summarised and partially quoted a piece former U.S.-President Richard Nixon wrote for the *Wall Street Journal*. The *FAZ*-article stated that Nixon criticised American policy towards Yugoslavia for not clearly distinguishing between 'aggressor' and 'victim', elaborating that "the communist falcons have practically launched a coup against Croatia with their offensive."[141] This colourful yet undefined term may have left the readers with the uncomfortable notion that all Serbs were aggressive communists.

In a *taz*-article, the author Roland Hofwiler reported that with Bosnia's independence, the country was no longer a 'socialist Republic', but a 'free state of Europe'.[142] This contrast between the shackles of communism and a

136 Anonymous: Kampf dem Vierten Reich. In: *Spiegel*, 09.12.1991, p. 26.

137 Anonymous: Auf Pferden reiten. In: *Spiegel*, 27.04.1992, pp. 176–177.

138 DW: Schutz für serbische Minderheiten. In: *Welt*, 05.12.1991, p. 10; Carl Gustaf Ströhm: Böse Lektion für De Michelis. In: *Welt*, 09.01.1992, p. 2; Astaf Domber: Ohne Mass und Ziel. In: *Welt*, 06.05.1992, p. 2; Anonymous: Auf Pferden reiten. In: *Spiegel*, 27.04.1992, p. 177; Jozsef Bata: Mobilisierung gegen Milosevic. In: *taz*, 09.03.1992, p. 8.

139 Astaf Domber: Ohne Maß und Ziel. In: *Welt*, 06.05.1992, p. 2.

140 Anonymous: Kampf dem Vierten Reich. Im: *Spiegel*, 09.12.1991, p. 26; Olaf Ihlau: Krakeel auf dem Balkan. In: *Spiegel*, 23.12.1991, pp. 137.

141 Leo Wieland: Eine amerikanische Stimme für Kroatien. In: *FAZ*, 19.12.1991, p. 10.

142 Roland Hofwiler: Bosniens Muslimanen leisten Widerstand. In: *taz*, 10.04.1992, p. 3.

free Europe epitomised the newspaper's intended negative association with communism. *BILD* also constructed linkages between Serbia and communism, referring to 'Serbia's communist government'[143], Belgrade's 'communist hardliners,'[144] the 'communist army,'[145] and simply the 'Serbian communists.'[146] None of these articles explained their juxtaposition of Serbia and communism, though a reader could assume that Belgrade's desire to uphold Yugoslavia as it had existed under Tito's communist reign caused these associations along with Milošević's initial career as a communist *apparatchik*. Primarily however, the sporadic and at times clumsy linkages of Serbia to communism may have served the defamation of Serbia by association with the recently failed ideology.

The fact that a simple word, laden with connotations from specific historical eras could subconsciously impact a reader's understanding of the subject-matter is a mechanism both journalists and editors were well aware of and may have used purposefully. Only one article considered here was a press-agency briefing, while all others were written by the newspapers' own correspondents.[147] This indicates that the dismissive language about Serbia was employed by individuals and was not a by-product from press agency briefings.

Authorship

The issue of authorship is worth considering in detail. The articles analysed here featured three forms: those authored by the publications' own correspondents, articles by press agencies such as AP or Reuters, and amalgamated press releases from different associations or organisations. In most cases the articles did not indicate what press release was consulted for the article, nor the organisation that had disseminated it. Some indicated their author by the acronym of the newspaper, such as 'F.A.Z.' for *Frankfurter Allgemeine Zeitung* or 'DW' for *Die Welt*. The attempt to identify authors is fraught with difficulties and only a partial analysis can be conducted. *Spiegel* and *BILD* rarely indicated individual authorship. In the case of *Spiegel* this stemmed from an

143 Vollrath von Heintze: Berlin, Kroatien, Kommunismus – drei Klarstellungen. In: *BILD*, 31.12.1991, p. 2.

144 Peter Meyer-Ranke: Kommunisten raus aus Kroatien. In: *BILD*, 04.01.1992, p. 2.

145 Vollrath von Heintze: Der verlogene Waffenstillstand. In: *BILD*, 08.01.1992, p. 2.

146 Rolf Bier: Unverschämtes Serbien. In: *BILD*, 24.01.1992, p. 2.

147 Spiegel did not indicate authorship. Thus the news-magazine's articles are excluded here.

editorial policy that all authors represent the publication's opinions and thus are not named individually.[148] *BILD* frequently published its Balkan-articles in news bulletins, which contain various 30 to 50 word-articles on different topics. None of these short 'news-blurbs' included any specification of individual authors. *AJW*, *Konkret* and *JF* did not publish enough articles in this timeframe to make a viable quantitative conclusion. In sum, only four publications examined here offered enough data for analysis.

Newspaper	Percentage of articles authored by correspondents	Percentage of articles authored by press agencies	Percentage of articles amalgamated from various press releases, etc.
Welt	48%	9%	40%
FAZ	43%	35%	21%
FR	30%	67%	0,46%
taz	47%	40%	8%

Table 1: Percentages of articles according to authorship.[149]

The above table shows that the majority of articles in daily papers except for *FR* had been authored by the papers' own correspondents. This dominant reliance in *Welt*, *FAZ* and *taz* implies a heightened interest in the region by these publications, as stationing a foreign correspondent on-site entailed a considerable financial commitment. However, simultaneously, all statistics for articles authored by correspondents lie below the 50%-mark, which indicates that the majority of the papers' resources in this respect still lay elsewhere. The only exception was *FR*, which primarily drew on press agencies as a main source of authorship. Usually these were collated briefings from various major press agencies, namely Agence France-Presse (AFP), Associated Press (AP), Reuters or Deutsche Presse Agentur (dpa).

148 John Jungclaussen: Liberal bis in die letzte Zeile. In: *Die Zeit*, 26.02.2004. http://www.zeit.de/2004/10/Economist (accessed 28.08.2014).

149 All numbers short of 100% are anonymous articles which cannot be categorised.

Brief Chronology of the Bosnian War: April 1992–July 1995

Following this first chapter about the early period of tension and violence in Bosnia, we will now turn to the Bosnian War in more depth. While a coherent historical narrative of the four-year-long Bosnian War goes beyond the scope of this book, a brief chronology will give the reader the necessary context to understand the next chapter.

In June 1992, just a few months after war broke out, UN-troops (UNPROFOR) entered Bosnia, initially to protect Sarajevo's airport, though their mandate was later expanded. The first year of the war was overshadowed by Bosnian-Serb concentration camps which were set up between May and August in the East-Bosnian towns Omarska, Keraterm, Trnoplje as well as other locations. These were discovered by Western reporters in the summer 1992 and were widely covered in the international media. 1993 was marked by international efforts to find a diplomatic solution to the on-going war. In January, the UN-Special Envoy Cyrus Vance and EU-representative Lord Owen began negotiating a peace treaty between Bosnia, Serbia and Croatia, known as the Vance-Owen Plan. However, this plan was pronounced officially failed on 18 June after a Bosnian-Serb referendum refused its terms. One month later, in July 1993, the UN-Special Envoy Thorvald Stoltenberg and EU-representative Lord Owen began negotiations for a further diplomatic effort, which was known as the Stoltenberg-Owen Plan. This in turn was rejected by the Bosnian Muslims on 29 August. Paralleled to these endeavours, the UN's presence in Bosnia was strengthened throughout 1993. In April NATO implemented a no-fly-zone ("Operation Deny Flight") over Bosnia following a UN-resolution. On 6 May 1993, the UN declared 'safe areas' in Sarajevo, Srebrenica, Goražde, Tuzla, Žepa and Bihać, which on 4 June UNPROFOR-troops were authorised to protect.

1994 was dominated by a combination of further atrocities and renewed attempts to find a peaceful solution. On 5 February, Sarajevo's civilians were shelled by Bosnian-Serb forces at Merkale Market. Four days later, NATO authorised air-strikes requested by UN of the Bosnian-Serb army in Sarajevo. In the same month, negotiations of the Contact Group[150] Plan began,

150 The Balkan Contact Group consisted of countries with a heightened interest in developments in the region, namely USA, UK, France, Germany and Russia.

attempting to construct a peace treaty. This in turn was rejected on 28 August 1994 after a referendum in the Bosnian-Serb Assembly. Nearly one year later, in July 1995, the Bosnian-Serb forces besieged Srebrenica, one of the 'safe areas' UNFROFOR-troops had been authorised to protect in 1993. The massacre that followed and its coverage in the German press will now be analysed in more depth.

Chapter 4
July 1995:
Srebrenica – Reporting Genocide

'Genocide', 'crimes against humanity' and 'extermination' appeared in the indictment of Radovan Karadžić and Ratko Mladić made by the International Criminal Tribunal for Former Yugoslavia (ICTY) on 14 November 1995 for the Bosnian-Serb attack on Srebrenica.[1] The synopsis of the atrocities in Srebrenica, which occurred between 6 and 13 July 1995, is widely covered in secondary literature as well as an extensive UN-report published in 1999.[2]

1 ICTY: The Prosecutor of the Tribunal against Radovan Karadžić [and] Ratko Mladić: Indictment. Case No. IT-95-18-I. http://www.icty.org/x/cases/karadzic/ind/en/kar-ii951116e.pdf (accessed 28.08.2014).

2 Fotini Bellou: Srebrenica – The War Crimes Legacy: International Arguments, Intervention and Memory. In: *Southeast European and Black Sea Studies* 7,3 (2007), pp. 387–398; Helge Brunborg / Torkild Hovde Lyngstad / Henrik Urdal: Accounting for Genocide: How Many Were Killed in Srebrenica? In: *European Journal of Population* 19,3 (2003), pp. 229–248; Smail Čekić / Muharem Kreso / Bećir Macić: *Genocide in Srebrenica. United Nations 'Safe Area', in July 1995.* Sarajevo: Institute for the Research of Crimes against Humanity and International Law 2001; Lisa DiCaprio: The Betrayal of Srebrenica: The Ten-year Commemoration. In: *The Public Historian* 31,3 (2009), pp. 73–95; Bob de Graaff: The Difference between Legal Proof and Historical Evidence. The Trial of Slobodan Milošević and the Case of Srebrenica. In: *European Review* 14,4 (2006), pp. 499–512; Jan Willem Honig / Nobert Both: *Srebrenica: Record of a War Crime.* London: Penguin 1996; Jan Willem Honig: Strategy and Genocide: Srebrenica as an Analytical Challenge. In: *Southeast European and Black Sea Studies* 7,3 (2007), pp. 399–416; Selma Leydesdorff: Stories from No Land: The Women of Srebrenica Speak out. In: *Human Rights Review* 8,3 (April–June 2007), pp. 187–198; Jelena Obradovic-Wochnik: Knowledge, Acknowledgement and Denial in Serbia's Responses to the Srebrenica Massacre. In: *Journal of Contemporary European Studies* 17,1 (2009), pp. 61–74; David Rohde: *Endgame: The Betrayal and Fall of Srebrenica, Europe's Worst Massacre since World War II.* Boulder: Westview 1998; Stevan Weine: *When History is a Nightmare: Lives and Memories of Ethnic Cleansing in Bosnia-Herzegovina.* New Brunswick: Rutgers University Press 1999; Ivan Zveržhanovski: Watching War Crimes: The

Before delving into the media coverage of the Srebrenica Massacre, a brief excursion will outline the historical background.

Firstly it must be noted that the primary perpetrators of the massacre was the army of the Republika Srpska (RS), or the Bosnian-Serb army rather than JNA, which had been in the foreground of the press-coverage analysed in the previous chapter. The Bosnian Serbs had united in a constituent republic, the RS, due to Bosnia's secessionist strivings. Radovan Karadžić was the President and based the Republic's headquarters in Pale, a town south-east of Sarajevo. General Ratko Mladić was Chief of Staff of the Bosnian-Serb army and spearheaded the attack on Srebrenica.

As can be deduced from the plethora of literature on Srebrenica, a predominantly Muslim town according to a 1992 census, it had been an embattled area since the beginning of the Bosnian War.[3] In 1993, when Srebrenica was on the verge of being captured by the Bosnian-Serb army, the town and its environs were declared one of six UN 'safe areas'. With several UN-bases in and around Srebrenica, this scheme was intended to protect the Bosnian Muslim civilians.[4] However, due to lacking consensus in the Security Council (UNSC), the UN-troops only had a peace-keeping mandate, and therefore could not use force to prevent the Bosnian-Serb offensive.[5]

Consequently, when the Bosnian-Serb army initiated the attack on Srebrenica under the military command of General Mladić and the political direction of Karadžić on 6 July 1995, there was no significant defence in Srebrenica and the Bosnian-Serb army quickly enveloped the enclave. The fierce shelling forced the UN-DUTCHBAT-troops "[…] to abandon their observation post on the southern edge of the enclave […]"[6] Horrified that the UN-soldiers were simply retreating from the Serbian offensive rather than defending themselves and the enclave's civilian population, Bosnian Muslim troops, who had also been unable to hinder the siege[7] threw grenades at the

Srebrenica Video and the Serbian Attitudes to the 1995 Srebrenica Massacre. In: *Southeast European and Black Sea Studies* 7,3 (2007), pp. 417–430; United Nations: The Fall of Srebrenica. In: *Report of the Secretary-General Pursuant to General Assembly Resolution* 53/35, Vol. A/54/549. New York: United Nations General Assembly 1999.

3 Honig / Both: *Srebrenica*, p. xvii.

4 DiCaprio: The Betrayal of Srebrenica, p. 78.

5 United Nations: The Fall of Srebrenica, pp. 6, 17; Brunborg / Lyngstad / Urdal: Accounting for Genocide, p. 232.

6 Honig / Both: *Srebrenica*, p. 232.

7 The Bosnian Muslim troops were unable to defend Srebrenica because they had been forced to turn over most of their weapons to the UN-troops who aimed to ensure that a negotiated cease-fire would be adhered to (Rohde: *Endgame*, p. 8).

DUTCHBAT-soldiers, attempting to stop their retreat.[8] As a result, the Dutch soldier Raviv Rensen was killed on 8 July 1995.[9] Indeed, the peacekeepers were so defenceless against the approaching army that several UN-soldiers were held hostage in the environs of Srebrenica and were used as human shields by the Bosnian-Serb army to protect strategically important buildings such as arms depots.[10] The caricaturist Horst Haitzinger depicted the helplessness of the UN soldiers in a very poignant cartoon.

Figure 9: Horst Haitzinger, "Who suggested that the blue helmets don't serve a purpose here anymore? ("*Wer hat da behauptet, die Blauhelme hätten hier keine Funktion mehr?*")[11]

Nevertheless, the local population poured into Srebrenica from the surrounding towns, hoping for protection on the UN-base. The town's inhabitants rapidly increased to 45,000 people, tripling the pre-war population.[12]

Based in an old battery factory in Potočari, near Srebrenica, the Dutch soldiers allowed between 3,000 to 4,000 refugees into their compound. However,

8 Honig / Both: *Srebrenica*, p. 3.

9 Rohde: *Endgame*, p. 36.

10 Honig / Both: *Srebrenica*, p. 36.

11 This cartoon was not published in any of the newspapers analysed in this book. A different cartoon by Haitzinger was published by *Spiegel*.

12 Leydesdorff: Stories from No Land, p. 192.

when it was judged to be full, the entrance was closed off, leaving around 20,000 people outside.[13] Due to the sheer number of people, the situation in and around the UN-base quickly turned into a humanitarian disaster. Beyond providing the most basic aid, the UN-soldiers could not do anything to stop the take-over of the enclave. Between 6 and 13 July, the Bosnian-Serb forces expelled and displaced 23,000 Bosnian women and children, who were transported to a nearby town, Tuzla, in buses. Thousands of Muslim men were detained and later executed, which now counts as the largest single war crime in Europe since the Second World War.[14] The 1999 UN-report on Srebrenica referred to the events in the enclave as 'attempted genocide' and stated that

> […] the Serbs began the systematic extermination of the thousands of Bosniac males being held in Bratunac [near Srebrenica] in the early morning hours of 14 July. [The only exception was…] a handful of individuals who survived by hiding under or among the dead bodies.[15]

EU forensic scientists would later determine that in the months following the initial massacres, the Bosnian-Serb army dug up the mass graves and reburied the bodies in 33 'secondary sites', attempting to hide the evidence of their atrocities.[16]

However, none of this information was available to the international community and media at the time. Immediately after the Bosnian-Serb army had besieged the enclave, neither representatives from international organisations nor journalists were granted access. Thus, there was no definitive proof for the extent of these atrocities until 1996, when the war had ended and EU forensic scientists began uncovering numerous mass graves. This fact is largely disregarded in the secondary literature, but becomes crucial when considering the media's understanding and coverage of the massacre as it was unfolding. Initially the displaced civilians gradually arriving in Tuzla were the only source of information. The regional UN-headquarters set up refugee camps on the airfield of Tuzla's airport, which were quickly "[…] swarming with Western journalists."[17] In late July the men who had fled from the mass executions and who arrived in Tuzla after a six-day march offered additional

13 Honig / Both: *Srebrenica*, p. 28.

14 Ibid., p. xix.

15 United Nations: The Fall of Srebrenica, pp. 109, 111, 200.

16 Ibid., p. 232.

17 Rohde: *Endgame*, p. 300.

information. DUTCHBAT-soldiers gradually returning to The Netherlands also provided primary insights into the events in Srebrenica.

Alongside the historical narrative, a harsh judgment of the UN's failure to protect Srebrenica's civilian population dominates the secondary literature.[18] For example, David Rohde cited a Bosnian Muslim man who stated "[...] that Srebrenica's Dutch peacekeepers were little more than greedy cowards. They had come here to make money [...] not to protect the safe area."[19] Significantly, the indignation regarding the UN's role in Srebrenica was not applied to the fatality of a peacekeeper. Due to the primary focus on the UN's failure to protect Srebrenica's civilian population, the reader is left with the impression that it was the UN's 'own fault' for retreating rather than protecting the enclave from the Bosnian-Serb attack. This outrage that the Srebrenica Massacre could unfold under the watchful eyes of the international community is important to keep in mind when analysing the contemporary German press coverage, which we turn to now.

The timeframe set out in this chapter – 6 July to 22 August 1995 – studies the German print media coverage commencing with the Bosnian-Serb attack on Srebrenica and the first weeks of the refugee crisis in Tuzla. The September 1995 issue of *Konkret* is also considered to trace if any information relevant to this chapter may have appeared later due to the editorial cycle of the monthly publication. In spite of the limited information available to the international community and German media immediately after the siege, the nature of the Srebrenica-coverage offers valuable insights regarding the state of knowledge at the time and what interpretations were offered in this limited context. After analysing how the publications pieced together the details of the massacre, this chapter will examine how the German press reported on the role of the UN and specifically Germany. Here the impact of Germany's National-Socialist past will be considered, as well as the language and images used throughout the coverage.

AJW will not be included in this chapter, as it did not report on Srebrenica at all. As noted previously, the weekly newspaper only reported on the Balkans when a connection could be made to the Jewish cultural sphere. Presumably the Srebrenica Massacre did not seem directly relatable to its Jewish readership. This is surprising, considering that the events in Srebrenica were

18 Particularly in DiCaprio: The Betrayal of Srebrenica; Rohde: *Endgame*; Leydesdorff: Stories from No Land.

19 Rohde: *Endgame*, p. 7.

regarded as genocide by some observers early on, which could have been an interesting angle to explore further by *AJW*.

Piecing Together the Events in Srebrenica

In light of the inaccessibility of the enclave, the manner in which the atrocities were reported and what sources were utilised to piece together the details are worth exploring. In spite of repeated appeals by the UN-Security Council (UNSC) to be granted access to the town, the Bosnian Serbs did not allow any UN-personnel to enter Srebrenica in July and August 1995.[20] Foreign journalists and employees from Non-Governmental Organisations (NGOs) such as the International Committee of the Red Cross (ICRC) and Doctors without Borders (MSF)[21] were subjected to the same restrictions. Consequently many NGOs based their spokespersons in Tuzla, where they communicated with the international media. One example was Ron Redmond, spokesman for the UN Refugee Agency (UNHCR), who was cited repeatedly in the German press.[22] However, this also meant that journalists had access to the same first-hand sources as multilateral organisations. While the German publications did not mention this advantage explicitly, it gives the journalists' reporting based on interviews with eyewitnesses expelled from Srebrenica more authority as this was the only first-hand information available at the time. Nonetheless, in general the limited state of knowledge about the events in Srebrenica cannot be stressed enough, as it rendered much of the reporting fragmentary and speculative.

Turning now to the coverage of the German publications, their treatment of the refugees and the atrocities in Srebrenica was very diverse, though it cannot be categorised along the lines of political leaning. The reporting in *BILD*, *Spiegel* and *taz* featured strong and prolonged interest in the enclave. In contrast, *Welt* and *FAZ* as well as *FR* were comparable in their reduced

20 UNSC: Security Council authorizes Secretary-General to use "all resources available" to restore Srebrenica's status as safe area, Press Release Security Council, SC/6066, 12.07.1995, p. 4; UNSC: Security Council demands Bosnian Serbs allow humanitarian agencies access to civilians in Srebrenica, Press Release Security Council, SC/6067, 14.07.1995, p. 1; UNSC: Security Council demands access to detainees in areas under Serb control in Bosnia, Press Release Security Council, SC/6082, 10.08.1995, pp. 1–2.

21 From the French: *Medicins sans Frontières.*

22 For example cited in dpa/afp/rtr: Flüchtlinge aus Srebrenica „überfordern" die UN. In: *FR*, 15.07.1995, p. 2; Welt-Nachrichtendienst: Serben erobern die Enklave Srebrenica. In: *Welt*, 12.07.1995, p. 1; AFP/dpa/Reuter: Bosnische Serben dringen in die Enklave Zepa ein. In: *FAZ*, 26.07.1995, p. 1.

interest. *JF* published a single article on Srebrenica, which focused on the DUTCHBAT-soldiers who were gradually returning to The Netherlands. This article quoted the Dutch foreign aid secretary Jan Pronk to have said that massacres were ensuing in Srebrenica and that "genocide was occurring."[23] *JF's* reproduction of this quote featuring the loaded term 'genocide' is striking, as the article did not include any other information about the events in Srebrenica. This loose utilisation in the anonymous article suggests a missing interest to grapple deeply with the subject-matter.

In comparison, *Welt* and *FAZ* as well as *FR* reported on Srebrenica much more extensively, though they significantly based all stories on various 'official' voices, such as statements made by spokespersons from UN, UNHCR, MSF and ICRC, or later returning Dutch soldiers. These articles primarily outlined the deteriorating humanitarian situation in Tuzla and gave preliminary numbers of people who had arrived from Srebrenica, however none cited refugees directly. Due to the similitude of sources, *Welt*, *FAZ* and *FR* reported comparable details, for example that all boys and men above the age of 16 were being held in the football stadium of Bratunac to determine whether they were war criminals.[24] Other articles reported that some refugees had seen men who had been shot and others who had their throats slit[25] and that some women bore signs of severe abuse.[26]

FAZ was particularly rigid in its editorial policy of exclusively citing official sources rather than refugee accounts. Consequently, the conservative

23 JF: „Das Schweigegebot gebrochen". In: *JF*, 28.07.1995, p. 6.

24 For example AFP/Reuter/AP: Bosnische Serben erobern Srebrenica – Zehntausende auf der Flucht. In: *FAZ*, 12.07.1995, p. 1; Reuter/AP/AFP: Der UN-Sicherheitsrat fordert den Abzug der Serben aus der Enklave. In: *FAZ*, 13.07.1995, p. 1; Reuter/dpa: Die Serben vertreiben Tausende aus Srebrenica. In: *FAZ*, 14.07.1995, p. 1; F.A.Z.: Die Serben verstärken den Druck auf die Bosnier und auf die Soldaten der Vereinten Nationen. In: *FAZ*, 15.07.1995, p. 1; E. L.: Redeverbot für Blauhelme. In: *FAZ*, 19.07.1995, p. 2; Carl Gustaf Ströhm: Die merkwürdige Rolle des UN-Beauftragten in Bosnien. In: *Welt*, 14.07.1995, p. 6; Carl Gustaf Ströhm: Enklaven in Not: Der Aussichtslose Kampf der Verteidiger von Zepa. In: *Welt*, 18.07.1995, p. 8; WeNa: 20 000 Flüchtlinge aus Srebrenica vermisst. In: *Welt*, 15./16.07.1995, p. 3; afp/ap/dpa: UN drohen mit Luftangriffen. In: *FR*, 11.07.1995, p. 1; ap/rtr/afp/dpa: Bosnische Serben erobern Srebrenica. In: *FR*, 12.07.1995, p. 1; afp/rtr/dpa/ap: Serben verjagen Moslems aus Srebrenica. In: *FR*, 13.07.1995, p. 1; dpa/ap/rtr/afp: Flüchtlingsdrama in Bosnien. In: *FR*, 14.07.1995, p. 1; rtr/ap/dpa/afp: Serben dringen in Zepa ein. In: *FR*, 17.07.1995, p. 1; dpa: „Kinder aus Srebrenica stehen unter Schock". In: *FR*, 27.07.1995, p. 7.

25 Carl Gustaf Ströhm: Die Hölle von Srebrenica. In: *Welt*, 12.07.1995, p. 3; WeNa: Serben vertreiben Moslems aus Srebrenica. In: *Welt*, 13.07.1995, p. 1; WeNa: Flüchtlings-Chaos in Bosnien. In: *Welt*, 14.07.1995, p. 1.

26 WeNa: Flüchtlings-Chaos in Bosnien. In: *Welt*, 14.07.1995, p. 1; WeNa: 20 000 Flüchtlinge aus Srebrenica vermisst. In: *Welt*, 15./16.07.1995, p. 3.

broadsheet solely conveyed carefully-worded official opinions which were constrained by diplomatic formulations or outright censorship. The result of this approach was that a sterile point of view dominated *FAZ's* articles about Srebrenica, rather than a grass-root, humanitarian approach. This was also mirrored in *FAZ's* selection of images, which shied away from showing the suffering civilians. Indeed, only three pictures from all 23 published in *FAZ* in this period featured the victims of Srebrenica.[27]

Significantly, two of these three images depicted the refugees receiving aid from UN-soldiers.[28] These images, while illustrating the refugees' desperate situation simultaneously conveyed a sense of reassurance, as their anguish was seemingly being eased through the international efforts. This selection underlines *FAZ's* superficial engagement with the subject-matter. Not only did the broadsheet's readers absorb only the official version of events in Srebrenica, but they also did not gain any pictorial insight into the extent of the catastrophe.

However, a significant departure from this policy could be found in various articles which cited returning DUTCHBAT-soldiers. Although they were subjected to a 'rule-of-silence' until all UN-soldiers had left Srebrenica for fear of their safety, some broke this rule and made statements in the media. One such *FAZ*-piece quoted a Dutch soldier who stated that the Bosnian-Serb forces abused their power, murdering and mutilating people. They "'[…] cut off the ears of some, others they raped.'"[29] Later reports featured equally graphic descriptions, for example that UN-soldiers saw "[…] a truck full of corpses […]" which were clearly adult men, or a tractor pulling a hanger full of corpses; a digger and tipper with corpses were also sighted and reported.[30]

The broadsheet's spotlight on peacekeepers rather than refugees was further underlined by an image, which was published in both *FAZ* and *BILD* on the same day. In the picture, the main focus is on 11 uniformed UN-soldiers lying on the grass. In the far left-hand corner of the image, one can see a group of civilians – a woman holding an infant is most visible – sitting right next to the soldiers. The caption accompanying the *FAZ*-image read: "The faces of the Dutch soldiers mirror the situation of the UN after the conquest of Srebrenica." Only the *BILD*-caption also drew attention to the

27 Pictures published in *FAZ*, 14.07.1995, p. 2; *FAZ*, 17.07.1995, p. 2; *FAZ*, 18.07.1995, p. 2.

28 Pictures published in *FAZ*, 17.07.1995, p. 2; *FAZ*, 18.07.1995, p. 18; *Welt*, 18.07.1995, p. 8.

29 AFP: Vorwürfe gegen die Eroberer Srebrenicas. In: *FAZ*, 18.07.1995, p. 2.

30 Reuter: Niederländer bezeugen neun Erschießungen. In: *FAZ*, 24.07.1995, p. 2; E. L.: Soldat hat Leichen gesehen. In: *FAZ*, 07.08.1995, p. 5.

Muslim refugees waiting next to the soldiers in the left corner of the picture. The photographer's preferred angle focusing on the Dutch soldiers rather than the civilians is sharpened by *FAZ's* failure to even mention them in the caption.

A definitive reason for *FAZ's* side-lining of Srebrenica's victims remains unclear, but it could have stemmed from a cautionary awareness to the limited reliable information available at the time. Moreover, refugees were perhaps deemed too entangled to be reliable sources for reports, especially combined with the inability to cross-check and confirm their accounts. While a hesitation to quote eye-witnesses due to their depth of involvement is comprehensible, the newspaper's reliance on statements given by soldiers who had officially been subjected to a 'rule-of-silence' is less comprehensible. Arguably, these soldiers would have recollected the incidents in Srebrenica selectively and perhaps aimed to present their own role in a positive light. Moreover, the motives of some soldiers to make press statements against official rules are never challenged in *FAZ's* pieces.

While also drawing primarily on official sources, *FR* and *Welt* featured some exceptions. For example, *Welt* published two articles, both written by its correspondent, Ströhm, who was based in Dubrovnik, Croatia. These pieces offered detailed reports of the atrocities perpetrated by Bosnian-Serb forces in Srebrenica and were significantly based on refugees' eyewitness reports. One such article reported that Bosnian-Serb soldiers had stolen uniforms from UN-soldiers in Srebrenica and wore them while rounding up Muslim men.[31] In Ströhm's second piece, he interviewed a female refugee in Tuzla, who had stated that many Muslim men from Srebrenica had been shot. She declared: "'In the morning we saw that in Potočari [...they] had been slaughtered and hung up like animals.'" The eyewitness continued that the buses, in which the women and children were deported to Tuzla, had frequently been stopped and the passengers were forced to watch how men – their husbands, fathers and sons – were being killed by the side of the road. "Mothers had to watch as their daughters were raped."[32] By using such accounts, *Welt* offered its readers a detailed view of the events in and around Srebrenica which was missing in *FAZ's* writing. However, it remains unclear why the two articles mentioned above were written while Ströhm was based in Croatia rather than Tuzla and how he could have gained in-depth insights without being on-site.

31 Carl Gustaf Ströhm: „Serben zogen sich UN-Uniformen an". In: *Welt*, 20.07.1995, p. 4.

32 Carl Gustaf Ströhm: „Vergewaltigt, getreten, abgeschlachtet". In: *Welt*, 17.07.1995, p. 3.

Another example was the publication of the same article in both *FR* and *Welt* on 14 July 1995, written by Zoran Radosavljevic, a Croatian journalist working for the Russian press agency rtr.[33] However, only *FR* provided the author's name, while *Welt* indicated the authorship as 'DW', which stands for '*Die Welt*', and even indicated the co-author to be *Welt's* own Ströhm. Though each article was slightly adapted, the majority of the content remained the same. Both started with the memorable description of the refugees from Srebrenica as: "ragged, hungry, disheartened and absolutely terrified [...]" They continued with stories told by individual refugees who recalled that they had to bribe Bosnian-Serb soldiers to gain access to the buses to Tuzla. However men of fighting age were detained to investigate whether they were war criminals.[34] The *Welt*-article featured additional details including that a "UN-spokesperson declared that he had witnessed accounts stating that Bosnian Serbs had raped at least two women before displacing them to the no man's land."[35] Perhaps this supplement warranted that Ströhm and '*Die Welt*' were identified as authors rather than rtr's Radosavljevic. This press-agency article is significant because it was the first and rare product of eyewitness accounts published in these newspapers. Written almost immediately after the siege on Srebrenica began, it offered the detailed information German publications perhaps could not obtain in other ways. In keeping with its rigid editorial stance not to include eye-witness reports, *FAZ* did not publish this rtr-story, which could have offered the readers a victims' perspective and which was evidently readily available to the German print media.

Similar to the textual exceptions in *Welt* and *FR*, which occasionally drew on refugee accounts, both papers also juxtaposed their written pieces with pictures of Srebrenica's victims, giving the reader a visual insight into their grief.[36]

These images depicting both the grief and desperation of the refugees, as well as the extent of the humanitarian disaster are very different from *FAZ's* pictures. Rather than emphasising the aspect of international aid, they conveyed the desolate misery and evoke much more empathy amongst the reader.

33 *taz* also published this article in a similar format: rtr: Die Vertriebenen von Srebrenica. In: *taz*, 14.07.1995, p. 8.

34 DW / Carl Gustaf Ströhm: „Wir hatten alle ganz schrecklich Angst". In: *Welt*, 14.07.1995, p. 4; Zoran Radosavljevic: „Sieben lange Tage haben wir in Keller verbracht". In: *FR*,14.07.1995, p. 2.

35 DW / Ströhm: „Wir hatten alle ganz schrecklich Angst". In: *Welt*, 14.07.1995, p. 4.

36 Imgages published in *FR*, 14.07.995, p. 2; *FR*, 15.07.1995, p. 2; *Welt*, 15.07.1995, p. 3; *Welt*, 18.07.1995, p. 8

Figure 10: Reuters; printed in *Welt*, 15 July 1995, p. 3, and *taz*, 15 July 1995, p. 1.

In contrast, *taz*, *BILD* and *Spiegel* relied heavily on first-hand reports from survivors in Tuzla, focusing more on the grass-roots, humanitarian angle than the previous newspapers, attempting to offer their readers as much insight into a convoluted series of events as was possible at the time. Taking *taz* first, a number of articles pieced together the "[…] new horror-stories [that] arrive[d] in Tuzla […] with every bus-load of new refugees."[37] Their stories contributed not just to a general understanding and evaluation of what had occurred in Srebrenica, but gave graphic insights into the horror they had endured. A good example of the vivid vignettes the paper painted for its readers is the interview with Muhira Z., who said that "her son was 'butchered with a knife', right in front of her eyes. Her daughters […] vanished […] 'they are probably dead, they have murdered them, I only heard their screams.'"[38] *taz* supplemented its striking articles with images that gave the reader a moving insight into the fate of the victims in Tuzla and by extension Srebrenica.[39]

37 Hera: Tausende vermisst, die wehrfähigen Männer interniert. In: *taz*, 17.07.1995, p. 3.

38 Erich Rathfelder: „Ich habe nur noch ihre Schreie gehört". In: *taz*, 17.07.1995, p. 3.

39 For example, images published in *taz*, 15.07.1995, p. 11.

A guest contribution in *taz*, authored by the famous American journalist Roy Gutman, who had written about the concentration camps in Bosnia, was also memorable. Having won a Pulitzer Prize in 1993 for this coverage, Gutman had gained great status and was considered an authority on the Bosnian War. His 1995 article drew on various interviews, in which refugees recounted different aspects of Srebrenica's siege. Several stated that they had heard Bosnian-Serb soldiers say repeatedly that their aim was to kill as many Muslims as possible. 42-year old Sadikovic recalled that "every night [...] young women were taken from the factory-building in Potočari. No one ever saw them again." Gutman wrote that these experiences were so severe that some of the survivors could not cope with them and committed suicide.[40] The author included more specific details of one case:

> A young girl from Srebrenica got on the bus half-naked. She had severe abrasions and one could safely assume that she had been raped [...] Upon arrival in Tuzla, she hung herself on a tree.[41]

Another *taz*-story, which had been published anonymously a few weeks earlier on 15 July, had also reported that "a 20-year old woman, who was separated from her family, hung herself in the forest."[42]

In spite of these repeated references to this fateful story, *taz* never accompanied its articles with an image. In contrast, *BILD* did so on the same day as *taz's* anonymous piece was published, namely 15 July and placed it on the first page (figure 11).

The *BILD*-article published along this image stated: "a picture accuses", proceeding to describe what the 20-year old girl was wearing and that she used a torn blanket to hang herself.[43] The image combined with this text indeed left the reader with a sense of being accused. This picture became widely-known and even iconic. For example U. S. Senator Dianne Feinstein, stated that upon seeing this picture, she truly comprehended that the Bosnian War was producing innocent victims and that this was not a civil war in which all parties were equally guilty, as she had presumed. Michael Sells, who quotes her remark from the *Congressional Record* explains that this realisation was spurred by "[...] what the picture left unsaid [...including answers to questions such as] what humiliations and depravations did she suffer, had she been raped,

40 Roy Gutman: General Mladić und der Todeskonvoi. In: *taz*, 11.08.1995, p. 11.

41 Ibid.

42 Anonymous: Wo sind die Männer von Srebrenica geblieben. In: *taz*, 15./16.07.1995, p. 1.

43 Anonymous: Als die Serben kamen, erhängte sie sich. In: *BILD*, 15.07.1995, p. 1.

Figure 11:
"In this July 14, 1995 photo, refugee Ferida Osmanovic from Srebrenica is found hanged in a forest outside the U.N. base at Tuzla airport. The woman who looked to be in her early 20s had hanged herself with a torn blanket." Photographer: Darko Bandic, dpa-ap; printed in *BILD*, 15 July 1995, p. 1.

did she witness loved ones being killed?"[44] The Senator's reactions emphasise the power of images and how this particular example influenced the world's perception of Srebrenica. This international acclaim of the picture renders its non-inclusion in almost all publications considered here even more surprising, though its absence in *FAZ*, *Welt*, *FR* and *JF* can be explained by the limited inclusion of the refugees' fate.

Returning to *BILD's* textual reporting, it included detailed eyewitness accounts similar to *taz*. Due to the habitual brevity of the tabloid's articles, these stories were not usually embedded in much contextual background, though they still gave the readers a reasonably coherent insight into the massacre. They predominantly featured the subject of rape, perhaps more prominently than other publications, which is in keeping with the tabloid's focus on sensational stories. Some reported that mass rapes took place while Srebrenica's women and children were cowering in the factory in Potočari, and other articles included more personal recollections.[45] For example one story

44 Sells: *Bridge Betrayed*, pp. 144–145.

45 Anonymous: Die Serben nahmen meine beiden Nichten mit: Ich sah sie nicht wieder. In: *BILD*, 14.07.1995, p. 2; Anonymous: Verzweiflung und Chaos in den UN-Flüchtlingslagern. In: *BILD*, 15.07.1995, p. 2.

cited Nurika Hrustanovic, who remembered that in Potočari she saw one girl being dragged off the bus by her hair and then raped by 30 Chetniks, while UN-soldiers merely stood by.[46] Here the referral to the Bosnian-Serb soldiers as Chetniks is particularly striking and perhaps intends to dismiss 'the Serbs' as raging war criminals. As most *BILD*-articles were written anonymously and did not include a locality of the author, it is not possible to deduce whether they stemmed from on-site correspondents who interviewed refugees. However, none of the stories featured here could be found in other publications, which suggests that they were unique and not based on press agencies.

Spiegel published two articles which offered vivid insights into the events in Srebrenica. On 24 July 1995, Renate Flottau gave a very graphic and detailed narrative of the refugees in Tuzla and what they had witnessed in Srebrenica. Though there was no geographic indication of where the story was researched and written, it was heavily based on oral accounts, suggesting that Flottau was in Tuzla, speaking directly to eye-witnesses. One refugee, Mukeleta, told the journalist about her husband and 13-year-old son who had been abducted. When attempting to run after her son, Serbian guards stopped her, saying: "'we are just contemplating which parts of your son we're going to cut off.'" The article continued that after she recapitulated her experiences, Mukeleta collapsed, weeping hysterically. Other refugees Flottau cited in her piece recalled that during their three-hour bus-ride from Srebrenica to Tuzla, the vehicles occasionally slowed down so the passengers could get a full view of the executed men on the side of the road.[47] The title, "I kissed the feet of the murderer", as well as the picture accompanying the piece of a sobbing woman, overcome by grief, sitting on the floor, summarised the horrors of what was occurring in Srebrenica in a very immediate manner.[48]

Other images published by *Spiegel*, evoked a similar emotional reaction in the readers.[49] For example one of the pictures showed an old woman being carried in a carpet by four younger people, unable to make the harrowing journey herself; another depicted a wailing woman with her arms thrown up in despair. The theme of wailing women appears regularly in these images. While this focus could be interpreted as a pre-selection on behalf of the

46 S. Bassewitz / M. Soyka: Serben zerrten junge Mädchen an den Haaren aus den Bussen. In: *BILD*, 20.07.1995, p. 2.

47 Renate Flottau: „Ich küsste die Füße des Mörders“. In: *Spiegel*, 24.07.1995, p. 112.

48 Image published in *Spiegel*, 24.07.1995, p. 112.

49 Anonymous: Beim ersten Schnee. In: *Spiegel*, 17.07.1995, p. 115; Walter Mayr: „Es ist keiner mehr übrig“. In: *Spiegel*, 31.07.1995, p. 118.

photographer or editors to feature a motif that would evoke strong empathy with the viewer, it must also be noted that the victims arriving in Tuzla *were* predominantly women and children, as most men had been detained, shot, or those who had managed to escape had not yet arrived in Tuzla.
One particularly striking image was published by the news-magazine in mid-July. This image depicts floods of refugees confronting two completely overwhelmed UN-soldiers sitting on a tank. One of the soldiers seems to have lowered his head in resignation. Of course one does not know if the soldier was not merely looking down or perhaps speaking to someone. Regardless, the instinctive mood conveyed by this *Spiegel*-image is one of a weak and resigned UN confronted with masses of people whom they cannot help. This is a very different – and perhaps more accurate – image of the UN as displayed in *FAZ's* images, which exclusively showed the international organisation as easing the pain of Srebrenica's victims.

Srebrenica's Men Arrive in Tuzla

In late July 1995, several thousand men who had managed to flee from the enclave by foot as the Bosnian-Serb siege unfolded, arrived in Tuzla.[50] *taz*, *BILD* and *Spiegel* were the only publications that covered the men's arrival, detailing what they had endured, and in doing so used this opportunity to continue piecing together the events.[51] The lack of interest in the remaining publications is striking, as these men provided new information on what had occurred in Srebrenica. *Spiegel's* account was based on the experiences of Mevludin Oric, a 25-year-old father of two. Speaking to the news-magazine's correspondent, Walter Mayr, Oric recalled that he was one of 10,000 men who had fled as the enclave fell. He recalled that he was supposed to be shot, but was saved by playing dead and hiding under corpses. During the night he stole away and embarked on the long trek to Tuzla.[52] A *BILD*-article featured a similar story, referring to a man who only succeeded in fleeing

50 Erich Rathfelder: *Sarajevo und danach: Sechs Jahre Reporter im ehemaligen Jugoslawien.* Munich: C. H. Beck 1998, p. 243.

51 taz: Todesmarsch nach Tuzla. in: *taz*, 19.07.1995, p. 1; Erich Rathfelder: Weitermarschieren – oder sterben. In: *taz*, 19.07.1995, p. 11; Anonymous: 100 Kilometer durch alle Fronten – ich überlebte. In: *BILD*, 18.07.1995, p. 1; Anonymous: Bosnien: Moslem-Staaten rufen zum Heiligen Krieg auf. In: *BILD*, 25.07.1995, p. 2; Walter Mayr: „Es ist keiner mehr übrig". In: *Spiegel*, 31.07.1995, pp. 117–118.

52 Walter Mayr: „Es ist keiner mehr übrig". In: *Spiegel*, 31.07.1995, pp. 117–118.

from Srebrenica because he had hidden under corpses of 'slaughtered' prisoners.[53] It remains unclear if both publications referred to the same individual. Another *BILD*-article published one week earlier had reported on the harrowing experiences of a Bosnian soldier who arrived in Tuzla after days of wandering through the forests following his escape from Srebrenica. He explained that once the Bosnian Serbs had arrived in the enclave, "[…] they hauled away all men of fighting age in trucks. […]Women were raped and mutilated. Laughing, the Serbs cut off the refugees' ears."[54]

taz's correspondent Rathfelder recounted Husan Hrustanovic's story. According to Rathfelder, the 38-year-old was initially reluctant to speak to the western journalist, but eventually did so. It emerged that on the way from Srebrenica many men were captured and arrested by Bosnian Serbs, while others were torn apart by landmines. From the 15,000 who initially left Srebrenica, between 3,000 and 4,000 men had survived the journey thus far. "The others are still struggling through the forest or have already been captured by the Serbs, perhaps murdered by them."[55] The contradicting numbers offered here – *taz's* eyewitness spoke of 15,000 men while *Spiegel's* testimony cited 10,000 men – strike an external observer, though the conflicting information may not have been noticed by a casual reader at the time. However, for the purposes of a media analysis, such instances underline the absence of concrete, provable facts, which continued to cloud the German media's understanding of the events in Srebrenica and perhaps explain why other publications chose not to report on the matter in much detail.

The articles in *Konkret* about Srebrenica differed decisively from the previous publications. Indeed, aside from some marginal remarks, the magazine's commentary on Srebrenica did not develop until September 1995, long after the other publications' coverage. At that point, the writing was dominated by the twin allegations that the German media "ranging from [the conservative] *FAZ* to [the left-leaning] *taz*,"[56] was manipulating information.[57] Another article pointed to the confusing coverage of missing people with figures ranging from 1,500 to 10,000, suggesting exaggeration and criticising that the media

53 Anonymous: NATO-Truppen marschieren auf – Serben schießen weiter. In: *BILD*, 25.07.1995, p. 2.

54 Anonymous: 100 Kilometer durch alle Fronten – ich überlebte. In: *BILD*, 18.07.1995, p. 1.

55 Erich Rathfelder: Weitermarschieren – oder sterben. In: *taz*, 19.07.1995, p. 11.

56 Jürgen Elsässer: Ein deutscher Krieg. In: *Konkret*, July 1995, p. 12.

57 Jürgen Elsässer: Augen zu und durch! Der Antifaschismus des dummen Kerls. In: *Konkret*, September 1995, p. 12; Klaus Bittermann: „Reife Leistung". In: *Konkret*, September 1995, p. 14.

reported that the Serbs were 'liquidating' Srebrenica's civilian population.[58] Significantly, none of the publications considered in this chapter used the term 'liquidation' in their coverage, as the author, Jürgen Elsässer, claimed, and the latter did not elaborate what specific publications he was accusing. Moreover, none of *Konkret's* articles informed their readers of the difficulties to secure reliable sources and the inaccessibility of the enclave. This information could have explained the fluctuating and at times contradictory numbers published in the daily newspapers. Instead, Elsässer repeatedly argued that the 'main-stream' German media manipulated events of the Bosnian War to fit their agenda.[59] However he did not expand what this agenda was, who set it, and with what intended effect. Consequently his allegations can be dismissed as unsubstantiated, especially considering the diverse coverage in the German press analysed here.

Nonetheless, one of Elsässer's articles must be considered, as it critiqued Roy Gutman's previously mentioned guest contribution to *taz*.[60] The author attempted to discredit Gutman at the outset, claiming that his discovery and coverage of the Bosnian concentration camps consisted of dubious eye-witnesses and questionable evidence.[61] Elsässer alleged that the same faulty methodology formed the basis of the *taz*-piece, which he claimed was based on suspiciously vague sources, such as a statement by a 'human rights investigator'.[62] The author evidently aimed to criticise and depreciate not just this particular piece of writing, but also the German print media coverage in general. As a result of this desire to attack fellow German journalists, *Konkret's* articles on Srebrenica failed to cover the fallen enclave in a significant fashion and thus did not offer their readers a general understanding of the matter. Entirely missing from its coverage was the plight of refugees in Tuzla and their experiences, not to mention the atrocities that were undoubtedly occurring in Srebrenica.

58 Elsässer: Augen zu und durch! Der Antifaschismus des dummen Kerls. In: *Konkret*, September 1995, p. 12.

59 For example: Jürgen Elsässer: Sache der Deutschen. In: Wolfgang Schneider (ed.): *Bei Andruck Mord.* Hamburg: Konkret 1997, pp. 69–75.

60 See chapter 4, fn. 40.

61 Elsässer: Augen zu und durch! Der Antifaschismus des dummen Kerls. In: *Konkret*, September 1995, p. 12.

62 Ibid.

Authorship

Having focused on the manner in which the atrocities were covered and what sources were drawn on to piece together the factual details, the quantitative distribution of the articles' authorship in the daily broadsheets must now be considered.

Newspaper	Percentage of articles authored by correspondents	Percentage of articles authored by press agencies	Percentage of articles amalgamated from various press releases, etc.
Welt	61%	5%	34%
FAZ	64%	31%	4%
FR	34%	64%	0,6%
taz	69%	25%	3%

Table 2: Percentages of articles according to authorship[63]

As the above table indicates, all daily newspapers aside from *FR* predominantly relied on pieces written by their own journalists rather than press agencies, in spite of the inaccessibility of the enclave and the difficulties of obtaining information. Moreover, *Welt* was the only paper which substantially drew on amalgamated press releases. The majority of *FAZ's* stories were written by the broadsheet's own correspondents, which indicates that the human resources were available to lead interviews with eyewitnesses and refraining to do so was perhaps the result of an inherent scepticism regarding the trustworthiness of eyewitnesses.

Srebrenica and the UN

Having analysed the way in which the various newspapers compiled their coverage of the uncertain events in Srebrenica, we turn to the press' evaluation of the UN, which all publications except *JF* included in their reporting. *Konkret* stood alone in its assessment that any German commentator lamenting the UN's inaction was an 'imperialist' who condoned the meddling in another country and indeed the fragmentation of a sovereign state.[64] All remaining publications took a more moderate stance and expressed a general consensus that the UN's reputation had suffered from mishandling the

63 All numbers short of 100% are anonymous articles which cannot be categorised.

64 Karl Held / Peter Decker: Krieg der Nationen. In: *Konkret*, August 1995, p. 16.

Srebrenica-crisis.[65] Perhaps a bit dramatically, *taz's* Erich Rathfelder concluded that "Bosnia [...was] turning out to be the UN's grave."[66]

Welt's articles were marked by a comparable approach, though they were more detailed and frequent than in the other publications. For example, numerous articles focused on the UN's 50th birthday, which it would celebrate in October that year, doubting the present-day effectiveness of the organisation.[67] Portraying the UN as being in a mid-life crisis, these articles sought to identify what problems had contributed to the DUTCHBAT's inaction. These included that the UN did not have independent financial resources, no standing and independent troops, and that national interests frequently dominated and conflicted with the decision-making process.[68]

Spiegel's reports were alone in presenting a more positive interpretation of the UN's role in Bosnia. While conceding that the UN had unquestionably failed to protect Srebrenica's civilian population,[69] the news-magazine's articles also called attention to Russia's interest in the conflict. One, for example, speculated that if the UN pulled out of Bosnia due to its failures in Srebrenica, what would follow would be terrifying: "Washington [would] lift the arms embargo, Moscow [would] arm Serbia, Belgrade [would] officially step into the war [...]"[70] By framing the UN's presence in Bosnia as an important counter-weight to Russia in the region, *Spiegel* introduced an alternative interpretation of the UN's role. However in doing so, it also re-introduced the Cold War-era opposition of Russia versus 'the West,' which had been present in the German coverage of the early 1990s, but had not re-appeared in 1995.[71] Nevertheless, *Spiegel's* argumentation demonstrated that there were various ways of interpreting the events in Srebrenica and Bosnia, cautioning the reader of jumping to one-sided conclusions.

65 Pierre Simonitsch: Das wahrscheinlichste Szenario: Der Abzug der Blauhelme. In: *FR*, 13.07.1995, p. 8; Günther Chalupa: Das Versagen der UNO bei Srebrenica. In: *taz*, 12.07.1995, p. 2; koc: Verteidigungsminister Rühe: „Glaubwürdigkeit der UNO steht auf dem Spiel". In: *BILD*, 14.07.1995, p. 2.

66 Erich Rathfelder: Bosnien wird zum Grab der UNO. In: *taz*, 21.07.1995, p. 10.

67 Hans-Peter Schwarz: Die UN in der Midlife-Krise: Abschied von hohen Zielen. In: *Welt*, 06.07.1995, p. 6; rtr: Die UNO-Resolution 824 zwischen Anspruch und Wirklichkeit. In: *Welt*, 13.07.1995, p. 4; Thomas Loeffelholz: Das Debakel der UNO. In: *Welt*, 17.07.1995, p. 4.

68 Hans-Peter Schwarz: Die UN in der Midlife-Krise: Abschied von hohen Zielen. In: *Welt*, 06.07.1995, p. 6.

69 Gerd Schmückle: Beistand ohne Verstand. In: *Spiegel*, 17.07.1995, p. 116; Anonymous: „Komplizen der Barberei". In: *Spiegel*, 24.07.1995, pp. 110–111, 113–114.

70 Anonymous: Beim ersten Schnee. In: *Spiegel*, 17.07.1995, pp. 114–115.

71 See pp. 78–79.

Beyond these deliberations, the consensus that the UN was ineffective and had failed in Srebrenica led to the disregard in most German publications of the UN-fatality in Srebrenica following a Bosnian-Muslim attack. The weekly or monthly publications *JF*, *Konkret* and *Spiegel* did not report on the death of the UN-soldier at all, underlining that it was not deemed important enough to include beyond the day-to-day news-cycle. The daily newspapers, *Welt*, *FAZ*, *FR*, *taz* and *BILD* covered the incident on 10 July, two days after it occurred. All articles were marked by their marginalised treatment of the matter, merely mentioning that a Dutch soldier had been killed by Bosnian governmental troops as the UN-soldiers had attempted to retreat from their position.[72] This was epitomised by the over-simplified *BILD*-article which reported that "[...] a grenade exploded [and] a Dutch died."[73] None of these newspapers identified the soldier by name, nor did they mention him beyond these initial articles.

In contrast, *Welt* reported on this incident with much more interest and most frequently, namely three times during July 1995.[74] Helmut Hetzel, the author of two pieces, was *Welt's* foreign correspondent in The Hague, which might account for his heightened interest in the fate of the Dutch UN-soldiers. Significantly, Hetzel's articles identified the deceased soldier by name, demonstrating an immediacy no other publication introduced.[75] This proximity is further underlined by a picture of Rensen's coffin being carried to an airplane by his comrades.[76] The conservative daily was the only publication to publish an image of Rensen. Notably it was very small and could have easily been missed by a casual reader. Nonetheless it is significant that the coffin of a UN-soldier killed in combat was shown at all.

Surprisingly the press releases published by the UN-Security Council (UNSC) at the time did not mention Rensen's death or his name either. Indeed it was not until 21 July – at a time when no German publication, not even *Welt*, covered the incident anymore – that a UNSC-press release even alluded to

72 dpa/Reuter: Serbische Truppen überrennen Stellungen der UN-Soldaten in Bosnien. In: *FAZ*, 10.07.1995, p. 1; dpa/ap/rtr/sim: Serben dringen in UN-Schutzzone ein. In: *FR*, 10.07.1995, p. 1; Anonymous: Holländischer UN-Soldat tot. In: *BILD*, 10.07.1995, p. 2; Erich Rathfelder: Serben greifen UNO-Schutzzone Srebrenica an. In: *taz*, 10.07.1995, p. 2.

73 Anonymous: Holländischer UN-Soldat tot. In: *BILD*, 10.07.1995, p. 2.

74 WeNa: Serbische Panzer stehen kurz vor Srebrenica. In: *Welt*, 10.07.1995, p. 3; Helmut Hetzel: „Tapfere Männer". In: *Welt*, 13.07.1995, p. 4; Hetzel: Trauma-Teams stehen niederländischen Blauhelmen zur Seite. In: *Welt*, 18.07.1995, p. 8.

75 Helmut Hetzel: Tapfere Männer. In: *Welt*, 13.07.1995, p. 4.

76 Picture published in: *Welt*, 13.07.1995, p. 8.

the role of the soldiers. In this statement made by the UN Secretary-General Boutros Boutros-Ghali, 13 days after the fatality, he paid tribute "'[...] to the sacrifice of those United Nations personnel who [...had] given their lives to defend peace and human dignity.'"[77] The content of the press release was unquestionably about Bosnia and Srebrenica, but the vague statement neither mentioned Rensen by name, nor the circumstances which caused his death. Moreover, Boutros-Ghali did not give any indication of the number of UN-personnel who had lost their lives. The lack of official engagement with the UN-fatality reveals how sensitive the subject was. Arguably the publicised death of a UN-soldier in Bosnia would have weakened public support for the mission, which could explain the reserved statements. The vague and almost uncomfortable treatment of the UN-fatality in Srebrenica in the German daily press, but also in official UN-communiqués underlines the uncertainty of how to assess the situation. Mirroring the secondary literature about this incident, the German press coverage is marked by its lack of outrage about the UN's loss.

The Publications' Opinion

Amidst the day-to-day coverage that attempted to piece together the convoluted events in Srebrenica and reported on the UN's role in the enclave, most articles did not offer a clear opinion or judgement. While nuances in their interpretation and argumentation indicated what perspective an author agreed with most, these were rather subtle. Editorials, cartoons and in one case a *Feuilleton*-article were much more explicit in expressing their opinion and are therefore worth considering in more detail. Commencing with the latter, the *Feuilleton* is a particularly unique section of the daily German newspaper. The genre allows the author more journalistic freedom with regard to content and style. Thematically the section traditionally picks up on current issues, focusing primarily on social, cultural and ethics questions. It is of particular relevance in this chapter due to the inaccessibility of the enclave. With missing or unproven information omnipresent in the press' understanding of Srebrenica, the *Feuilleton* could have offered ample space for long exposés and discussions concerning the implications of Srebrenica on Germany, 'the West' in general and how this instance of extreme violence would affect German foreign policy in the region. However, only *FR* made use of its *Feuilleton* section, publishing a single, but very memorable article.

77 UNSC: At London Meeting, Secretary-General Stresses Need for UNPROFOR to Remain in Bosnia with Clearer Mandate. UNSC Press Release, SG/SM/5689, 21.07.1995, p. 1.

Authored by Nenad Popović, it was provocatively entitled 'Addio, Bosnia', which picked up on a headline of the Italian newspaper *La Repubblica* from 14 July, as the author explained. Indignant about the UN's inaction in Srebrenica, the piece's most poignant section was the bitter comment accusing no one in particular and yet everyone: "while we are enjoying the summer of 1995 (this July has been particularly hot, hasn't it?), the screams from the torture dungeons below us are getting quieter." The author continued that gradually the only noise that remained was a faint humming, just like the noise that came out of the "[…] shower rooms in concentration camps filled with humans and Cyclone B […]"[78] This article, striking for its direct reference to the Nazi gas chambers and concentration camps, confronted the reader with the moral outrage about Srebrenica which no other article either in *FR* or other German publications articulated. In this case the *Feuilleton*-section gave the author more opportunity to make emotive cross-references, as the guest author was not confined by journalistic etiquette.

Editorials and cartoons – both formats which equally allow more editorial freedom – were featured much more frequently. *JF* and *Konkret* did not utilise either to comment on Srebrenica and the weekly *Spiegel* featured only one cartoon and no editorials. However, all daily newspapers employed caricatures very frequently to voice their opinions. One theme found in the cartoons of all daily publications were scathing comments on the weakness of international organisations such as the UN and ICTY which were unable to stop Karadžić's and Mladić's siege of Srebrenica.

Figure 12: Walter Hanel; 'printed in *FAZ*, 28 July 1995, p. 3.

78 Nenad Popovic: Addio, Bosnia. In: *FR*, 28.07.1995, p. 7.

One *FAZ*-cartoon (figure 12) showed Karadžić and Mladić laughing impishly and viewing the ICTY, the UN and EU as mere scarecrows rather than real threats. Similarly, a cartoon printed in *taz* depicted Karadžić as a school-master and UN as a scrawny, helpless school boy who repeatedly wrote "I shall not disturb" on the blackboard.[79]

Figure 13: Felix Mussil; printed in *FR*, 18 July 1995, p. 1.

The above *FR*-cartoon (figure 13) showed Karadžić ablating the UN's Bosnia-presence one safe-zone at a time – starting in this case with Srebrenica and Žepa. The portrayal of the UN-soldier whose helmet is too big and has fallen into his face, but continues to hold his presence even though he is completely useless, strikes the viewer as pathetic. A *Welt* cartoon characterised Karadžić as a tank, shooting in the direction of Srebrenica. Three chicken wearing UN-helmets are depicted as hearing, seeing and saying nothing, again underlining their incompetence and indeed the UN's deplorable behaviour.[80]

These caricatures are very interesting, as they featured a level of indignation and judgement regarding the UN's role in Srebrenica, which was not present in the articles at the time. The stark contrast between the textual coverage, which generally reported that the UN had mishandled the situation,[81] and the

79 Cartoon published in: *taz*, 22 July 1995, p. 10.

80 Cartoon published in: *Welt*, 13.07.1995, p. 8.

81 See pp. 100–101.

accusatory caricatures is striking. This underlines the freedom of the latter. Two further cartoons found in *FAZ* and *Spiegel* must also be considered. Both conveyed the blanket-accusations of 'the Bosnian Serbs' or Serbia in opposition to the UN, already discussed in the previous chapter.

Figure 14: Walter Hanel; printed in *FAZ*, 17 July 1995, p. 3.

The *FAZ*-cartoon (figure 14) was published on 17 July, just as the atrocities of Srebrenica were becoming known to the world through the refugees arriving in Tuzla. Serbia was crudely portrayed as the omnipotent figure of death against whom the angel of peace is powerless. The miniscule figure representing the UN underlines the international community's complete insignificance as well as its difficult task to attain peace in the region. *Spiegel's* single caricature (figure 15) published in this period shows a menacing figure representing the 'Bosnian Serbs' on a pile of skulls with the UN's 'declaration of bankruptcy' framed on the wall behind him. Moreover, the words written at the bottom of the image, "Srebrenica, etc." implied that the fallen enclave is only one of many war-crimes the Bosnian Serbs were guilty of.

This placement of blame with Serbia was also mirrored in *FAZ's* editorials, which introduces the third format used to express opinions. These were frequently authored by one of its five editors and repeatedly focused on Serbia. For example, on 13 July, Dr. Günter Nonnenmacher wrote that the lesson learned from Srebrenica was that the UN would have to decide whether to

Figure 15: Horst Haitzinger, "Nicer Living" ("*Schöner Wohnen*"); printed in *Spiegel*, 24 July 1995, p. 115.

engage actively in the war and would thus become a "warring party", or pull out completely. Immediately the editorial stressed that UN-soldiers had been used as human shields.[82] This juxtaposition served as a reminder that they had been exposed to horrific experiences and a withdrawal could be justified. Reißmüller, another *FAZ*-editor, published an editorial explaining the fall of Srebrenica as the consequence of 'Greater Serbian' politics.[83] This is particularly significant when compared to a 'normal' *FAZ*-article published the same day. In it, Matthias Rüb stated that the causes for the fall of the enclave were difficult to explain and that it was not clear what the Bosnian Serbs had gained from capturing the small enclave.[84] This cautious coverage was not at all congruent with the definitive explanations and accusations expressed in Reißmüller's editorial just a few pages later, emphasising the extent of freedom to publish the author's personal opinion in editorials. Moreover Reißmüller's opinion piece underlines the broadsheet's continuing anti-Serbian stance, which had already been established in the newspaper's coverage in the early 1990s.

82 Nm: Im Sumpf. In: *FAZ*, 13.07.1995, p. 2.

83 Rm: Um Srebrenica. In: *FAZ*, 12.07.1995, p. 12.

84 Matthias Rüb: Sieg über Srebrenica, die Nato und Vereinten Nationen. In: *FAZ*, 12.07.1995, p. 2.

FR's Roman Ares warned that if the West did nothing, "[...] genocide [...would] lose its reprehensibility."[85] The concerted use of the term 'genocide' in conjunction with the editorial's publication date – 10 July – is striking. Mere days after the siege of Srebrenica, the fate of the thousands of missing men was not yet determined. While the mass displacement of thousands of women and children arriving in Tuzla was self-evident, the extermination of Srebrenica's male population was merely speculative at this point. These subtle distinctions of language will be explored with more detail later in this chapter. However, for now it is worth noting that the format of an editorial was used in *FR* to introduce this loaded term.

Editorials in *BILD* and *Welt* used their platform to launch appeals for a more active intervention from the West.[86] Emphasising the aspect of human suffering, *BILD's* editorial by Dana Horakova is particularly interesting. The German-Czech journalist and politician articulated disgust and contempt, stating that she could no longer stand the misery in Srebrenica, "because I cannot nor want to believe that this war cannot be ended." Explaining her outrage, Horkova described scenes from Srebrenica: "Children, who [...hung] on their mothers' hands, and they march[ed] and march[ed]. [...] Stony roads. Death. It is so horrible."[87] It remains unclear whether the author had been to Tuzla or Bosnia, but this was not crucial at this point. The vivid image of the human suffering in Srebrenica presented was the main message the author wanted her readers to comprehend.

Ströhm's *Welt*-editorial is particularly striking, in which he asserted that certain "[...] voices [...were] becoming more audible which suppose[d] that the UN and the major powers had consciously played Srebrenica into the Serbians' hands."[88] This drastic accusation that the UN had purposefully allowed the enclave to be taken over, implying back-door deals, is singular in the conservative broadsheet and reminiscent of *Konkret's* articles proposing conspiracy theories of imperialist schemings. Ströhm's editorial continued that it was increasingly disappointing that the Croatian and Muslim actions were reprimanded so severely by the international community, while Serbian atrocities were largely overlooked. Significantly the author did not specify who

85 Roman Arens: Serbisches Hintertor. In: *FR*, 10.07.1995, p. 3.

86 Dana Horakova: Bosnien: Zorn und Ohnmacht. In: *BILD*, 15.07.1995, p. 2; Ralf Georg Reuth: Bosnien – Was will Moskau. In: *BILD*, 25.07.1995, p. 2; Hans-J. Schmahl: Die UNO am Scheideweg. In: *Welt*, 12.07.1995, p. 1; Carl Gustaf Ströhm: Für den Fall von Gorazde. In: *Welt*, 18.07.1995, p. 1.

87 Dana Horakova: Bosnien: Zorn und Ohnmacht. In: *BILD*, 15.07.1995, p. 2.

88 Carl Gustaf Ströhm: Für den Fall von Gorazde. In: *Welt*, 18.07.1995, p. 1.

exactly he was accusing. With this vague yet severe argument, Ströhm's editorial counters his paper's previously empathetic treatment of the UN-soldier's death in early July, which had specifically accused the Bosnian Muslim army for causing the soldier's death.

The message conveyed in the cartoons, editorials and *Feuilleton*-article is marked by its focus on the UN's failure and subsequent moral outrage about Srebrenica. Both elements had been missing in the day-to-day coverage, which was dedicated to piecing together the events surrounding the fallen enclave. Perhaps this stemmed from the remaining ambiguity regarding Srebrenica and the inability to cross-check much of the information. It is commendable that emotional debates did not impact the press' everyday reporting and that any expression of opinion was limited to artistic formats (cartoons) or ones allowing more editorial freedom (*Feuilleton*-article and editorials). This is particularly noteworthy when considering how emotionally and morally charged the Srebrenica Massacre and the UN's failure to protect its civilian population is today, both in the public conscience and in much of the secondary literature, which professes assessments such as "[...that] Srebrenica will forever be associated with the triumph of evil."[89]

Srebrenica and Germany: The Weight of History

With the increasingly prevalent understanding that the UN had failed to protect the civilian population of Srebrenica, the international community debated whether NATO should launch a military intervention in Bosnia with the primary goal of instating a no-fly-zone over the country and thus disabling the Bosnian-Serb forces.[90] As the German press reported, plans were made for a 'Rapid Reaction Force' to be deployed to Bosnia, consisting of British and French troops, as well as German Tornado air-crafts. In addition, *Bundeswehr*-medics would support the mission with a military hospital in Split, Croatia.[91] This military contribution to a NATO-intervention would have

89 DiCaprio: The Betrayal of Srebrenica, p. 74.

90 As reported for example in Rmc: Deutsche Tornados auf dem Sprung zum Balkan-Einsatz. In: *Welt*, 18.07.1995, p. 8.

91 For example: Anonymous: Beim ersten Schnee. In: *Spiegel*, 17.07.1995, p. 114; Anonymous: Komplizen der Barberei. In: *Spiegel*, 24.07.1995, p. 111; Marc Weller: In Bosnien ein diffuser Auftrag für Blauhelme und Nato. In: *FAZ*, 12.07.1995, p. 11; Sto.: Fischer sieht Übereinstimmung. In: *FAZ*, 13.07.1995, p. 2; Martin S. Lambeck: Der Westen streitet über Bosnien-Einsatz. In: *Welt*, 15./16.07.1995, p. 1; Rüdiger Moniac: Bundeswehr startet Bosnieneinsatz. In: *Welt*, 18.07.1995, p. 1; Franz Uhle-Wettler: Bundestag beschließt Kampfeinsatz der Bundeswehr: Einsatz im Ungewissen. In: *JF*, 07.07.1995, p. 1; Anonymous: Deutsche Piloten fliegen über Bosnien. In: *BILD*, 10.08.1995, p. 1.

been a significant departure from German foreign policy since the Second World War, which had been marked by non-intervention and an emphasis on diplomacy. Unsurprisingly, this controversial departure from German foreign policy marked by non-intervention and indeed justifying this shift with the country's National-Socialist past was picked up by the German print media.

Before analysing the discussion it provoked at the time, special attention must be drawn to a prominent politician from the pacifist Green Party, Joschka Fischer. As the Co-Chairman of his party in the *Bundestag*, he was a strong proponent of an international intervention following Srebrenica, in spite of his party's pacifist roots.[92] Moreover, as discussed in the introduction, the 1968-generation, to which Fischer belonged, had been instrumental in propelling the collective memory of post-war Germany into the direction of assuming responsibility for its National-Socialist past. As Hans Kundnani has elaborated in his monograph, the Green Party and indeed Fischer as an individual had identified their political *raison d'être* through the paradigm 'never again war.' However, as Fischer revealed in an interview with Kundnani, after he had heard the news about Srebrenica,

> […] he had difficulties looking at himself in the mirror. [He asked himself:…] 'How could it happen? What have you done?' […] 'I was asking myself the same question that I had once asked my parents.'[93]

This ominous statement was a direct reference to the shift of collective memory effected by the 1968-generation, Fischer's first political home, whose followers had frequently accused their parent-generation of having allowed the Nazi-genocide to unfold and having 'looked the other way.'

Following the catalytic wake-up-call, as Fischer viewed the Srebrenica Massacre, he wrote an open letter, which was widley reported on and cited by various newspapers, in which he supported a German military contribution.[94] The controversial and indeed radical political shift cannot be over-stated. First, Fischer outlined the previous diplomatic endeavours which had attempted to find a peaceful solution in Bosnia without using military force. By the end of the first page, Fischer concluded that these peaceful undertakings had failed,

92 Schwab-Trapp: *Kriegsdiskurse*, p. 151.

93 Kundnani: *Auschwitz or Utopia*, p. 241.

94 Joschka Fischer: Die Katastrophe in Bosnien und die Konsequenzen für unsere Partei Bündnis 90/Die Grünen, 30.07.1995. http://www.gruene.de/fileadmin/user_upload/Dokumente/Gr%C3%BCne_Geschichte/JoschkaFischer_Die_Katastrophe_in_Bosnien_und_die_Konsequenzen_fuer_unsere_Partei_1995.pdf (accessed 30.08.2014).

which was epitomised in the Bosnian-Serb siege of Srebrenica.[95] Repeatedly referring to 'ethnic cleansing' and 'ethnic war', it is remarkable that Fischer distanced his assertions from the term 'genocide'. In the first instance this seems to deliberately disassociate the events in Bosnia from those perpetrated by Nazi-Germany. However, he quietly introduced a linkage to this historical era by stating that 50 years after the end of the Second World War, "war has returned [to Europe] with all its gruesomeness and barbarity […]"[96]

All publications aside from *BILD* reported on the controversial letter.[97] However, only *FAZ* supported Fischer's moral interpretation of the Germany past. In an article written by Freimut Duve, a Social Democratic (SPD) member of the German *Bundestag*, the author lamented that after the Second World War, Germany had vowed 'never again Auschwitz', but was now watching the 'genocide' in Bosnia without intervening.[98] Duve continued with a plea that while Germany would need to be apprehensive about intervening in the Balkans due to its past, equally the country's past must not be used as an excuse to accept further atrocities.[99] This linkage was unique amongst the German print media. Interestingly Duve's father, Bruno Herzl – great-nephew of the father of Zionism Theodor Herzl – came from a Jewish family in Osijek, Croatia. Duve's father had been killed by the Croatian *Ustashe* during the Second World War. Perhaps this family background inclined him to link Germany's past to Srebrenica when other authors did not.

Duve's personal interest is further underlined with a second article he wrote for *taz*, a few weeks earlier, which echoed Fischer's moral arguments based on Germany's history. On 15 July already, Duve and three colleagues from the *Bundestag*, Christian Schwarz-Schilling (CDU), Marieluise Beck (Green Party) and Hildebrecht Braun (FDP), had launched a public cross-party appeal in

95 Ibid., p. 1.

96 Ibid., p. 7; also discussed in Schwab-Trapp: *Kriegsdiskurse*, pp. 154–158.

97 Articles on this matter include Karl-Ludwig Günsche: Grüne Gewalt. In: *Welt*, 02.08.1995, p. 1; oe: „Wir müssen für den Schutz der UN-Schutzzonen sein". In: *Welt*, 03.08.1995, p. 7; Sto.: Fischer für militärische Sicherung der bosnischen Schutzzonen. In: *FAZ*, 02.08.1995, p. 2; Olaf Ihlau / Paul Lersch: Das wäre blutiger Zynismus. In: *Spiegel*, 21.08.1995, pp. 27–29; Thomas Schmid: Pflöcke eingeschlagen: Joschka Fischer analysiert den Krieg in Bosnien. In: *taz*, 02.08.1995, p. 10; Christian Rath: Moralisches Punktesammeln: Joschka Fischer bringt die Debatte der Grünen nicht weiter. In: *taz*, 02.08.1995, p. 10; Joschka Fischer: Bosnische Konsequenz: Auszüge des Briefes, den Joschka Fischer gestern an die Bundestagsfraktion schickte. In: *taz*, 02.08.1995, p. 11; Klaus Bittermann: Augen zu und durch! „Reife Leistung". In: *Konkret*, September 1995, p. 14.

98 Freimut Duve: Ohne Konzept gegen Völkermord. In: *FAZ*, 04.08.1995, p. 10.

99 Ibid., p. 10.

taz, articulating the same arguments Fischer expressed in letter-form several weeks later. In the *taz*-piece the three authors stated that "we grew up in a country, which has aggregated endless guilt. Many of us only realised upon growing up that Germany is responsible for the most inhumane genocide in history." The appeal continues that 50 years after the victory over fascism, 'genocide' was unfolding again in Europe and "Europe can no longer claim to have learned from its history."[100] Importantly, this letter did not spark any reaction in other publications; this only occurred when Fischer put forward the same arguments. In both articles, Duve referred to 'genocide' unfolding. He never specified whether this was in reference to Srebrenica specifically or to the Bosnian War in general. Regardless, the author seemingly employed the term to shock the reader and increase the sense of urgency to intervene.

Aside from Duve's article, which is noteworthy due to its timing, *taz* did not engage further with the debate and indeed did not pick up on it again when Fischer published his letter. Other than vague comments such as that Fischer had initiated a debate that was vital for his party and for Germany as a whole,[101] the paper completely distanced itself from the topic. This retraction from the debate is striking, especially since *taz* had previously represented the interpretation that Germany's history created a moral obligation to intervene. Perhaps now that this issue had touched the very core of the Green Party's philosophy and had split its members into opposing factions, the newspaper was unsure which side to take, especially in light of the fragmentary information available about Srebrenica. Nonetheless, the complete omission of the debate seems incomprehensible and even unprofessional for a daily newspaper.

Duve's echo of Fischer's claims from August 1995 in his *FAZ*-article sparked strong disagreement in *Konkret's* September issue, which referenced them in two of the three articles on Srebrenica.[102] Klaus Bittermann's piece explicitly criticised Duve, stating that "anyone who has the faintest idea about this conflict knows that this is a conventional war for territory [...]", not 'genocide.'

100 Freimut Duve / Christian Schwarz-Schilling / Marieluise Beck / Hildebrecht Braun: Europa hat nichts gelernt. In: *taz*, 15./16.07.1995, p. 10.

101 Thomas Schmid: Pflöcke eingeschlagen: Joschka Fischer analysiert den Krieg in Bosnien. In: *taz*, 02.08.1995, p. 10; also in Christian Rath: Moralisches Punktesammeln: Joschka Fischer bringt die Debatte der Grünen nicht weiter. In: *taz*, 02.08.1995, p. 10.

102 Jürgen Elsässer: Augen zu und durch! Der Antifaschismus des dummen Kerls. In: *Konkret*, September 1995, p. 12; Klaus Bittermann: Augen zu und durch! „Reife Leistung". In: *Konkret*, September 1995, p. 14; Gerhard Stuby: Augen zu und durch! Wenigstens Gerechtigkeit? In: *Konkret*, September 1995, p. 16.

The author went on to say that rape and displacement were inevitable side-effects of war and thus the Bosnian War must not be compared to the Nazis' crimes, which had left the world in ruins. Bittermann then launched into a number of conspiracy theories allegedly perpetuated by the 'bourgeois press' regarding the extent of the atrocities in Srebrenica, which was being (mis) used to justify a military intervention.[103] Moreover he made the sweeping declaration that "their engagement in the Balkans has made the Germans a people in war fever."[104]

The magazine's September-issue underlined Germany's alleged enthusiasm for war with its front cover image, which featured Joschka Fischer in military uniform. The satirical portrayal of the pacifist politician in a military uniform and a comical facial expression becomes even snider with the realisation that the uniform belonged to the Croatian President Tudjman, who had frequently been associated with the fascist Ustasha.[105] Perhaps an average reader would not have immediately comprehended that the uniform was Tudjman's. However, with this photo-alteration, *Konkret's* editorial staff clearly intended to associate any military endeavour in Bosnia with fascism. Moreover, the poor quality of the photo-montage with which Fischer's head is placed on Tudjman's uniform – underlined by the tilted hat – may have encouraged any reader to wonder to whom the uniform belonged.

JF's single article also criticised any interpretation of a potential German involvement based on moral arguments. The paper featured an interview with Kurt Waldheim, former UN-Secretary General (1971–1981), who had been stationed in the Balkans as a *Wehrmacht*-officer in 1942–1944. In light of the recent events in Srebrenica, Waldheim concluded that "[…] the German policy until now […had] been right: not to engage militarily, and only give humanitarian support […]"[106] While this conclusion was not very controversial, *JF's* choice of interviewee is striking. In 1986 it was disclosed that the Austrian diplomat Waldheim had concealed "[…] the fact that for three years he had served as a Nazi officer in combat zones and places of atrocities

103 Klaus Bittermann: Augen zu und durch! „Reife Leistung". In: *Konkret* , September 1995, p. 14; also discussed in Jürgen Elsässer: Augen zu und durch! Der Antifaschismus des dummen Kerls. In: *Konkret*, September 1995, p. 12.

104 Klaus Bittermann: Augen zu und durch! „Reife Leistung". In: *Konkret* , September 1995, p. 14.

105 This picture is to be compared with a portrait of Tudjman published in *Spiegel* on 07.08.1995, p. 112 .

106 Andreas Mölzer: „Nation ist stärker als Klasse". In: *JF*, 04.08.2995, p. 3.

against Jews, Serbs, Italians and others."[107] Waldheim, who was soon associated with anti-Semitic remarks, was put on the 'Watch List' of the United States in 1987, barring him from entering the country.[108] The article readily drew on Walheim as a source to comment on the prospect of German military participation in the Balkans without mentioning any of these details surrounding his person, though presumably the readers at the time would have been aware of them. Moreover, considering that Waldheim was Austrian and arguably did not have a note-worthy insider's perspective on Germany's foreign policy, *JF's* choice could be seen as an attempt to reinstate Waldheim as a respected commentator on foreign policy.

While most publications concentrated on evaluating whether Fischer's argument of linking Germany's past to the need for an intervention in Bosnia was valuable or faulty, *Spiegel* was the only example in the main-stream press which was overtly critical of Fischer's proposition. In an interview with the Green politician – importantly the only one published in this period – Fischer asserted that 'Never again War' and 'Never again Auschwitz' were two important pillars of his political ideology and while these paradigms stood in diametrical opposition to waging war, at this point military interaction was necessary in Bosnia. Notably, the two *Spiegel*-correspondents who led the interview inquired whether this change in policy was a symptom of Fischer aiming to become a more viable and 'electable' candidate for a coalition-party in the 1998 elections.[109] Though Fischer quickly denied this motivation, the news-magazine's confrontational approach was unique. Though this was never fully articulated, *Spiegel's* interview insinuated that perhaps Srebrenica was being (mis)used by Fischer to shift his party's foreign policy stance to a position more suitable for governing, implying that the calls for an intervention due to 'genocide' could be inflated and serving a political agenda. As much of this appears to be conjecture, these implications were left unsaid. However, the leading questions in this interview suggested this interpretation to the reader.

This interview was not the only instance in which the news-magazine expressed its opposition to Fischer's policy proposal. In mid-July *Spiegel* published an article guest-authored by Gerd Schmückle, who had been NATO's deputy commander-in-chief for Europe until 1980. Surprisingly this former

107 Avi Beker: Building up a Memory: Austria, Switzerland, and Europe Face the Holocaust. In: Eric Langenbacher / Yossi Shain (eds): *Power and the Past: Collective Memory and International Relations*. Washington, D.C.: Georgetown University Press 2010, pp. 97–120, here p. 102.

108 Ibid., p. 105.

109 Olaf Ihlau / Paul Lersch: „Das wäre blutiger Zynismus". In: *Spiegel*, 21.08.1995, pp. 28–29.

high-ranking NATO-official voiced his scepticism towards Germany's departure from its post-war foreign policy coined by diplomacy and non-intervention. Primarily the author criticised that German politicians presented the military engagement as a 'moral responsibility', basing their arguments on Germany's obligation stemming from the past as well as of being part of an alliance like NATO. Furthermore he criticised that the hypothesis was gaining prominence that "for 50 years the others protected us, now we also need to protect them".[110]

Welt and *FR* were also sceptical of Fischer's reinterpretation of Germany's foreign policy, though they did not criticise him directly. Rather, they stubbornly placed any German contribution into the wider context of alliance politics. For example, *Welt's* Rüdiger Moniac detailed that the task of the German air force would be to help the UN-ground troops 'earn respect at the front'.[111] This was underlined again in another article, which stated that the German military would naturally be a part of an overall UN-strategy and would not be acting independently.[112]

Along with the national press, the German politicians' treatment of Srebrenica must be considered. It is worth noting that only one parliamentary session took place in the timeframe considered in this chapter, presumably due to the summer recess that followed. Consequently, there was little opportunity for a profound political debate. This single session took place on 13 July 1995; mere days after the siege of Srebrenica had begun. Dr. Rita Süssmuth (CDU), President of the *Bundestag*, opened the session with remarks on events unfolding in the enclave. Condemning the Bosnian-Serb attacks, Süssmuth stated that "this week's Serbian attacks show[ed] that the Bosnian Serbs [...were] planning nothing less than displacement, annihilation of the Bosnian-Muslim culture in the Balkans and concerted genocide."[113] This use of 'genocide' is surprising considering how little information was officially available at the time of the debate. Apart from Süssmuth's opening remarks, there was no mention of Srebrenica in this session.

110 Gerd Schmückle: Beistand ohne Verstand. In: *Spiegel*, 17.07.1995, p. 116; also discussed in Anonymous: Beim ersten Schnee. In: *Spiegel*, 17.07.1995, pp. 114–115.

111 Rüdiger Moniac: Bundeswehr startet Bosnieneinsatz. In: *Welt*, 18.07.1995, p. 1; Moniac: Luftbrücken nach Piacenza. In: *Welt*, 18.07.1995, p. 8.

112 Rmc: Deutsche Tornados auf dem Sprung zum Balkan-Einsatz. In: *FAZ*, 18.07.1995, p. 8.

113 *Deutscher Bundestag*, Plenarprotokoll 13/49, Stenographischer Bericht, 49. Sitzung, 13.07.1995, p. 4045.

The interpretation of Germany's foreign policy and whether this should be considered in combination with the country's past can be embedded in the larger context of Holocaust memory. As discussed in the previous chapter, much of the literature argues that by the 1990s, the shame through the *Betroffenheitsdiskurs* had abated to a more general, 'meta-physical guilt', which could be traced in the German coverage of 1991/92 already. However, the genocide in Srebrenica seemed to reinvigorate the sense that Germany's past shaped its foreign policy. Significantly, this revitalised discourse predominantly occurred in the political sphere rather than in the print media. It was Joschka Fischer as well as Freimut Duve and his colleagues who interpreted German foreign policy through the lens of the Second World War, not journalists or editors. This presents an interesting disjoint between the German print media and simultaneous political discourse, emphasising how independently the press operated from the political sphere.

The Language of the Media

We turn to the last section of this chapter, namely the use of specific terms throughout the print media's coverage. As considered in the previous chapter, language constitutes an important and subtle dimension to the writing. Firstly it must be noted that *Welt* and *FAZ* used 'Bosnian Serbs' and 'Serbs' interchangeably. *Spiegel's* reports predominantly referred to 'Serbs', even calling Mladić and Karadžić '*Serben-Chefs*' meaning 'Serb-bosses.'[114] This erroneous generalisation emphasises the superficial categorisations the press employed which implied an anti-Serbian tendency. *FR* and *taz* did so less frequently, indeed some of *taz's* articles referred to 'Karadžić-Serbs' to make this distinction.[115]

The term '*Völkermord*', or 'genocide' was used immediately in most publications except in *BILD*, *Spiegel* and *Konkret*, and it appeared primarily in the context of information regarding the missing men presumed to have been killed.[116] While the Srebrenica Massacre has officially been termed 'genocide',

114 Anonymous: Komplizen der Barberei. In: *Spiegel*, 24.07.1995, p. 114.

115 Erich Rathfelder: Verraten und verkauft. In: *taz*, 11.07.1995, p. 10; Andreas Zumach: Das Doppelspiel von Paris und London. In: *taz*, 13.07.1995, p. 3; Zumach: Uno entmachtet Yasushi Akashi. In: *taz*, 14.07.1995, p. 8.

116 For example: Helmut Hetzel: Lob für Mladic, der sie demütigte. In: *Welt*, 25.07.1995, p. 1; Reuter: Niederländer bezeugen neun Erschießungen. In: *FAZ*, 24.07.1995, p. 2; Freimut Duve / Christian Schwarz-Schilling / Marieluise Beck / Hildebrecht Braun: Europa hat nichts gelernt. In: *taz*, 15./16.07.1995, p. 10; Tomislav Sunic: Srebrenica und die bosnischen Lektionen: Der Krieg hat erst begonnen. In: *JF*, 28.07.1995, p. 6; Roman Arens: Srebrenica – Ende der Lüge. In: *FR*, 13.07.1995, p. 3.

for example in the ICTY's indictment of Karadžić and Mladić,[117] this could only be asserted with certainty once it was proven that the 8,000 missing men from Srebrenica had been massacred. This was not the case in mid-July, mere days after the siege, and shows that in this instance many publications hastily jumped to conclusions.

Consequently, when placed within the context of the limited information available at the time, the immediate utilisation of the word could be termed a hyperbole. Moreover, little reflection occurred regarding the legal implications of its usage. As noted earlier, applying the term 'genocide' creates the legal obligation arising from the 1948 Genocide Convention to terminate it.[118] This link, while implied by Fischer, was never made in the German press coverage, which indicates a certain lack of profound engagement with the subject matter by those publications reporting on it. In contrast, the displacement of thousands of civilians from Srebrenica was evident by the waves of refugees arriving in Tuzla. The German press frequently used the term 'ethnic cleansing' to describe their fate.[119] This semantic differentiation indicates that in some instances, the publications analysed here deliberated very carefully what to report and what terminology to employ.

During the coverage of the Srebrenica Massacre, Cold War analogies found in the early phase of the war were no longer utilised. Rather, links to the Second World War were constructed frequently.[120] For example, *FAZ* and *FR* reported on protests at the memorial site of the Buchenwald concentration camp.[121] As *FR's* article stated, the protestors carried a banner that read: "Europe has learned nothing from the Holocaust – Bosnia is a posthumous victory for Hitler."[122] The use of Buchenwald as a setting to perpetuate political causes could have caused indignation. However, neither *FAZ* nor *FR*

117 See chapter 4, fn. 1.

118 See pp. 25–28.

119 For example: Joschka Fischer: Bosnische Konsequenz: Auszüge des Briefes, den Joschka Fischer gestern an die Bundestagsfraktion schickte. In: *taz*, 02.08.1995, p. 11; Reuter/dpa: Die Serben vertreiben Tausende aus Srebrenica. In: *FAZ*, 14.07.1995, p. 1; Wgl.: Doch schon wieder. In: *FAZ*, 18.07.1995, p. 1; Anonymous: Serben-General: Wohin bringt er die 30 000 Frauen und Kinder? In: *BILD*, 13.07.1995, p. 1; rtr/dpa: Kinkel unterstützt Hilfe für Bosnien. In: *FR*, 17.07.1995, p. 2; Carl Gustaf Ströhm: Bosnische Kroaten werfen Paris „perfides Spiel" vor. In: *Welt*, 21.07.1995, p. 3.

120 Bernt Conrad: Von Wahrheit und „Schande im Balkan-Krieg". In: *Welt*, 16.08.1905, p. 6; Sto.: Kopelew ruft zum Einmischen auf. In: *FAZ*, 21.07.1995, p. 2; Anonymous: Komplizen der Barberei. In: *Spiegel*, 24.07.1995, p. 110.

121 dpa: Bosnier besetzen Buchenwald. In: *FAZ*, 28.07.1995, p. 2; dpa: Bosnier demonstrieren in Gedenkstätte Buchenwald. In: *FR*, 28.07.1995, p. 5.

122 dpa: Bosnier demonstrieren in Gedenkstätte Buchenwald. In: *FR*, 28.07.1995, p. 5.

commented on these crude associations or how they interpreted this linkage between Bosnia and the Holocaust, although the sensationalist setting was presumably the primary reason for the coverage of this relatively small protest of 30 Bosnian activists, as *FAZ* reported.[123] This demonstrates how effective such cross-references were in terms of publicity.

Welt and *FAZ* utilised analogies to the Holocaust in the bluntest manner, both in their articles and in their selection of official statements to quote from.[124] The UNHCR-spokesperson, Ron Redmond, and *Welt's* correspondent Ströhm both compared Srebrenica's inhabitants to inmates in a concentration camp.[125] After Redmond made this comparison in Geneva on 12 July, presumably during a press conference, Ströhm utilised the exact analogy a day later when he wrote on 13 July that the inhabitants of the enclave were in reality "[…] a kind of concentration camp prisoner […]"[126] Similarly a brief *BILD*-piece published on 24 July used the word 'concentration camp' to describe Mladić's tactics in Srebrenica while a *FAZ*-editorial on 15 July compared the separation of males and females in Srebrenica to the methods used in a concentration camp.[127] None of the articles explained their comparisons further, nor did they contextualise them. Undeniably, they sought to elucidate a sense of commiseration and shock amongst their readership.

These comparisons and analogies to the Second World War and the Holocaust irrefutably coloured the content. However, considering the high number of articles published in July and August 1995, these modest examples must be considered in this quantitative context, especially as the majority of these examples stemmed from two papers, namely *Welt* and *FAZ*. Nonetheless it is safe to assume that the presence of these analogies and comparisons were examples of a prevailing discourse which continually influenced German

123 dpa: Bosnier besetzen Buchenwald. In: *FAZ*, 28.07.1995, p. 2.

124 Walter H. Rüb: „Nur politischer Druck kann die Barbarei beenden". In: *Welt*, 10.07.1995, p. 7; Carl Gustaf Ströhm: Die Hölle von Srebrenica. In: *Welt*, 12.07.1995, p. 3; Ströhm: Der serbische Sieg. In: *Welt*, 13.07.1995, p. 8; Ströhm: Bosnische Kroaten werfen Paris „perfides Spiel" vor. In: *Welt*, 21.07.1995, p. 3; WeNa: Marschbefehl für Eingreiftruppe. In: *Welt*, 24.07.1995, p. 1; Sto.: Fischer sieht Übereinstimmng. In: *FAZ*, 13.07.1995, p. 2; Sto.: Bundestag: gezielter Völkermord. In: *FAZ*, 14.07.1995, p. 2; wgl.: Aus Rumelien. In: *FAZ*, 17.07.1995, p. 8; E. L.: Minister durchbricht das Schweigegebot über Greueltaten. In: *FAZ*, 20.07.1995, p. 2; Sto.: Kopelew ruft zum Einmischen auf. In: *FAZ*, 21.07.1995, p. 2; Freimut Duve: Ohne Konzept gegen Völkermord. In: *FAZ*, 04.08.1995, p. 10.

125 Carl Gustaf Ströhm: Die Hölle von Srebrenica. In: *Welt*, 12.07.1995, p. 3.

126 Carl Gustaf Ströhm: Der serbische Sieg. In: *Welt*, 13.07.1995, p. 8.

127 S. von Bassewitz and M. Soyka: Serben-General Mladić: Er hat sogar seine Tochter auf dem Gewissen. In: *BILD*, 24.07.1995, p. 2; Nm: Die Ehre verteidigen. In: *FAZ*, 15.07.1995, p. 10.

perception. There was not, however, a particular intensification of this discourse as the German print media reported on Srebrenica.

As this chapter has demonstrated, the events in Srebrenica were cloaked in ambiguity as they were occurring, which impacted the German press' and thus the public's understanding of the event. Nonetheless, Srebrenica's role as a turning point in the war was not questioned or underestimated. To the present day, the Srebrenica Massacre remains central and indeed shapes the media's discourse and commentary on foreign policy. This was particularly evident in the debate about a potential NATO-intervention in Libya during the 2011 Arab Spring and arose again in 2012, in connection with Syria. For example an opinion piece authored by Brendan Simms for the British newspaper *The Independent* in May 2011 was entitled "Road to Libya runs through Srebrenica."[128] Similarly, the German weekly newspaper *Die Zeit* published an article about Syria in March 2012 poignantly entitled "Srebrenica-Moment."[129] Another featured the sub-title "Back then Srebrenica, today Homs."[130] The continued relevance of the Srebrenica Massacre until the present day emphasises how shocking the extent of the war crimes were and that Srebrenica will forever be associated with debates about international interventions.

128 Brendan Simms: Road to Libya Runs through Srebrenica. In: *The Independent*, 29.05.2011. http://www.independent.co.uk/opinion/commentators/brendan-simms-road-to-libya-runs-through-srebrenica-2290326.html (accessed 30.08.2014).

129 Andrea Böhm: Srebrenica-Moment. In: *Die Zeit*, 26.03.2012. http://www.zeit.de/2012/13/Eliasson (accessed 30.08.2014).

130 Emir Suljagic / Reuf Bajrovic: Keine Schutzzone ohne Schutz. In: *Die Zeit*, 02.03.2012. http://www.zeit.de/2012/10/P-oped-Suljagic (accessed 30.08.2014).

Chapter 5
November–December 1995: Peace in Bosnia – The Dayton Agreement

Following the Srebrenica Massacre in July 1995, the international community and specifically the United States were increasingly determined to end the war in Bosnia. Exerting diplomatic pressure, combined with three weeks of NATO-air strikes ('Operation Deliberate Force'), the international community intensified the urgency of ending the Bosnian War. In November 1995, the Balkan Contact Group (consisting of the United States of America, the United Kingdom, France, Germany and Russia) convened in Dayton, Ohio with Milošević, Izetbegović and Tudjman to find a peaceful solution after nearly four years of war. The agreement, which was drawn up at Dayton, was much more than a mere peace treaty. It was a plan to rebuild political structures "on the basis of little more than the ruins and rivalries of a bitter war," making it "[…] the most ambitious document of its kind in modern history […]" as Carl Bildt, Co-Chairman of the Dayton Peace Conference summarised.[1]

On 1 November 1995, the Presidents of Bosnia, Croatia and what was left of Yugoslavia – Izetbegović, Tudjman and Milošević – commenced peace negotiations in Dayton. Milošević represented the Bosnian Serbs because Karadžić and Mladić had been banned due to their instrumental role in the Srebrenica Massacre, for which they had been indicted by the ICTY. Furthermore, this was part of an American strategy to hold Milošević accountable for the Bosnian Serbs' actions and ensure their cooperation.[2] The talks were

1 Carl Bildt: *Peace Journey: The Struggle for Peace in Bosnia.* London: Orion 1998, p. 392.

2 Richard Holbrooke: *To End a War.* New York: Modern Library 1998, p. 98.

steered by representatives of the international community, most prominently by the American diplomat Richard Holbrooke. However, all five countries of the Balkan Contact Group sent a delegation to Dayton. The German committee was led by Wolfgang Ischinger, at the time Political Director of the Federal Foreign Office.

In Dayton, the Serbian, Croatian and Bosnian representatives were confined to a military air base, which was secluded from the outside world and the international media. The negotiations were intended to last 8–10 days, but took three weeks. During this time there were various moments at which the talks seemed to have reached an irreversible dead end.[3] Particularly crucial and discordant topics included whether Sarajevo would be divided amongst the three entities, the right of return for refugees, and most importantly the territorial partition of Bosnia in general. The avoidance of pivotal themes such as officially determining the fate of the indicted war criminals Mladić and Karadžić indicates a certain hesitance to further complicate the negotiations. Similarly, the exclusion of Kosovo's status in the talks, which some diplomats viewed as the next imminent crisis in the Balkans, suggests an urge to avoid too many contentious topics, which could prevent a peace treaty for Croatia and Bosnia.[4] The negotiations were concluded with the initialling of the agreement on 21 November 1995; the official signing ceremony took place on 15 December in Paris.

Weeks of discussions concluded that Bosnia would not be divided into separate states with Bosniak, Serbian and Croatian populations, but would rather consist of a Bosnian-Croatian Federation, which was forged in Dayton and a Serbian sub-entity, the Republika Srpska (RS). The RS – similar to the political status of a Swiss canton – was a legal entity within the federal structure of Bosnia and was allocated the right, for example to create an independent police force and school system, while remaining part of Bosnia. The 'inter-entity boundary line' allotted 49% of the territory to the Bosnian Serbs and 51% to the Bosnian-Croat Federation.[5] Moreover the treaty established "[…] a central three-man [rotating] presidency with representatives from each of

3 Auswärtiges Amt (ed.): *Deutsche Außenpolitik 1995: Auf dem Weg zu einer Friedensregelung für Bosnien und Herzegowina: 53 Telegramme aus Dayton.* Bonn: Auswärtiges Amt, Referat Öffentlichkeitsarbeit 1998, p. 30; Petritsch / Pichler: *Kosovo-Kosova*, p. 94.

4 Telegram Nr. 8, 04.11.1995, 1649 local time. In: Auswärtiges Amt (ed.): *Deutsche Außenpolitik 1995*, p. 67.

5 Elizabeth Cousens / Charles Cater: *Toward Peace in Bosnia: Implementing the Dayton Accords.* Boulder: Lynne Rienner 2001, p. 34; Patrice McMahon / Jon Western: The Death of Dayton. In: *Foreign Affairs* 88,5 (2009), pp. 69–83.

the three ethnic groups, a Council of Ministers and a central Parliament."[6] A further stipulation was the deployment of an international Implementation Force (IFOR) formed by NATO, which would ensure that the cease-fire was adhered to and that the peace agreement was fully implemented.[7]

The content of the Dayton Accords has been analysed widely in a plethora of secondary literature, most of which was published several years after the negotiations. All concentrate on the political stipulations laid out in the agreement, their implementation, how effective this process was and where its faults lay. Almost unanimously the key literature agrees that the Dayton Accords, which formulated a peace treaty and simultaneously laid out the constitution for post-war Bosnia, did not conclusively address all problems in Bosnia. While the immediate violence subsided, the systemic problems such as tensions and antagonism amongst Serbians, Croatians and Bosniaks, which had been exacerbated by years of war, remained.[8] Moreover, the literature questions the agreement's efficacy, arguing that Serbia, Croatia and Bosnia only committed half-heartedly after giving in to pressure from the United States.[9] Perhaps the most significant criticism was that

> two of the belligerents – the Bosnian Serbs and the Bosnian Croats – did not even properly sign the agreement but rather were 'represented' by the presidents of their respective patron states, Yugoslavia [Milošević] and Croatia [Tudjman].[10]

In addition to the predominantly negative assessment, another commonality in the secondary literature is the authors' approach marked by political science. None of the works unlock the historical process of these negotiations and the intricate developments leading to the peace conference. Equally, there is no literature detailing the policies or perspectives with which the international delegations approached the discussions, what their objectives

6 Fiona Watson / Tom Dodd: The Dayton Agreement: Progress in Implementation. In: *International Affairs and Defence Section, House of Commons Library*. London, Resarch Paper 96/80 (09.07.1996), p. 5; also explored in McMahon / Western: The Death of Dayton.

7 Watson / Dodd: The Dayton Agreement, p. 6; Cousens / Cater: *Toward Peace in Bosnia*, p. 37.

8 Cousens / Cater: *Toward Peace in Bosnia*; Watson / Dodd: The Dayton Agreement; Marc Weller / Stefan Wolff: Bosnia and Herzegovina Ten Years after Dayton: Lessons for Internationalized State Building. In: *Ethnopolitics* 5,1 (2006), pp. 1–13.

9 Cousens / Cater: *Toward Peace in Bosnia*; Lenard Cohen: The Balkans Ten Years After: From Dayton to the Edge of Democracy. In: *Current History* 104,685 (2005), pp. 365–373; Richard Dannatt: *Leading from the Front: The Autobiography*. London: Corgi 2010; Sumantra Bose: *Bosnia after Dayton: Nationalist Partition and International Intervention*. London: Oxford University Press 2002, p. 2.

10 Weller / Wolff: Bosnia and Herzegovina Ten Years after Dayton, p. 1; Cousens / Cater: *Toward Peace in Bosnia*, p. 43.

and negotiating-tactics were, and how they perceived their own role in comparison to the other delegations. Such insights are only offered by two primary sources, namely the seminal accounts produced by active participants at Dayton: Wolfgang Ischinger and Richard Holbrooke.[11]

Holbrooke's minute record of the weeks leading up to the negotiations and the discussions themselves gives the reader a unique insight into the 'shuttle diplomacy' practiced by the American delegation. Acting as the intermediary between the three Balkan countries, Holbrooke and his American colleagues 'shuttled' back and forth between Sarajevo, Belgrade and Zagreb to broker compromises. This candid account reveals how difficult it was to bring the representatives from Bosnia, Croatia and Serbia together and emphasises how divided and at times internally competitive the Bosnian delegation was in Dayton. Such revelations contribute to the wider context of the peace talks, underlining how laborious the process was.[12]

Ischinger's work is a collection of 53 telegrams he sent to Bonn during the on-going negotiations. Published in 1998 by the German Foreign Ministry, this compilation offers a unique first-hand insight that can neither be found in any other literature, nor in the media coverage of the time. Some sensitive information remains censored and is blacked-out in the publication. Nevertheless, the crucial insight the reader takes away from this collection of telegrams is the tenacity of the discussions and how often they were on the brink of failing. As Ischinger writes, "we worked almost around the clock for three weeks, including Saturday and Sunday, without any breaks. We usually wrote [these telegrams] in the evening or during the night […]"[13]

One aspect that proves particularly important for the purposes of this chapter is how aware both diplomats were of a media presence. In his preface, Ischinger wrote that America's Western partners were angered by the American media policy. On the one hand Holbrooke and his colleagues attempted to prohibit other delegations' contact to the press. Simultaneously however, Ischinger noted, Holbrooke "consistently fed certain journalists [crucial information], of course emphasising America's central role" in the negotiations.[14]

Ischinger's telegrams also featured an acute media-awareness. For example, at

11 Ivo Daalder's book *Getting to Dayton: The Making of American's Bosnia Policy*. Washington, D.C.: Brookings Institution Press 2000, gives an outsider's account of the American policy at Dayton, but does not include the German or European perspectives.

12 Holbrooke: *To End a War*.

13 Auswärtiges Amt: *Deutsche Außenpolitik 1995*, p. 30.

14 Ibid., p. 32.

times he advised his superiors in Bonn when to publish a press-release for the German media and what key points this communication should entail.[15] Equally, the diplomat mentioned explicitly whether a meeting or conversation occurred in the presence of the media or not.[16]

Media Censorship and Authorship

This introduces the important issue of the media policy implemented during the on-going discussions, which were deliberately held on a restricted American army base. The resulting media blackout was enforced to prohibit that any representative used and misused the public sphere to promote certain agendas, endangering the peace negotiations.[17] The international media was only invited to carefully chosen events, for example at the beginning and end of the talks, for a press-conference and photo opportunity. While all daily newspapers except for *BILD* mentioned and acknowledged this censorship, it was not criticised by any.[18] In his memoirs, Holbrooke also addressed the topic of media censorship, explaining that

> [...] State Department Spokesman Nick Burns [...was] the only authorised spokesman on Dayton, and he [...briefed] the world from Washington. We did not even have a press briefing officer in Dayton.[19]

This press policy resulted that the international media could not report on the negotiations when they deemed it important, but rather when the US-State Department chose to reveal details of the process. This dynamic retracted a lot of power from the media, constructing a clear hierarchy between the political establishment and the news outlets.

Unsurprisingly this blackout impacted the articles' authorship. While all daily newspapers published pieces written in Dayton, none of these were authored by their own correspondents, perhaps because it was too costly to keep a correspondent on site when there was so little information available and it remained unclear how long the discussion would last. Rather, most articles submitted from Dayton were amalgamations from various press agencies,

15 Telegram Nr. 3, 02.11.1995, 1443 local time. In: Ibid., p. 54.

16 For example: Telegram Nr. 2, 01.11.1995, 2302 local time. In: Ibid., pp. 49–53.

17 Auswärtiges Amt: *Deutsche Außenpolitik 1995*, p. 32.

18 For example: Manfred Rowold: Bosnien: Clinton spürt Gegenwind. In: *Welt*, 01.11.1995, p. 4; AP/dpa: Fünf Militärbaracken um einen Parkplatz. In: *FAZ*, 01.11.1995, p. 6; Martin Winter: Das Irrlicht am Ende des Tunnels. In: *FR*, 22.11.1995, p. 3; Andreas Zumach: Warten auf den weißen Rauch über Dayton. In: *taz*, 01.11.1995, p. 8.

19 Holbrooke: *To End a War*, p. 236.

frequently citing three agencies as the author. Consequently, the product would have been less shaped by the interpretations of specific newspapers' correspondents. This qualitative nuance is important to keep in mind, as it disappears in the quantitative considerations below.

Newspaper	Percentage of articles authored by correspondents	Percentage of articles authored by press agencies	Percentage of articles amalgamated from various press releases, etc.
Welt	54%	10%	36%
FAZ	67%	32%	1%
FR	48%	51%	0%
taz	69%	27%	0,78%

Table 3: Percentages of articles according to authorship[20]

Comparing this distribution with the preceding chapter,[21] the censorship seemingly had no impact on the authorship. In spite of the extenuating circumstances surrounding Dayton, more than half of the articles in *Welt*, *FAZ* and *taz* were written by the newspapers' correspondents and *FR* still used more press-agency articles than the other papers. However, it is worth noting that while a large number of articles were authored by the newspapers' own correspondents in this timeframe, most of these did not address the negotiations themselves, but rather more general topics such as the on-going violence in Bosnia. These were frequently authored by the newspapers' correspondents based in Washington, D.C. or the Balkans. This distinction underscores the limitations of purely quantitative considerations.

The selection of images published at this time is a further testament to the effects of the media blackout. The only pictures of the on-going negotiations were clearly staged events which had been opened to international media. The initialling of the Dayton Agreement on 21 November was one example for a carefully-staged photo opportunity.[22] Consequently the same image was printed in various German newspapers. The scarcity of images available of the actual negotiations is underlined by *FR's* recycling of the same image,

20 All numbers short of 100% are anonymous articles which cannot be categorised.

21 See chapter 4, fn. 63.

22 Images published in *FAZ*, 23.11.1995, p. 3; FR, 23.11.1995, p. 3; Welt, 23.11.1995, p. 1.

which it published twice within less than two weeks and depicted Milošević and Izetbegović shaking hands.[23]

The Dayton Agreement in the Press

The articles that form the basis of the analysis for this chapter range from 1 November to 20 December 1995, encompassing the negotiations in Dayton (1–21 November) as well as the timespan until a few days after the treaty was officially signed in Paris on 15 December 1995. In addition to the coverage of the talks themselves, various themes that played a prominent role in the German press at the time will be considered. These include Germany's role in the negotiations, Milošević's position, the Srebrenica Massacre, and the debate about the deployment of German soldiers. As this chapter will demonstrate, these topics influenced and coloured the media's over-all perception and coverage of the Dayton process.

Before delving into these themes, *AJW's* coverage must be considered separately, as it did not explore any of these topics. In the six-week timeframe determined for this chapter, *AJW* only published two articles on Bosnia, neither of which specifically addressed the Dayton negotiations. Both were written by the press-agency dpa and covered the Jewish community in Sarajevo. One reported that Ivan Ceresnjes, its chairman, had now left the country and had emigrated to Israel. It continued that Ceresnjes and Sarajevo's Jewish community in general had always ensured its neutrality amongst the "opposing parties" and never taken sides in the conflict.[24] Similarly, the article itself did not give any indication of which side it identified with most. The second piece reported on 'La Benevolencija', a charity run by Sarajevo's Jewish community and that it aimed to help the civilian population now that peace had been restored.[25]

The two pieces clearly avoided the political perspective of the conflict and the on-going peace negotiations and instead concentrated exclusively on cultural aspects pertaining to Jewish life in Bosnia. This stands in stark contrast to a *taz*-article which asked Ignatz Bubis, chairman of the Central Council of Jews in Germany to respond briefly to the question: "Are military interventions justified to stop genocide?" Bubis responded with a clear "[…] absolutely

23 Images published in *FR*, 03.11.1995, p. 1; *FR*, 22.11.1995, p. 1. The same picture (though taken from a different angle) was published in *Spiegel*, 06.11.1995, p. 174.

24 dpa: Sarajevo: Kapitän geht von Bord. In: *AJW*, 16.11.1995, p. 8.

25 dpa: Helfer geehrt. In: *AJW*, 14.12.1995, p. 1.

yes" and referred to the Srebrenica Massacre to support his argument.[26] This public answer to a contentious issue in Germany proves that the official representative of the Jewish community in Germany did not shy away from the topic. As *AJW* was published by the Central Council of Jews in Germany and could thus be considered its mouthpiece, the newspaper's avoidance of this topic indicates an editorial policy specific to the publication rather than a general stance taken by the Council.

JF and *Konkret* also refrained from reporting about the peace talks. However, both publications contributed to the other debates mentioned previously, such as the re-evaluation of the Srebrenica Massacre and the contribution of German soldiers to NATO's IFOR-troops in Bosnia. All other publications considered here closely covered the Dayton negotiations and their intermittent progress. *BILD's* characteristically short and superficial coverage of international affairs meant that the tabloid only reported on Dayton when a breakthrough occurred, for example when the opposing parties agreed on the creation of a Bosnian-Croatian Federation or the right of return for refugees.[27] Consequently the *BILD*-reader was left with the perception of steady progress without knowing about the convoluted background. Moreover, these articles – on average 33 words long – did not offer its readers any form of evaluation, for example whether this agreement was fair or not.

The remaining publications' coverage was more discerning. For example, various articles covering the opening event, to which the international media had been invited, focused on the profound differences dividing the three Balkan leaders. *Welt's* Manfred Rowold described the atmosphere as 'clammy' while the three Balkan politicians avoided eye contact with each other. The handshake initiated by Holbrooke between Izetbegović, Tudjman and Milošević visibly cost a lot of effort, especially for the Bosnian President, Rowold reported.[28] Similarly a *FAZ*-article explained that "the insistence on individual translators is a further sign for the seemingly insurmountable divide between the three parties."[29] This detail was considered particularly remarkable, as Bosnian, Serbian and Croatian are different dialects of one Yugoslav language and could have been understood by all Balkan participants. Thus,

26 Ignatz Bubis: Sind Militäreinsätze bei Völkermord gerechtfertigt? In: *taz*, 01.12.1995, p. 12.

27 Anonymous: Flüchtlinge dürfen zurück. In: *BILD*, 04.11.1995, p. 1; Anonymous: Föderation. In: *BILD*, 10.11.1995, p. 2.

28 M. Rowold: Dayton – Synonym für Frieden oder Krieg. In: *Welt*, 03.11.1995, p. 3.

29 AP/dpa: Fünf Militärbaracken um einen Parkplatz. In: *FAZ*, 01.11.1995, p. 6.

the insistence on individual translators seemed to suggest a political message to establish each country as a completely separate entity.
While the difficult conditions of the negotiations were clearly recognised, the German press evidently did not see them as a sufficient explanation for what was deemed a sub-optimal outcome of the agreement. Rather than presenting the Dayton Accords as a successful first step towards peace in the region, all publications except *Konkret* pointed out the faults of the treaty. *Welt* for example lamented that 'the Serbs' only made up 30% of the population, but were allocated 49% of the territory. Even though "the Serbian territory is spread out to an economical and strategic disadvantage," the Serbians could still record a considerable success.[30] A *FAZ*-editorial took a stronger stance, stating that Dayton rewarded "[…] the Serbian aggressors at the expense of the victims," suggesting that the fundamental divide between aggressor and victims would continue to separate Bosnian society.[31] While *JF* did not cover the talks at all, an editorial published after they were concluded echoed *FAZ's* assessment, labelling the outcome as "horse-trading" from which Milošević benefitted the most. Peter Lattas commented emphatically that Milošević was a "power and survival-genius" whose primary goal was to stay in power.[32]
While the conservative and right-wing papers interpreted the short-comings of the agreement through the prism of how much Milošević and Bosnia's Serbian population benefitted from it, the left-leaning publications focused on the mistakes they believed the international community had made. Along these lines, a *Spiegel*-article criticised that the fate of war criminals was not discussed in any detail, rendering the Muslims the losers in this international power play, although they were 'in the right.'[33] *FR* and *taz* focused on the negative aspects of America's involvement in the peace process. Various articles stated that the peace treaty was forced by the USA rather than being an organic process. Thus, they argued, it remained unclear how serious the three Balkan politicians were about working towards a long-lasting peace[34] – a theory also postulated in the academic literature.[35] *taz* took a more extreme stance, arguing that the insufficient results were a sign of a faulty American

30 Carl Gustaf Ströhm: Vom erträumten Großserbien blieb am Ende nur Banja Luka. In: *Welt*, 25.11.1995, p. 4.

31 Rm: Falsche Züge. In: *FAZ*, 02.12.1995, p. 14.

32 Peter Lattas: Der Kuhhandel von Dayton. In: *JF*, 01.12.1995, p. 2.

33 Anonymous: Ein bitterer Friede. In: *Spiegel*, 27.11.1995, p. 145.

34 paa: Einig in Dayton. In: *FR*, 22.11.1995, p. 3; Ada Brande / Charima Reinhardt / Knut Pries: Ein schmallippiges Lob von den Zahlmeistern. In: *FR*, 23.11.1995, p. 3.

35 See chapter 5, fn. 3–10.

negotiation strategy.[36] One *taz*-article assessed that "the US-diplomacy in Dayton had to fail, because it attempted to unite demands which are fundamentally contradictory."[37] This evaluation strikes an external observer as absurd. Naturally Bosnia, Serbia and Croatia, which had engaged in violent wars for nearly four years, represented deeply contrary demands. By blaming America for attempting to bridge these differences, *taz's* anti-American evaluation seems to avoid a more profound analysis.

Another article criticised the agreement more generally stating that the "[…] ethnically 'cleansed' areas […would] stay 'clean'. Or do people seriously expect that a banished Muslim will return to his village in the (Bosnian) Serb Republic […]?" the *taz*-editor Thomas Schmid asked sarcastically.[38] This interpretation was underlined with a caricature printed the following day.

Figure 16: Klaus Stuttmann, "The form is preserved" ("*Die Form bleibt gewahrt*"); printed in *taz*, 24 November 1995, p. 10.

With the words "the form is preserved", it expressed the opinion that while Bosnia still looks the same – alluding to its shape on the map – it had changed fundamentally following the years of mass violence. The cross on the 1995-version of Bosnia could either represent an urn or could stand for the largely Christian population – whether Catholic or Orthodox – in a country that had previously been colourfully mixed.

36 Jürgen Gottschlich: Friedensvertrag ohne Frieden? In: *taz*, 02.11.1995, p. 10; Erich Rathfelder: Kriegsgefahr noch nicht gebannt. In: *taz*, 11.11.1995, p. 10; Thomas Schmid: Sarajevo ist der erst Prüfstein. In: *taz*, 15.12.1995, p. 10.

37 Erich Rathfelder: „Wer sind die Träumer?" In: *taz*, 22.11.1995, p. 1.

38 Thomas Schmid: Das völkische Prinzip. In: *taz*, 23.11.1995, p. 10.

In spite of the varying interpretations along the lines of political orientation, the reader – irrespective of which publication – was left with a vivid sensation that the agreement was fundamentally unfair. For example, articles in various publications quoted Izetbegović's assessment that it was 'bitter medicine' for Bosnia.[39] Only one *FR*-editorial concluded: "But who cares? Now there is electricity, gas and water in Sarajevo and the children can go to school again."[40] This summary re-aligned the critical perspective of the peace agreement, reminding the reader how disturbed everyday life in the war-torn city had been. However, apart from this exception, much of the German press-coverage at the time presented a similar interpretation of Dayton as the secondary literature produced several years later, namely a focus on the negative aspects of the peace agreement.

Another commonality found in the evaluations offered by the secondary literature and the German press-coverage of the time was that the tenacity of the negotiations was completely ignored. As mentioned previously, both 'insider accounts' by Holbrooke and Ischinger revealed how often the talks were on the brink of failing and how contentious and troublesome some of the seemingly small issues were. This context was missing in the literature on Dayton as well as throughout the coverage which consequently neglected to offer the reader viable reasons for what they deemed an underwhelming outcome. It could be argued that the media at the time did not have detailed knowledge of the on-going negotiations, explaining this missing context. Equally however, none of the publications featured interviews with Holbrooke, Ischinger or other high-ranking officials who had been present in Dayton after the agreement had been signed. These interviews could have offered additional insights into the peace process and perhaps explained why certain – seemingly unacceptable – compromises had been made. Possibly no such interviews were published because by the time Ischinger had returned from the hermetically closed-off army-base in Dayton, the peace treaty was deemed 'old news' and its implementation appeared more relevant.

39 Anonymous: Ein bitterer Friede, *Spiegel*, 27.11.1995, pp. 144–149; Klaus-Dieter Frankenberger: Bittere Medizin. In: *FAZ*, 15.12.1995, p. 1; Pierre Simontisch: Eiserne Mienen und etwas Lyrik von Clinton. In: *FR*, 15.12.1995, p. 3; DW: „Dieser Frieden ist wie eine bittere Medizin". In: *Welt*, 15.12.1995, p. 9.

40 Nenad Popovic: Das Ereignis von Dayton. In: *FR*, 23.11.1995, p. 10.

Use of Images

We turn now to the images published in this timeframe. As discussed previously, the diplomatic negotiations and an occasional picture depicting international statesmen shaking hands or signing a piece of paper were not the same interesting and evocative images other aspects of the war had offered. Interestingly, rather than omitting images from their Balkan or Dayton coverage altogether, all publications except for *JF* sought to pictorially remind their readers of the on-going violence in Bosnia. These focused on the civilian suffering in Bosnia.[41]

Figure 17:
"Croatia- Bosnia-War in former Yugoslavia; In reaction to the "Operation Storm" (Liberation of the Krajina region) the Serbs displaced remaining Muslims and Croats in northern Bosnia from the city of Banja Luka (on 15.08.95, 1.736 refugees were registered according to UNHCR) border river Sava; A man accuses: his teeth were knocked out and his money stolen before he was deported." Photographer: Christian Jungeblodt.

41 For example images published in *Welt*, 08.11.1995, p.3 and p.6; *Spiegel*, 27.11.1995, pp.144–145; *Spiegel*, 06.11.1995, p.176; FR, 27.11.1995, p.2; FAZ, 23.11.1995, p.3; *BILD*, 27.11.1995, p.2.

Figure 18:
MOSTAR / BIH 1995, "Cease fire after three years of bloody war. The town is destroyed and most of the people are living among debris." Photographer: Livio Senigalliesi; printed in *taz*, 11–12 November 1995, p. 8.

These images presented various scenes of destruction, desperation and human suffering caused by the war while simultaneously showing the reader the state of chaos in Bosnia. They consequently demonstrated – perhaps more tellingly than any article citing statistics – how difficult the post-Dayton path of reconstruction would be. Significantly, aside from the two pictures pictured above (figures 17 and 18), none of the captions accompanying the images elaborated whether the victims were Bosnian Muslims, Croats or Serbs. This augmented the sense of universal suffering. Two images printed in *taz* were the only ones that explicitly showed Muslim civilians, as was explained in the respective captions. Equally however, the paper portrayed scenes of every-day-misery from a Serbian perspective, as did *FR* and *Welt*.[42] These pictures were especially meaningful, as they conceded that Serbian civilians had also suffered under the war.

42 Images published in *FR*, 09.12.1995, p. 3; *taz*, 30.11.1995, p. 11.

Figure 19:
"Bosnia – War in former Yugoslavia; "Operation Storm" (liberation of the Krajina region); Near the city of Banja Luka – after the displacemnt oft he Serbs from the Kraijna region. Serbian cross; 28.08.1995." Photographer: Christian Jungeblodt.[43]

Figure 20:
picture alliance/AP Images: "An unidentified Serbian woman holds a skull she believes to be that of a relative during a reburial in the Bosnian village of Fakovici in this May, 1993." picture alliance/AP Images; printed in *Welt*, 14 December 1995, p. 1.

43 This precise image was not printed, though it is a good example of an image portraying the suffering of Serbian civilians. Other images by the photographer were published in *taz*.

The *Welt*-image (figure 20) of a grieving woman cradling a skull is particularly heart-wrenching and reminded the reader that Srebrenica was not the only instance of mass murder during the four-year-war. This approach is a surprising departure from *Welt's* previous coverage, which had eagerly blamed 'the Serbs' for the violence and its lamentation that they had benefitted too much from the Dayton Agreement. The readiness of *taz*, *FR* and *Welt* to portray Serbian suffering, even if these examples were isolated cases, suggest an understanding that the post-Dayton reconstruction of the country would have to address and include Croats, Serbs and Muslims living in Bosnia.

Germany in the Back Seat

Throughout the coverage of the negotiations, the disregard of Germany's role in the national media itself becomes apparent; Germany was deemed unimportant by omission. Instead the German press consistently focused on America and its representative, Holbrooke.[44] This side-lining of Germany was manifested in nuances such as some articles quoting statements by the Russian and French Presidents, as well as US-Secretary of State Warren Christopher, but not Chancellor Helmut Kohl or Foreign Minister Klaus Kinkel.[45] This was also the case in *FR* and *taz*, which had conveyed a strong anti-American evaluation of the Dayton Agreement.

The predominant focus on America's role is comprehensible considering not only the locality of the negotiations, but also the engagement of high-ranking US-politicians in the peace process. As mentioned in Ischinger's telegrams and Holbrooke's memoir, when the discussions faltered, either Secretary of State Christopher or at one occasion even President Bill Clinton travelled to Dayton to signal their prevailing dedication to and interest in finding a peaceful solution.[46] Moreover, Holbrooke's memoir reveals that a number of American officials joined the negotiations intermittently to address specific problems. For example the Deputy Assistant Secretary of the Treasury

44 For example: Anonymous: Teuflischer Plan. In: *Spiegel*, 27.11.1995, pp. 150–151; Andreas Zumach: Bosnien-Marathon geht in die Verlängerung. In: *taz*, 22.11.1995, p. 1; Rolf Paasch: Riskantes Pokern um die Teilung Bosniens. In: *FR*, 01.11.1995, p. 5; WeNa: Neue Hoffnung im zerstörten Bosnien. In: *Welt*, 23.11.1995, p. 6; Matthias Rüb: Kongress gegen Entsendung von Truppen. In: *FAZ*, 01.11.1995, p. 6; Anonymous: Frieden schon perfekt? In: *BILD*, 18.11.1995, p. 2.

45 For example: WeNa: Neue Hoffnung im zerstörten Bosnien. In: *Welt*, 23.11.1995, p. 1; Anonymous: Serben wollen abziehen. In: *BILD*, 13.11.1995, p. 2.

46 For example: Telegram Nr. 47, 20.11.1995, 0158 local time. In: Auswärtiges Amt: *Deutsche Außenpolitik 1995*, p. 131; Holbrooke: *To End a War*, p. 274.

helped construct a unified currency for Bosnia.[47] This high-level commitment in the peace process was not demonstrated by any other country and thus the focus on America's role in the German press coverage of Dayton could be seen as a reflection of reality, in which Germany simply did not play an important role.

This evaluation of Germany's role in the region is corroborated by Michael Libal who had been the head of the Southeast European Department of the German Foreign Ministry between 1991 and 1995.[48] Drawing on his personal and professional knowledge, Libal authored a book exploring the diplomacy conducted by the EC, OSCE and Germany, concluding that the latter was not the dominant actor in the region, in spite of its initially prominent role during the recognition process.[49] However, the German press' focus on America could also be the result of the American media policy, Ischinger had criticised in his telegrams, which highlighted America's position in the peace process.[50]

FAZ, *Spiegel* and *BILD* were the only publications that mentioned the German delegation in Dayton at all, and each did so in only a single piece. *FAZ's* article outlined what questions and themes would be most pertinent to Ischinger's German delegation, such as the fate of the refugees and post-conflict arms control.[51] The *Spiegel*-article reported that the Political Director of the Federal Foreign Office [Ischinger] had been instructed only to leave Dayton if the negotiations had reached a dead end and the opposing parties were unwilling to compromise. The same article later elaborated that "the Germans would rank last […]" at the festivities in Paris surrounding the signing of the agreement, due to their relatively unimportant role.[52] However, the anonymous author did not include a judgement of this fact – for example whether this was justified.

The *BILD*-article attributed the most importance to Ischinger and his German colleagues, writing that approximately half of the 140-page long agreement resulted from the contribution of the German delegation. Significantly the tabloid did not explain how the author reached this conclusion, rendering the information questionable. The author then continued by

47 Holbrooke: *To End a War*, pp. 256–258.

48 Michael Libal: *Germany and the Yugoslav Crisis, 1991–1992.* Westport: Praeger 1997, p. ix.

49 Ibid., pp. 101–148.

50 See chapter 5, fn. 14–16.

51 C. G.: Es soll so lange verhandelt werden, bis ein Friedensabkommen erreicht ist. In: *FAZ*, 01.11.1995, p. 7.

52 Anonymous: Ein bitterer Friede. In: *Spiegel*, 27.11.1995, p. 149.

exploring Ischinger's career development and personal life, ending with the information that he would be taking a four-day skiing holiday over Christmas.[53] This mirrors the tabloid's habit of focusing on one individual's story to explain wider themes and correlations. The details of a German diplomat's private life offered an opportunity to avoid the complex world of international relations while still alluding to it.

The diminished interest of national newspapers in Germany's involvement was a significant shift from the media coverage at the beginning of the conflict, particularly about Germany's early recognition of Croatia and Slovenia.[54] Here, many of the arguments put forward by *Welt*, *BILD*, *FAZ* and *taz* had stated that Germany had a unique diplomatic acumen while its European allies were naïve in their insistence on a unified Yugoslavia. However, none of these publications lamented that Germany's knowledge and pioneering diplomacy was relegated to the background during the 1995 peace talks. This could suggest that the national media agreed with the retreat of German foreign policy into the realms of alliance-politics after this initial *Alleingang*.

Milošević's Role

Turning to a theme that strongly captured the German print media's interest, the role of Slobodan Milošević and his questionable transformation from a 'war-monger' to a respectable politician who was integrated in international diplomacy, received a lot of attention.[55] In this matter the German press strongly disagreed with the *modus operandi* of the international politicians – an opinion frequently expressed in editorials. While the politicians willingly overlooked Milošević's past role in the Balkan Wars and concentrated on the necessity of including him in the peace-process to make the agreement binding, the print media considered here was less forgiving. Interestingly, the previously mentioned hierarchy established due to the politicians' monopoly of

53 Mainhardt Graf Nayhauss: Friedensvertrag für Bosnien: Ein Genscher-Mann strickte mit. In: *BILD*, 01.12.1995, p. 2.

54 See pp. 70–74.

55 For example: Matthias Rüb: Kongress gegen Entsendung von Truppen. In: *FAZ*, 01.11.1995, p. 6; wie.: Pendeldiplomatie Christophers zwischen Milosevic, Izetbegovic und Tudjman. In: *FAZ*, 20.11.1995, p. 1; Johann Georg Reißmüller: Ungerecht und unsicher. In: *FAZ*, 22.11.1995, p. 1; Leo Wieland: Vom Kriegstreiber zum Dayton-Darling. In: *FAZ*, 25.11.1995, p. 3; Johann Georg Reißmüller: Erst mussten Hunderttausende sterben. In: *FAZ*, 14.12.1995, p. 1; WeNa: Rühe nennt Zeitplan für Bosnien. In: *Welt*, 28.11.1995, p. 1; Carl Gustaf Ströhm: Serbische Preistreiber. In: *Welt*, 16.11.1995, p. 1; Rolf Paasch: Sie möchten heim, aber nicht mit den Mördern leben. In: *FR*, 09.12.1995, p. 3.

information,[56] did not stop the German press from taking a diametrically opposite stance on Milošević's inclusion in the peace process.

Various articles cautioned that Western politicians were willing to overlook crucial facts about the depth of Milošević's involvement in war crimes to secure peace.[57] Indeed all publications except for *JF* and *Konkret* linked Milošević to the Srebrenica Massacre. For example, articles in *FR*, *FAZ* and *Spiegel* cited witnesses who allegedly confirmed the participation of JNA-soldiers in the 'ethnic cleansing' of Srebrenica.[58] This stood in stark contrast to Milošević's previous claims that his troops had nothing to do with the massacre and that he had lost control over Karadžić and Mladić. Other articles were less specific, reporting that rumours were brewing in America which suggested Holbrooke and other American politicians were holding back information regarding the depth of Milošević's involvement in the Srebrenica Massacre to ensure that the peace process would not be disturbed.[59] *Welt* and *Spiegel* explained that these allegations had been made by the Bosnian foreign minister, which could suggest a political agenda.[60] However neither article further examined this facet. Both publications later cited UN-General Secretary Boutros-Ghali, who according to *Welt* and *Spiegel* had stated that the peace process had 'absolute priority' to the prosecution of war criminals.[61]

This political pragmatism was the main concern and crucial criticism in all publications except for *JF* and *Konkret*. Using terms such as 'war-monger',[62]

56 See pp. 125–127.

57 Leo Wieland: Vom Kriegstreiber zum Dayton-Darling. In: *FAZ*, 25.11.1995, p. 3; Roy Gutman: Friedensstifter Milosevic? In: *taz*, 15.11.1995, p. 15; azu/dpa/AFP: Klagt Den Haag Milosevic an? In: *taz*, 28.11.1995, p. 1; Hans Monath: Zurück zur Sache! In: *taz*, 28.11.1995, p. 1.

58 Pierre Simontisch: UN-Bericht belegt Greueltaten. In: *FR*, 01.12.1995, p. 7; km: Beweise für serbische Verbrechen. In: *FAZ*, 01.12.1995, p. 2; Anonymous: Jagd auf die Mörder. In: *Spiegel*, 06.11.1995, p. 175.

59 Rolf Paasch: Riskantes Pokern um die Teilung Bosniens. In: *FR*, 01.11.1995, p. 5; rtr/wps/taz/b. s.: USA weisen Goldstones Kritik zurück. In: *taz*, 09.11.1995, p. 8; wie.: Kühler Handschlag im Hope-Hotel. In: *FAZ*, 03.11.1995, p. 3; rtr: Vorbehalte gegen Milosevic bei Bosnien-Gesprächen. In: *Welt*, 01.11.1995, p. 1; Anonymous: Ein bitterer Friede. In: *Spiegel*, 27.11.1995, p. 147.

60 Rtr: Vorbehalte gegen Milošević bei Bosnien-Gesprächen. In: *Welt*, 01.11.1995, p. 1; also in Anonymous: Ein bitterer Friede. In: *Spiegel*, 27.11.1995, p. 147.

61 Manfred Rowold: Warren Christopher will Bosnien-Gipfel retten. In: *Welt*, 15.11.1995, p. 5; Erich Folath / Volkhard Windfuhr: Nachtwächter für Uno? In: *Spiegel*, 11.12.1995, pp. 151–156.

62 Manfred Rowold: Der Tag, als Dayton Geschichte wurde. In: *Welt*, 23.11.1995, p. 3; Matthias Rüb: Kongress gegen Entsendung von Truppen. In: *FAZ*, 01.11.1995, p. 6; Anonymous: Ein bitterer Friede. In: *Spiegel*, 27.11.1995, p. 147.

the 'father of the war',[63] and the 'primary instigator of the war'[64] who spoke with 'angels' tongues'[65] to describe Milošević, the publications agreed that he should not have been invited to the negotiations. The anger expressed in *Welt* and *FAZ* editorials was particularly memorable. *Welt's* Ströhm argued that Milošević should be in The Hague (at the ICTY) rather than Dayton and that his presence at the peace talks was an 'unreasonable imposition' for any 'half-way righteous person'.[66] Similarly, *FAZ*-editor Reißmüller called it 'grotesque' to force the victims to sit at the same table with the aggressors.[67] Indeed *FAZ* underlined this point pictorially with a cartoon depicting Milošević as a badly disguised peace dove, flying above a burning mosque.

Figure 21:
Fritz Behrendt;
printed in *FAZ*,
7 November 1995, p. 7.

While Ströhm had held Milošević responsible for the violence since the lead-up to the Bosnian War,[68] Reißmüller's focus on Milošević was a shift away from his previous stance that vehemently attributed the war to a renewal of 'ancient hatreds' in the region.[69]

63 Rolf Paasch: Riskantes Pokern um die Teilung Bosniens. In: *FR*, 01.11.1995, p. 5; Roman Arens: Ein fauler Friede. In: *FR*, 23.11.1995, p. 3.

64 Johannes Vollmer: „Das ist eine ethnische Teilung". In: *taz*, 23.11.1995, p. 2.

65 W. A.: Der Auftakt von Dayton. In: *FAZ*, 03.11.1995, p. 1.

66 Carl Gustaf Ströhm: Brücke zum Frieden. In: *Welt*, 23.11.1995, p. 4.

67 Johann Georg Reißmüller: Ungerecht und unsicher. In: *FAZ*, 22.11.1995, p. 1.

68 See chapter 3, fn. 82–86.

69 See chapter 3, fn. 27–29.

The Srebrenica Massacre Re-appears

In addition to linking Milošević personally to Srebrenica, all publications aside from *JF* also re-examined the massacre in more general terms. *Konkret* only did so in one article, reminding its readers that there were various contradicting facts about Srebrenica and that a military intervention was in no way justified due to the so-called 'genocide' in the enclave.[70] However at this point, the enclave itself was still inaccessible to international observers, so the death toll remained an estimate and was usually quoted at around 6,000 (as opposed to ca. 8,000, which is more accurate).[71] In spite of these prevailing uncertainties, there was mounting evidence of Bosnian-Serb war crimes perpetrated in the enclave in July 1995, which had been supported by Serbia.

FR, *FAZ* and *taz* covered a UN-report that had been commissioned in early November to investigate the details of the Srebrenica Massacre and assess who had been responsible for the crimes committed. In the words of *FAZ*, the UN-report "[...] described 'scenes of unfathomable barbarity'. Thousands of men were executed and buried in mass graves, hundreds of men burned alive, men and women mutilated and 'butchered'."[72] All three daily newspapers drew on the same graphic example from the UN-report to portray the horrific war crimes that had been perpetrated, namely that a grandfather had been forced to eat the liver of his own grandson.[73]

taz, *Spiegel* and *FAZ* chose to visually portray the suffering of Srebrenica's expelled civilians who were still persevering in Tuzla in late 1995, unable to return home. An image published in *FAZ* showed desolate-looking Muslim – predominantly female – refugees.[74] In contrast, *taz* published the image below of refugees receiving aid from a UN-truck.

Both themes, which had already appeared in the pictorial coverage of the Srebrenica Massacre analysed in the previous chapter. However, an inversion is worth noting. As discussed in the preceding chapter, *FAZ* had not published a single image showing the anguish of Srebrenica's victims or the

70 Jürgen Elsässer: Mladics Katyn? In: *Konkret*, December 1995, p. 20.

71 For example: WeNa: Rühe nennt Zeitplan für Bosnien. In: *Welt*, 28.11.1995, p. 1; km: Beweise für serbische Verbrechen. In: *FAZ*, 01.12.1995, p. 2; Pierre Simontisch: UN-Bericht belegt Greueltagen. In: *FR*, 01.11.1995, p. 5; dpa: „Unvorstellbare Barbarei". In: *taz*, 17.11.1995, p. 8; rtr/AFP: Chirac: Schutz für Serben. In: *taz*, 01.12.1995, p. 8; Anonymous: Nachtwächter für Uno? In: *Spiegel*, 11.12.1995, p. 134; Anonymous: Bosnien. In: *BILD*, 01.12.1995, p. 2.

72 E. L.: Neue Anklagepunkte. In: *FAZ*, 17.11.1995, p. 7; dpa/AP: UN: Unangreifbare Beweise für serbisches Massenmorden. In: *FAZ*, 30.11.1995, p. 1

73 E. L.: Neue Anklagepunkte. In: *FAZ*, 17.11.1995, p. 7; dpa: Unvorstellbare Barbarei. In: *taz*, 17.11.1995, p. 8; dpa: „Wahrhaft Szenen aus der Hölle". In: *FR*, 17.11.1995, p. 2.

74 Image published in *FAZ*, 23.11.1995, p. 3.

Figure 22: "Bosnia – War in former Yugoslavia; Srebenica; Bosnian women who fled from Srebrenica are at the Tuzla airport refugee camp; UNPROFOR. The Bosnian Enklave Srebrenica – back then a UN-safe area – was the scene of a massacre perpetrated by the Bosnian-Serb army under the command of General Ratko Mladic. Bosnian (Muslim) men were murdered; mainly women, children and elderly fled from the massacre, ending in Tuzla, at the UN-airport. 23.07.1995" Photographer: Christian Jungeblodt; printed in *taz*, 15 November 1995, p. 8.

refugees in Tuzla.[75] Rather the dominant motif of the broadsheet's images had depicted instances of international aid alleviating the refugees' suffering. Now for the first time, *FAZ* published an image focusing solely on the human grief, typical of *taz's* previous visual coverage, while *taz* published a picture reminiscent of *FAZ's* previous pictures. *FAZ's* shift in visual policy could result from the inescapable reality of the extent of the Srebrenica Massacre about which there was no doubt in late 1995, even though the enclave remained sealed-off.

Another theme which recurs in various articles was the DUTCHBAT-soldiers' depth of involvement at the time. This subject matter was fuelled by refugees' statements, which fiercely accused the UN-soldiers of immoral actions. One example cited by *Welt* and *Spiegel* claimed that soldiers had refused to provide

75 See chapter 4, fn. 27.

medical assistance to the Muslim civilians.[76] This serious incrimination can be qualified with the explanation presented in a *FAZ*-article that the commanding UN-officer feared an exhaustion of medical supplies for the soldiers themselves, especially since it remained unclear how long the Bosnian-Serb siege would continue.[77] More severe allegations were reported by *FAZ*, *FR* and *taz*, citing refugees from Srebrenica who had arrived in Germany and who claimed in a press conference that the peacekeepers had sold food, cigarettes and other supplies, such as clothing, for exorbitant prices.[78] A *taz*-article further elaborated that to prove this allegation, one young man, Ekrem, who spoke at the press conference, held up a T-shirt with 'Royal Dutch Army' written on it. He claimed to have paid the Dutch soldiers 360 Mark for that T-shirt and a pair of socks.[79] Both *taz* and *FR* went even further, stating that young girls were 'persuaded' to prostitute themselves. The Dutch soldiers usually paid two cigarettes, according to the statements made by these refugees.[80] Considering the severity of these charges, it is surprising that *Konkret* did not pick up on this topic. Judging from the magazine's previous coverage, this kind of information usually sparked *Konrekt's* interest.

Official sources, especially the UN and the Dutch government denied these allegations and the newspapers reported this in a single sentence.[81] In contrast, the accusations themselves were reported in much more detail. Consequently the reader was left with an over-whelming sense that the Dutch soldiers had acted immorally. This matter has not been re-examined in the existing secondary literature on Srebrenica (discussed in chapter four) nor in the 2014 trial holding the Netherlands responsible for the death of 300 boys and men in Srebrenica.[82] Of course these allegations remain very hard to

76 Htz: Erneute Vorwürfe gegen UN-Soldaten aus Holland. In: *Welt*, 28.11.1995, p. 6; Anonymous: Nachtwächter für Uno? In: *Spiegel*, 11.12.1995, p. 134.

77 As mentioned in dpa: Abermals schwere Vorwürfe gegen niederländische Blauhelme. In: *FAZ*, 28.11.1995, p. 7.

78 E. L.: Den Haag: Beschuldigungen unrichtig. In: *FAZ*, 03.11.1995, p. 2; dpa/tro: Neue Vorwürfe gegen UN-Truppe. In: *FR*, 04.11.1995, p. 2; tro/ap/afp: Neue Vorwürfe gegen niederländische Blauhelm-Soldaten. In: *FR*, 28.11.1995, p. 2; Karin Nink: Prostitution und Schwarzhandel in Srebrenica. In: *taz*, 04.11.1995, p. 2.

79 Karin Nink: Prostitution und Schwarzhandel in Srebrenica. In: *taz*, 04.11.1995, p. 2.

80 dpa/tro: Neue Vorwürfe gegen UN-Truppe. In: *FR*, 04.11.1995, p. 2; Karin Nink: Prostitution und Schwarzhandel in Srebrenica. In: *taz*, 04.11.1995, p. 2.

81 For example: WeNa: „Srebrenica – das schlimmste Kriegsverbrechen seit Stalins Tod". In: *Welt*, 01.11.1995, p. 4; tro.: Minister will Anhörung zu Srebrenica vermeiden. In: *FR*, 07.12.1995, p. 7; AFP: Srebrenica: Beweise vernichtet. In: *taz*, 18./19.11.1995, p. 2.

82 Dan Bilefsky / Marlise Simons: Netherlands Held Liable for 300 Deaths in Srebrenica

prove or disprove with any certainty, and many details remain inconclusive. For example, the reader was never informed why the refugee had so much money to buy a T-shirt and socks, or why he found it necessary to purchase these items of clothing for such an exorbitant amount. These important questions were not explored or even mentioned in the articles at the time. Rather the newspapers presented the alleged immoral actions of the DUTCHBAT-troops with such certainty that few readers would have been left with doubts of their culpability. These remaining questions and inconsistencies indicate a continuing tendency amongst the German press to present the UN-soldiers as guilty onlookers rather than victims of larger politics which had prohibited military engagement in Srebrenica. The near-omission of a UN-fatality explored in the previous chapter adds to this assessment.

This was further underlined by numerous articles in *taz* and *Konkret*, which reported that indeed the American, French and German intelligence services had known about the imminent siege, but had deliberately chosen not to interfere.[83] These incriminations were not echoed in any other publications considered here, but unquestionably left the reader with a sense of fault regarding the international community. This would have been reinforced by the reproachful articles of the faulty negotiations in Dayton and particularly *taz's* condemning portrayal of America in the peace process. *taz's* intensified interest in Srebrenica, even in late 1995 was further exemplified in an article written by a nurse from 'Doctors without Borders', Christine Schmitz, about her experiences in the enclave, almost in diary format. The content of the article did not necessarily add to the state of knowledge about the massacre. However, its style offered a sense of immediacy, which newspaper articles and editorials did not convey. The author painted a vivid picture for her readers when she wrote that "while heavily armed soldiers with German Shepherd dogs guarded and watched the displacement, horrible scenes occurred […] as men were separated from their wives and children."[84] Schmitz witnessed the horrors of mass-displacements and heard shots coming from abandoned houses where Muslim men had been taken. She reflected: "What a strange feeling to be in this evidently empty city, pass by Serbian check-points and

Massacre. In: *New York Times*, 16.07.2014. http://www.nytimes.com/2014/07/17/world/europe/court-finds-netherlands-responsible-for-srebrenica-deaths.html?_r=1 (accessed 29.07.2014).

83 *Konkret*, December 1995, p. 20; *taz*, 01.11.1995, p. 8; *taz*, 08.11.1995, p. 15; *taz*, 09.11.1995, p. 8; *taz*, 13.11.1995, p. 10; *taz*, 15.11.1995, p. 8.

84 Christine Schmitz: Die letzten Stunden von Srebrenica. In: *taz*, 04.11.1995, p. 24.

witness looting."[85] Such reflections offered the reader a much closer understanding to what had happened in the enclave.

In contrast to *taz*, the massacre found almost no place in *BILD's* articles produced in late 1995. Indeed, only three pieces mentioned the massacre at all – each in only a few sentences. In November, one *BILD*-article reported that eight refugees who had been hiding in the forest around Srebrenica for 130 days had now been found.[86] However, no further details are offered about new insights gained about the atrocities that had been committed in the previous months.

The coverage of Srebrenica in late 1995 not only underscored the continuing restrictions of information, but also arguably influenced the readers' perception of the on-going Dayton negotiations. While international diplomats were locked away on an American air-base, negotiating a peaceful outcome of the Bosnian War, the German public read about new details of the Srebrenica Massacre, which the national newspapers linked to Milošević. While this connection gained a lot of attention at this point, it is important to remember that *Spiegel* had already identified this connection several months before, as the events were unfolding in July 1995. Written several months earlier, on 24 July 1995, an anonymous *Spiegel*-article had stated in relation to Srebrenica that "Western diplomats [...] are ignoring that the Belgrade government is still generously supporting [...the Bosnian Serbs...] with weapons and military-technical help."[87] Though at the time this was only mentioned in a single side-note, which may have easily been overlooked, this indicates a level of investigative reporting and analysis neither UNSC-press releases nor the other German publications presented. This link between Milošević and Srebrenica tainted the Dayton Agreement as insufficient and too advantageous for the Serbs, who were presented to be the initial aggressors of the war. It also created a sense of urgency to ensure such violence would never occur again. This second argument strongly influenced the domestic debate in Germany that followed the signing of the Dayton Accords in December 1995.

85 Christine Schmitz: Die letzten Stunden von Srebrenica. In: *taz*, 04.11.1995, p. 24.

86 Anonymous: Flüchtlinge lebten 130 Tage im Wald. In: *BILD*, 20.11.1995, p. 1.

87 Anonymous: „Komplizen der Barbarei". In: *Spiegel*, 24.07.1995, p. 114.

The Domestic Debate: German Soldiers Deployed to the Balkans?

One stipulation pledged by the agreement was the deployment of troops to Bosnia to ensure that the various elements of the peace treaty would be implemented and the cease-fire adhered to. The Implementation Force (IFOR), as it was known, was formed by NATO and Russia, comprised 60,000 troops and was legitimised through a UN-mandate.[88] "Its main task was to guarantee the end of hostilities and separate the armed forces […]"[89] by controlling a four-kilometre wide demilitarised zone in Bosnia.[90] With the previously feeble attempts of international peacekeeping in mind, this peace force "[…] had very robust rules of engagement […]", as British General Richard Dannatt recalls in his autobiography.[91] Consequently the deployed troops were more likely to engage in combat than their predecessors, the UN-troops, which only had a peace-keeping mandate. As a partner in this alliance, Germany was faced with the difficult and controversial dilemma whether to send troops to Bosnia, as this would be a clear departure from post-war foreign policy marked by non-intervention. This controversy reignited the domestic debate already analysed in the previous chapter.[92]

As all publications except *JF* and *Konkret* reported, Chancellor Kohl and his cabinet proposed to contribute approximately 4,000 *Bundeswehr*-soldiers to IFOR after the agreement had been signed.[93] The majority of these soldiers were to be stationed in Split, Croatia rather than Bosnia and would primarily be responsible for transportation and logistics.[94] The troop-deployment was ratified by the *Bundestag* with a large political majority, as various newspapers

88 JG: Weihnachten gehört Papi Bosnien. In: *taz*, 29.11.1995, p. 1.

89 NATO: Peace Support Operations in Bosnia and Herzegovina. http://www.nato.int/cps/en/natolive/topics_52122.htm (accessed 30.08.2014).

90 Toal / Dahlman: *Bosnia Remade*, p. 159.

91 Dannatt: *Leading from the Front*, p. 149.

92 Jonathan Bach produced a useful discourse analysis of the two German *Bundestag* debates: Bach: *Between Sovereignty and Integration*, pp. 147–175.

93 WeNa: Bosnien-Einsatz beschlossen. In: *Welt*, 29.11.1995, p. 1; dpa: Rühe verabschiedet Soldaten vor Einsatz. In: *FAZ*, 06.12.1995, p. 7; ap/afp: Rühe schließt Aufstockung aus. In: *FR*, 30.11.1995, p. 1; Andreas Zumach: „Frieden in Bosnien voll entbrannt". In: *taz*, 23.11.1995, p. 1; Anonymous: Weites Herz. In: *Spiegel*, 27.11.1995, p. 26; Anonymous: Bosnien-Einsatz: Im Bundestag alles klar. In: *BILD*, 07.12.1995, p. 1; also discussed in Schwab-Trapp: *Kriegsdiskurse*, p. 211.

94 Karl Feldmeyer: Tagesordnung bleibt geheim. In: *FAZ*, 14.11.1995, p. 4; Rüdiger Moniac: Nato-Friedenstruppe rüstet sich für Bonn. In: *Welt*, 23.11.1995, p. 6; Andreas Zumach: Die Friedenstruppen der Nato. In: *taz*, 07.12.1995, p. 9; Anonymous: Weites Herz. In: *Spiegel*, 27.11.1995, p. 26; Einar Koch: Bosnien: Bundeswehr probt Winterkrieg. In: *BILD*, 23.11.1995, p. 2.

reported.[95] Before delving deeper into this subject matter, it is important to highlight one particular controversy covered in all daily newspapers. In early December 1995, General Klaus Naumann, the *Bundeswehr's* Inspector General, referred to the engagement of German troops in the Balkans as a 'combat mission' in a television interview. This term was rapidly picked up by various newspapers, causing considerable controversy in political circles.[96] The German Minister of Defence, Volker Rühe, quickly denied the accurateness of the term, stating that Naumann had no authority to make such an assessment and that German soldiers would not be part of a 'combat mission'. Various daily papers elaborated that this distinction was important because members of the opposition had declared their support for the deployment of German troops, but only under the condition that it was not a 'combat mission'.[97] However, the newspapers did not comment on this controversy beyond reporting on the political debate about it. Indeed, while the print media mentioned on the nuances of this debate, the articles did not include judgment.

The politicians' panic-stricken reaction to the misplaced use of a single term underlines how uneasy the German politicians were about the prospect of deploying troops into active combat. While this reluctance almost certainly resulted from Germany's National-Socialist past and the hitherto preferred civilian or diplomatic foreign policy neither the press nor politicians explicitly stated this. Chancellor Kohl's speech given in the *Bundestag* on 6 December 1995 about the possible deployment emphasised this. In it, Kohl barely mentioned Germany's past. Only in one side-note Kohl remarked that "in many families the memories of the horrible, bitter […] Second World War are still

95 Martin Lambeck: Breiter Konsens bestimmte Bosnien-Debatte. In: *Welt*, 07.12.1995, p. 2; Sto.: Der Bundestag mit großer Mehrheit für die Entsendung der Bundeswehr-Soldaten nach Bosnien. In: *FAZ*, 07.12.1995, p. 1; dpa/rtr: Bundeswehr steht zum Abmarsch bereit. In: *FR*, 06.12.1995, p. 4; Anonymous: Bosnien-Einsatz: Im Bundestag alles klar. In: *BILD*, 07.12.1995, p. 1.

96 Knut Pries: EU bittet USA für Bosnien zur Kasse. In: *FR*, 05.12.1995, p. 1; dpa/Reuter: Erstes Kontingent der Friedenstruppen in Bosnien eingetroffen. In: *FAZ*, 05.12.1995, p. 1; Anonymous: Die Bosnien-Generäle – der erste muss schon gehen. In: *BILD*, 05.12.1995, p. 2.

97 For example: Armin Fuhrer: Grüne für Friedenstruppe, gegen Kampfeinsätze. In: *Welt*, 04.12.1995, p. 1; Martin Lambeck: Breiter Konsens bestimmte Bosnien-Debatte. In: *Welt*, 07.12.1995, p. 2; Helmut Lölhöffel: SPD-Spitze stimmt Bosnien-Einsatz zu. In: *FR*, 14.11.1995, p. 4; Knut Pries: EU bittet USA für Bosnien zur Kasse. In: *FR*, 05.12.1995, p. 1; ban: Im SPD-Streit über Bundeswehreinsätze in Bosnien setzt sich Lafontaine durch. In: *FAZ*, 18.11.1995, p. 1; dpa: Rühe verabschiedet Soldaten vor Einsatz. In: *FAZ*, 06.12.1995, p. 7; JG: Weihnachten gehört Papi Bosnien. In: *taz*, 29.11.1995, p. 1; Hans Monath: Fischer grollt im Hintergrund. In: *taz*, 01.12.1995, p. 4.

alive."[98] However his most central argument was the concept of '*Bündnissolidarität*', or alliance-solidarity, which he argued compelled German troop deployment. Consequently he emphasised that "[…] we cannot refuse a peace mission […] which is expected by all of our friends and partners."[99] Significantly, Kohl spoke of a 'peace mission', calling attention to the peace treaty which had been agreed upon several days earlier and which laid the foundation for the deployment of the IFOR-troops. Therefore the utilisation of this term was not an embellishment by Kohl. Most significantly the Chancellor seemed to consciously circumvent the moral dimension of the debate and instead emphasised the political realities of being a member of NATO.

However, while Kohl was exceedingly prudent in weighing the words used to describe the prospective mission, *BILD* was much more blatant. The tabloid's avid support for the deployment of German soldiers was manifested in the 'our boys' sentiment created in various articles. Publishing statements such as "a clear majority [in the *Bundestag*] for *our* soldiers!"[100] and "Take good care of yourselves!"[101], the tabloid constructed a sense of communal support for the troops which is highly unusual for German discourse about soldiers and could not be found in any other publication. Moreover, *BILD* underlined its message with a picture printed on the first page, arguably awakening patriotic sentiments. In it, a long line of uniformed German soldiers can be seen, standing to attention. The headline read: "*Deutsche Soldaten heute nach Bosnien: Passt gut auf euch auf!*", or "German soldiers today to Bosnia: Take care of yourselves!"[102] However, *BILD* was the only publication to express such a strong opinion in favour of the troop deployment. Most publications merely reported that initially there had been political opposition to the cabinet's proposition, but that eventually a broad political consensus had been reached in its favour.[103] No articles, editorials or cartoons entailed any form

98 *Deutscher Bundestag*, Plenarprotokoll 13/76, Stenographischer Bericht, 76. Sitzung, 06.12.1995, p. 6632.

99 Ibid.

100 Anonymous: Bosnien-Einsatz: Im Bundestag alles klar. In: *BILD*, 07.12.1995, p. 1. Emphasis added by author.

101 Anonymous: Deutsche Soldaten heute nach Bosnien. In: *BILD*, 06.12.1995, p. 1.

102 Image published in *BILD*, 06.12.1995, p. 1.

103 Martin Lambeck: Breiter Konsens bestimmte Bosnien-Debatte. In: *Welt*, 07.12.1995, p. 2; Sto.: Für „Abrüstung" der Bosnien-Debatte. In: *FAZ*, 30.11.1995, p. 2; Sto.: Auch die SPD hat nichts gegen den Einsatz der Bundeswehr in Bosnien. In: *FAZ*, 01.12.1995, p. 1; Sto.: Der Bundestag mit großer Mehrheit für die Entsendung der Bundeswehr-Soldaten nach Bosnien. In: *FAZ*, 07.12.1995, p. 1; rei/afp/dpa: Bonn schickt 4000 Soldaten. In: *FR*, 29.11.1995, p. 1; dpa/rtr: Bundeswehr steht zum Abmarsch bereit. In: *FR*, 06.12.1995, p. 4; Anonymous: „Tränen auf allen Seiten". In: *Spiegel*, 11.12.1995, pp. 36–37.

of opinion. The only other clear manifestation of opinion was in opposition, which was published by *taz*- and *JF*-editorials.

Starting with the latter, a *JF*-editorial argued that the deployment of the IFOR-troops was not an example of simple *Realpolitik*, but rather morally justified politics. This, Robert Hepp continued, was always based on the interpretation of the party with the stronger battalion, as "us Germans had figured out since Nürnberg [...]"[104] The author implied that the Nürnberg trials that started in 1946 with the aim to bring the leaders of the Third Reich to justice, were not morally justified, but rather the result of the winners of the Second World War imposing their ethical standards. This not only underlines *JF's* far-right leaning, but equally emphasises the different interpretations and perspectives found in the press' coverage of the on-going events. Ekkehart Krippendorff, a Professor at Berlin's Freie Universität, articulated his critical view in a *taz*-editorial, stating that the "militarily organised political career criminals" ("*militärisch organisierte Polit-Berufsverbrecher*") only followed one goal, namely to support "[...] legal and semi-legal arms manufacturers [...]" in their mercantile endeavours by initiating this international peace force.[105] It is uncertain who the author referred to with his polemical term "political career criminal" – German politicians specifically or Western statesmen in general. Nonetheless, the article's title "Intervene! *Civilian* Europe is now called upon in Bosnia" underlined the author's rejection of a military deployment.[106] However, Krippendorff did not outline what specifically civilian measures should be taken in addition to the recently negotiated peace treaty.

Another issue which neither Krippendorff nor any other articles considered here mentioned was that the soldiers to be deployed would be part of a peace force. With the initialling of the Dayton Accords on 23 November 1995, the war in Bosnia had ended and the IFOR-troops would not be deployed into active combat. While fighting could not be precluded completely, the matter at hand was not whether German soldiers should engage in active combat, as they would in the Kosovo War (1999). Rather they would contribute to a peace-force, a mission sanctioned by a UN-mandate, as they had numerous times before, for example in Kenya (1991), Somalia (1993–94) or Ruanda

104 Robert Hepp: Abkehr vom Pazifismus. In: *JF*, 08.12.1995, p. 2.

105 Ekkehart Krippendorff: Intervenieren! Das zivile Europa ist jetzt in Bosnien gefordert. In: *taz*, 30.11.1995, p. 10.

106 Emphasis added by author.

(1994).[107] Significantly, none of the publications analysed here picked up on these points.

The Green Party and the 'Genocide Clause'

While eventually a wide-ranging political consensus supported the German troop deployment, the opposition parties – SPD and Bündnis 90/Die Grünen (the Green Party) – launched into internal discussions regarding their position on this matter. Both convened in a party convention, which was covered extensively by the German press. The SPD convention, which took place on 14–17 November 1995, was reported on, but did not cause much sensation. The different factions within the party eventually found a consensus and agreed to support the decision to deploy German troops as long as this would not be a 'combat mission.'[108] Hans Monath commented in a *taz*-editorial that the speed at which a consensus was found in the SPD indicated that there was no profound debate on the subject matter, which on the contrary was the case in the Green Party.[109]

The Green Party convention (1–3 December 1995) was significantly more controversial in nature and was thus covered in much more detail. As discussed in the previous chapter, the Green Party in Germany had traditionally been a pacifist party since its foundation. However, by 1995, it was strongly divided between the '*Fundis*', who wanted the party line to stay true to its fundamental ideology of pacifism and wanted to vote against the deployment, and the '*Realos*', who aimed for a more 'realistic' integration in politics and supported the deployment. Joschka Fischer, who would become Germany's Foreign Minister in 1998, was the primary representative of the latter faction. As discussed in the previous chapter, Fischer had publicly vocalised his support for Germany contributing in international interventions in a letter to his party.[110] As this debate touched the very core of the Green Party, numerous

107 Bundeswehr: Friedensschaffende Einsätze. http://www.einsatz.bundeswehr.de/portal/a/einsatzbw/!ut/p/c4/04_SB8K8xLLM9MSSzPy8xBz9CP3I5EyrpHK9pPK-U1PjUzLzixJIqIDcxKT21ODkjJ7-4ODUPKpFaUpWql1aUmZqC4OsXZDsqAgBQaGH7 (accessed 30.08.2014).

108 ban.: Im SPD-Streit über Bundeswehreinsätze in Bosnien setzt sich Lafontaine durch. In: *FAZ*, 18.11.1995, p. 1; Sto.: Auch die SPD hat nichts gegen den Einsatz der Bundeswehr in Bosnien. In: *FAZ*, 01.12.1995, p. 1; Helmut Lölhöffel: SPD-Spitze stimmt Bosnien-Einsatz zu. In: *FR*, 14.11.1995, p. 4; Anonymous: Weites Herz. In: *Spiegel*, 27.11.1995, p. 26; Anonymous: Bundestag für Bosnien-Einsatz. In: *BILD*, 01.12.1995, p. 2.

109 Hans Monath: Zurück zur Sache! In: *taz*, 28.11.1995, p. 1.

110 See chapter 4, fn. 92–96.

articles spoke of a '*Zerreißprobe*', a crucial test; and with political ideology at the heart of this discussion, many of the themes were emotive and readily picked up by the media. The most prevalent themes were the concept of intervening militarily to stop 'genocide,' and what role Germany's historical past played in this respect.

The dilemma of using force to stop 'genocide' versus upholding Germany's post-war foreign policy that shied away from military interventions resonated heavily in the Greens' debate and was fully reflected in the press coverage. The main arguments which were relayed and emphasised in the newspapers were the following: Joschka Fischer and his supporters ('*Realos*') argued that genocide demanded military force to stop it, while Ludger Volmer's '*Fundi*' faction argued that economic sanctions should be the most extreme measures the international community should implement.[111] This faction further argued that Srebrenica and Bosnia in general was being (mis)used as a reason to 'militarise German foreign policy' as *FAZ*, *FR* and *Spiegel* reported.[112] Fischer in turn criticised his party colleagues for being 'isolationist' and demanded that a 'genocide clause' be introduced into German foreign policy. As various articles reported, Fischer frequently referred to the Srebrenica Massacre as an example in which the international community should have intervened militarily.[113] Judging that '"in Bosnia, pacifism has failed,"' Fischer called for a new attitude in Germany's foreign policy.[114] Simultaneously, Fischer frequently referred to the Third Reich and the Holocaust, arguing that Germany's past compelled them now to intervene in Bosnia, and to stop genocide in the future. In doing so, Fischer initiated a debate on what impact Germany's past should have on its perceptions of Bosnia.

111 Armin Fuhrer: Grüne für Friedenstruppe, gegen Kampfeinsätze. In: *Welt*, 04.12.1995, p. 1.

112 Dt.: Was tun beim Völkermord? In: *FAZ*, 20.11.1995, p. 4; Peter Ziller: Streit um Krieg und Frieden. In: *FR*, 09.11.1995, p. 4; Edgar Auth: Vorschläge für eine Friedenspraxis nach dem Krieg in Ex-Jugoslawien. In: *FR*, 01.12.1995, p. 7; Paul Lersch: „Den Menschen helfen". In: *Spiegel*, 27.11.1995, pp. 41–47; Anonymous: „Tränen auf allen Seiten". In: *Spiegel*, 11.12.1995, pp. 36–37.

113 gue.: Fischer warnt seine Partei vor Isolationismus. In: *Welt*, 28.11.1995, p. 1; Karl-Ludwig Günsche: Grüne kämpfen um das Prinzip der Gewaltfreiheit. In: *Welt*, 29.11.1995, p. 2; AP: Grüne streiten über Bosnien-Einsatz. In: *FAZ*, 27.11.1995, p. 2; AP: Grüne streiten über Bosnien-Einsatz. In: *FAZ*, 28.11.1995, p. 2; Charima Reinhardt / Peter Ziller: Fischer wirft Linken Opportunismus vor. In: *FR*, 28.11.1995, p. 1; Hans Monath: Zwischen Intervention und Embargo. In: *taz*, 07.11.1995, p. 4; Monath: Joschka Fischer ist der wahre Internationalist. In: *taz*, 28.11.1995, p. 1; Monath: „Klare Konfliktlinien vor dem Grünen-Parteitag". In: *taz*, 30.11.1995, p. 4.

114 Armin Fuhrer: Grüne für Friedenstruppe, gegen Kampfeinsätze. In: *Welt*, 04.12.1995, p. 1.

The publications analysed here expressed clear opinions on the Green debate and can be categorised by their political affiliations. While the conservative newspapers agreed with Fischer and drew heavily on Germany's past to justify a possible military mission, the left-leaning publications were very reluctant to do so, arguing that it would qualify and perhaps minimise the unique horrors of the Holocaust. However it must be noted that while the left-leaning publications rejected the equivalence of the Holocaust to intervening in Bosnia, they did not at any point disagree with the deployment itself. *JF*, although far-right in its political affiliation agreed with the left-leaning publications, as it generally rejected Germany's participation in multi-national endeavours.

Even though *Welt* and *FAZ* speculated whether Fischer was merely engaged in a political game of coalition-politics, both, along with *BILD*, supported the interpretation that the Third Reich and Holocaust created an obligation to stop genocide in the future and to deploy troops to Bosnia. Various *FAZ*-articles stated that the situation in Bosnia required Germany to consider the 'lessons from its past' and intervene in Bosnia in the name of the 'genocide clause'.[115] A *Welt*-editorial reminded its readers that Europe had failed miserably in stopping the violence in the Balkans when it had a chance in the early 1990s. Rather, it needed America to get involved. "And now the Germans of all people […] are supposed to say 'without me'?", the author asked sceptically. Such a foreign policy would only create mistrust and incomprehension amongst Germany's neighbours, Peter Phillips' editorial argued.[116] *BILD's* articles reminded its readers in its usual declamatory manner that "we [the Germans] know what genocide is" and that Germany had to support the UN's attempts to stop the Bosnian 'genocide.'[117] Michael Wolfssohn, a Professor at the Freie Universität in Berlin, cautioned in a further *BILD*-article that "our rejection of the genocide back then [Third Reich] would not be credible if we allowed genocide to continue to unfold today."[118]

While all three conservative newspapers readily used references to the Holocaust to justify German troop deployment to Bosnia, only one single editorial (in *Welt*) explored if the term 'genocide' was even applicable to the Bosnian case. Here Herbert Kremp argued that "in spite of all the atrocities, genocide in its exact definition cannot be discerned in Bosnia," as the Bosnian

115 AP: Grüne streiten über Bosnien-Einsatz. In: *FAZ*, 28.11.1995, p. 2; G. H.: Gemeinsame Führung. In: *FAZ*, 07.12.1995, p. 1.

116 Peter Phillips: Vernunft und Augenmaß. In: *Welt*, 29.11.1995, p. 1.

117 Peter Bönisch: Bosnien-Einsatz: Eine Verpflichtung. In: *BILD*, 29.11.1995, p. 2.

118 Michael Wolffssohn: Ein Wort zu unseren Soldaten in Bosnien. In: *BILD*, 12.12.1995, p. 2.

Serbs did not "[…] systematically exterminate the Muslims, as for example had happened to the Armenians or Jews […]". The author further accused Fischer's faction of the Green Party of manipulating this term to their advantage.[119] Unfortunately, this crucial consideration of whether 'genocide' was the correct term did not find any further resonance in other newspapers or in the political discourse. However, while the application of the term to the entire Bosnian War must be questioned, Kremp's article disregarded that Srebrenica had been officially labelled genocide and indeed the ICTY had indicted Karadžić and Mladić on 14 November 1995 for perpetrating genocide in Srebrenica.[120] While the *Welt*-article disregarded this important aspect, the author's questions are important and underline how confused and confusing the coverage of this matter was. All three conservative papers stated that Germany should deploy soldiers to Bosnia and that Germany's past obliged the country to stop 'genocide.' However, this argumentation merged two wholly different issues. The German soldiers' mission in Bosnia was not to stop 'genocide', but to implement a previously signed peace treaty. While the Srebrenica Massacre a few months earlier may have warranted such a debate, at this point a cease-fire existed and 'genocide' was no longer being perpetrated, rendering this discussion unnecessary.

The missing differentiation of these two matters in the conservative coverage indicates two tendencies. Firstly, how omnipresent the trauma of Srebrenica remained in the analysis of Bosnia. The shock of what had unfolded in the enclave, which was labelled 'genocide' by the ICTY, and that the international community had not intervened spilled over into this debate on peace implementation in Bosnia. This creates a strong sense of needing to reconcile previous failures. Secondly, the merging of these two issues shows that the German past and the interpretation that it created a responsibility to act remained a strong influence in the conservative press' coverage of Bosnia. Indeed, one could argue that it was not possible to entertain the thought of German military involvement without linking it to a larger moral debate.

In spite of their support for Fischer's arguments, various editorials in *Welt* and *FAZ*, as well as a *Konkret*-article explained Fischer's shift in policy with the politician's long-term goal to make the Green Party a viable candidate to form a coalition-government with the centre-left SPD in the 1998 elections.[121] The

119 Herbert Kremp: Primat der Außenpolitik: eine unrühmlich verendete Idee. In: *Welt*, 06.12.1995, p. 4.

120 See chapter 4, fn. 1.

121 Karl-Ludwig Günsche: Grüne kämpfen um das Prinzip der Gewaltfreiheit. In: *Welt*,

Konkret-article linked Fischer's policy specifically to his intention of becoming foreign minister.[122] This notion, which had also been addressed in a *Spiegel*-interview with Fischer a few months earlier,[123] was never explored in more detail – the speculative nature of such arguments presumably preventing a more in-depth discussion. Understandably, the journalists did not want to risk their professional reputation by publishing too far-reaching conjecture without supporting facts. Moreover, the scope of a newspaper article or editorial was perhaps too restrictive to elaborate on the above points.

Contrary to the conservative press, the left-leaning publications *taz* and *Spiegel* disagreed with linking Germany's past to the debate about troop deployment. Sibylle Toennis' *taz*-editorial focused on Fischer and criticised his argumentation because it drew on Germany's past. She disapproved of the fact that "[…] Fischer refers to his biography, which also belongs to all of us" when justifying his stance. "He had parents who had tolerated genocide in their own country. The mission in Bosnia is supposed to compensate for Auschwitz."[124] By bluntly juxtaposing Bosnia and Auschwitz, the author aimed to underline the absurdity of attempting to reconcile one atrocity by intervening in another country. A further *taz*-article, published on 27 November by Paul Parin, was dedicated exclusively to the question of whether Bosnia and the Holocaust could and should be compared. Entitled "A comparison is a comparison is a comparison", Parin criticised the perception that Bosnia "[…] is a posthumous victory for Hitler." Indeed, he postulated that Bosnia and the Holocaust are as profoundly different "[…] as the Holocaust is from the atomic annihilation of Hiroshima and Nagasaki […]"[125] This criticism of using 'the history argument' to justify military engagement in Bosnia indicates a prevailing sense in *taz* that the horrors of the Holocaust and Third Reich should not be diminished through comparisons.
A *Spiegel*-article also drew on Germany's National-Socialist past to argue against a German troop-deployment, though its argument did not focus on the Holocaust as *taz's* articles had. It stated that German soldiers should under no circumstances be stationed on Bosnian territory, because *Wehrmacht*-soldiers

29.11.1995, p. 2; fy: Rot-Grün auf der Probe. In: *FAZ*, 29.11.1995, p. 1; Sto.: Eine starke Minderheit der Grünen einverstanden mit einem Bosnien-Einsatz der Bundeswehr. In: *FAZ*, 04.12.1995, p. 1; Pascal Beucker: Pazifist der Reserve. In: *Konkret*, November 1995, p. 12.

122 Pascal Beucker: Pazifist der Reserve. In: *Konkret*, November 1995, p. 12.

123 See chapter 4, fn. 109.

124 Sibylle Toennies: Viel Pazifisimus bleibt nicht übrig. In: *taz*, 05.12.1995, p. 10.

125 Paul Parin: Ein Vergleich ist ein Vergleich ist ein Vergleich. In: *taz*, 27.11.1995, p. 12.

had been there 'only recently'.[126] The distinct and presumably conscious use of the term 'recent' to describe events that occurred 50 years earlier underlines the publications' endeavour to use the 'history argument' to reject future deployments. Though *FR's* articles did not specifically comment on 'the history argument', one editorial harshly criticised Foreign Minister Kinkel's claim that Germany's military engagement in Bosnia was 'morally justified'. Sarcastically entitled 'Leaseholder of Morality', it questioned why Kinkel had to introduce the 'heavy-weight concept' of ethics and why he painted a black and white image rather than admitting that this debate was nuanced by many shades of grey.[127] With this criticism, the editorial rightfully drew attention to the problematic fusion of politics and morality. Interestingly however, this criticism was not applied to the debate within the Green Party, which equally merged the two concepts.

Amidst the depths of the heated discussion of linking the German past to its contemporary foreign policy, we must return to the crux of the Green Party's debate: namely whether a 'genocide clause' should be included in German foreign policy. Considering the subject-matter from afar, this debate appears largely unnecessary. Having ratified the 1948 UN-Genocide Convention in 1954, Germany had already bound itself by international law to stop genocide when it occurred anywhere in the world.[128] Consequently the debate initiated by Fischer and his '*Realos*' appears redundant. Moreover, it is important to remark that the depth of coverage regarding 'the Green debate' was not congruent with its political importance. The *Bundestag,* which according to German law needed a 50% vote to deploy the soldiers, had the following compilation at the time:[129]

CDU/CSU	294 seats
FDP	47 seats

SPD	252 seats
Green Party	49 seats
PDS	30 seats

126 Anonymous: Weites Herz. In: *Spiegel*, 27.11.1995, p. 26.

127 AH: „Pächter der Moral". In: *FR*, 01.12.1995, p. 3.

128 United Nations: Convention on the Prevention and Punishment of the Crime of Genocide, Article VIII, p. 3.

129 N/A: Wahl zum 13. Deutschen Bundestag am 16. Oktober 1994. http://www.bundeswahlleiter.de/de/bundestagswahlen/frühere_bundestagswahlen/btw1994.html (accessed 12.12.2014).

Accordingly, the CDU/FDP coalition claimed more than 50% of the 672 seats. Thus the government would have had enough votes, especially with SPD's support, irrespective of the Green Party's stance. This in turn rendered the internal party debate interesting, but not crucial to the political decision. However, considering the highly contentious nature of the troop deployment, it was of course in the government's interest to ensure as much cross-party support as possible, especially to avoid waves of protest that could be initiated by the Green Party and find popular support. Nonetheless this political constellation introduces the question why the subject-matter was covered so extensively. Though the discussion only occurred within the Green Party, it was indeed representative of a larger debate about Germany's collective conscience. In a persistent effort to grapple with the past, Germany had to clarify its position on military interventions. This in turn underlines that while the secondary literature claimed that Germany's collective memory had diluted and 'internationalised' since the early 1990s, the country's past was still very present in 1995 and significantly shaped the discourse on Bosnia.

This debate regarding a 'genocide clause', linked with the deployment of German soldiers shows how many layers of discourse influenced the German print media's coverage of the Dayton Agreement in November and December 1995. With the signing of the peace treaty, the Bosnian War was officially terminated – after nearly four years. However, this peace treaty would throw a longer shadow than many external observers initially presumed and in some ways led directly to the renewed violence in Kosovo.

Chapter 6
March–June 1998: Renewed Violence – The Kosovo Conflict

After the Dayton Agreement was signed in December 1995, international attention in the Balkans turned to the implementation of the peace treaty and rebuilding the war-torn Bosnia and Croatia. However, by February 1996 – only two months after Dayton – violent conflict returned to the region, this time in Kosovo, a southern province of Serbia. This was manifested by the bombing of a Serbian refugee camp in the Krajina region, which was the first 'declared action' of the Kosovo Liberation Army (KLA).[1] Their proclaimed goal was to use violent means to attain Kosovo's independence from Serbia. The quest for sovereignty resulted from years of oppression and mal-treatment by the Serbian minority of the Kosovo-Albanians who made up 90% of Kosovo's population.[2]

This chapter will analyse the German press coverage of the violence in Drenica and other parts of Kosovo. By studying the four-month timeframe considered in this chapter – 1 March to 30 June 1998 – the way in which primary sources portrayed the causes of the Kosovo conflict as well as the Serbian forces and the KLA will be considered. Moreover, the historical comparisons made by the press to the Bosnian War and World War Two will be analysed. Before proceeding, it must be mentioned that *AJW* will not be included in this chapter. The newspaper published by the Central Council of Jews in Germany did not feature a single article on Kosovo in this four-month

1 Matthew Bennett: The Kosovo Liberation Army. In: Matthew Bennett / Paul Latawski (eds): *Exile Armies*. London: Routledge 2005, pp. 159–168, here p. 162.

2 Amnesty International: *Kosovo: The Evidence*, p. 8.

period. While *AJW's* interest in the Balkans had already been sparse during the Bosnian War, there had been occasional articles using Sarajevo's Jewish Community as an entry-point to the topic. However, since Kosovo did not have a significant Jewish community, there was no interest in Kosovo as the conflict was developing. Moreover, by 1998, *AJW* had become a bi-weekly publication (as opposed to weekly until 1995). Falling circulation numbers and scarce finances could have been another reason for the reduced reporting of international affairs. However, the access to news agency reports and a previous limited interest in the Bosnian War rather suggest a continued disinterest in the Balkans. The other two publications with a targeted readership, *JF* and *Konkret*, did not report much on the conflict as it was developing. *JF* published various articles, though these are not relevant until the latter part of this chapter; *Konkret* published only one article about Kosovo in this timeframe, which will be discussed where relevant. However, all remaining publications reported on the violence with heightened interest.

Causes of the Kosovo Conflict in the German Media

With the advent of a further Balkan conflict within the same decade, the reasons drawn on by the German print media to explain the renewed violence will be considered first. The publications considered here contextualised the violence by drawing on the 1389 battle and on Milošević's 1989 revocation of Kosovo's autonomy. Before delving into the historical context given by the German publications, *BILD* must be considered separately, as there was only one instance where the tabloid explored the causes of the conflict. Almost as a side-note the single tabloid-article explained: "[…] Kosovo is the legendary Field of the Blackbirds, where the Turks conquered the Serbs and then the Hungarians."[3] This allusion to the 1389 Battle of Kosovo was not expanded upon, nor was the reader offered an explanation why it would still be relevant in the 1990s. The sparse mention of historical context is congruent with the tabloid's general coverage of international affairs. While the conflict itself was reported, the causes of the violence were not.
Four other publications, *FAZ*, *FR*, *taz* and *Spiegel* drew on the historic battle more deeply, convincingly presenting it as a fundamental reason for Serbia's determination to refuse Kosovo's autonomy, let alone independence.[4] For example, a *FAZ*-article stated that

3 B. Kalnoky / W. Kramer: Kosovo – droht ein neues Bosnien? In: *BILD*, 07.03.1998, p. 2.
4 Anonymous: Der Fluch der eigenen Geschichte. In: *taz*, 06.03.1998, p. 3; Erich Rathfelder:

> this battle offer[ed] the historical background to understand the crisis and the manner in which Serbia…[was] clinging on to Kosovo. No Serbian politician would ever give up Kosovo voluntarily.[5]

Some *FR*-articles labelled Kosovo as the 'symbol of eternal Serbdom' and the 'historic heartland' of the Serbian nation.[6] Explaining that "history is more alive in the Balkans than anywhere else […]", these *FR*-articles underlined the prevailing importance of the 1389 battle to Serbia's national self-perception.[7]

In addition to giving this historical context, three publications, *Spiegel*, *FR* and *taz* introduced a further facet, stating that the 1389-milestone would not be so relevant in the present day if Slobodan Milošević had not manipulated this 600-year-old battle to fuel Serbian nationalism and incite violence.[8] As an anonymous *Spiegel*-article stated, "until the present day, this territory […was] the grail of Serbian nationalism […] which Milošević wanted to exploit to maintain his power."[9] With this important slant to the debate on the causes of the conflict, the three left-leaning papers portrayed Milošević to be stirring ancient hatreds and evoking violent nationalism and thus held him responsible for the renewed violence. Although the notion of long-standing antagonism between Kosovo-Albanians and Serbs was repeatedly alluded to, significantly, the concept of 'ancient hatreds' was never used explicitly. This is surprising considering how frequently it had been drawn on in the coverage of the Bosnian War in the early 1990s[10] and indicates a clear development in the way in which the Balkan violence was explained.

The increased focus on Milošević found in the press' historical background can be seen as a continuation of the publications' previous coverage during

Die Dynamik des Krieges. In: *taz*, 27.04.1998, p. 12; Anonymous: Front im Süden. In: *Spiegel*, 16.03.1998, p. 176; Renate Flottau: Krieg der Waldmenschen. In: *Spiegel*, 08.06.1998, p. 150; Wolfgang Günter Lerch: „Wir werden sie zu Serben machen". In: *FAZ*, 07.03.1998, p. 12; Hans-Georg Ehrhart / Matthias Z. Karadi: Wann brennt der Balkan? Plädoyer fuer eine komplexe Präventionspolitik im Kosovo-Konflikt. In: *FR*, 25.03.1998, p. 9; Rolf Paasch: Warum das Amselfeld anders ist. In: *FR*, 10.06.1998, p. 3.

5 Wolfgang Günter Lerch: „Wir werden sie zu Serben machen". In: *FAZ*, 07.03.1998, p. 12.

6 Hans-Georg Ehrhart / Matthias Z. Karadi: Wann brennt der Balkan? Plädoyer für eine komplexe Präventionspolitik im Kosovo-Konflikt. In: *FR*, 25.03.1998, p. 9; Rolf Paasch: Warum das Amselfeld anders ist. In: *FR*, 10.06.1998, p. 3.

7 Rolf Paasch: Warum das Amselfeld anders ist. In: *FR*, 10.06.1998, p. 3.

8 Roman Arens: In Kosovo wie in Bosnien. In: *FR*, 10.03.1998, p. 3; Erich Rathfelder: Serben stimmen über Kosovo ab. In: *taz*, 23.04.1998, p. 10.

9 Anonymous: Jeder gegen jeden. In: *Spiegel*, 09.03.1998, p. 149.

10 See pp. 49–52.

which the Serbian leader had increasingly become the press' focal point to explain the wars. Significantly, almost all German publications considered here intertwined Milošević and his nationalist policies with a second historical milestone, namely the 1989 revocation of Kosovo's autonomy. *Welt*, *FAZ*, *FR*, *Spiegel* and *taz* all mentioned this policy very frequently, implicitly deeming it the most important cause of the conflict.[11] However, these references were very repetitive and also distinctly superficial. For example, one *Welt*-article reported that "the EU demand[ed] that Milošević would re-introduce Kosovo's autonomy, which had been revoked in 1989."[12] Almost all references were of this nature and significantly failed to explain what the effects of this revocation of autonomy were or why this could cause a violent conflict ten years later. Only one *Spiegel*-article elaborated that a parallel state had evolved under the auspices of Ibrahim Rugova after Kosovo's autonomy had been revoked.

> The Albanians boycotted the Serbian institutions in Kosovo, founded their own hospitals, schools and even a university; the classes took place in private apartments [...] In this manner they compensated for the loss of their autonomy, which had been granted by Tito in 1974 and had been revoked by Milošević in 1989.[13]

The article went on to explain that the parallel state constructed after 1989 offered the Kosovo-Albanians a sense of self-government which ten years later they wanted to actualise. These details helped the reader understand what the direct effects of the revoked autonomy were and why they could have played a key role in perpetuating violence.

11 AFP/rtr: Belgrad lässt Panzer im Kosovo auffahren. In: *Welt*, 02.03.1998, p. 6; Boris Kalnoky: USA stellen sich vor Kosovo-Albaner. In: *Welt*, 04.03.1998, p. 7; Katja Ridderbusch: Nur gegen Kompromisse sind sich alle einig. In: *Welt*, 07.03.1998, p. 6; rtr: Bonn und Washington einig. In: *Welt*, 18.04.1998, p. 2; DW: Neue Sanktionen gegen Belgrad. In: *Welt*, 30.04.1998, p. 6; Matthias Rüb: Auf dem Amselfeld eskaliert die Gewalt. In: *FAZ*, 03.03.1998, p. 10; Wolfgang Günter Lerch: „Wir werden sie zu Serben machen". In: *FAZ*, 07.03.1998, p. 12; afp/rtr: Tote bei Kämpfen im Kosovo. In: *FR*, 02.03.1998, p. 2; Gerd Hoehler: Manche erträumen sich Groß-Albanien. In: *FR*, 07.03.1998, p. 5; Hans-Georg Ehrhart / Matthias Z. Karadi: Wann brennt der Balkan? Plädoyer für eine komplexe Präventionspolitik im Kosovo-Konflikt. In: *FR*, 25.03.1998, p. 9; Anonymous: „Kollektiver Selbstmord". In: *Spiegel*, 09.03.1998, p. 148; Renate Flottau: „Sie sollen Krieg haben". In: *Spiegel*, 04.05.1998, p. 150; Gregor Meyer: Für die Freiheit ist jedes Opfer recht. In: *taz*, 05.03.1998, p. 11; Erich Rathfelder: Milosevic zieht ein Referendum aus seiner Trickkiste. In: *taz*, 04./05.04.1998, p. 11; Erich Rathfelder: Die militärische Option. In: *taz*, 25./26.04.1998, p. 12; Erich Rathfelder: Die Dynamik des Krieges. In: *taz*, 27.04.1998, p. 12; Andreas Zumach: Das Dilemma der Nato im Kosovo. In: *taz*, 13./14.06.1998, p. 10.

12 AP/rtr: EU fordert Autonomie für Kosovo. In: *Welt*, 05.03.1998, p. 6.

13 Anonymous: Front im Süden. In: *Spiegel*, 16.03.1998, p. 177.

As this section has demonstrated, the violence in Kosovo immediately sparked the German press' interest, though its explanation was limited to Milošević's nationalist policies of reigniting the 1389-myth and revoking Kosovo's autonomy. The birth of the KLA and its guerrilla warfare was not seen as a catalyst for the violence by any of the publications, although this is such a prominent issue in the secondary literature. Only *FAZ*, *FR* and *taz* explored alternative explanations, mentioning that Kosovo had not been included in the Dayton negotiations, though these were merely single references and would have been lost in the coverage.[14] However, just like the secondary literature, the publications did not accuse 'the West' for this exclusion. It is worth noting at this point that *Welt's* articles published in this four-month timeframe focused solely on Milošević's policies. This narrow interpretation is reminiscent of the newspaper's early coverage of the Bosnian War, in which *Welt's* main Balkan-correspondent, Carl Gustaf Ströhm, accused Milošević personally for the outbreak of violence long before other journalists.[15] While Ströhm was no longer Balkan-correspondent at this time and indeed did not write any of the articles considered here, there appears a similar stance in this later coverage.

Kosovo-Albanian Civilians

Turning now to the publications' coverage of the violence itself, this was portrayed with a lot of detail, focusing primarily on the suffering of the Kosovo-Albanian civilians. Concrete numbers of casualties for the four-month timeframe of this chapter remain unknown, though between February 1998 and March 1999 a total of circa 400,000 civilians were forced to leave their homes and more than 1,000 civilians were killed by Serbian police forces.[16] All publications reported on this violence. For example, *FAZ's* Matthias Rüb reported in mid-June that Kosovo-Albanians had been "massacred with axes [and] ripped apart by grenades [...]" in the killings that had taken place in the small town Prekaz during February and March.[17] Similarly *taz's* Balkan-correspondent Erich Rathfelder painted a vivid picture of the violence in the

14 Matthias Rüb: Instabilitätsexport. In: *FAZ*, 15.06.1998, p. 16; Daniel Riegger: „Gezielte Sanktionen gegen Milosevic sind möglich". In: *FR*, 16.03.1998, p. 5; Anonymous: Der Fluch der eigenen Geschichte. In: t*az*, 06.03.1998, p. 3.

15 See chapter 3, fn. 82–86.

16 Commission on Kosovo: *The Kosovo Report*, p. 2.

17 Matthias Rüb: Auf der in Prishtina gestalteten Web-Site „Arta" erfährt man alles über die Krise. In: *FAZ*, 16.06.1998, p. 7.

Drenica region, specifically Prekaz, writing that the Kosovo-Albanian civilians were distressed at a funeral "[…] by the shattered skull of a woman, the children whose mouths were crying out in agony and the disfigured faces of the men."[18] Another *taz*-article reported that "one inhabitant [of an attacked village] had his throat slit […]"[19] Several days later, Rathfelder described those fleeing "[…] from the hell in Kosovo: The shapes are emaciated. Two days and two nights they have been in transit since leaving their village […]"[20] The adjective 'emaciated' may strike the reader as overly dramatic to describe people who had been on the run for two days, but the images these words conjured were very effective.

A *BILD*-article, notably co-authored by *Welt's* Boris Kalnoky reported that "crying women, streaming with blood […ran] into the open, carrying crying babies. Rocket-launchers and mines rip[ped] apart those who […fled]."[21] Other articles reported of "mass executions, mass rapes, mass flight,"[22] as well as mass graves.[23] The fate of thousands of Kosovo-Albanian refugees fleeing their villages was encapsulated in the moving story of one 12-year-old girl called Shipe Caca. The anonymous piece in *BILD* reported that "after grenades hailed down on her village, she suddenly stood alone with five small *Mitflüchtlinge* [co-refugees]. Shipe took the children by their hands and made her way across the meadows."[24] This same story was reported in *Welt*,[25] demonstrating a further over-lap of the two papers, both produced by the Axel-Springer publishing house.

This replication of the same content in a broadsheet and tabloid offers an interesting opportunity to compare the coverage in different types of newspapers. *BILD's* tendency to sensationalise can be found in the use of descriptions such as "grenade showers, hailing on the village" and children being left "utterly alone". Moreover, the method of reporting that focuses on a personal story can often be found in the tabloid. The broadsheet's article on the other hand, refrained from such staggering word-choices. While featuring the same details about Shipe's fate, it also included more general news on the

18 Erich Rathfelder: Gewehre zum letzten Geleit. In: *taz*, 12.03.1998, p. 10.

19 AP/AFP: Flucht aus dem Kosovo. In: *taz*, 02.06.1998, p. 4.

20 Erich Rathfelder: Auf der Flucht vor der Hölle im Kosovo. In: *taz*, 06./07.06.1998, p. 10.

21 B. Kalnoky / W. Kramer: Kosovo – droht ein neues Bosnien? In: *BILD*, 07.03.1998, p. 2.

22 Georg Gafron: Fünf vor Zwölf. In: *BILD*, 28.04.1998, p. 2; Anonymous: Massenflucht vor den Serben. In: *BILD*, 08.06.1998, p. 2.

23 Anonymous: Massengrab entdeckt. In: *BILD*, 07.06.1998, p. 2.

24 Anonymous: Kosovo: Die Flucht der Kinder. In: *BILD*, 14.06.1998, p. 3.

25 Boris Kalnoky: Hauptsache Richtung Albanien! In: *Welt*, 09.06.1998, p. 3.

developments in Kosovo, for example the KLA's mobilisation, embedding the suffering of a single girl in the larger context of the on-going violence. This awareness of the larger conflict surrounding one individual's narrative cannot be found in the tabloid which only focused on the personal fate of a single girl whose story could have occurred in any war-torn country.

Continuing with *Welt's* reporting on the fighting in the Drenica region, Boris Kalnoky wrote in a *Welt*-article that "the children's corpses [...did] not look like they had been killed in battle by stray bullets or grenades. Their little bodies [...were] mostly unharmed, only their heads are shattered."[26] The author continued that the youngest victim was three years old and the eldest 92, suggesting that children and elderly were the primary targets. This is encapsulated by the article's title: "Children and elderly were the victims." Another piece described a Kosovo-Albanian video that had become available to the author, showing victims of the recent violence. "In a bullet-ridden room lie the corpses of the Ahmeti family; a pregnant woman without head; the other bodies full of bullet wounds."[27] Articles in *taz* and *FR* emphasised the same perspective.[28] For example *FR's* Stephan Israel wrote that "in the hills and woods surrounding Drenica, journalists have found whole groups of terrorised and traumatised women and children."[29] Various *FR*-articles underlined that the victims were not 'terrorists', as claimed by Serbian propaganda, but mostly women, children and elderly.[30] This argument was conveyed succinctly in Israel's article entitled "For the Serbs, also women, children and elderly are terrorists".[31] This significantly polemical and sarcastic condensation of the on-going violence was strongly anti-Serbian and very memorable to the reader.

In early March a *Spiegel*-article reported on an old Kosovo-Albanian woman who was about to bury her sons, nephews and grandsons after an attack by Serbian policemen. The account described the victims: "one of them they battered to death in front of the house, teeth and bits of brain [...lay] under

26 Boris Kalnoky: Kinder und Greise waren die Opfer. In: *Welt*, 10.03.1998, p. 6.

27 Boris Kalnoky: Serben lassen Panzer rollen. In: *Welt*, 06.03.1998, p. 8.

28 Erich Rathfelder: „Wir sind bereit, für den Kosovo zu sterben". In: *taz*, 10.03.1998, p. 3; Rathfelder: Gewehre zum letzten Geleit. In: *taz*, 12.03.1998, p. 10.

29 Stephan Israel: Serbiens Polizei will keine Zeugen. In: *FR*, 10.03.1998, p. 3.

30 dpa/afp/rtr: Nato setzt auf Diplomatie. In: *FR*, 12.03.1998, p. 1; Stephan Israel: Für die Serben sind auch Frauen, Kinder und Greise „Terroristen". In: *FR*, 12.03.1998, p. 8; dpa: UN-Berichte: Serbische Polizei folterte Albaner. In: *FR*, 16.04.1998, p. 2.

31 Stephan Israel: Für die Serben sind auch Frauen, Kinder und Greise „Terroristen". In: *FR*, 12.03.1998, p. 8.

a pile of brushwood, next to it a large, blood-stained stone."[32] This very graphic description reporting on the brute force administered by Serbians against Kosovo-Albanians featured one significant difference from the other German publications: it focused on young, able-bodied men and thus potential soldiers as victims, rather than emphasising the suffering of women, children and elderly. While this was an interesting distinction, it was singular and various other cases concentrated on female victims in the *Spiegel*-articles' narratives. For example, a piece written by Renate Flottau described the fate of a Kosovo-Albanian woman in the late stages of pregnancy who had to flee from a Serbian attack and spend two nights in the cold without any bread or water.[33] Another article authored by Flottau focused on the 28-year-old Merita who "[…] ran her shaking hands through her hair and cried out of anger" because her entire village had been destroyed.[34]
Interestingly, none of the stories published in the German press at this time featured interviews with the victims, but instead consisted of the correspondents' observations as external onlookers. This unusual manner of reporting allowed the reader to learn about the details of the on-going violence, however only through the eyes of the correspondent. With no citations by local eye-witnesses, the journalists became the only medium through which the readers learned about the fighting. Due to this reporting style, the shock experienced by the correspondents upon witnessing the violence stood in the forefront of their pieces. On the one hand this contributed to their immediacy, while simultaneously adding a layer of interpretation to the coverage which confined the readers' understanding of the events. The journalist's role as a 'gate-keeper' of information is consequently emphasised. While correspondents always select the narratives the readers learn about, by omitting direct citations of eye-witnesses, the reader is more subjected to the journalists' personal interpretation than in previous instances.

The graphic descriptions found in the textual coverage about crushed skulls and slit throats were comprehensibly not translated to the visual representation of the Kosovo-Albanian victims. Rather than showing instances of such brute force, the images found in all publications except *JF* pictured refugee treks to portray the human suffering. The focus on quantity showing the large

32 Anonymous: Jeder gegen jeden. In: *Spiegel*, 09.03.1998, pp. 148–149.

33 Renate Flottau: Angst hinter Mauern. In: *Spiegel*, 16.03.1998, pp. 178–179.

34 Renate Flottau: Krieg der Waldmenschen. In: *Spiegel*, 08.06.1998, pp. 150, 153.

numbers of displaced people perhaps circumvented the individual horrors.[35] While there seems to be a disjoint between the graphic articles and the images, by focusing on numbers, indeed the visual and textual analysis complemented each other. Through the pictorial coverage, the reader grasped the extent of displacements, while the articles revealed the horrific details of the violence and specifically of fatalities. When combined, the textual and visual coverage gave a detailed overview and evoked deep empathy with the fate of the Kosovo-Albanian civilians in the readers.

This identification with the Kosovo-Albanian perspective is brought out further through various images published in this timeframe which frequently showed Kosovo-Albanians partaking in peaceful demonstrations during which they were confronted with Serbian policemen.

Figure 23: Reuters; printed in *FAZ*, 17 March 1998, p. 6.[36]

Strikingly, all pictures were taken from a perspective that emphasised the difference in strength, contrasting defenceless Kosovo-Albanian civilians to large, armed Serbian soldiers. The viewer was left with the sensation that the Kosovo-Albanian population had no choice but to rebel, being oppressed by

35 Anonymous: Deutsche als Degen der USA? In: *Spiegel*, 22.06.1998, p, 125; Anonymous: Massenflucht vor den Serben. In: *BILD*, 08.06.1998, p. 2; Matthias Rüb: Der Brandstifter spielt nun den Feuerwehrmann. In: *FAZ*, 09.03.1998, p. 8.

36 Other examples with this motif were published in *Welt*, 02.05.1998, p. 6; *Spiegel*, 04.05.1998, p. 150.

an exceedingly powerful police force. Furthermore, all three images featuring this motif were taken from the same perspective, namely from behind the Serbian policemen; the two images in *Welt* and *Spiegel* even showed the same policeman. This implies that the photographers were only granted access to a certain segment of the event, underlining how limited the coverage was that eventually reached the German reader. Mere snapshots of the full extent were conveyed. The amount of information these images expressed simply through the place and angle from which they were taken, is quite astounding.

A second setting featured heavily in the pictorial coverage of Kosovo-Albanian civilians in this time-period was funerals.[37] The accompanying articles explained that these frequently turned into spontaneous demonstrations against the violence perpetrated by Serbian forces in Kosovo.

Figure 24: An unidentified ethnic Albanian flashes a V-sign at a mass funeral in the village of Cirez, some 50 kilometres (31 miles) west of Priština in the Yugoslav province of Kosovo Tuesday March 3, 1998. AP; printed in *Spiegel*, 9 March 1998, p. 149.

37 Stephan Israel: Töten unter Ausschluss der Öffentlichkeit. In: *FR*, 29.04.1998, p. 2; Gregor Meyer: Für die Freiheit ist jedes Opfer recht. In: *taz*, 05.03.1998, p. 11; Anonymous: Für die Freiheit ist jedes Opfer recht. In: *Spiegel*, 09.03.1998, p. 148.

Spiegel chose to illustrate this theme by singling out the young boy seen standing in the above picture. Wrapped in the Kosovo-Albanian flag, he might be seen as a symbol of the despairing population and hopeless future of the Kosovar youth. However, what in the first instance appears to be a spontaneous and genuine expression of grief and solidarity, which was confirmed in the accompanying article,[38] has to be qualified upon closer inspection. Three months later, on 8 June, *Spiegel* published another picture of the same boy at the same event.[39]

Taken from a different position, the viewer realises that he was the only individual amongst the masses to be wrapped in a Kosovo-Albanian flag. It also shows that he was standing alone amongst the corpses, which were also cloaked in the flag and placed between the crowd and organisers. It is now evident that the whole event was more choreographed than suggested in the first article. The stage area was also draped in the same flag and equipped with amplifiers and microphones, in the background of this second image published in June, emphasised this. This suggests that the funeral was also used as a political rally. Considering these images together, the placement of a young boy cloaked in a flag as the protagonist of such a politicised gathering evokes a sense of sinister nationalism that utilises youth to mobilise masses. However, a casual reader at the time probably would not have realised this connection especially as the images were published three months apart. Nonetheless, for our purposes it underscores how carefully choreographed some of these seemingly casual or spontaneous pictures were.

Serbian Civilians

Considering that the province's population consisted of 90% Kosovo-Albanians, combined with more institutionalised and well-equipped Serbian forces, it is unsurprising that the majority of the victims were Kosovo-Albanian. Nonetheless, one must not disregard the militarised activities of KLA, which specifically targeted Serbian forces, but also civilians living in Kosovo. However, featuring Serbian civilians as victims of targeted violence was a dimension barely found in the German publications considered here. *JF*, *Konkret* and *FR* did not cover this theme at all. *FAZ*, *Spiegel* and *taz* were the only publications to report that the Serbian civilians also suffered from

38 Anonymous: Jeder gegen jeden. In: *Spiegel*, 09.03.1998, pp. 148–149.

39 Image published in *Spiegel*, 08.06.1998, p. 153.

the violence and indeed were forced to flee their homes due to KLA's operations.[40] A *taz*-article guest-authored by the Belgrade-based journalist Andrej Ivanji quoted a Serbian civilian who was afraid that the Serbian cultural and religious sites which were "Orthodox islands floating helplessly in the Albanian ocean" would now be looted and burned down by the KLA.[41] This aspect was underlined with a picture published the following month.[42] As the picture's caption explained, this Serbian woman had fled to a Christian-Orthodox monastery to seek refuge from the on-going violence. While the short description detailed that elderly Serbian women – clearly not combatants – were victims of this conflict, the image itself did not have the same effect as the previously discussed pictures of the affected Kosovo-Albanian. This underscores the effect of quantity in some images. The masses of Kosovo-Albanian refugees or of mourners were the most memorable feature from the other images. This in turn evoked such sympathy amongst the viewers, which was not generated by this picture of a single victim.
Other articles in *FAZ* and *Spiegel* also reported on Serbian civilians suffering, but took a different perspective. They clearly circumvented the link to KLA and rather focused on Milošević's policies as the primary cause for their misery. For example, *Spiegel's* Renate Flottau wrote that "the Serbs [living] in Kosovo […felt] like Belgrade has deserted them in the middle of their enemy's land." The article asserted that 70% of the Serbs living outside of Kosovo had no interest in going to war over this 'historical outpost.'[43] Similarly, *FAZ's* Matthias Rüb revisited the wars Serbia had led against Slovenia, Croatia, Bosnia and now Kosovo, underlining how exasperated and frustrated the Serbian people presumably were with Milošević for dragging them into so many wars – all of which had been lost.[44] Almost contrary to this picture of helplessness, Rüb also described Serbian civilians as accessories to the police, who he claimed had "[…] systematically armed the Serbian civilians."[45] *Welt* exclusively featured this dimension. For example, Boris Kalnoky reported that both sides were preparing for violence and "[…] Serbian civilians were

40 Matthias Rüb: Kosovo-Albaner lehnen Gespräche weiter ab. In: *FAZ*, 17.04.1998, p. 1; Renate Flottau: „Sie sollen Krieg haben". In: *Spiegel*, 04.05.1998, pp. 149–150.

41 Andrej Ivanji: Der ewige Kampf um den Kosovo. In: *taz*, 06.03.1998, p. 3.

42 Image published in *taz*, 27.04.1998, p. 11.

43 Renate Flottau: Angst hinter Mauern. In: *Spiegel*, 16.03.1998, pp. 178–179.

44 Matthias Rüb: Auch der Krieg im Kosovo ist für Serbien nicht zu gewinnen. In: *FAZ*, 25.06.1998, p. 3.

45 Matthias Rüb: Russland setzt Milošević unter Druck. In: *FAZ*, 07.05.1998, p. 9.

equipped with weapons." This implied a militarisation of the civilian population and thus their direct involvement in the armed conflict.[46]
The lack of interest for Serbian civilian suffering is presented most clearly when considering the quantity of the pictorial coverage of this theme.

Publication	No. of images between 1 March and 30 June 1998	No. of pictures showing Kosovo-Albanians as victims	Percentage	No. of images showing Serbians as victims	Percentage
Welt	51	17	33%	1	2%
FAZ	47	19	40%	0	0%
FR	24	17	71%	0	0%
taz	38	18	47%	2	5%
BILD	15	4	27%	0	0%
Spiegel	42	12	29%	0	0%

Table 4: Number of images showing victims of violence.[47]

As table 4 demonstrates, only *Welt* and *taz* featured images of Serbians as victims, although even these were so marginal that a casual reader at the time could have easily over-looked them. However, only one of the three pictures of Serbian victimhood was of a Serbian civilian suffering from the conflict. The other two images showed Serbian soldiers who had died in combat.[48] While this still portrayed them as victims rather than perpetrators, their active involvement in the war – rather than being innocent bystanders – was likely to have diminished the readers' sympathy.

The Serbian Forces

Departing from the German press' coverage of the civilians, equally the depiction of the perpetrators is worth considering. Surprisingly, detailed information about the Serbian forces did not find much attention in the German publications. Accordingly, none mentioned how many policemen were in Kosovo, who important commanders were and how many people they had killed. This omission portrayed them as an undefinable, threatening and omnipresent

46 Boris Kalnoky: Rätselraten über Ziele der Serben. In: *Welt*, 09.03.1998, p. 6.

47 Excluding maps and cartoons.

48 Erich Rathfelder: Schlechte Zeiten für Verhandlungen. In: *taz*, 23.05.1998, p. 10; DW: Neue Gewalt im Kosovo löst Fluchtwelle aus. In: *Welt*, 03.06.1998, p. 1.

entity.[49] This was emphasised by the images featured in almost all publications at this time, featuring heavily-armed soldiers in armoured vehicles and tanks, frequently driving in a motorcade.[50] The primary message conveyed in these pictures was the Serbian supremacy, for example how heavily they were armed. This becomes particularly prevalent when considered in conjunction with the previous images of the waves of Kosovo-Albanian refugees. Such an opposition created a distinct sense of the victims being Kosovo-Albanian and Serbian perpetrators. Judging from these images, Milošević's distinction that these were police units and not soldiers was merely formal.[51]

The textual coverage portrayed the Serbian army in an equally negative light. In one *Welt*-article, poignantly entitled, "Singing Serbian troops celebrate their 'slaughter party,'" the author described the heavily-armed squads moving from one village to the next, wreaking havoc.[52] Significantly, this piece referred to 'troops' rather than the official description of police forces. Perhaps this distinction was included consciously to make a statement about this artificial distinction. Another explanation could be that to eyewitnesses such as the author, they simply appeared more like troops than policemen. A *FAZ*-article was more explicit on this matter, stating that it had become clear "[…] that Belgrade […was] not pursuing legitimate police-operations in Kosovo to uphold order […] but that they […were] carrying out war."[53] *FR* did not mention the Serbian soldiers at all while *Spiegel* and *BILD* only did so once, in a very cursory manner.[54]

49 Boris Kalnoky: Rätselraten über Ziele der Serben. In: *Welt*, 09.03.1998, p. 6; fy: Die Nato setzt auf das Treffen Jelzins mit Milosevic; Heute Luftmanöver an den Grenzen zum Kosovo. In: *FAZ*, 15.06.1998, pp. 1–2; Erich Rathfelder: Freie Hand für Belgrad. In: *taz*, 07.05.1998, p. 2; Erich Rathfelder: Falsches Zeichen. In: *taz*, 27.05.1998, p. 12.

50 Anonymous: Kehr um, Milosevic! In: *Spiegel*, 15.06.1998, p. 135; Boris Kalnoky: Milosevic lässt US-Vermittler abblitzen. In: *Welt*, 11.05.1998, p. 5; Erich Rathfelder: Albanische Dörfer unter Beschuss. In: *taz*, 24.04.1998, p. 10; Renate Flottau: Angst hinter Mauern. In: *Spiegel*, 16.03.1998, p. 179.

51 See chapter 2, fn. 32–39.

52 Boris Kalnoky: Singend feiern die serbischen Truppen ihr „Schlachtfest". In: *Welt*, 09.03.1998, p. 3.

53 Wolfgang Günter Lerch: Der Kosovo-Knoten ist kaum zu lösen. In: *FAZ*, 12.06.1998, p. 14.

54 Anonymous: Kosovo: Serben starten Großoffensive mit Panzern. In: *BILD*, 30.06.1998, p. 2; Renate Flottau: Angst hinter Mauern. In: *Spiegel*, 16.03.1998, pp. 178–179.

Milošević – The Main Culprit?

In spite of these occasional references in the textual and visual coverage, the Serbian forces did not play a very prominent role in the German press' understanding of the violence. Rather they repeatedly held Milošević personally responsible for the violence. *JF* was the only exception, mentioning him only once in this period.[55] As the previous section on the causes of the conflict has shown, the German press frequently linked historical causes with Milošević's policies. However, blaming him for the renewed violence in Kosovo was not merely embedded within the historical context, but was presented in a much more direct manner. For example, *Welt's* Boris Kalnoky wrote that Milošević was not a "[…] guarantee for stability, but rather for violence in the Balkans."[56] Other articles portrayed him as a manipulative political gambler, or as *FR's* Rolf Paasch stated "a tactician"[57] who would appear to make concessions in negotiations while continuing the process of 'ethnic cleansing'.[58] Various pieces in *FAZ*, *BILD* and *Spiegel* referred to him as simply the 'Serb-leader'[59] and reminded the reader of Milošević's decade-long wars of aggression in the Balkans.[60] *BILD's* characterisation of Milošević was particularly memorable due to its tabloidesque bluntness. For instance, one editorial referred to him as a 'butcher'.[61] Numerous other articles featured over-simplified language which portrayed Milošević personally to be the perpetrator. Whether this was intentional or not cannot be determined. For example on 13 June, one anonymous article stated that "[…] 65,000 people […had] been displaced since the

55 Alexander Beermann: Wie Elefanten im Porzellanladen. In: *JF*, 27.03.1998, p. 8.

56 Boris Kalnoky: „Rote Linie". In: *Welt*, 03.03.1998, p. 4; also discussed in Stephan Israel: Der Guerillakampf im Kosovo hat bereits begonnen. In: *FR*: 03.03.1998, p. 1; afp/ap/dpa/rtr: Kinkel fordert von UN Eingreifen in Kosovo. In: *FR*, 07.03.1998, p. 1; Roman Arens: In Kosovo wie in Bosnien. In: *FR*, 10.03.1998, p. 3; dpa/afp: US-Gesandter gibt Milosevic Schuld. In: *FR*, 27.03.1998, p. 2; paa: Lieber leiden. In: *FR*, 08.04.1998, p. 3.

57 Paa: Lieber leiden. In: *FR*, 08.04.1998, p. 3.

58 Katja Ridderbusch: Milosevic oder Das Doppelspiel von Konzession und Härte. In: *Welt*, 10.03.1998, p. 4; Boris Kalnoky: Spielen auf Zeit. In: *Welt*, 07.04.1998, p. 4; Kalnoky: Albaner-Parlament voller Serben? In: *Welt*, 08.05.1998, p. 7; Kalnoky: Doppeltes Spiel. In: *Welt*, 25.05.1998, p. 4; Stephan Israel: Serbiens Polizei will keine Zeugen. In: *FR*, 10.03.1998, p. 3; Israel: Die Einladung zum Dialog klingt wie ein Hohn. In: *FR*, 13.03.1998, p. 3.

59 W. A.: Nagelprobe. In: *FAZ* ,15.06.1998, p. 1; W. A.: Leere Worte. In: *FAZ*, 18.06.1998, p. 16; Anonymous: Kosovo. In: *BILD*, 13.06.1998, p. 2; Anonymous: Jeder gegen Jeden. In: *Spiegel*, 09.03.1998, p. 149.

60 Johann Georg Reißmüller: Kein Ausweg für das Kosovo? In: *FAZ*, 16.04.1998, p. 1; Gerald Livingston: Ein Husar auf dem Balkan. In: *Spiegel*, 01.06.1998, pp. 160, 162.

61 Georg Gafron: Die NATO muss handeln! In: *BILD*, 06.06.1998, p. 2.

Serbian dictator Slobodan Milošević [...] expelled Albanians from the South-Serbian province Kosovo."[62]

Interestingly, *taz's* treatment differs from the publications considered above. While various articles portrayed Milošević to have manipulated the international community to attain exactly what he wanted in Kosovo,[63] he was never directly linked to the violence. This is surprising, especially considering the newspaper's unhalted accusations of Milošević being a war-criminal in previous chapters. Moreover, Erich Rathfelder and Andreas Zumach, both *taz*-correspondents during the Bosnia War, authored the majority of these articles. Consequently one could suspect that their portrayal of Milošević would have been influenced by the Serbian President's involvement in the Srebrenica Massacre, for example. However, the utmost connection Rathfelder made between the on-going violence and Milošević was in an editorial, where he stated: "Milošević has settled for the military solution."[64] One explanation for this detachment could be the attempt to re-assess the new conflict in Kosovo without any preconceptions stemming from previous wars.

It must be noted that almost all treatment of Milošević as the main culprit was featured in editorials, which allowed more personal interpretation than 'normal' articles. Perhaps the larger political context could explain this peculiarity. After the Bosnian War had ended, Milošević had not been indicted for war-crimes, nor had he been ousted from power in Belgrade. Consequently the publications could have seen him as more politically stable. As a result, linking Milošević personally to the renewed violence in Kosovo could have been deemed more interpretation or conjecture than fact at this early stage in the conflict and thus been predominantly published in editorials rather than articles. This preference of a format that allowed more editorial freedom is further underlined with the use of cartoons. All four daily newspapers, except for *BILD* which did not use this medium at all, published caricatures

62 Anonymous: Kosovo: Die Flucht der Kinder. In: *BILD*, 14.06.1998, p. 3; also in Georg Gafron: Fünf vor Zwölf. In: *BILD*, 28.04.1998, p. 2; Gafron: Die NATO muss handeln! In: *BILD*, 06.06.1998, p. 2; Lothar Loewe: Kein NATO-Einsatz um jeden Preis. In: *BILD*, 13.06.1998, p. 2; Anonymous: Pulverfass Kosovo. In: *BILD*, 15.06.1998, p. 2.

63 For example: Andreas Zumach: Slobodan Milosevic kann erst einmal abwarten. In: *taz*, 07./08.03.1998, p. 10; Martin Brusis: Grenzen des Dialogs. In: *taz*, 10.03.1998, p. 12; AP/AFP: Milosevic düpiert Gelbard. In: *taz*, 28./29.03.1998, p. 5; Erich Rathfelder: Milosevic zieht ein Referendum aus seiner Trickkiste. In: *taz*, 04./05.04.1998, p. 11; Rathfelder: Die militärische Option. In: *taz*, 25./26.04.1998, p. 12; Rathfelder: Holbrookes Mission droht zu scheitern. In: *taz*, 12.05.1998, p. 12.

64 Erich Rathfelder: Die militärische Option. In: *taz*, 25./26.04.1998, p. 12.

to present a direct causal link between Milošević and the violence. The cartoons published in this timeframe can be categorised into abstract and graphic styles. Starting with the former, the more detached examples could be found in *FR*, for example.

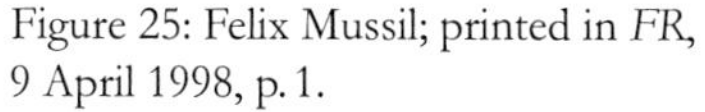

Figure 25: Felix Mussil; printed in *FR*, 9 April 1998, p. 1.

Figure 26: Felix Mussil: printed in *FR*, 13 June 1998, p. 1.

Both caricatures depicted Milošević as the omnipotent ruler over Kosovo while simultaneously criticising the international community's failure to stop him. This denigration was significantly absent in the articles, which as mentioned previously, never accused 'the West' of failing in Kosovo.[65]

The second category also focused on Milošević, but presented the violence he was blamed for much more explicitly. A *Welt*-cartoon was the most explicit in some respects, featuring him with blood-stained hands and armed with a gun. However, it also used more abstract commentary through the introduction of 'ethnic cleansing,' showing Milošević hanging up a 'cleansed' shirt labelled 'Serbia'.[66] Similarly, the caricatures in *FAZ* and *taz* also emphasised the brute force administered by the Serbian President very graphically.

65 See chapter 2, fn. 34.

66 Image published in *Welt*, 06.06.1998, p. 4.

Figure 27: Fritz Behrendt; printed in *FAZ*, 4 March 1998, p. 10.

Figure 28: Klaus Stuttmann; printed in *taz*, 30 June 1998, p. 12: "Would you kindly get out of here, this is my domestic concern!!"

Both showed Milošević holding a blood-covered club. Considering the previous analysis of *taz's* textual reporting, which did not link Milošević to the on-going violence, this cartoon expresses the opposite. However, it must be emphasised that *taz's* cartoon was singular and can be seen as an exception and perhaps expressed the personal opinion of the caricaturist. This in turn underlines the artistic freedom cartoons offered and that their message did not necessarily have to mirror other interpretations offered in the newspaper. *FAZ's* cartoon on the other hand reinforced the broadsheet's textual coverage, portraying Milošević as a General who after Vukovar, Sarajevo and Srebrenica had also added Kosovo to his victories. This is particularly meaningful, as it distinctly linked Milošević to past war-crimes such as Srebrenica and simultaneously placed the violence in Kosovo on the same level as this instance of Bosnian genocide. A further *FAZ*-cartoon is also worth noting, as it introduced a hitherto dormant issue.

Figure 29: Fritz Behrendt; printed in *FAZ*, 18 March 1998, p. 9.

Portraying Milošević as a Chetnik soldier holding an old-fashioned weapon, and Kosovo dressed in a traditional Muslim outfit, it underlined the perception of outdated, savage violence and implied that the region was 'different' and backward. Moreover, Milošević's sign, "We do not tolerate interference" commented on his repeated insistence that Kosovo was a domestic issue. In the background, Muslim villages are burning, identifiable by the minaret and mosque.

With this detail the cartoon raised the religious dimension of the conflict which was missing nearly completely in the articles: Kosovo-Albanians are predominantly Muslim while Serbians are largely Christian-Orthodox. However the former were not simply referred to as 'Muslims', as had been the case with Bosniaks in the German print coverage of the Bosnia War. Indeed, a reader at the time, gathering his knowledge about Kosovo exclusively from the German newspapers studied here would not even have been aware of this religious divide; it was mentioned in only two articles. A *FAZ*-article stated that "most of the Albanians are Sunni Muslims, though there are also around 50,000 Christians among them."[67] A *Spiegel*-article quoted a Serbian living in Kosovo who stated that until 1996, "[…] Serbian and Albanian families celebrated the holidays together, in spite of different religions." However, now each group was segregated and barricaded themselves behind a wall of fear, as the article's title, "*Angst hinter Mauern*", indicates.[68] While both articles alluded to religion as a potential cause for the conflict, it was not explored in more depth. This over-sight could be explained with the focus on Milošević and his destructive policies to explain the renewed violence in early 1998. Presumably this resulted from his role in the preceding wars in Bosnia and Croatia. However, by placing him in the centre of the narrative, the Kosovo conflict was portrayed as a 'simple' war of nationalist aggression, disregarding possible larger systemic issues.

The Kosovo Liberation Army

This heightened interest in Milošević as an individual and subsequent disregard for possible alternative causes of the conflict introduces a further theme: the German press' representation of the KLA. The portrayal of the Kosovo-Albanian combatants was a contentious issue, as the army had been labelled a 'terrorist organisation' by Robert Gelbard, Bill Clinton's special envoy to the Balkans in early 1998.[69] This was harshly criticised in all newspapers except for *FR*, *Konkret* and *BILD*. The argumentation brought forth – mostly in editorials – stated that while the attribute 'terrorist' may be

67 Wolfgang Günter Lerch: „Wir werden sie zu Serben machen". In: *FAZ*, 07.03.1998, p. 12.

68 Renate Flottau: Angst hinter Mauern. In: *Spiegel*, 16.03.1998, p. 179.

69 As reported in Nened Sebak: The KLA – Terrorists or Freedom Fighters? In: *BBC*, 28.06.1998. http://news.bbc.co.uk/2/hi/europe/121818.stm (accessed 31.08.2014); Michael Moran: Terrorist Groups and Political Legitimacy. In: *Council on Foreign Relations*, 16.03.2006. http://www.cfr.org/terrorism/terrorist-groups-political-legitimacy/p10159#p4 (accessed 31.08.2014).

accurate, officially calling it such gave the Serbian forces reason to continue the massacres and persecution of Kosovo-Albanians.[70] Perhaps as a reaction to Gelbard's negative assessment, the publications used a plethora of explicitly positive terms, ostentatiously avoiding the label 'terrorist'. Accordingly, terms including 'independence fighters',[71] 'freedom fighters'[72] or 'underground army'[73] replaced more accurate labels such as 'soldiers.' This nomenclature used in almost all publications suggests a positive disposition towards the KLA's cause.

Only four exceptions could be found, namely in *Welt*, *BILD*, *Konkret* and *JF*. While one *Welt*-article referred to 'Albanian nationalists,' which had negative over-tones, a *BILD*-article described the KLA as outright 'illegal.'[74] The articles in *Konkret* and *JF* were much more explicit. *JF's* Alexander Beermann asserted that the KLA had contributed to the escalating conflict, reminding his reader that "[…] no ethnic conflict only has 'good guys' on one side and 'bad guys' on the other." He continued that while this was sometimes forgotten in the German news coverage, "[…] some of the […] UÇK's actions were utter terror, which cost the lives of innocent Serbian civilians […]"[75] This phrasing was the closest even these more sceptical articles came to labelling the KLA a 'terrorist organisation.' Similarly, *Konkret's* Ralf Schröder expressed his disbelief that the Kurdish PKK, the Irish IRA and Basque ETA were all deemed 'terror organisations' while in Kosovo "[…] a bandit […becomes a] 'fighter', a gang of murderers a 'liberation army' […]"[76]

In spite of this evasive treatment of KLA, *Welt* and *FAZ* offered their readers comprehensive dossiers about the army, while simultaneously acknowledging

70 Martin Brusis: Grenzen des Dialogs. In: *taz*, 10.03.1998, p. 12; Boris Kalnoky: Kriegsgefahr. In: *Welt*, 06.03.1998, p. 4; Anonymous: Jeder gegen Jeden. In: *Spiegel*, 09.03.1998, pp. 148–149; rüb: Feuergefechte im Kosovo. In: *FAZ*, 06.03.1998, p. 2; Johann Georg Reißmüller: Und wieder versagte der Westen. In: *FAZ*, 10.03.1998, p. 1.

71 Katja Ridderbusch: Milosevic oder Das Doppelspiel von Konzession und Härte. In: *Welt*, 10.03.1998, p. 4; cho.: Milosevic lehnt in Moskau den Rückzug serbischer Truppen aus dem Kosovo ab. In: *FAZ*, 17.06.1998, p. 1; dpa/afp: Schwere Gefechte mit Dutzenden Toten. In: *FR*, 02.06.1998, p. 1.

72 Boris Kalnoky: Milošević setzt auf serbischen Zusammenhalt. In: *Welt*, 23.04.1998, p. 5.

73 DW: Großoffensive der Serben gegen Armee der Kosovo-Albaner. In: *Welt*, 30.06.1998, p. 1; Richard Meng: Kinkel und Albright drohen Belgrad mit Strafe. In: *FR*, 09.03.1998, p. 1; Erich Rathfelder: Schlechte Zeiten für Verhandlungen. In: *taz*, 23.05.1998, p. 10; Anonymous: Gefechte im Kosovo werden immer heftiger. In: *JF*, 12.06.1998, p. 9.

74 WeNa: Fronten im Kosovo bleiben verhärtet. In: *Welt*, 14.03.1998, p. 1; Anonymous: Massenflucht vor den Serben. In: *BILD*, 08.06.1998, p. 2.

75 Alexander Beermann: Wie Elefanten im Porzellanladen. In: *JF*, 27.03.1998, p. 8.

76 Ralf Schröder: Blutrausch. In: *Konkret*, April 1998, p. 42.

that many details remained unknown. In fact, the depth of knowledge that could be obtained from these articles is equal to what is now available in the academic literature on the KLA. *FAZ*'s Rüb reported that in 1996 the KLA first came into appearance with assassinations of Serbian policemen and political functionaries and that 'KLA-fighters' were pursuing guerrilla tactics rather than a conventional conflict with front-lines.[77] Rüb's referral to fighters manifests a more straightforward treatment of KLA than other *FAZ*-articles featured. *Welt's* Kalnoky also authored an in-depth dossier, reporting that "a 'Kosovo Liberation Army', which no one [...seemed] to know anything about – [for example] who its leader [...was] and who [...was] fighting for them – had their first battle in November." Now they were becoming increasingly active in Drenica, a heavily embattled region in Kosovo, which they "[...] triumphantly declared 'Serb-free territory.'"[78] This article succinctly summarised the problem regarding the KLA: on the one hand they undeniably existed and were militarily active; on the other hand very few details were known about them. As a result it was very difficult to know how best to portray them.

Nonetheless, both *FAZ* and *Welt* attempted to offer as many details as was possible at this time. *Welt's* Kalnoky demonstrated his diligent research by drawing on a report by "a Western secret service" which stated that the KLA allegedly consisted of several hundred exiled Albanians and had its headquarters in Germany. The man in charge was thought to be Bujar Bukoshi, the Kosovo-Albanian Prime Minister who lived in Geneva. The army was known to have training camps in Northern Albania, from where they also obtained their weapons.[79] This indicates an increasing level of organisation and of professional skill, which is reiterated by other articles published in April, reporting that KLA-soldiers could now be seen wearing uniforms.[80] Various *FAZ*-articles drew on official KLA-communiqués, which described their recent military actions.[81] While they did not give many details regarding

77 Matthias Rüb: Auf dem Amselfeld eskaliert die Gewalt. In: *FAZ*, 03.03.1998, p. 10; Rüb: Bewunderung für die Befreiungsarmee. In: *FAZ*, 04.03.1998, p. 5.

78 Boris Kalnoky: Serben lassen Panzer rollen. In: *Welt*, 06.03.1998, p. 8.

79 Boris Kalnoky: Rätselraten über Ziele der Serben. In: *Welt*, 09.03.1998, p. 6; Kalnoky: Die Kosovo-Albaner in der Defensive. In: *Welt*, 05.05.1998, p. 6; Kalnoky: Jeder Mann im Kosovo ist zum Kämpfen bereit. In: *Welt*, 19.06.1998, p. 8.

80 Boris Kalnoky: „Stunde der Pessimisten". In: *Welt*, 02.04.1998, p. 4; Kalnoky: Milošević setzt auf serbischen Zusammenhalt. In: *Welt*, 23.04.1998, p. 5.

81 Stephan Lipsius: Bewaffneter Widerstand formiert sich. In: *FAZ*, 04.03.1998, pp. 10–11; rüb: Solana gegen militärisches Eingreifen im Kosovo-Konflikt. In: *FAZ*, 12.03.1998, pp. 1–2;

for example the number of Serbian policemen or civilians they had killed, they did provide information such as where and when the Serbian forces had been pushed back. Though the *FAZ*-correspondents mentioned that these communiqués were sent directly to the newspaper's local office – indicating an easy access to the information – no other daily newspapers utilised them. *Spiegel* was the only other publication to cite these communiqués.[82] The broadsheets' active interest to research and assess the Kosovo-Albanian combatants suggests a very straight-forward approach to the subject matter. However, what also becomes clear is that these dossiers functioned as a survey of the mysterious KLA and its origins. None included any prognostic analyses of how the KLA may develop or how this could impact the conflict in general.

Both broadsheets published pictures of Kosovo-Albanian soldiers, demonstrating that they did not shy away even from visual representations. The *FAZ*-image showed two men in camouflage armed with machine guns and their faces covered in black masks.[83] The *Welt*-image portrayed two soldiers in helmets running through a street amidst a manoeuvre.[84] On the one hand, these two images also functioned as proof for the KLA's existence while simultaneously corroborating that the KLA-soldiers were uniformed and well-armed, indicating a high level of organisation. However, particularly the *FAZ*-image of two men wearing face masks leaves an uncomfortable notion of rebellious separatists who fear indication rather than a legitimate and official armed force.

While this level of investigative reporting was unique to *Welt* and *FAZ*, other publications also devoted their attention to the Kosovo-Albanian combatants. Here two main themes were prevalent: the smuggling of weapons and contrasting or even justifying KLA's activities with civilian suffering. Commencing with the latter *FAZ*, *FR* and *taz*[85] all offered an explanation for this increased militarisation of the conflict by juxtaposing Kosovo-Albanian civilian suffering with the army's activities. For example, various *FAZ*-articles published in

Matthias Rüb: Zweifel am demokratischen Kampf für die gerechte Sache. In: *FAZ*, 21.03.1998, p. 8.

82 Anonymous: Front im Süden. In: *Spiegel*,16.03.1998, pp. 176–178; Anonymous: Drohungen der Partisanen. In: *Spiegel*, 23.03.1998, p. 159.

83 Image published in *FAZ*, 04.03.1998, p. 10.

84 Image published in *Welt*, 24.06.1998, p. 8.

85 Erich Rathfelder: Sieben Tote bei Schießerei in Kosovo. In: *taz*, 02.03.1998, p. 10; AP/rtr/taz: Befreiungsarmee ruft Kosovo-Albaner zu Kampf gegen Serben auf. In: *taz*, 05.03.1998, p. 1; Rathfelder: „Wir sind bereit, für den Kosovo zu sterben". In: *taz*, 10.03.1998, p. 3.

March had mentioned that the Drenica region was a KLA-stronghold where its soldiers were heavily armed and highly respected by the local population.[86] Only a few weeks later, in late-March, Rüb revisited the region. The correspondent reported that various 'operations' by the Serbian police had led to 80 civilians losing their lives; many people now lived in refugee camps. Such events, Rüb wrote, strengthened the support for the KLA, which would fight back against the "overpowering Serbian police."[87] This contrasting of the Kosovo-Albanian suffering and the hope given by the KLA created the impression that the latter, while an illegal military formation, was the only hope for the civilians to gain security.

Similarly *FR's* articles portrayed the KLA as taking "[…] revenge for the Albanians who had been killed during the weekend"[88] and that it was "[…] finding more and more adherents due to the increasing oppression from the Serbs."[89] A further *FR*-article quoted Venton Surroi, the editor of a Kosovar newspaper, *Koha Ditore*, who called the KLA "[…] 'a kind of peasant-guerrilla that is trying to protect its own villages and families.'" The same article also stated that it "[…] has prevented larger massacres […]"[90] An account by Stephan Israel echoed that many young men were joining the KLA. Quoting the 18-year-old Adnan Fetahu who stated "[…] 'we don't just want to allow ourselves to be butchered' […]"[91] their armed struggle was presented as comprehensible.

Spiegel's articles took a slightly more nuanced approach. The news-magazine explained KLA's popularity by illuminating the social problems of Albanians in Kosovo, especially young people, such as high unemployment and a frustration with politics.[92] However, unlike other publications, *Spiegel* portrayed the KLA as having a negative effect on the region. It argued that the attacks initiated by the "mysterious 'Liberation Army'" in turn provoked revenge

86 For example: rüb: Viele Tote bei Zusammenstößen im Kosovo. In: *FAZ*, 02.03.1998, p. 1; Matthias Rüb: Auf dem Amselfeld eskaliert die Gewalt. In: *FAZ*, 03.03.1998, p. 1; Rüb: Bewunderung für die Befreiungsarmee. In: *FAZ*, 04.03.1998, p. 5.

87 Matthias Rüb: Wo sind die Kämpfer der „Befreiungsarmee Kosova"? In: *FAZ*, 19.03.1998, p. 3; Rüb: Zweifel am demokratischen Kampf für die gerechte Sache. In: *FAZ*, 21.03.1998, p. 8.

88 Stephan Israel: Polizei greift Dörfer an. In: *FR*, 06.03.1998, p. 1.

89 Gerd Höhler: Manche erträumen sich Groß-Albanien. In: *FR*, 07.03.1998, p. 5.

90 Stephan Israel: Die Einladung zum Dialog klingt wie ein Hohn. In: *FR*, 13.03.1998, p. 3.

91 Stephan Israel: Mit dem Kopf im Sand sieht man keinen Krieg. In: *FR*, 30.04.1998, p. 3.

92 Anonymous: Jeder gegen jeden. In: *Spiegel*, 09.03.1998, pp. 148–149; Renate Flottau: „Sie sollen Krieg haben". In: *Spiegel*, 04.05.1998, pp. 149–150; also in Flottau: Krieg der Waldmenschen. In: *Spiegel*, 08.06.1998, pp. 150–153; Barbara Supp: Stramm und sauber in den Krieg. In: *Spiegel*, 22.06.1998, pp. 128–129.

massacres by the Serbian police and was consequently pushing the region closer to war. Writing that "these fanatics use[d] all means, no number of victims [...was] too high", the anonymous author painted what appears to be an extraordinarily detrimental picture of the KLA.[93] However, it only seems to stand out as negative when compared to the overwhelmingly positive coverage in other publications. When considering the assessment independently, it actually reflects some of the findings in other sources, for example the Amnesty International report.[94]

The second theme prominent in the coverage of the KLA was the smuggling of weapons. As mentioned in the secondary literature, the army obtained its weapons from Albanian arms depots, which could be accessed after the government had collapsed in 1997 and chaos ensued.[95] While the smuggling of weapons from Albania to Kosovo seemed to be the only viable option to increase its military power, this was naturally a controversial matter, as the source was a collapsed state and the smuggling of weapons can be seen as a main element of a terrorist organisation – a label the media was avoiding. *BILD*, *Welt* and *FR* covered the smuggling in a very superficial manner, merely alluding to its existence in side-notes.[96] This cursory treatment linked with *FR's* previously mentioned portrayal of the KLA as the only hope for the oppressed Kosovo-Albanians suggests sympathy for its activities. *Welt's* omission of the army's illegal procurement of weapons in light of the broadsheet's previously mentioned detailed dossier also indicates a mild treatment of the Kosovo-Albanian combatants. *BILD's* single reference to the topic was embedded in an interesting piece marked by the omission of certain details. In late June an anonymous article reported that at least 22 people died in the last days; including "[...] 10 Albanians in Kosovo [who] were shot by Yugoslav border troops."[97] The mention of the border troops linked with the timing of the account makes it clear that this incident occurred in the course of smuggling weapons from Albania to Kosovo. However, this was not

93 Anonymous: Front im Süden. In: *Spiegel*, 16.03.1998, pp. 176–178.

94 Amnesty International: *Kosovo: The Evidence*.

95 See chapter 2, fn. 36.

96 Boris Kalnoky: Im Kosovo stehen die Zeichen auf Krieg. In: *Welt*, 25.04.1998, p. 7; Kalnoky: Albanien im Bann der Krise. In: *Welt*, 05.06.1998, p. 6; Kalnoky: Jeder Mann im Kosovo ist zum Kämpfen bereit. In. *Welt*, 19.06.1998, p. 8; Gerd Höhler: Manche erträumen sich Groß-Albanien. In: *FR*, 07.03.1998, p. 5; Stephan Israel: Serbiens Polizei will keine Zeugen. In: *FR*, 10.03.1998, p. 3; rtr/afp/dpa/ap: Tote bei Kämpfen im Kosovo. In: *FR*, 25.03.1998, p. 1; rtr/ap: Kinkel und Talbott erhöhen Druck auf Milosevic. In: *FR*, 18.04.1998, p. 2.

97 Anonymous: Kosovo Einsatz: Rühe bleibt bei seiner Meinung. In: *BILD*, 19.06.1998, p. 2.

mentioned by this or any other *BILD*-article, leaving the theme unexplored and allowing the reader to have the impression that ordinary Albanians were being massacred.

Spiegel, *taz* and *FAZ* on the other hand devoted more attention to this topic. In an article by *taz's* Erich Rathfelder, he reported new attacks with fatalities. "The dead, aged between 20 and 37, had tried to smuggle weapons across the border a week earlier […]" This statement was quickly qualified with the assessment: "these are amateurs who have prepared themselves to stand against professionals."[98] Rathfelder repeated this contrast between laypersons and experts in a later article published in June.[99] Equally, by including their age, Rathfelder emphasised the youth and therefore the innocence of the victims. Interestingly, he did not emphasise that these young men were actually of fighting age, may have been KLA-members and not simply 'in the wrong place, at the wrong time.'

Various *FAZ*-articles portrayed KLA's activities in a similarly favourable manner.[100] However, the most ardent support was articulated in an editorial written by *FAZ*-editor, Johann Georg Reißmüller:

> the fewer weapons arrive from Albania and elsewhere for the Albanians in Kosovo, the more peaceful it will get, because the Serbs will encounter less and less defence in their oppression of the Albanians. Is this the kind of peace the West wants?[101]

This outright endorsement for KLA's smuggling of weapons is underlined by a picture showing mules carrying small loads of weapons.[102] This image – remarkably the only picture in all newspapers showing the smuggling – aimed to underline how futile the attempts were and that the KLA probably did not have much hope of winning its cause if this was how their supplies were being replenished. This is especially brought to the fore when compared with the portrayal of Serbian forces and tanks considered earlier.

Spiegel's articles also portrayed KLA's procurement of weapons as a useless endeavour, which could not effectively counter the organised Serbian military forces. Learning about mules that carried Kalashnikovs and anti-tank rocket launchers from Albania, the reader gained the sense that the process was very

98 Erich Rathfelder: Die Angst vor dem großen Schlag. In: *taz*, 29.04.1998, p. 11; also in Rathfelder: „Wir kämpfen hier gegen den Islam". In: *taz*, 27.04.1998, p. 11.

99 Erich Rathfelder: Die serbische Strategie im Kosovo. In: *taz*, 04.06.1998, p. 10.

100 For example: Oliver Hoischen: „Das ganze Volk der Kosovo-Albaner ist die UCK". In: *FAZ*, 15.06.1998, p. 3.

101 Rm: Artenvielfalt. In: *FAZ*, 13.05.1998, p. 10.

102 Image published in *FAZ*, 17.06.1998, p. 11.

hard and ungrateful.[103] Moreover, such descriptions portrayed the KLA to be rather quaint and unperilous. In that sense it qualifies the written reports of attacks on Serbian soldiers because the image rather evokes a sense of optimistic and somewhat futile efforts against an unconquerable opponent.

JF differed from all publications above, as its articles neither addressed the smuggling of weapons, nor did they justify civilian suffering with the KLA's activities. However, in mid-March 1998, *JF* published an interview with Bujar Bukoshi, the elusive Prime-Minister of the Kosovo-Albanian shadow-state who was thought to be in charge of the army. In this unique interview, *JF's* Gerhard Quast asked Bukoshi who was to blame for the conflict, which the interviewee attributed to "[...] Serbian politics [and its] criminal politicians [...]" After rejecting that Kosovo was Serbia's internal affair, as Milošević continually claimed, Bukoshi continued that the KLA was gaining support from the Kosovo-Albanian population and was developing into their "[...] only beacon of hope [...]"[104] This interview is remarkable because it de-mystified Bukoshi who was frequently portrayed as one of many unattainable KLA-leaders in exile. If *JF*, being a relatively small German newspaper with presumably limited funds, was able to reach him, surely other publications with more resources for investigative reporting could also have interviewed him. Moreover, this interview – which did not contain any sceptical or critical questions – departed from *JF's* previous more pro-Serbian stance. While KLA was deemed a military organisation, it also conveyed Bukoshi's view that this was the only hope for the Kosovo-Albanians.

As the above section has shown, the Kosovo-Albanian combatants were acknowledged and reported on in all publications, though the coverage was dominantly in favour of KLA's activities. In spite of these detailed insights about the army's structure and acquisition of weapons produced by the German press, Kosovo's leader, Ibrahim Rugova, who insisted that his pacifist policies were the only correct path to attain independence, continually denied that a militarised formation existed.[105] For example, *FAZ* and *Spiegel* reported Rugova's claim that the KLA was an invention of Serbian propaganda.[106] When it was no longer possible to deny the army, Rugova made

103 Renate Flottau: Krieg der Waldmenschen. In: *Spiegel*, 08.06.1998, pp. 150–153; Barbara Supp: Stramm und sauber in den Krieg. In: *Spiegel*, 22.06.1998, pp. 128–129.

104 Gerhard Quast: „Unsere Geduld ist am Ende". In: *JF*, 13.03.1998, p. 2.

105 Petritsch / Pichler: *Kosovo-Kosova*, p. 102.

106 Matthias Rüb: Spannungen zwischen Belgrad und Tirana. In: *FAZ*, 20.04.1998, p. 7; Anonymous: „Kollektiver Selbstmord". In: *Spiegel*, 09.03.1998, p. 148.

declarations such as: "the KLA mostly consists of normal civilians, who want to defend their homes"[107] or "I am convinced that the KLA would also listen to my command,"[108] which articles in *FAZ* and *Spiegel* cited. Rugova's assertions disregarded the independent command structure the KLA had established and its systematic expansion through training camps. Interestingly, none of the publications criticised Rugova for these naïve assessments of the developments in his own country. Arguably undermining and discrediting Rugova publicly would have hurt the cause of Kosovo's struggle for autonomy or even independence, which the print media – in this case very partial – found easier to avoid.

This publication of Rugova's claims without further queries or criticisms introduces the question if his statements were truly naïve, or rather a deliberate deceit by the publications reporting them to uphold clear categories and a linear narrative. One could speculate that Rugova was publicly presenting himself as a pacifist to please 'the West' while secretly supporting the KLA. Such musings can never be confirmed without a personal interview with Rugova, who passed away in 2006; though one could not be assured of the veracity of his answers. However, during the later Rambouillet peace talks (March 1999), where Rugova as well as KLA-delegates were represented, it became clear that the former truly was opposed to the army's violent means and belonged to a very different faction of Kosovar politics. Indeed, some accounts revealed that Rugova refused to speak to and negotiate with his KLA-counterparts, enraging the EU and American diplomats.[109]

Language and Authorship

In the course of this coverage, the intricacies of language in the different publications are worth considering; starting with the simple nomenclature utilised to refer to the two sides. As the violence was unfolding, all newspapers except *Spiegel* and *Konkret*, published details of ambushes. Due to their weekly or monthly publication cycles, neither reported on the day-to-day fighting and rather covered larger themes. The choice of words used to describe these incidents is revealing. All referred to the "fighting between Albanians and Serbian police". In other words, the Serbian side consisted of armed forces, which were juxtaposed with the general term 'Albanians', rather than its equivalent,

107 AFP/AP/Reuters/epd: Aufruf zur Kontrolle der UCK. In: *FAZ*, 20.06.1998, p. 7.

108 Anonymous: „Wir wollen Luftangriffe“. In: *Spiegel*, 22.06.1998, p. 126.

109 Petritsch / Pichler: *Kosovo-Kosova*, pp. 176–178.

KLA-soldiers.[110] There were some exceptions, for example various articles referred to 'armed Albanians.'[111] Moreover the dossiers in *Welt* and *FAZ* discussed previously intermittently referred to KLA's members as combatants. However, these were rare exceptions and were clearly outweighed by the day-to-day reporting which avoided terms such as 'KLA-soldiers' or 'Kosovo-Albanian fighters.'

The early stages of the Kosovo conflict were marked by massacres and the expulsion of the civilian population. All newspapers except *JF* used the phrase 'ethnic cleansing' for the violence, although its specific utilisation differed. Firstly, *Welt*, *FAZ* and *Spiegel* always used the term in quotation marks. *FR* and *BILD* were not consistent, at times using quotations marks and omitting them at other times. *taz* on the other hand never used quotation marks. This suggests a conscious assertion that 'ethnic cleansing' was indeed taking place and was not merely an abstract term. Moreover *FAZ*, *taz* and *Spiegel* only used the term when they were reporting on assessments made by politicians, frequently quoting the Kosovo-Albanian President Ibrahim Rugova.[112]

110 DW: EU beschließt neue Sanktionen gegen Belgrad. In: *Welt*, 28.04.1998, p. 1; AP: Dutzende Tote bei bislang schwersten Kämpfen im Kosovo. In: *Welt*, 02.06.1998, p. 7; rüb: Tränengas und Schlagstöcke gegen Kosovo-Albaner. In: *FAZ*, 03.03.1998, p. 1; AFP/AP/dpa: Rugova fordert mehr Engagement der Kontaktgruppe. In: *FAZ*, 28.03.1998, p. 2; rtr/afp/dpa/ap: Tote bei Kämpfen im Kosovo. In: *FR*, 25.03.1998, p. 1; ap/dpa: Erneut Tote in Kosovo. In: *FR*, 18.05.1998, p. 2; rtr/AFP: Fünf Tote bei erneuten Auseinandersetzungen im Kosovo. In: *taz*. 25.03.1998, p. 1; AP/AFP: Flucht aus dem Kosovo. In: *taz*, 02.06.1998, p. 4; Anonymous: Kosovo Einsatz: Rühe bleibt bei seiner Meinung. In: *BILD*, 19.06.1998, p. 2; Anonymous: Kosovo: Neue Eskalation ethnischer Spannungen. In: *JF*, 06.03.1998, p. 11; Anonymous: Kosovo: ethnische Fronten verhärten sich weiter. In: *JF*, 13.03.1998, p. 10.

111 afp/dpa: Armee und Albaner liefern sich Kämpfe. In: *FR*, 27.04.1998, p. 2; Erich Rathfelder: Im Kosovo brennen wieder Häuser. In: *taz*, 26.03.1998, p. 10; rüb: Kämpfe im Kosovo gehen weiter; Albright droht Milosevic mit neuen Sanktionen. In: *FAZ*, 09.03.1998, p. 1; Anonymous: Gefechte im Kosovo werden immer heftiger. In: *JF*, 12.06.1998, p. 9.

112 Matthias Rüb: Kosovo-Führung um Beruhigung der Lage bemüht. In: *FAZ*, 05.03.1998, p. 7; Rüb: Belgrad setzt Angriffe auf Dörfer im Kosovo fort. In: *FAZ*, 07.03.1998, p. 1; AP/dpa: Rugova wirft Belgrad „ethnische Säuberungen" vor. In: *FAZ*, 14.03.1998, p. 1; wie.: Talbott reist auf den Balkan. In: *FAZ*, 14.03.1998, p. 2; Matthias Rüb: Der Spielraum für eine Lösung wird immer enger. In: *FAZ*, 02.06.1998, p. 5; fy: Die Nato setzt auf das Treffen Jelzins mit Milosevic; Heute Luftmanöver an den Grenzen zum Kosovo. In: *FAZ*, 15.06.1998, pp. 1–2; cho.: Im Westen Misstrauen gegenüber Belgrads Zusagen: Primakow: Es wurde das Maximum getan. In: *FAZ*, 18.06.1998, p. 1; AFP/AP/Reuters/epd: Aufruf zur Kontrolle der UCK. In: *FAZ*, 20.06.1998, p. 7; AFP/AP: EU berät Sanktionen gegen Serbien. In: *taz*, 14./15.03.1998, p. 4; Erich Rathfelder: Die Angst vor dem großen Schlag. In: *taz*, 29.04.1998, p. 11; Rathfelder: Die Nato hilft nach. In: *taz*, 15.05.1998, p. 2; AP/AFP/taz: Tausende Zivilisten fliehen aus dem Kosovo. In: *taz*, 03.06.1998, p. 10; Erich Rathfelder: Die serbische Strategie im Kosovo. In: *taz*, 04.06.1998, p. 10; AFP/dpa: Nato erwägt Einsatz im Kosovo. In: *taz*, 08.06.1998, p. 4; Rathfelder: Auf der Flucht vor der Hölle im Kosovo. In: *taz*, 06./07.06.1998,

This could indicate a certain avoidance to use the term on their own accord. Considering the wider context, this reluctance to refer to 'ethnic cleansing' is inconclusive. While the term had been used constantly during the Bosnian War, there had not been any incidents where the application of the term had been criticised, let alone contested. Conversely, the more post-war information was becoming available about mass-graves being found in Bosnia, the more the use of the term was legitimated. Perhaps there was a general awareness not to overindulge the term.

Nonetheless, *FR*, *Welt* and *BILD*[113] also used the term independently, both in articles as well as editorials, though not very frequently. For example one *FR*-article stated that "the Belgrade regime [...did] not want any witnesses of the 'ethnic cleansing.'"[114] Similarly, *Welt's* Kalnoky wrote that observers were starting to fear that Milošević would "[...] solve the problem like he had in Bosnia, namely 'ethnic cleansing'."[115] This use of the term again suggests the perception that 'ethnic cleansing' was being implemented by Belgrade. Moreover the *Welt*-article implied a heightened awareness of the subject due to the previous Bosnian War. This will be explored later in this chapter.

Conversely, the term 'genocide' was scarcely used. *taz* did not include the term at all in this four-month-period, and *FR* only used it once, when directly quoting Rugova.[116] *Spiegel* and *FAZ* only employed it in the context of the debate regarding a potential UN or NATO intervention and under what circumstances this would be justified.[117] The context for these articles was

p. 10; Rathfelder: Intervention für die Menschenrechte. In: *taz*, 15.06.1998, p. 12; Rathfelder: In Decani herrscht nackte Angst. In: *taz*, 22.06.1998, p. 11; Rathfelder: „Wir alle sind die Kosovo-Befreiungsarmee". In: *taz*, 24.06.1998, p. 13; Rathfelder: Allein gelassen. In: *taz*, 27./28.06.1998, p. 12; Anonymous: „Kollektiver Selbstmord". In: *Spiegel*, 09.03.1998, p. 148; Anonymous: „Wir wollen Luftangriffe". In: *Spiegel*, 22.06.1998, p. 126.

113 B. Kalnoky / W. Kramer: Kosovo – droht ein neues Bosnien? In: *BILD*, 07.03.1998, p. 2; Anonymous: Kosovo-Krieg: Serben zünden wieder Dörfer an! In: *BILD*, 05.06.1998, p. 1.

114 Stephan Israel: Serbiens Polizei will keine Zeugen. In: *FR*, 10.03.1998, p. 3.

115 Nikolaus Blome: Milosevic' Messer. In: *Welt*, 28.04.1998, p. 4. Other references in Boris Kalnoky: Kriegsgefahr. In: *Welt*, 06.03.1998, p. 8; Kalnoky: Rätselraten über Ziele der Serben. In: *Welt*, 09.03.1998, p. 6; WeNa: Fronten im Kosovo bleiben verhärtet. In: *Welt*, 14.03.1998, p. 1; Boris Kalnoky: Milosevic setzt auf serbischen Zusammenhalt. In: *Welt*, 23.04.1998, p. 5; Kalnoky: An der Front dominiert die Propaganda. In: *Welt*, 29.04.1998, p. 6; Lothar Rühl: Klärungsbedarf. In: *Welt*, 26.06.1998, p. 4.

116 afp/rtr: Tausende fliehen vor serbischen Angriffen. In: *FR*, 04.06.1998, p. 1.

117 Matthias Rüb: Belgrad setzt Angriffe auf Dörfer im Kosovo fort. In: *FAZ*, 07.03.1998, p. 1; Reuters/AP: Systematische Vertreibungen aus dem Kosovo. In: *FAZ*, 04.06.1998, p. 2; Nm.: Grüne Fassaden. In: *FAZ*, 12.06.1998, p. 14; E. L.: Hinweise auf Lager im Kosovo. In: *FAZ*, 17.06.1998, p. 2; Anonymous: Deutsche als Degen der USA? In: *Spiegel*, 02.06.1998, pp. 124–127.

the on-going debate amongst international politicians whether it would be legitimate to initiate a NATO-intervention in Kosovo even without a UN-mandate. Russia and China had indicated very clearly that they would veto any resolution in the UN-Security Council that would give NATO a mandate to intervene militarily, stating that Kosovo was part of Yugoslavia and thus an 'internal affair.' Consequently many international politicians – including Bill Clinton and Klaus Kinkel – were advocating a NATO-intervention without a UN-mandate, even though this would be against international law. They believed that the extensive human rights violations, and as *Spiegel* and *FAZ* reported, the threat of genocide, could justify such an international initiative.

There is one remarkable article published by *FAZ* which reported that an OSCE-ambassador in Tirana had received a "truly horrible report" about people being put in camps "[…] which possibly resemble those we have seen in other parts of the world."[118] This ominous yet indirect reference to the concentration camps in Bosnia of the early 1990s and perhaps the Third Reich was not mentioned by any other newspaper, nor did *FAZ* follow up on this matter, implying that the initial report was not substantiated. However, the willingness to publish this suspicion underlines the sensitivity of the newspaper to elements resembling 'genocide'.

However, the conservative *Welt* and *BILD* were not as discerning, using the term sparingly, but with considerable force.[119] For example, in early March *Welt's* Kalnoky alleged that the Serbian policy of massacres carried "[…] the signature of a coolly organised genocide."[120] The *BILD*-article explicitly stated that Milošević was pursuing genocide in Kosovo.[121] It is worth to pause and think about these allegations. With the benefit of hindsight, one can consult various documents by the UN and Amnesty International to find that the crimes perpetrated by Serbian police forces between March and June 1998 did not constitute 'genocide'.[122] While this can be said with certainty now, it remains incomprehensible why the two Springer-publications *Welt* and *BILD* chose to utilise the term. The evidence available at the

118 E. L.: Hinweise auf Lager im Kosovo. In: *FAZ*, 17.06.1998, p. 2.

119 Lothar Rühl: Klärungsbedarf. In: *Welt*, 26.06.1998, p. 4; Boris Kalnoky: Serbischer Ungeist. In: *Welt*, 09.03.1998, p. 4.

120 Boris Kalnoky: Serbischer Ungeist. In: *Welt*, 09.03.1998, p. 4.

121 Einar Koch: Kosovo: Heute steigen deutsche Kampfflieger auf. In: *BILD*, 15.06.1998, p. 1.

122 For example: OSCE: Kosovo/Kosova: As Seen, As Told; Independent International Commission: *The Kosovo Report.*

time indicated that Kosovo-Albanian civilians were being expelled from their homes and at times massacred. While observers confirmed a certain system in the Serbian course of action, there had been no accounts of 'genocide' thus far. While the hyperbole of utilising the term could be brushed off as sensationalism typical for the tabloid *BILD*, the same cannot be said for the broadsheet *Welt*. Perhaps a continued desire to discredit Milošević fuelled the misplacement of this term. Significantly, these idiosyncrasies were largely found in articles written by the publications' own correspondents rather than those authored by press agencies or pieced together from press releases. This reveals that the articles featuring particularly significant terms or embellished references to KLA-soldiers were not by-products of other sources or casual references, but rather mirrored the interpretation sanctioned by the publications' editors-in-chief.

These considerations introduce the wider theme of authorship. The distribution of these articles according to their source is best presented by quantity.

Newspaper	Total number of articles published	Percentage of articles authored by correspondents	Percentage of articles authored by press agencies	Percentage of articles amalgamated from various press releases, etc.
Welt	230	54%	27%	5%
FAZ	299	73%	26%	0.3%
FR	198	43%	56%	0%
taz	174	57%	43%	0%

Table 5: Percentages of articles according to authorship[123]

The above table indicates that in this timeframe, all daily broadsheets aside from *FR* published the majority of their articles authored by the publications' own Balkan-correspondents. The presence of international correspondents in the Drenica region and the expenses associated with this indicates a heightened level of interest at this early stage of the Kosovo conflict amongst the German media. Unfortunately, none of the articles produced by the publications' correspondents offered any insights into their daily work routine amidst this renewed violence in Kosovo or how they gathered information for their pieces.

123 All numbers short of 100% are anonymous articles which cannot be categorised.

However, Rathfelder's memoir, *Kosovo* (2010), offers a unique understanding regarding the method of research he and probably his colleagues from other publications were pursuing. One must make allowances when considering this information that the author presumably used his memoir to present himself in a favourable way. Writing about his experiences in Drenica in early March 1998, Rathfelder recalls that they were exploring the region in a cross-country vehicle, driving through forests and hidden roads to avoid Serbian forces.[124] Dodging Serbian military jeeps and shots fired at his car, Rathfelder underlines how adventurous and dangerous his investigative reporting was.[125] No such background details were published in the correspondents' articles at the time, which underlines how little the reader learned about the perils of journalism in Kosovo.

The Weight of History: Bosnia and World War Two

While such information remained unknown to the reader at the time, a more present feature was the cross-references to the Bosnian War and the Second World War in the German press' coverage of the violence in Kosovo. Starting with the former, all publications except *JF* and *Konkret* repeatedly referenced the previous Bosnian War during the emerging Kosovo conflict. In various cases, these were introduced in citations of speeches by international politicians, including Richard Holbrooke, Bill Clinton, Javier Solana, Joschka Fischer and Kofi Annan. All of them warned that Kosovo could become a 'second Bosnia', as was reported in various publications.[126] This caution was frequently deemed self-explanatory, though some contained a reference to the Serbian massacres of Bosnian civilians to further explain these comparisons. In addition, some of the newspapers' own correspondents also drew on this analogy. Significantly, these instances were marked by the overriding

124 Erich Rathfelder: *Kosovo*. Berlin: Suhrkamp 2010, p. 172.

125 Rathfelder: *Kosovo*, p. 174.

126 Lothar Rühl: Klärungsbedarf. In: *Welt*, 26.06.1998, p. 4; Matthias Rüb: Warum sollte Milosevic zu Zugeständnissen bereit sein? In: *FAZ*, 10.03.1998, p. 2; Rüb: „Starkes Signal" an Belgrad. In: *FAZ*, 10.03.1998, p. 2; Rüb: Milosevic „unnachgiebig wie üblich". In: *FAZ*, 11.05.1998, p. 2; fy: Notfalls Einsatz militärischer Mittel im Kosovo. In: *FAZ*, 29.05.1998, pp. 1–2; ul: Fischer fordert Intervention im Kosovo-Konflikt. In: *FAZ*, 10.06.1998, p. 6; Richard Meng: Bonn will Belgrad Chance geben. In: *FR*, 18.06.1998, p. 1; afp/dpa: Serbische Truppen greifen in Kosovo an. In: *FR*, 30.06.1998, p. 1; AP/AFP: Nato zeigt Balkan Flagge. In: *taz*, 29.05.1998, p. 4; AFP/dpa: Weiter Drohungen Richtung Belgrad. In: *taz*, 18.06.1998, p. 10; Anonymous: „Wir wollen Luftangriffe". In: *Spiegel*, 22.06.1998, p. 126.

message that 'the West' was once again allowing Milošević to wreak havoc, as he had in Bosnia.[127]

However, the strongest accusation and most emotive comparisons to Bosnia appeared in editorials. For example, Rathfelder's *taz*-editorial published in late-May accused: "as [had] already occurred in Bosnia, Europe [...was] acting irresponsibly [...] the war in Kosovo continue[d] unabated, even with increased intensity. However, Europe [...was] looking away."[128] A month later, *BILD's* Georg Gafron deplored in an editorial:

> again massacres against innocent people! [...] This time the butchers of Serb-President Milošević are going about their business in Kosovo. [...] NATO must act now, even though it's almost too late again. A second Bosnia must not happen![129]

Various examples in *Welt* evoked a similar sense of urgency by comparing Kosovo to Bosnia.[130] In early March Kalnoky wrote two separate editorials stating that just like in Bosnia, we were seeing "depressing pictures of fleeing civilians on tractors"[131] and as in the previous war, the Serbian tactic did not "[...] allow mercy for the victims and does not want witnesses for is crimes."[132] These loaded analogies to the Bosnian War helped the reader recall the images seen just a few years ago, making the events in Kosovo more pressing. These conjured images created a sense of urgency to act which may else not have appeared this early on.

In addition to the allusions made to the previous war in Bosnia, *taz*, *Spiegel*, *FR* and *FAZ* also made specific references to the Srebrenica Massacre.[133] The two *Spiegel*-articles referred to Srebrenica as the central reason for why NATO was considering an intervention in Kosovo much more quickly than

127 Boris Kalnoky: Milosevic setzt auf serbischen Zusammenhalt. In: *Welt*, 23.04.1998, p. 5; Wolfgang Günter Lerch: Der Kosovo-Knoten ist kaum zu lösen. In: *FAZ*, 12.06.1998, p. 14; Matthias Rüb: Instabilitätsexport. In: *FAZ*, 15.06.1998, p. 16; Erich Rathfelder: Freie Hand für Belgrad. In: *taz* 07.05.1998, p. 2.

128 Erich Rathfelder: Falsches Zeichen. In: *taz*, 27.05.1998, p. 12.

129 Georg Gafron: Die NATO muss handeln! In: *BILD*, 06.06.1998, p. 2.

130 Boris Kalnoky: Kriegsgefahr. In: *Welt*, 06.03.1998, p. 4; Kalnoky: Serbischer Ungeist. In: *Welt*, 09.03.1998, p. 4; Katja Ridderbusch: Milosevic oder Das Doppelspiel von Konzession und Härte. In: *Welt*, 10.03.1998, p. 4.

131 Boris Kalnoky: Kriegsgefahr. In: *Welt*, 09.03.1998, p. 4.

132 Boris Kalnoky: Serbischer Ungeist. In: *Welt*, 09.03.1998, p. 4.

133 Erich Rathfelder: Freie Hand für Belgrad. In: *taz*, 07.05.1998, p. 2; Rathfelder: „Menschenrechte sind keine innere Angelegenheit". In: *taz*, 13./14.06.1998, p. 10; Rathfelder: Intervention für die Menschenrechte. In: *taz*, 15.06.1998, p. 12; Stephan Israel: Serbiens Polizei will keine Zeugen. In: *FR*, 10.03.1998, p 3; Rolf Paasch: Endlosspule des Versagens. In: *FR*, 12.06.1998, p. 3; fy: Militärische Einsätze im Kosovo? In: *FAZ*, 10.06.1998, p. 2.

in Bosnia, possibly even without a UN-mandate.[134] A potential NATO-intervention without a UN-mandate was naturally controversial and had also been picked up in a *FAZ*-article on 10 June, which quoted Germany's Minister of Defence, Volker Rühe, who, remembering Srebrenica stated that "[…] there are situations in which it could be immoral not to deploy soldiers."[135] Two days later, in his *FR*-editorial, Rolf Paasch asked the poignant question: "an intervention in breach of international law or a second Srebrenica? What would you rather have to answer to?"[136]

However, Srebrenica and the recent Bosnian War were not the only historical milestones alluded to in the coverage. References to the Second World War could also be found in the coverage, though significantly only in *FR* and *Welt*. *FR's* correspondent Paasch warned that Germany should not get too involved in a potential military response against Milošević. After all, Serbia was a country "[…] in which German bombers and German troops caused a lot of destruction in the past."[137] The conservative *Welt* took a different stance on the matter. In an editorial, Kalnoky addressed an accusation made frequently by Serbian propaganda that Germany was pursuing a 'Fourth Reich' by getting involved in the Balkans. This term had been used in 1991 already, when Germany recognised Croatia's independence before the other EU-countries. From then on, Serbian politicians and state-controlled media outlets voiced this accusation regularly throughout the Bosnian War. When the Serbian media accused Germany of constructing a "[…] fascist 'fourth Reich'[…]" again in 1998, *Welt's* correspondent dismissed these allegations as Serbian propaganda reminiscent of the Bosnian War, instead emphasising Milošević's continual rampages in the Balkans.[138] Comparing these sparse references to the coverage in 1991/92, as the Bosnian War was developing, it is clear that significantly less attention was paid to the Second World War as the Kosovo conflict was unfolding. The scant references are highly significant and suggest that after initial difficulties, the German print media no longer saw Germany's active involvement in Europe's foreign affairs, even military involvement, as problematic due to the country's past.

134 Anonymous: „Kehr um, Milošević!" In: *Spiegel*, 15.06.1998, pp. 134–135; Anonymous: Deutsche als Degen der USA? In: *Spiegel*, 02.06.1998, pp. 124–127.

135 Fy: Militärische Einsätze im Kosovo? In: *FAZ*, 10.06.1998, p. 2.

136 Rolf Paasch: Endlosspule des Versagens. In: *FR*, 12.06.1998, p. 3.

137 paa: Mit Falken-Augen. In: *FR*, 16.06.1998, p. 3.

138 Boris Kalnoky: Serbischer Ungeist. In: *Welt*, 09.03.1998, p. 4.

Chapter 7
January 1999:
The 'Račak Massacre'

On 15 January 1999, 45 people were killed in a Kosovo-Albanian village called Račak, though it remains contested whether the fatalities were massacred civilians, as the KLA and Organisation for Security and Cooperation in Europe (OSCE) claimed, or if they were KLA-soldiers who died in combat as Belgrade asserted. This incident has found considerable attention in the secondary literature and is frequently included as one of the important milestones that led to NATO's military intervention in March 1999.[1] Numerous secondary sources[2] and primary accounts[3] mention Račak, emphasising the catalytic role it had in the international community's engagement in Kosovo. For example, Heinz Loquai alleged in his monograph that Račak was exploited "[...] for an increased intensification of the conflict and as a justification for

1 For example: Wolfgram: Democracy and Propaganda; Michael Ignatieff: *Virtual War: Kosovo and Beyond*. London: Picador 2000; Loquai: *Der Kosovo-Konflikt*, p. 45; Jochen Hils: *Manipuliertes Volk? Mediendemokratie und die militärische Interventionspolitik der USA am Beispiel der Kosovokriege*. Baden-Baden: Nomos 2007, pp. 174–208; Judah: *Kosovo*, pp. 193–194; Petritsch / Pichler: *Kosovo-Kosova*, pp. 159–166.

2 Including Friedrich: *Die deutsche Außenpolitik im Kosovo-Konflikt*, pp. 64–65; Günter Hofmann: Wie Deutschland in den Krieg geriet. In: *Die Zeit*, 12.05.1999. http://www.zeit.de/1999/20/199920.krieg_.xml, p. 2 (accessed 27.08.2014); Wolfgram: Democracy and Propaganda; Edward Herman / David Peterson: CNN: Selling NATO's War Globally. In: Philip Hammond / Edward Herman (eds): *Degraded Capability: The Media and the Kosovo Crisis*. London: Pluto 2000, pp. 111–122; Ignatieff: *Virtual War*.

3 Rudolf Scharping: *Wir dürfen nicht wegsehen: Der Kosovo-Krieg und Europa*. Munich: Ullstein 2001; Rathfelder: *Kosovo*; Petritsch / Pichler: *Kosovo-Kosova*; Loquai: *Der Kosovo-Konflikt*.

a further military escalation."[4] Wolfgang Petritsch echoed this interpretation, stating that "the pressure to find a quick solution in light of the developments which had spun out of control was reinforced by the media's handling of the events around Račak/Reçak."[5]

In spite of this increased international interest and the importance of Račak attributed by the secondary literature, this controversial incident has not received much attention in the field of media analyses. While there are several well-researched studies, particularly on the months of NATO's bombardment,[6] very few scholars have considered the events that preceded it, including the Račak incident. Mark Wolfgram's media analysis entitled "Democracy and Propaganda: NATO's War in Kosovo" is the only exception, though its academic usefulness is limited aside from its background information. In the abstract, Wolfgram explained his project as follows:

> This article uses [...] the fighting at Račak [as one of three examples...] to illustrate how democratic governments in the US and Germany attempted to manipulate public perceptions of the Kosovo conflict to justify the 1999 war.[7]

Yet the author does not quote a single German government document or protocol of a *Bundestag*-debate to substantiate his bold claim of manipulation on behalf of the German government. Moreover he only quoted three articles from the German print media, two from *Spiegel* and one from the daily broadsheet *Süddeutsche Zeitung*. This small sample size combined with limited primary sources renders his conclusions questionable.

Analysing the German press coverage between 15 January to 24 March 1999[8] – from the day of the killings until the first day of the NATO-intervention – this chapter examines the coverage of three important developments: firstly, the Račak incident itself, secondly, the publication of the autopsy examination and lastly, the domestic debate surrounding German involvement in a potential NATO-intervention. *AJW* will not be included in this chapter, as the newspaper did not publish any articles about Račak, Kosovo, or the German involvement in a prospective NATO-intervention in this timeframe. This complete lack of interest is congruent with the development already traced in the previous chapter and can likely be explained with the absence of

4 Loquai: *Der Kosovo-Konflikt*, p. 51.

5 Petritsch / Pichler: *Kosovo-Kosova*, p. 165.

6 To be discussed in the following chapter.

7 Wolfgram: Democracy and Propaganda, p. 153.

8 The April 1999 issue of *Konkret* will also be considered, as relevant information may have appeared later due to the editorial cycle of a monthly magazine.

a notable Jewish community in Kosovo. The closest the paper came to reporting any events in Kosovo was on 22 January 1999 in an article that covered the Jewish community in Sarajevo and what it meant to re-build a life after a war. However the piece did not contain any cross-references to Kosovo.[9]

The Račak Incident in the German Press

All other publications analysed here devoted considerable attention to Račak. Remarkably, all daily newspapers except for *BILD* reported on 16 January 1999 – one day after the incident and before further information had become available – that there had been fighting in Račak and according to the Serbian information centre in Priština, 15 KLA-fighters had died.[10] The willingness on behalf of *Welt*, *FAZ*, *FR* and *taz* to publish information based on Serbian sources indicates that these newspapers' correspondents did not exclusively rely on Kosovo-Albanian information. Following a weekend during which more information had become available and the head of the OSCE-mission in Kosovo, Walker, had issued his statement condemning the Serbian atrocities, all daily papers stated from 18 January onwards that the incident in Račak was a 'massacre' of 45 Kosovo-Albanian civilians. None qualified that this term was Walker's personal assessment. Numerous articles elaborated that OSCE-observers had found the fatalities; most had been shot in the head or neck. The articles also detailed that there were three women and one twelve-year-old boy amongst the victims.[11] The weekly *Spiegel* published this information a few days later, on 25 January 1999.[12]

Following Walker's statement, the previous information that KLA-soldiers had died in the Račak incident re-appeared in three of the papers which had initially reported it; *Welt* did not pick up on it again. *FAZ*, *FR* and *taz* all reported that the KLA itself had openly stated that it had lost 7–8 soldiers

9 Phillip Dreyer: „Ich weiß, was es heißt, nichts mehr zu haben". In: *AJW*, 22.01.1999, p. 5.

10 DW: Nato: Belgrad plant Offensive im Kosovo. In: *Welt*, 16.01.1999, p. 7; Reuters/AFP/AP: Heftige Kämpfe im Kosovo. In: *FAZ*, 16.01.1999, p. 1; ap: OSZE-Beobachter angeschossen. In: *FR*, 16.01.1999, p. 1; rtr/AP/AFP: Erneut schwere Kämpfe im Kosovo. In: *taz*, 16.01.1999, p. 5; also in Judah: *Kosovo*, p. 193.

11 DW: Kosovo-Massaker alarmiert die Nato. In: *Welt*, 18.01.1999, p. 1; Matthias Rüb: Empörung über Massaker im Kosovo: Nato-Rat zu Dringlichkeitssitzung einberufen. In: *FAZ*, 18.01.1999, p. 1; isr/ap/dpa/afp: Serben greifen Racak nach Massaker erneut an. In: *FR*, 18.01.1999, p. 1; Thomas Schmid: Kosovo-Massaker einhellig verurteilt. In: *taz*, 18.01.1999, p. 1; Anonymous: Massaker im Kosovo. In: *BILD*, 17.01.1999, p. 3.

12 Renate Flottau / Olaf Ihlau / Roland Schleicher: Im Teufelskreis der Gewalt. In: *Spiegel*, 25.01.1999, pp. 136–138.

during the fighting in Račak.[13] One of the *FR*-articles was accompanied by a map of Kosovo which contained an arrow with the description "Massacre of Albanian UÇK-fighters and civilians".[14] In spite of this acknowledgement of combatants amongst the fatalities, all following articles continued to refer to 45 civilian victims, rather than reducing the number to 37 or 38. Moreover, after 18 January, none mentioned the KLA-fatalities again. This inconsistency implies a subtle preference of the Kosovo-Albanian side of the story, which was further underlined by the utilisation of the term 'massacre' in their headlines.[15]

Many of the articles covering the incident immediately included graphic details.[16] Unlike the initial coverage of the violence in Kosovo, these articles drew heavily on eyewitness reports. A *Welt*-article cited a survivor who stated that many of the corpses exhibited traces of abuse, for example a decapitated man with a smashed skull and gauged-out eyes. "The perpetrators had even removed the brain from the skull with a spoon," he was quoted as saying.[17] The opening line of a *Spiegel*-article was equally striking. A local eye-witness, Bedri Azemi stated amidst sobs: "Only the bottom jaw still hung on the neck [...] that's how I found my beloved brother Banush out on the field; his head had been chopped off with an axe."[18] Similarly *taz's* Schmid quoted a man who recounted that "'my brother was executed right next to me', pulling a

13 Matthias Rüb: Nach dem Massaker von Recak steht die OSZE-Mission im Kosovo hilflos da. In: *FAZ*, 18.01.1999, p. 3; Rüb: Die Nato zeigt sich abermals zum Einsatz im Kosovo bereit. In: *FAZ*, 22.01.1999, pp. 1–2; isr/ap/dpa/afp: Serben greifen Racak nach Massaker erneut an. In: *FR*, 18.01.1999, p. 1; Stephan Israel: Jedes Massaker führt vom Frieden weg. In: *FR*, 18.01.1999, p. 1–2.

14 Image published in *FR*, 18.01.1999, p. 2.

15 For example: DW: Kosovo-Massaker alarmiert die Nato. In: *Welt*, 18.01.1999, p. 1; Matthias Rüb: Empörung über Massaker im Kosovo: Nato-Rat zu Dringlichkeitssitzung einberufen. In: *FAZ*, 18.01.1999, p. 1; Wgl.: Das Massaker. In: *FAZ*, 18.01.1999, p. 1; Matthias Rüb: Nach dem Massaker von Recak steht die OSZE-Mission im Kosovo hilflos da. In: *FAZ*, 18.01.1999, p. 1; isr/ap/dpa/afp: Serben greifen Racak nach Massaker erneut an. In: *FR*, 18.01.1999, pp. 1–2; Stephan Israel: Jedes Massaker führt vom Frieden weg. In: *FR*, 18.01.1999, pp. 1–2; Thomas Schmid: Kosovo-Massaker einhellig verurteilt. In: *taz*, 18.01.1999, p. 1; Anonymous: Massaker im Kosovo. In: *BILD*, 17.01.1999, p. 3.

16 For example: Anonymous: Massaker im Kosovo. In: *BILD*, 17.01.1999, p. 3; Matthias Rüb: Nach dem Massaker von Recak steht die OSZE-Mission im Kosovo hilflos da. In: *FAZ*, 18.01.1999, p. 3.

17 Boris Kalnoky: Serbien riskiert den nächsten Krieg auf dem Balkan. In: *Welt*, 18.01.1999, p. 3.

18 Renate Flottau / Olaf Ihlau / Roland Schleicher: Im Teufelskreis der Gewalt. In: *Spiegel*, 25.01.1999, pp. 136–138.

piece of skull, stained with dry blood from his pocket […]"[19] The *FR*-article underscored the victims' ages and gender, perhaps to suggest that they were not KLA-soldiers. "The grandfather lies dead in front of the barn […] An 18-year-old woman was obviously shot from behind."[20]

Along with the graphic descriptions of alleged Serbian savagery, the press' coverage of Račak was immediately accompanied by a sense of outrage. *Welt's* Kalnoky wrote that the 'massacre' was 'perverse'[21] while a *FAZ*-editorial referred to the 'Belgrade extermination-machine'.[22] This blunt and forceful word-choice demonstrated a sense of indignation which could not fail to register with readers. To further underline the horrific nature of the events, various pieces included emotive evaluations made by German politicians. For example, a *Welt*-article cited Foreign Minister Joschka Fischer that "[…] the massacre filled him with disgust."[23] A *Spiegel*-article quoted Minister of Defence Rudolf Scharping who had stated that the 'massacre' had to be explained in its "entirety of abomination."[24] Articles in *FAZ*, *FR* and *taz* all quoted Walker who declared that Račak exceeded everything he had ever seen, even in other war zones.[25] It is striking that the journalists readily published these evaluations without including qualifications of their own, perhaps in editorials. Many of these correspondents – Matthias Rüb of *FAZ* and *taz's* Thomas Schmid to name two – had also covered the Bosnian War and Kosovo's surge of violence in October 1998. It would seem that in these long years of witnessing and reporting on violent warfare and in the case of Srebrenica, genocide, they would have found Walker's assessment of 45 fatalities being worse than anything else he had seen in other wars slightly hyperbolic. Only *taz's* Erich Rathfelder wrote that Račak was "not entirely surprising"[26] which he later echoed in his memoirs.[27] However, this vague implication that considering the preceding Serbian violence Račak was not extraordinary would

19 Thomas Schmid: Aus nächster Nähe erschossen. In: *taz*, 18.01.1999, p. 3.

20 Melissa Eddy: Jeder Schritt führt zu einer neuen Greueltat. In: *FR*, 18.01.1999, p. 2.

21 Boris Kalnoky: Will Milošević einen Militärschlag? In: *Welt*, 21.01.1999, p. 7.

22 wgl.: Das Massaker. In: *FAZ*, 18.01.1999, p. 1.

23 DW: Kosovo-Massaker alarmiert die Nato. In: *Welt*, 18.01.1999, p. 1.

24 Olaf Ihlau / Siegesmund von Ilsemann: Geduld und Zähigkeit. In: *Spiegel*, 25.01.1999, pp. 138–140.

25 Matthias Rüb: Empörung über Massaker im Kosovo: Nato-Rat zu Dringlichkeitssitzung einberufen. In: *FAZ*, 18.01.1999, p. 1; isr/ap/dpa/afp: Serben greifen Racak nach Massaker erneut an. In: *FR*, 18.01.1999, p. 1; Thomas Schmid: Kosovo-Massaker einhellig verurteilt. In: *taz*, 18.01.1999, p. 1.

26 Erich Rathfelder: Die USA drohen mit einem Militäreinsatz. In: *taz*, 18.01.1999, p. 3.

27 Rathfelder: *Kosovo*, p. 225.

have easily been overlooked by many readers. The general reluctance of the correspondents to publish their own opinions and preference to reflect what politicians stated could result from the sparse concrete evidence available at the time. However, none of the articles presented their information as sparse, unreliable or limited. Consequently the lack of published personal opinion and interpretation on this matter, including in editorials or cartoons, where more editorial freedom is granted, remains curious.
The articles about the atrocities in Račak were accompanied by various images, which offer another perspective to the textual coverage.

Figure 30: An unidentified OSCE verifier, right, and ethnic Albanian rebel of KLA-Kosovo Liberation Army, left, count the bodies of as many as 40 men that were found on a hillside in the village of Racak, some 25 km (16 miles) south of Priština. AP; printed in *FAZ*, 18 January 1999, p. 3.

The above picture was *FAZ's* only visual of the incident. However, *Spiegel*, *BILD*, *taz*, FR and *Welt* published similar images of this ditch at roughly the same time, making it one of the most recognizable visuals of the incident.[28] *Welt*, *taz* and *FR* have indicated that the picture was taken by a news agency; AP, Reuters and dpa respectively. This gives a sense of how many journalists and photographers must have been on-site in Račak shortly after the bodies were found. The ditch-image corroborated the content of the textual

28 Images published in *BILD*, 17.01.1999, p. 3; *Spiegel*, 25.01.1999, p. 136; *taz*, 18.01.1999, p. 1; *FR*, 19.01.1999, p. 3; *Welt*, 18.01.1999, p. 3.

coverage. It is clearly visible in this image that the corpses were wearing civilian clothing and did not have weapons on them, which was the central narrative in many of the articles.[29] In addition, *BILD* published a more gruesome picture in which all the victims were laid out on the street. Especially the corpses lying closest to the camera show blood-covered faces. This visual is also very striking because it gives a clearer impression of the large number of victims involved.[30]

While the primary focus of the picture is the fatalities in the foreground, the groups of people found in the background – presumably journalists, though the image is too grainy to be sure – underlines the international attention Račak attracted. *taz* published a similar image, showing the corpses laid out in the local mosque, as the caption explained.

Figure 31:
Reuters; printed in *taz*,
12 February 1999, p. 10,
and 18 March 1999, p. 3.

taz's image featured some of the corpses' heads covered with pieces of white cloth, implying mutilations, but leaving specifics unsaid. In contrast, *BILD*'s picture (not shown here) was taken from an angle where precisely these more sanguine and gory details were in the foreground. The intended effect of shock and horror, especially in the visual coverage, was not unusual for the

29 Images published in *Welt*, 18.01.1999, p. 10; *FAZ*, 18.01.1999, p. 1; *FR*, 10.02.1999, p. 2; *taz*, 18.01.1999, p. 1; *Spiegel*, 25.01.1999, pp. 136–138; *BILD*, 18.03.1999, p. 1.

30 Image published in *BILD*, 30.01.1999, p. 1.

tabloid. However, comparing it to the more sombre *taz*-picture, in which the mourning of an elderly man and young child are more prominent than the mutilations, the plethora of messages that can be conveyed through images is underscored.

An interesting commonality could be found in *BILD*, *Spiegel*, *taz* and *Welt*, all of which featured images of this ditch showing the same elderly man wearing a white hat, seemingly guiding the journalists.[31] None of the publications explained who this man was. His repeated appearance raises questions about his identity: were international journalists only granted access if they were guided by a local? Judging from his attire, the man was Kosovo-Albanian. Did his narrative influence the content of the articles? These questions unfortunately remain unanswered, though they underline how many unknown factors influenced the article that ultimately reached the reader.

JF did not publish any pictures of Račak, nor did it offer the same detailed and gruesome information about the atrocities. However, in the single article that mentioned the incident, *JF* uniquely embedded Račak into the wider context of on-going violence in Kosovo. Reminding the reader that both the KLA and the Serbian forces had been using the cease-fire to re-organise their troops, the author indicated that Račak was one of many examples of violence.[32] This balanced reporting resembles the accounts in some of the secondary sources discussed at the beginning of this chapter, but is an extraordinary exception compared to the other publications' coverage at the time. Interestingly, this deliberate content of the article was contradicted by the article's title: "The goal is genocide." Combined with the information derived from the article that Serbian police had 'massacred' Račak's civilian population, the title and terminology expressed an underlying message that Belgrade was ultimately aiming to exterminate the Kosovo-Albanian population in Kosovo, and that Račak was just one of many more incidents to come. Though the article itself did not explicitly state this, the utilisation of the term 'genocide' and 'massacre of civilians' implied this. Such subtleties in language and terminology will be explored in more depth later in this chapter.

31 The man can be seen in the background of Figure 30 and more prominently in a number of pictures not printed here, for example, *BILD*, 17.01.1999, p. 3; *taz*, 18.01.1999, p. 1; *Welt*, 18.01.1999, p. 3.

32 Victor Capé: Das Ziel ist der Genozid. In: *JF*, 22.01.1999, p. 10.

Račak: The Serbian Perspective

As mentioned previously, the events surrounding Račak were contested almost immediately, with the Serbian narrative differing from the Kosovo-Albanian version.[33] However, given the general inclination to the Kosovo-Albanian perspective found in the previously discussed articles, the German mainstream press did not entertain the idea that Račak was manipulated or staged by the KLA. *Welt*, *Spiegel*, *FR*, *taz* and *FAZ*, all included the Serbian interpretation in their articles, though all but *Welt* dismissed it very quickly. Significantly, none of the articles openly stated that the Serbian version was untrue or unreliable. Rather, through subtle techniques such as discrediting the Serbian source or unequally contrasting one version with the other left the reader with an unmistakeable conclusion that had never actually been articulated.[34]

For example, the single *Spiegel*-article that mentioned the different versions of events primarily focused on the Kosovo-Albanian interpretation, outlining the Serbian atrocities that had been committed in Račak. Only later it alluded to the Serbian point-of-view in a single sentence, stating: "Milošević insisted [...] that all victims were killed in combat."[35] This side-note received comparably little attention and indeed was buried in other details of the article. The authors continued that the "radical nationalist" Vojislav Šešelj had accused the Albanians of changing the "UÇK-terrorists' [clothing]" to make them look like civilians. After introducing this Serbian version, the authors reminded the readers that Šešelj's favoured war tactic included "[...] massacres of civilians as well as ethnic cleansing and the torching of Albanian settlements." This immediate discrediting of the source automatically dismissed his assessment and thus rendered the Serbian version of events mere propaganda.[36]

In *FAZ* and *FR*, the technique of unequal juxtaposition was utilised. In all cases the Serbian narrative was included, however their structure was laid out in such a way that the reader was confronted with overwhelming evidence to the contrary. For example, on 18 January, *FAZ's* Matthias Rüb started his article with the Serbian assertions that the attack on Račak was a search-and-punish-action by the Serbian police, looking for what they called KLA-terrorists

33 See chapter 2, fn. 45–52.

34 Thomas Schmid: Serbische Versionen über das Massaker. In: *taz*, 19.01.1999, p. 11; Andrej Ivanji: Serbien setzt weiter auf Härte. In: *taz*, 20.01.1999, p. 5.

35 Renate Flottau / Olaf Ihlau / Roland Schleicher: Im Teufelskreis der Gewalt. In: *Spiegel*, 25.01.1999, pp. 136–138, here p. 137.

36 Ibid.

who had shot a Serbian policeman in the region just a few days before. The article continued that "according to eyewitnesses and the OSCE-mission, the incident was *naturally* portrayed differently"[37] and ended with Walker's quote "Jesus Christ, at least cover them", which Rüb wrote he spluttered when he saw the corpses, some of which had been mutilated.[38] By structuring the article in this way, the author leaves no question which version of events he found more plausible. Indeed by the time the reader had finished the article, the beginning about KLA-soldiers being involved could have easily been forgotten. Similarly a *FR*-article wrote that *Washington Post* had reported its possession of live recordings of 'Serb-leaders' in which the Deputy Prime Minister Nikola Šainović called General Sreten Lukić in Kosovo to inquire how the 'attack' was proceeding. With shots being fired in the background, Lukić was heard to answer that so far 22 people had been shot, suggesting cold murder taking place during a casual phone conversation. The *FR*-article ended with the information that according to the official Serbian account, the 45 people who had been shot in Račak had been KLA-soldiers.[39] However, a reader would have easily forgotten this version amidst the more memorable – though difficult to verify – story of the phone conversation.

In contrast, various *Welt*-articles repeated the Serbian account without using subtle devices to counter them.[40] This made the conservative broadsheet the only German publication to seriously present the Serbian point-of-view. This is particularly striking as it is a significant shift from the paper's previous anti-Serbian and anti-Milošević inclination found in the articles dating from the early to mid-1990s, as well as earlier articles that had called Račak 'a perverse massacre.'[41] This discrepancy within the same timeframe could be explained with the differing authors. All articles that included the Serbian perspective were authored by 'DW' or '*Die Welt*' and were amalgamations of several press releases. In contrast, the memorable description of Račak being 'perverse' was produced by Boris Kalnoky, though significantly not in an editorial. This

37 Emphasis added by author.

38 Matthias Rüb: Nach dem Massaker von Recak steht die OSZE-Mission im Kosovo hilflos da. In: *FAZ*, 18.01.1999, p. 3. Other articles include Rüb: Empörung über Massaker im Kosovo: Nato-Rat zu Dringlichkeitssitzung einberufen. In: *FAZ*, 18.01.1999, p. 1; Rüb: OSZE protestiert gegen Ausweisung Walkers. In: *FAZ*, 20.01.1999, p. 12; Rüb: Die Nato zeigt sich abermals zum Einsatz im Kosovo bereit. In: *FAZ*, 22.01.1999, pp. 1–2.

39 afp/dpa: Tonbänder belegen angeblich Massaker-Befehl. In: *FR*, 29.01.1999, p. 2.

40 DW: Nato will Kosovo-Massaker aufklären. In: *Welt*, 19.01.1999, p. 7; DW: Nato droht Milosevic mit einem Militärschlag. In: *Welt*, 20.01.1999, p. 1; DW: Massaker von Racak weiter umstritten. In: *Welt*, 26.01.1999, p. 7.

41 See chapter 7, fn. 21.

matter of authorship and its influence on the articles will be discussed in more detail at a later point, however here it is worth noting that *Welt* uniquely included several articles featuring the Serbian perspective.

In addition, *Welt* and *taz* reported that various French and British newspapers, for example *Le Monde* or *The Guardian*, were publishing articles which claimed that some of the information on Račak was inconclusive, assessing that the 'massacre' may have been staged. In a *Welt*-article, the author went as far as posing the question whether the fatalities in Račak were "[...] part of a macabre play staged by the underground army UÇK to motivate the West to intervene".[42] *Welt* cited a *Guardian*-article which had reported that the OSCE had provided information revealing that while some of the corpses did exhibit close-range bullet-wounds, other victims had clearly been killed at a different location from where they were found. "[...] Skid marks and trails of blood or brain-mass allow the conclusion that the corpses had been moved from elsewhere."[43] Equally *taz's* article referred to the doubts raised by two French newspapers, *Liberation* and *Le Monde*. The German daily reported that *Le Monde's* articles wondered why there was "so little blood" in the ditch where the corpses were found and whether this was an indication that the event had been staged.[44] While *Welt* and *taz* reported that these international news-outlets doubted the linear narrative of events in favour of the Kosovo-Albanians, both detached themselves from such musings. Neither published further articles in this direction. Nonetheless, their engagement – though only in one article each – suggests that the authors were intrigued if nothing else by the two interpretations of the Račak incident.

Konkret also cited French newspapers – in this case *Le Monde* and *Le Figaro* – to present the interpretation that the events in Račak could have been manipulated and were perhaps being misused by the international community to justify armed intervention in Kosovo. In March Otto Köhler published an article about Račak, questioning whether "[...] the massacre was really a massacre." Preferring the more neutral term '*Leichenfund*' or 'discovery of corpses', Köhler's article stated that *Le Figaro's* journalists had not found many shell casings near the corpses, which they concluded indicated that they had not been massacred. Köhler then turned to the article in *Le Monde*, which claimed that the 'massacre' was simply 'too perfect'. There was too little blood in the ditch for the killings to have taken place there. Moreover "the village had

42 nik: Krieg um die 40 Toten von Racak im Kosovo. In: *Welt*, 22.01.1999, p. 7.

43 Ibid.

44 bo: US-französischer Stellvertreterkrieg. In: *taz*, 29.01.1999, p. 10.

[…] been observed the whole day and no one had noticed anything indicating a 'massacre.'"[45] Though Köhler himself stopped short of offering a personal view, his choice of citations left little doubt as to his intended argument. Moreover, as this was the only *Konkret*-article about Račak in this timeframe, the readers were presented with a one-sided narrative.

In connection with the predominant preference of the Kosovo-Albanian narrative in most publications, the distribution of the articles' authorship is worth considering.

Newspaper	**Total number of articles published**	**Percentage of articles authored by correspondents**	**Percentage of articles authored by press agencies**	**Percentage of articles amalgamated from various press releases, etc.**
Welt	158	51%	18%	31%
FAZ	173	78%	21%	1%
FR	147	54%	46%	0%
taz	165	70%	29%	0%

Table 6: Percentages of articles according to authorship.[46]

As the above table shows, these daily newspapers preferred to publish articles authored by their own correspondents. This suggests that the pieces produced for the reader were frequently based on eyewitness accounts collated by the correspondent himself; the sources he or she chose to give a voice to and ultimately the journalists' personal interpretations. This in turn suggests that the quick dismissal of the Serbian narrative or the unchallenged replication of Walker's assessment were examples of the publications' and correspondents' pro-Kosovo-Albanian interpretation.

The Autopsy Report

Soon after the fatalities had been discovered in Račak, a forensic examination of the corpses took place. Directly after the incident, the bodies had been examined by a Serbian-Belorussian forensic team, which the international community deemed unreliable and biased. Consequently, approximately ten days later, the European Union Forensic Expert Team (EU-FET) was appointed to conduct what they deemed neutral examinations. The Finnish

45 Otto Köhler: Mass Murder Inc. In. *Konkret*, March 1999, p. 31.

46 All numbers short of 100% are anonymous articles which cannot be categorised.

experts, led by Dr. Helena Ranta began their work on 22 January and summarised their findings in a document produced by Ranta on 17 March.[47] The presentation of the forensic report on 17 March revived the German press' interest, which had abated after the initial surge. *JF* was the only publication not to pick up on the matter.

First a summary of the autopsy report itself, as well as an article published in the journal *Forensic Science International* by members of the Department of Forensic Medicine, University of Helsinki will give a sense of the forensic inquests that followed.[48] The report itself was only six pages long, though Ranta also submitted the ca. 3000 photographs and 10 hours of film taken during the autopsies.[49] While brief, it featured some notable clarifications regarding the controversies that had surrounded Račak. It stated that

> most of the victims wore several warm jackets and pullovers. No ammunition was found in the pockets […] The clothing bore no identifying badges or insignia of any military unit. No indication of removal of badges or insignia was evident. Based on autopsy findings […] it is highly unlikely that clothes could have been changed or removed.[50]

The report further stated that "there were no indications of people being [anything] other than unarmed civilians."[51] However, it concluded that the mutilations which had been cited by many newspapers as proof of the brutality of Serbian criminals occurred post-mortem and "[…] most likely related to animal activity – such as stray dogs […] and other wild animals."[52] This could also account for the decapitations that had frequently been reported on in the German press coverage. "Gnaw marks were presented on the vertebrae and base of the fractured skull."[53] Other instances of mutilations mentioned by eyewitnesses, such as that a brain had been scooped out with a spoon[54] was not discussed by Ranta. This in turn introduces questions regarding the reliability of eyewitness accounts.

47 Anonymous: Report of the EU Forensic Expert Team on the Račak Incident, 17.03.1999. http://www.ess.uwe.ac.uk/Kosovo/Kosovo-Massacres2.htm (accessed 07.06.2012) [henceforth abbreviated to EU-FET Report].

48 EU-FET Report; J. Rainio / K. Lalu / A. Pentillä: Independent Forensic Autopsies in an Armed Conflict: Investigation of the Victims from Racak, Kosovo. In: *Forensic Science International* 116,3 (2001), pp. 171–185.

49 Rainio / Lalu / Pentillä: Independent Forensic Autopsies, p. 172.

50 EU-FET Report, p. 3.

51 Ibid., pp. 3–4.

52 Rainio / Lalu / Pentillä: Independent Forensic Autopsies, p. 183.

53 Ibid., pp. 182–183.

54 See chapter 7, fn. 17.

Dr. Ranta also drew attention to problems and limitations of her findings. As the opening sentence clarified, this was a 'medicolegal investigation' which constituted "[…] only a part – but […did] not cover the whole spectrum – of criminal investigations."[55] Consequently, based on this report alone, it was not possible to definitively assess whether the victims in Račak were indeed 'massacred', as that "[…] is a legal description of the circumstances surrounding the deaths of persons […]" and could only be applied after "a full criminal investigation [was] combined with the interrogation of witnesses […]"[56]

The German print media responded in a variety of ways. The daily publications reported that the Račak-victims were deemed civilians by Ranta and her team, which was the most important conclusion the newspapers featured.[57] Other details, for example that the mutilations had been considered to be inflicted by animals could be found in some articles.[58] All newspapers except for *FAZ* and *Spiegel* mentioned that the forensic team did not explicitly label the incident a 'massacre' because there had been no criminal investigation.[59] *FR* made this fact most explicit by including it in its article-title: "Medics leave the word massacre for the jurists".[60] In spite of qualifications expressed in *FR's* headline, significantly the term 'massacre' was not placed in quotation marks, implying that it still could not be dismissed altogether. Similarly, the conservative broadsheets *Welt* and *FAZ* stubbornly included 'massacre' in their titles, although the articles reported that Ranta had not used the term.[61] Indeed, *Welt's* title, "The report about Račak-Massacre leaves questions open"

55 EU-FET Report, p. 4.

56 Ibid.

57 Jochen Hehn: Serben stellen neue Forderungen. In: *Welt*, 18.03.1999, p. 8; Matthias Rüb: Massaker von Recak als Verbrechen gegen die Menschlichkeit bezeichnet. In: *FAZ*, 18.03.1999, p. 2; Stephan Israel: Das Wort Massaker überlassen die Mediziner den Juristen. In: *FR*, 18.03.1999, p. 2; AFP/taz: Opfer von Racak waren Zivilisten. In: *taz*, 18.03.1999, p. 1; Anonymous: Kosovo-Krise: Serben bereiten sich auf Krieg vor! In: *BILD*, 18.03.1999, p. 1.

58 Matthias Rüb: Massaker von Recak als Verbrechen gegen die Menschlichkeit bezeichnet. In: *FAZ*, 18.03.1999, p. 2; Thomas Schmid: Racak – ein Verbrechen gegen die Menschlichkeit. In: *taz*, 18.03.1999, p. 3.

59 kk/rtr: Der Bericht über Kosovo-Massaker lässt Fragen offen. In: *Welt*, 18.03.1999, p. 8; Stephan Israel: Das Wort Massaker überlassen die Mediziner den Juristen. In: *FR*, 18.03.1999, p. 2; Thomas Schmid: Racak – ein Verbrechen gegen die Menschlichkeit. In: *taz*, 18.03.1999, p. 3.

60 Stephan Israel: Das Wort Massaker überlassen die Mediziner den Juristen. In: *FR*, 18.03.1999, p. 2.

61 Mattias Rüb: Massaker von Recak als Verbrechen gegen die Menschlichkeit bezeichnet. In: *FAZ*, 18.03.1999, p. 2; kk/rtr: Der Bericht über Kosovo-Massaker lässt Fragen offen. In: *Welt*, 19.03.1999, p. 8.

directly refuted the article's content which stated that Ranta refused to utilise the word. The continued appearance of the term 'massacre' in *Welt's* and *FAZ's* titles, even after Ranta had distanced herself from the term suggests that the publications aimed to preserve the understanding of events they had presented in January. Conversely, *taz* did not place the term in its title, instead proclaiming: "Račak-victims were civilians".[62]

Both *FAZ* and *Spiegel* covered the autopsy report and its contents very superfically and instead used its publication as an opportunity to summarise the events in Račak.[63] Rüb's *FAZ*-article only devoted the last few sentences to the report and even then failed to include any of the limitations Ranta had warned of.[64] The *Spiegel*-article took the same approach, mentioning the document in only one sentence.[65] Due to this limited coverage, both publications included a factual error: they stated that Walker's assessment (that Račak had been a 'massacre'), had been confirmed by the autopsy report.[66] While the *Spiegel*-article did not give any indication of the author's locality, the *FAZ*-article was written from Budapest rather than Priština, where Ranta had presented her findings, which could explain the superficial reporting. Rüb himself was clearly not in Priština, leaving the impression that Ranta's presentation was deemed unimportant by either the newspaper, the journalist, or both.

A *Konkret*-article mentioning the autopsy report was equally superficial. Otto Köhler dismissed it as unreliable, stating that from the beginning, Ranta's examinations had served the purpose of proving what OSCE's Walker had alleged right away, namely that Račak was a 'massacre'. Disgruntled the author wrote: "never mind that the Serbian and Belorussian forensic scientists have already eliminated the option that Račak was a massacre. Serbs! Russians!"[67] The forensic findings were presented as proving Walker right, which – by refusing to use the term 'massacre' – was clearly incorrect. However, the article's subtitle, "[…] Such lustfulness for war has not existed since 1914",

62 AFP/taz: Opfer von Racak waren Zivilisten. In: *taz*, 18.03.1999, p. 1.

63 Renate Flottau / Roland Schleicher: Marsch in die Sackgasse. In: *Spiegel*, 22.03.1999, pp. 196–198; Matthias Rüb: Massaker von Recak als Verbrechen gegen die Menschlichkeit bezeichnet. In: *FAZ*, 18.03.1999, p. 2.

64 Matthias Rüb: Massaker von Recak als Verbrechen gegen die Menschlichkeit bezeichnet. In: *FAZ*, 18.03.1999, p. 2.

65 Renate Flottau / Roland Schleicher: Marsch in die Sackgasse. In: *Spiegel*, 22.03.1999, pp. 196–198.

66 Matthias Rüb: Massaker von Recak als Verbrechen gegen die Menschlichkeit bezeichnet. In: *FAZ*, 18.03.1999, p. 2; Renate Flottau / Roland Schleicher: Marsch in die Sackgasse. In: *Spiegel*, 22.03.1999, pp. 196–198.

67 Otto Köhler: Joschka brennt. In: *Konkret*, April 1999, p. 16.

demonstrates the author's intention to prove that 'the West' was moving towards a NATO-intervention, no matter what the 'facts' were. However, *Konkret's* Köhler did correctly point to a certain prejudice against the Serbo-Belorussian forensic team. Ranta's report made a point to state that "at the professional level, the team experienced no problems in collaboration with Yugoslav or Belorussian pathologists." Indeed, according to Ranta, there was a "[...] cooperative working atmosphere," which was not mentioned in any publication.[68]

In contrast, *FR*'s coverage was much more detailed. Here the correspondent, Stephan Israel, included a description of the presentation: that Ranta stood on a stage, flanked by diplomats, to present the report. Such vivid details of the proceedings suggest that the journalist was present. He wrote that after relentless questions by the journalists, Ranta deemed Račak a 'crime against humanity', though she did not want to attribute the label 'massacre.'[69] In this respect, *FR's* coverage of the report was the most discerning and accurate. However, one interpretation was not included in the article, namely what it could mean that Ranta made her presentation in the presence of diplomats. Perhaps this interest of the international community to witness and possibly steer the event could have been viewed as an affirmation that manipulation – in whatever form – was taking place.

The Press' Language

Throughout this coverage of Račak, some changes in language became evident; for example the vocabulary used in reference to the KLA. While previous articles (considered in chapter 6) had been cautious and even protective of the KLA, this had partly changed. For example, all mainstream publications spoke of 'KLA-fighters'[70] in their coverage, rather than referring to them ambiguously as 'Kosovo-Albanians', as they had before. Moreover the use of quotation marks around 'Kosovo Liberation Army' is revealing.

68 EU-FET Report, p. 5.

69 Stephan Israel: Das Wort Massaker überlassen die Mediziner den Juristen. In: *FR*, 18.03.1999, p. 2.

70 For example: nik: Krieg um die 40 Toten von Racak im Kosovo. In: *Welt*, 22.01.1999, p. 7; Matthias Rüb: Tausende sind im Kosovo auf der Flucht. In: *FAZ*, 19.03.1999, p. 5; ap: OSZE-Beobachter angeschossen. In: FR, 16.01.1999, p. 1; rtr: Nato-Einsatzplan für Kosovo steht. In: *taz*, 27.01.1999, p. 4; Renate Flottau / Rainer Pörtner: Poker an der roten Linie. In: *Spiegel*, 01.03.1999, p. 155; Anonymous: Neues Blutbad im Kosovo. In: *BILD*, 30.01.1999, p. 1.

Publication	Use of quotation marks in 1998 (chapter 4)	Use of quotation marks during Račak-coverage
Welt	Yes	No
FAZ	Occasionally	No
BILD	Occasionally	No
FR	Occasionally	Occasionally
taz	No	No
Spiegel	No	No
Junge Freiheit	Yes	No
Konkret	Yes	No reference to KLA

Table 7: Use of quotation marks around 'Kosovo Liberation Army'.

This table demonstrates that the conservative newspapers *Welt*, *FAZ* and *BILD* as well as the far-right *JF* all shifted in their use of quotation marks. During their coverage of the initial violence in Kosovo, analysed in the previous chapter, these publications had occasionally or consistently placed quotation marks around 'Kosovo Liberation Army,' indicating an uncertainty about how to label this army and whether they deemed it a legitimate formation or not. However, by January 1999, all papers except occasionally *FR* no longer used quotations marks. This suggests a more straightforward treatment with the army as an actor in the violence.
Additionally, *JF* continually referred to KLA-fighters as 'partisans' and called their military actions 'partisan-strikes.'[71] This may have been aimed to evoke connotations of World War Two, where communist partisans led by Tito fought against the fascists. An interview with Zoran Jeremić, the Yugoslav ambassador in Bonn reiterated this. When the term 'partisan' was used in a question posed to Jeremić, he replied: "according to our perception, partisans are those who fought against fascism during the Second World War. However regarding the UÇK, we are speaking of terrorists […]"[72] The continued use of this misplaced term, even after Jeremić's correction is puzzling. While the term 'partisan' alluded to the KLA's guerrilla tactics, perhaps *JF's* utilisation was an attempt to avoid the term 'terrorist.' However, as discussed in the

71 For example: Victor Capé: Das Ziel ist der Genozid. In: *JF*, 22.01.1999, p. 10; Karl Gerigk: „Der Kosovo wird missbraucht". In: *JF*, 05.02.1999, p. 3.

72 Karl Gerigk: „Der Kosovo wird missbraucht". In: *JF*, 05.02.1999, p. 3.

previous chapter, a *JF*-article had described KLA's tactics as 'utter terror,' rendering this new term jarring.[73]

Moreover, an idiosyncrasy of *FAZ's* coverage is noteworthy. All articles consistently used the Albanian spelling of Račak and Priština, namely Reçak and Prishtina. In the early coverage, *FAZ's* articles – all authored by the newspaper's Balkan-correspondent, Matthias Rüb – had continued to include the Serbian version in brackets.[74] This could be a desire to express the broadsheet's sympathy for the Kosovo-Albanian side, while simultaneously reassuring the reader that this was not merely a spelling mistake. However, the newspaper persistently used the Serbian version for Kosov*o*, rather than switching to Kosov*a*, probably as this was more familiar to the reader.

The concerted utilisation or avoidance of the terms 'genocide' and 'ethnic cleansing' are also worth considering. The latter was used sparingly; indeed only in *FAZ* and *taz*.[75] These articles – predominantly published in *FAZ* – merely reported that 'ethnic cleansing' was occurring in Kosovo, but did not refer specifically to Račak. While *Welt* and *FR* each used 'genocide' once, this was not in connection to the Račak incident. The *Welt*-article, for example, stated that Milošević could end up perpetrating 'genocide' in Kosovo if things continued as they were, while the *FR*-article called Milošević a 'suspected genocidaire' or '*Völkermörder*.'[76] However *FAZ* and *JF* specifically linked 'genocide' to Račak. The latter alleged that Belgrade's ultimate goal was 'genocide' and even used this word in the title of an article, as mentioned previously.[77] *FAZ* reported that a lobby group called 'International Helsinki Federation' had attributed this label in its assessment of Račak.[78] Significantly, the article did not qualify this evaluation, which it could have done simply by citing someone with the opposite view. Even if the fatalities in Račak had

73 See chapter 6, fn. 75.

74 wgl.: Das Massaker. In: *FAZ*, 18.01.1999, p. 1; Matthias Rüb: Nach dem Massaker von Recak steht die OSZE-Mission im Kosovo hilflos da. In: *FAZ*, 18.01.1999, p. 3; Rüb: OSZE protestiert gegen Ausweisung Walkers. In: *FAZ*, 20.01.1999, pp. 1–2; Rüb: Der serbische Wahnsinn folgt einer inneren Logik. In: *FAZ*, 20.01.1999, p. 3.

75 Thomas Schmid: Wer A sagt, muss nicht B sagen. In: *taz*, 05.03.1999, p. 12; bko: Am Pranger. In: *FAZ*, 17.03.1999, p. 16; bko: Hilflos in Paris. In: *FAZ*, 20.03.1999, p. 12; Matthias Rüb: Großoffensive serbischer Einheiten. In: *FAZ*, 22.03.1999, p. 2; Rüb: Die demonstrative Zuversicht der Albaner will mit dem Vormarsch der jugoslawischen Armee nicht zusammenpassen. In: *FAZ*, 23.03.1999, p. 3.

76 Boris Kalnoky: Die Diplomaten sind gescheitert. In: *Welt*, 22.03.1999, p. 3; also in Rolf Paasch: Irrweg der Diplomatie. In: *FR*, 22.01.1999, p. 3.

77 Victor Capé: Das Ziel ist der Genozid. In: *JF*, 22.01.1999, p. 10.

78 E. L.: Aktive Antwort auf Massaker gefordert. In: *FAZ*, 19.01.1999, p. 2.

been 'massacred,' the employment of the term 'genocide' in this respect is erroneous and highly inflated, perhaps utilised to present the Serbian forces as negatively as possible by linking them to 'genocide.' In this context it must be noted that the Srebrenica Massacre continued to reappear in *Welt*, *FR*, *taz* and *Spiegel*. These references reminded their readers that the 'last time,' during the Bosnian War it had taken 8,000 deaths in Srebrenica to convince NATO to finally intervene. They continued by expressing their hope that this time the international community would not wait as long.[79]

Use of Images

Aside from the Račak incident itself, the on-going violence in other parts of Kosovo continued to interest the German press. The images accompanying these articles portrayed various different themes, though three are worth considering in more detail: the depiction of Serbian forces, KLA-soldiers, and the victims of the violence. The latter theme presented a clear polarisation: there were almost no pictures showing Serbian victims, except in *taz* and *Welt*.[80]

The two visual representations featured grieving women – a favoured theme perhaps to evoke sympathy. The image printed in *taz* showed the funeral of a Serbian man who had been killed by the KLA, as the caption explained; the *Welt*-image showed the mourning family of a Serbian policeman who had been killed. These singular pictorial exceptions showing Serbians as victims could have been easily over-looked at the time. As the violence ensued in Kosovo, where 90% of the population was Kosovo-Albanian, one could argue that inevitably there were significantly fewer Serbian victims of violence, explaining the reduced visual coverage. However, the two images which were published tell an important narrative otherwise missing in the German press-coverage: that the KLA killed Serbians whose families mourned and suffered, just as the Kosovo-Albanians. This dimension – if covered in more detail – would have given the reader a more complete understanding of the violence in Kosovo and the KLA's activities.

In contrast, the visual presentation of the Kosovo-Albanian victims of the violence was much more prominent. Refugee treks were a common theme,

79 Nikolaus Blome: Gehört Milosevic Europa? In: *Welt*, 20.01.1999, p. 10; Rolf Paasch: Irrweg der Diplomatie. In: *FR*, 22.01.1999, p. 3; Thomas Schmid: Wer A sagt, muss nicht B sagen. In: *taz*, 05.03.1999, p. 12; Olaf Ihlau / Siegesmund von Ilsemann: Geduld und Zähigkeit. In: *Spiegel*, 25.01.1999, p. 140.

80 Images published in *taz*, 05.03.1999, p. 5; *Welt*, 02.02.1999, p. 7.

which underlined the dimensions of the humanitarian catastrophe unfolding. Various images showed families loaded on truck beds; others pictured long treks of civilians carrying nothing but the clothes on their bodies.[81] The unmistakeable message communicated through these pictures was that civilians – frequently women and children – were the primary victims of forced expulsions.

Upon closer consideration, some images in *Welt*, *FR* and *taz* presented an odd mixture of messages. Three images published by *taz*, *Welt* and *FR* printed pictures of a dead KLA-soldier and their mourning relatives.[82] As one of the captions explained, one particular image was the first prize winner of the prestigious photo-journalism contest 'World Press Photo' of the year 1998.[83] Originally published in the American broadsheet *Washington Post* in November 1998,[84] this picture shows the widow of a KLA-commander at his funeral. It is interesting that the papers were willing to value the emotions of the survivors of KLA-combatants as much as they would have done had the person who had been killed been an innocent bystander or a civilian. In light of the absence of comparable images featuring grieving Serbian widows and children of fallen Serbian combatants, this could suggest sympathy with the KLA. The publications' pronounced emphasis on the Kosovo-Albanian suffering rather than the KLA-induced violence coincides with the near-complete omission of picturing Serbian civilians as victims mentioned previously.

Congruent with the one-sided portrayal of the victims of the violence, the visual representation of the perpetrators was imbalanced.

81 Rolf Paasch: Es gibt keinen Platz mehr zwischen den Fronten. In: *FR*, 10.03.1999, p. 3; Renate Flottau / Olaf Ihlau: Die Alternative heißt Krieg. In: *Spiegel*, 15.03.1999, p. 208; Oliver Santen: Reißt dieser Mann ganz Europa in den Krieg? In: *BILD*, 22.03.1999, p. 2.

82 Images published in *taz*, 10.02.1999, p. 10; *Welt*, 25.01.1999, p. 6; *FR*, 13.02.1999, p. 2; *Welt*, 13.02.1999, p. 7.

83 Images published in *FR*, 13.02.1999, p. 2; *Welt*, 13.02.1999, p. 7.

84 Dayna Smith, World Press Photo of the Year 1998. http://www.archive.worldpressphoto.org/search/layout/result/indeling/detailwpp/form/wpp/q/ishoofdafbeelding/true/trefwoord/year/1998 (accessed 02.09.2014).

Publication	Number of images in total excluding maps	Number of images showing KLA-soldiers	Number of images showing Serbian forces
Welt	53	3	8
FAZ	37	2	3
FR	29	0	4
taz	48	7	3
BILD	11	0	1
Spiegel	35	2	6

Table 8: Number of images showing Serbian and Kosovo-Albanian force.

As the table above demonstrates, *JF*, *FR* and *BILD* did not publish any images of KLA-soldiers. Moreover, all publications aside from *taz* published more images of Serbian forces, making them a more memorable cause for the violence. While quantitatively the KLA was barely represented, the few images that did portray the army must be considered from a qualitative perspective. The publications frequently published pictures showing the KLA heavily armed and in an organised, militarised manner.[85] One particularly poignant image printed in *FAZ* depicted an armed KLA-soldier standing in front of a house with "UÇK" smeared on it. It is striking that this house was intact while the neighbouring house without these three letters was completely destroyed.

This pictorial evidence of the KLA emphasised its strong presence in Kosovo, monitoring checkpoints, and engaging in close-range combat. Comparing these images with the visual coverage of KLA in the preceding chapter, such as the image of a man smuggling weapons on a mule,[86] the Kosovo-Albanian army was portrayed as much more professional and dangerous here. This mirrored the linguistic changes relating to the KLA, as discussed previously.[87]

85 Images published in *Spiegel*, 25.01.1999, p. 139; *taz*, 18.02.1999, p. 10; *Welt*, 05.02.1999, p. 1; *FAZ*, 15.01.1999, p. 6.

86 See chapter 6, fn. 102.

87 See pp. 203–211.

Račak – A Catalyst?

Before proceeding to the German print media's discussion about the imminent NATO-intervention, it is worth considering the distribution of articles pertaining to Račak in a graph. The horizontal axis lists each day analysed in this timeframe and the vertical axis indicates the number of articles published per day, ranging from zero to six.

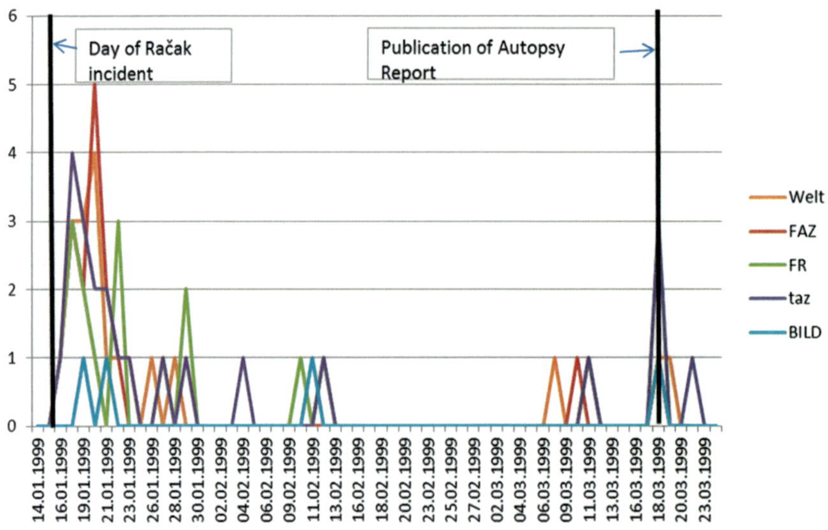

Figure 32: Publication of articles in daily press between 15 January and 24 March 1999

As this graph indicates, all daily newspapers featured a heightened interest in Račak just after the corpses had been discovered. However, after this initial surge, Račak was barely mentioned in the print media and by mid-February was omitted entirely. Only the publication of the long-awaited autopsy report in mid-March, caused a renewed interest in the press. Thus, while Račak may have 'woken up' the international community and initiated a debate about terminating the violence in Kosovo using military force, the incident's influence did not extend beyond this catalytic function. This was further underlined in the analysis of editorials and cartoons which called for a military intervention to stop Milošević – none of which, with the exception of one *FAZ*-cartoon, referred to Račak specifically. Rather the general violence which continued to dominate the day-to-day coverage of Kosovo initiated these appeals. The complete omission of Račak in the *Bundestag*-debate on

25 February 1999 – the only parliamentary session in this timeframe that discussed the situation in Kosovo – further corroborates this point. As this chapter has demonstrated, the causal link between Račak and the NATO-intervention frequently claimed in the secondary literature was not prevalent in the German press coverage.[88]

However, the Račak incident did directly lead to a peace conference in Rambouillet, France. Similar to the Dayton Accords, representatives from the opposing parties were confined to the negotiation venue for a designated time-period (in this case between 6 and 23 February 1999). In addition to delegations from the Balkan Contact Group, Serbian and the Kosovo-Albanian politicians were present. Significantly, Ratko Markovič, Serbia's Deputy Prime Minister represented Serbia rather than Milošević and the Kosovo-Albanian delegation was comprised of both KLA-representatives and President Rugova. The media was excluded from these talks, though *taz's* Erich Rathfelder claimed that there were some leaks to the press without detailing who disclosed what information.[89] As can be read in the extensive literature covering Rambouillet,[90] the negotiations were unsuccessful and both parties left France on 23 February without signing a peace treaty. After the Balkan Contact Group exerted diplomatic pressure on both sides, the Kosovo-Albanian delegation eventually returned to Paris and signed the peace-treaty on 18 March, while Markovič continued to refuse. Serbia's reasons for this rejection were manifold. They included that civilian and military implementations laid out in annexes infringed on Serbian sovereignty and that "[…] the Albanian delegation was provided with concessions amounting to the guarantee of an independent referendum."[91] Nevertheless, as a result, Serbia was blamed for the failure to settle the Kosovo-conflict peacefully. As the threat of NATO-bombardment was omnipresent if no agreement to end the violence was found, Serbia's refusal to sign this peace treaty immediately introduced the option of a NATO-intervention.[92]

88 *Deutscher Bundestag*, Plenarprotokoll 14/22, Stenographischer Bericht, 22. Sitzung, 25.02.1999, pp. 1699–1713.

89 Erich Rathfelder: Beratungen in getrennten Räumen. In: *taz*, 08.02.1999, p. 8.

90 For example: Günther Hofmann: Warum Deutschland in den Krieg geriet. In: *Zeit*, 12.05.1999. http://www.zeit.de/1999/20/199920.krieg_.xml (accessed 02.09.2014); Friedrich: *Die deutsche Außenpolitik*, pp. 58–72; Loquai: *Der Kosovo-Konflikt*, pp. 68–90; Petritsch / Pichler: *Kosovo-Kosova*, pp. 175–176; Elizabeth Allen Dauphinee: Rambouillet: A Critical (Re)Assessment. In: Florian Bieber / Židas Daskalovski (eds): *Understanding the War in Kosovo*. London: Routledge 2003, pp. 101–121.

91 Dauphinee: Rambouillet: A Critical (Re)Assessment, p. 107.

92 Maull: German Foreign Policy, Post-Kosovo, p. 3.

NATO-Intervention and German Politics

This prospective bombardment of Serbian forces in Kosovo and Serbia itself was controversial because Russia and China – both veto-powers in the UN-Security Council – deemed Kosovo Serbia's internal affair and had indicated that they would not pass any UN-mandate. Consequently, NATO had declared its prospective operation a 'humanitarian intervention' and thus circumvented the UN Security Council.[93] According to NATO, the alarming humanitarian catastrophe in the region caused by the hundreds of thousands of displaced persons justified such an intervention.[94] Moreover, the majority of the displaced persons found refuge in neighbouring Albania and Macedonia, which strained these already instable countries, threatening to weaken the region even further.[95] In spite of the ambiguous framework regarding international law, Germany agreed to contribute 14 Tornado-airplanes and 500 soldiers to NATO-operations in Kosovo and therefore potentially deploy German soldiers into active combat for the first time since the Second World War.[96] Before delving into the analysis of how the German press reported on this issue, it is worth considering the political situation in Germany at the time.

After 16 years in office, the conservative Chancellor Helmut Kohl (CDU) lost the elections to Gerhard Schröder (SPD) in October 1998, just as the violence in Kosovo intensified. The SPD formed a coalition government with the Green Party, which made Joschka Fischer Deputy Chancellor and Foreign Minister. This red-green coalition, which according to party lines was traditionally sceptical of war – or in the case of the Green Party fundamentally pacifist – had to face the difficult decision of including German soldiers in a potential NATO-intervention against Serbia. While the German contribution to the NATO-intervention was controversial, it was supported by all parties in the German parliament aside from the left-wing *Partei des Demokratischen Sozialismus* (PDS). This was largely due to the humanitarian catastrophe which was at the centre of the political debate at the time.[97] Irrespective of political inclinations, Germany's post-war foreign policy had generally shied away from using military force. For example Hanns Maull argued that this foreign policy was "[…] shaped by Germany's traumatic past: the lessons of

93 Jones: *Genocide*, p. 575.

94 Ibid., p. 331

95 Webber: The Kosovo War: A Recapitulation, p. 451.

96 Maull: German Foreign Policy, Post-Kosovo, p. 3.

97 Jones: *Genocide*, p. 575.

history led to aversion, or at least profound scepticism, vis-à-vis any use of military force […]"[98] However, Schröder and Fischer significantly departed from this conventional foreign policy, which was further amplified when it became clear that NATO would potentially launch its intervention without a UN-mandate.[99]

Significantly, the German press was not as sceptical of German involvement due to the country's past, as might be expected. Indeed, only *JF* and *Konkret* disagreed with a possible strike against Serbia, though for different reasons. *Konkret* expressed its disapproval of a NATO-intervention in various articles, drawing on Germany's National-Socialist past to oppose war, while simultaneously cautioning that the information about the events in Račak was still fragmentary and that it was too early to jump to conclusions.[100] *JF's* articles were decidedly in opposition to a potential intervention, though none gave a coherent reasoning for this position or offering any detailed information to the reader. For example, one article expressed the decisive assertions such as 'the bombardment of Belgrade is out of the question,'[101] without offering supporting facts or explaining why this was an unfathomable development. Similarly, Peter Lattas stated in early February that "[…] as long as the grandfathers of the prospective soldiers […were] defamed as murderers of the *Wehrmacht*, […] such a deployment […was] not worth […] a single bone of a German grenadier."[102] With this forceful statement Lattas alluded to Otto von Bismarck's famous quote that "the Balkans […were] not worth the bones of a Pomeranian grenadier."[103] Moreover, Lattas reminded his readers that due to the mandatory draft of the *Wehrmacht* during the Second World War, not all soldiers who had fought for Hitler were Nazis and the soldiers' service to their country should not be forgotten. However, the cryptic message Lattas was attempting to convey with this link did not contribute to the reader's understanding of the potential deployment of soldiers to Kosovo. Perhaps the contributor to the weekly *JF* assumed that the readers obtained details to contextualise this debate through other channels such as television

98 Maull: Germany and the Use of Force, p. 56.

99 Ibid., p. 58.

100 For example: Otto Köhler: Mass Murder Inc. In: *Konkret*, March 1999, p. 31; Köhler: Joschka brennt. In: *Konkret*, April 1999, p. 16.

101 Karl Gerigk: Belgrad eingrenzen. In: *JF*, 26.02.1999, p. 2.

102 Peter Lattas: Serbische Sackgasse. In: *JF*, 05.02.1999, p. 2.

103 Rene Ristelhüber: *A History of the Balkan Peoples*. Boston: Twayne 1971, p. 180. Other transcriptions of this citation refer to "Pomeranian musketeers", see E. J. Feuchtwanger: *Bismarck*. London: Psychology Press 2002, p. 198.

or other publications. Nonetheless, the coverage given by the paper itself appears disjointed and superficial in this respect.
While *JF* and *Konkret* disagreed with Germany's involvement in a NATO-intervention, their limited circulation and targeted readership prevented their arguments from being widely recognised. All other mainstream newspapers, ranging from conservative to left-wing, unanimously supported a NATO-intervention and Germany's involvement in it.[104] Their articles voiced two main arguments to explain their support: firstly, that the 'civilised world' needed to take a stance and stop the mass killings; and secondly that Milošević needed clear actions and not empty words.

Starting with the former, *Welt*, *FAZ*, *Spiegel* and *FR* introduced the moral dimension to their articles, contrasting Serbia to 'the West.' Markedly, a *Welt*-editorial authored by Katja Ridderbusch encapsulated this opposition by presenting Milošević as an autocratic, backward politician and the West as 'civilised.' Ridderbusch argued that "bit by bit the West has to urge Serbia towards a civilised political co-existence […]"[105] Numerous other articles conveyed the same message, simply by portraying Milošević's policies as barbaric and most importantly something 'the West' had matured from since the Second World War. For example, articles published in *Welt* and *FR* cited Germany's Foreign Minister Joschka Fischer who had stated that "[…] 'we will not accept a development towards mass murder and war in Europe […]'"[106] Another *Welt*-article quoted Scharping's proclamation that "we will not allow new heaps of corpses,"[107] which the Defence Minister had uttered during a parliamentary debate on 25 February 1999.[108] *FAZ* and *Spiegel* also cited Scharping, who at a different occasion stated "we will not watch as humans are being butchered."[109] Fischer articulated this moral dimension in the bluntest manner in a speech he gave in the *Bundestag*. Here he professed that

104 For example: rtr: Bundestag soll Kosovo-Einsatz zustimmen. In: *Welt*, 23.02.1999, p. 4; elo: Bundestag stimmt Einsatz im Kosovo zu. In: *FAZ*, 26.02.1999, p. 2; Richard Meng: Bundestag stimmt für Kosovo-Einsatz. In: *FR*, 26.02.1999, p. 1; Bettina Gaus: Den Weg in den Kosovo geebnet. In: *taz*, 27.02.1999, p. 2.

105 Katja Ridderbusch: Das große Ringen von Rambouillet. In: *Welt*, 22.02.1999, p. 10.

106 mdl/DW: Fischer: Wir nehmen Krieg und Massenmord nicht hin. In: *Welt*, 15.03.1999, p. 8; also in dpa/Vbn: Kriegsparteien in Klausur. In: *FR*, 08.02.1999, p. 1; Rolf Paasch: Irrweg der Diplomatie. In: *FR*, 22.01.1999, p. 3.

107 Andreas Middel: Nato vertagt Entscheidung über Kosovo. In: *Welt*, 22.03.1999, p. 9.

108 *Deutscher Bundestag*, Plenarprotokoll 14/22, Stenographischer Bericht, 22. Sitzung, 25.02.1999, p. 1700.

109 ban: Regierung zur Entsendung von Bodentruppen ins Kosovo bereit. In: *FAZ*,

> Europe is currently divided in half. When we look to the Balkans, we see the Europe of the past [...] of wars and of ethnic cleansing, when we look to Brussels, we see [...] the Europe of the future [...and] integration.[110]

Such normative arguments, present in the political discourse as well as the press' coverage, constructed clear oppositions between good and bad; 'the West' and Serbia or specifically Milošević; the defender of human rights and the perpetrator of war crimes. With such clear-cut categories presented to the reader, a military intervention seemed easily comprehensible and appeared to be the only logical solution to the current situation. Nonetheless, it must be noted that these moral arguments generally addressed the violence in Kosovo; none mentioned Račak specifically.

A multitude of articles produced in all mainstream publications – *Welt*, *FAZ*, *FR*, *taz*, *Spiegel* and *BILD* – echoed this normative argument with the interpretation that Milošević was to be blamed personally for the violence. This in turn created a sense of urgency that NATO had to stop him through strong actions and not half-hearted threats. Various articles portrayed the Serbian President as manipulating the international community to gain his ends.[111] For example *Spiegel* published an article entitled '*Milošević pokert hoch*' or 'Milošević is pushing his luck,' which portrayed him as persistently breaking ceasefires and unflinchingly manipulating the international community.[112] An interview *Welt* published with NATO-General Naumann after he had visited Milošević cited the former: "we are sensing a complete insensitivity towards our arguments [...they] all [...] completely bounced off of President Milošević,"[113] confirming the impression that Milošević was not taking the international community seriously. This message was also conveyed in several other articles, which frequently explained Milošević's non-cooperation with his political audacity.[114] Headlines such as 'Holbrooke-Mission in Belgrade

23.01.1999, pp. 1–2; Olaf Ihlau / Siegesmund von Ilsemann: „Geduld und Zähigkeit". In: *Spiegel*, 25.01.1999, p. 140.

110 *Deutscher Bundestag*, Plenarprotokoll 14/22, 25.02.1999, p. 1705.

111 Nikolaus Blome: Stöckchen für die Nato. In: *Welt*, 23.01.1999, p. 1; afp/rtr/dpa: Nato kündigt Angriff auf Serben an. In: *FR*, 24.03.1999, p. 1; Knut Pries: Nato rüstet sich für Luftangriffe. In: *FR*, 21.01.1999, p. 1; *taz*, 22.02.1999, p. 10; Renate Flottau / Olaf Ihlau / Roland Schleicher: Im Teufelskreis der Gewalt. In: *Spiegel*, 25.01.1999, p. 137.

112 Anonymous: Milošević pokert hoch. In: *Spiegel*, 22.02.1999, p. 157.

113 Rüdiger Moniac: „An Milošević prallen alle Argumente völlig ab". In: *Welt*, 23.01.1999, p. 7.

114 For example: AFP/dpa: Belgrad weicht keine Handbreite. In: *Welt*, 12.03.1999, p. 7; F.A.Z.: Holbrooke in Belgrad erfolglos: Clinton: Militärschlag ist die richtige Entscheidung. In: *FAZ*,

unsuccessful'[115] and 'Holbrooke failed in Belgrade, Clinton: Military-strike is the right decision'[116] underlined this. However, one particular reason for his attitude was not considered at all. Richard Holbrooke, who had been the chief architect of the Dayton peace treaty, had published his memoirs *To End a War* in 1998. This insightful book, which was a seminal source in the previous chapter on the Dayton negotiations,[117] outlined in detail what negotiating tactics he had used with Milošević and how difficult it had been to convince NATO to bomb Bosnian-Serb forces in 1995, even for just a few days to add pressure to the ongoing diplomatic negotiations.[118] It is plausible that Milošević, who was fluent in English, or his advisors read the book, and could have deduced that NATO's renewed threats against him were equally half-hearted. While *FAZ* and *taz* mentioned that Holbrooke had published this book,[119] these were only cursory remarks and did not include any speculations how such a revealing publication could influence the on-going diplomatic efforts in Kosovo.

Irrespective of this possible link, all daily newspapers continued to focus exclusively on Milošević's uncooperative policies, issuing forceful calls to 'finally intervene,' which primarily appeared in editorials and in some cases cartoons. The freedom these formats offered to publish opinions and interpretations more bluntly was perhaps fitting for these personal interpretations expressed by the respective authors. For example, *Welt's* Nikolaus Blome asked impatiently: "how often has the time run out for Slobodan Milošević? Twice? Four times?"[120] *FR's* Rolf Paasch echoed this: "how many 'last chances' can one person get?"[121] *FAZ's* editorials were more forceful, comparing Milošević to Saddam Hussein, even calling him "the Saddam of the Balkans."[122] Here the

24.03.1999, pp. 1–2; afp/rtr/dpa: Nato kündigt Angriff auf Serben an. In: FR, 24.03.1999, p. 1; Andreas Zumach: Harnäckiger Kampf um den Erfolg. In: *taz*, 24.02.1999, p. 3.

115 DW: Holbrooke-Mission in Belgrad gescheitert. In: *Welt*, 24.03.1999, p. 1.

116 F.A.Z.: Holbrooke in Belgrad erfolglos: Clinton: Militärschlag ist die richtige Entscheidung. In: *FAZ*, 24.03.1999, pp. 1–2.

117 See chapter 5, fn. 11–12.

118 For example Holbrooke: *To End a War*, pp. 118–119, 131–134.

119 Matthias Rüb: Unsichtbar in Rambouillet. In: *FAZ*, 09.02.1999, p. 9; Rüdiger Rossig: Ein Karrierist auf Reisen. In: *taz*, 12.03.1999, S. 9.

120 Nikolaus Blome: Milošević hat sich gewappnet. In: *Welt*, 19.03.1999, p. 10. Also see Katja Ridderbusch: Angeschlagene Nato. In: *Welt*, 25.02.1999, p. 10.

121 Paa: Letzte Drohung. In: *FR*, 01.02.1999, p. 3; also in Georg Gafron: Kosovo-Verhandlungen: Uralte Taktik. In: *BILD*, 22.02.1999, p. 2; W.A.: Bittsteller. In: *FAZ*, 21.01.1999, p. 1.

122 W.A.: Bittsteller. In: *FAZ*, 21.01.1999, p. 1; Günther Nonnenmacher: Wie sich Saddam und Milošević ähneln. In: *FAZ*, 24.02.1999, p. 1.

freedom offered by editorials bordered on name-calling. Two *taz*-editorials, both authored by Rüdiger Rossig, also expressed a clear call for the international community to stop Milošević. Rossig wrote hopefully:

> the time has come: almost eight years after the war began in Former Yugoslavia, NATO is ready to bomb targets in Serbia. Considering that [...] Milošević has constantly jerked around the international community since 1991, lying to them and provoking them, this is not surprising.[123]

However, when the international community decided instead to continue applying political pressure rather than resorting to military force, Rossig aired his disappointment in a second editorial.

> So, Serbia will not be bombed. The Albanians in Kosovo have to continue living in a police regime. The West has still not understood [...] after eight years [...] that Serbia's leadership only reacts to threats of military action when [...] they are put into action.[124]

In both cases the author referred to an eight-year war, emphasising that Milošević had also been responsible for the violence in Bosnia and Croatia, which his readers would have been familiar with. Later Rossig reiterated that Milošević was pursuing a 'war of extermination,'[125] underlining the urgency to stop him as soon as possible. It must be reiterated that for *taz*, a left newspaper that was usually sympathetic to pacifist arguments, such calls for military intervention were highly remarkable. However, throughout the paper's coverage of the Balkan violence, a heightened interest in the human dimension of the war has been traced, for example in its coverage of the Srebrenica Massacre. This focus on human suffering and the West's inability to stop it – for example in Srebrenica – could explain a gradual movement towards condoning a military intervention.
An accusation which permeated the editorials was that the West was allowing Milošević to pursue his manipulative and destructive policies. This message was also conveyed in various cartoons that satirised NATO and other Western institutions as impotent 'paper-tigers.'

123 Rüdiger Rossig: Die Zeit der Pazifisten. In: *taz*, 23.02.1999, p. 1.

124 Rüdiger Rossig: Die Grenzen militärischer Gewalt. In: *taz*, 25.02.1999, p. 12.

125 Rüdiger Rossig: Ziellos in den Status quo. In: *taz*, 23.03.1999, p. 1.

Figure 33: Felix Mussil; printed in *FR*, 19 January 1999, p. 1.

Figure 34: Felix Mussil; printed in *FR*, 24 March 1999, p. 1.

Figure 33 presented NATO, EU and OSCE as clueless characters, dithering between protests, threats, negotiations, condemnations and indignation, indicating how pathetic their collective response was. Similarly, figure 34 featured a NATO-fire fighter without water standing helplessly before a burning house labelled 'Kosovo.' A similar image of a fireman standing in front of a burning house labelled Kosovo had already been featured in April 1998 and effectively contrasted the urgency of intervening alongside NATO's profound inability to end the mayhem.[126]

Welt's depiction of a victorious Milošević covered in a pile of paper labelled 'ultimatum' communicated a similar message, namely that diplomacy would not stop the violence.[127] A less humorous stance was taken in a second *Welt's* caricature (not pictured), which illustrates fax machines in Belgrade and Brussels: while Belgrade received one ultimatum after another from Brussels, the latter collected endless death notices from Belgrade.[128] Two *FAZ*-cartoons linked the bloody violence in Kosovo more bluntly to Milošević.

126 See figure 25.

127 Cartoon published in *Welt*, 25.02.1999, p. 10.

128 Cartoon published in *Welt*, 04.03.1999, p. 10.

Figure 35: Burkhard Mohr; printed in *FAZ*, 23 February 1999, p. 2.

Figure 36: Walter Hanel; printed in *FAZ*, 20 January 1999, p. 3.

The first cartoon (figure 35) showed Milošević as a brutish butcher caught in the act of killing someone – presumably representing Kosovo – and angrily shouting at the international community, which is depicted as terrified and powerless to stop him. Figure 36 was both macabre and poignant. Two images of death as the grim reaper look over Račak and say: "We should at least write Mr. Milošević a thank you letter." The tabloid *BILD* did not confine such accusations of Milošević to its formats allowing a more liberal dissemination of personal opinions, such as cartoons or editorials. In late March it published a page-long article acutely entitled: "Is this man dragging all of Europe to war?"[129] Alongside the article was a picture of Milošević and one of tanks, visually linking him to destruction and suffering of the civilian population, especially women and children.[130]

Amongst these forceful charges against Milošević and advocating military strikes to stop him personally, only *Spiegel*, *Welt* and *FAZ* voiced cautionary counter-arguments. For example *FAZ's* articles reminded the readers that a bombardment of Serbian troops in Kosovo and Serbia proper was a complex matter that could raise new issues. The authors cautioned that questions needed to be considered, such as how Milošević would react once he was under attack. Perhaps this would motivate him to intensify the violence against the Kosovo-Albanians.[131] A further concern was that NATO would inadvertently become the KLA's air force and perhaps be misused to carry out the army's military goals.[132] This fear was also voiced in various *Spiegel*-articles.[133] In an interview with Scharping, *Spiegel's* correspondents asked why Milošević was seen as the primary problem when he had been portrayed as a factor for stability at Dayton just a few years ago. Scharping conceded that there were more problems in the Balkans than just Milošević, but that he was primarily responsible, as he ruined, or as Scharping termed it, 'torpedoed' every agreement.[134]

In spite of these appeals for caution in three publications, the dominant argument remained that ultimately NATO would have to end the suffering of the Kosovar people and that it should do so as quickly as possible. Arguably, the bluntly formulated, accusatory editorials and poignant cartoons had a more profound effect on the reader's opinion than some of the more carefully phrased articles. The strength of these arguments in forming the reader's

129 Oliver Santen: Reißt dieser Mann ganz Europa in den Krieg? In: *BILD*, 22.03.1999, p. 2.

130 Image published in *BILD*, 22.03.1999, p. 2.

131 bko: Hilflos in Paris. In: *FAZ*, 20.03.1999, p. 12; also in Renate Flottau: „Die Serben werden fauchen". In: *Spiegel*, 08.02.1999, pp. 150–151; Nikolaus Blome: Milošević hat sich gewappnet. In: *Welt*, 19.03.1999, p. 10.

132 wie: Nato nicht Luftwaffe der UÇK. In: *FAZ*, 22.01.1999, p. 2; W. A.: Bittsteller. In: *FAZ*, 21.01.1999, p. 1.

133 Olaf Ihlau / Siegesmund von Ilsemann: „Geduld und Zähigkeit". In: *Spiegel*, 25.01.1999, p. 138–139; Walter Mayr: Im Reich von König Slobo. In: *Spiegel*, 15.03.1999, pp. 210–213, here p. 210; Renate Flottau / Roland Schleicher: Marsch in die Sackgasse. In: *Spiegel*, 22.03.1999, p. 198.

134 Olaf Ihlau / Siegesmund von Ilsemann: „Geduld und Zähigkeit". In: *Spiegel*, 25.01.1999, p. 139.

opinion could be seen in a *Welt*-article from mid-February which published a poll answering the question: "Do you see a military strike against Serbia as necessary?" From the 2,008 people asked, 65% said yes and 30% voted for no.[135] While this poll did not represent the German population as a whole, as it only questioned *Welt*-readers, it nevertheless illustrates a profound support in Germany for military intervention.

The Weight of History

Amidst the press' arguments for and against a potential NATO-intervention, the predominant focus was clearly on Milošević. Accordingly, most German publications no longer saw the country's National-Socialist past as an influential factor in assessing Germany's foreign policy in Kosovo. For example, *JF* published an interview with former *Bundeswehr* General Gerd Schultze-Rhonhof, in which he was asked: "[…] how do you evaluate the *Bundeswehr*-mission in Kosovo considering the experiences in the Balkans during the Second World War?"[136] He responded that the contemporary problems in the Balkans had nothing to do with the past and therefore the *Wehrmacht* did not play any role. The two issues should be considered completely separately.[137] With this clear separation of past and present foreign policy, the article did not address the question whether the deployment of German soldiers was the right decision, but rather if the debate should be linked to Germany's past. *FR's* article took a similar approach, quoting Chancellor Schröder. In a speech justifying Germany's involvement in a potential NATO-strike, Schröder stated that he understood that some would question whether German soldiers should participate due to the "National-Socialist crimes of German soldiers" in the past. However, "the German debt in the Balkans could also be 'paid' by German soldiers 'preventing more murder.'"[138] This citation of Schröder's speech at the Munich Security Conference of 1999 was not questioned or criticised by *FR*. The quote, not found in any other daily newspaper, could thereby be seen as a stance the paper supported. The speech was only mentioned in one other publication, namely *Konkret*. In the March-edition, Otto Köhler criticised the speech for showing too much eagerness to forget the past. He dismissed the

135 Jochen Hehn: Keine Geduld mehr in Rambouillet. In: *Welt*, 15.02.1999, p. 7.

136 Karl Gerigk: „Gefahr eines zweiten Vietnams". In: *JF*, 12.03.1999, p. 6.

137 Ibid.

138 Von unseren Korrespondenten: Kanzler: Eine neue Außenpolitik. In: *FR*, 25.02.1999, p. 1.

Munich Security Conference as "NATO's annual intimidation-event", and vented his dismay at Germany's involvement in a NATO-intervention.[139]

Moreover, the two conservative broadsheets *Welt* and *FAZ* casually stated that Germany was staying in the background due to what *FAZ* termed its "special historical situation."[140] A *Spiegel*-article reminded its readers that when thinking of bombardments, the Belgrade-residents reverted to 6 April, 1941 "[…] when Hitler's pilots attacked the city and according to Serbian information 15,000 people died […]" However, the same article also mentioned that the Serbians had since constructed a myth out of this with the underlying message of "us against the rest of the world."[141] With this the article quickly dismissed the importance still attributed to 1941 as part of a Serbian propaganda effort.

The diminished importance of Germany's National-Socialist past in evaluating the country's impending deployment of soldiers to Kosovo is particularly noticeable when comparing the discussion to the debate about German soldiers supporting the international peace force in November and December 1995.[142] Interestingly, editorials in *Welt*, *FR* and *taz* lamented the missing context in the debate whether German soldiers should be involved in a possible NATO-intervention. For example, *Welt's* Jacques Schuster wrote that "for the first time in the country's recent history, Germany faced a war, faced a combat mission […]" and instead of debating the implications of this, Germans preferred to discuss Michael Jackson, a possible tax-raise or the bickering within the coalition government.[143] *taz's* Rossig noted that it was "odd that those who had fought over the sense of a military intervention in Bosnia and Croatia […] have fallen completely silent now."[144] A *Konkret*-article entitled "Steelhelmet Pacifists" was much more straightforward in naming those who had fallen silent. Andreas Spannbauer criticised the Green Party specifically for abandoning its founding pacifist principles for a new German foreign policy. The author primarily viewed the fact that the Green Party was now in government and had made certain promises during its election campaign as the main reason for this shift.[145]

139 Otto Köhler: Mass Murder Inc. In: *Konkret*, March 1999, p. 31.

140 elo: Fischer: Jetzt entscheidet sich, ob ein „Dayton II" gelingt. In: *FAZ*, 29.01.1999, p. 2; also Martin Lambeck: Das Kosovo und der Wehretat. In: *Welt*, 26.02.1999, p. 10.

141 Walter Mayr: Im Reich von König Slobo. In: *Spiegel*, 15.03.1999, pp. 210–213, here p. 212.

142 See pp. 145–149.

143 Jacques Schuster: Die Deutschen und der Krieg. In: *Welt*, 23.03.1999, p. 10.

144 Rüdiger Rossig: Die Zeit der Pazifisten. In: *taz*, 23.02.1999, p. 1.

145 Andreas Spannbauer: Stahlhelm-Pazifisten. In: *Konkret*, April 1999, p. 25.

FR's editorial also held the Green Party responsible to ensure that such a discourse occurred. Richard Meng's first sentence was perhaps the most striking: "of course it would be too easy to simply reproach [...the Greens] with their slogans from yesterday. [For example] the 'make peace without weapons'-slogans or the 'all soldiers are potential murderers'-quotes."[146] Meng consented that the times had changed and with it the individuals in the Green Party, such as Fischer. However, he could not understand that this disengagement with earlier principles was happening so quickly and that as a result there was no thoughtful or serious debate about a possible Kosovo-intervention. Meng feared that in spite of their biographies – alluding to Fischer's past as a pacifist revolutionary in the 1960s – the individuals were trying to "free themselves from the inhibitions of the post-war years."[147] Without ever naming the individuals he was referring to, Meng alluded to the 1968-generation in Germany whose *raison d'être* had been not to allow Germany's past to be forgotten. However with the absence of historical debate about a potential NATO-involvement, this was exactly what was occurring.

It is striking that after mentioning the missing historical context in the debate, these authors did not offer it themselves. After all, they were the contributors to the forums where such debates could have been initiated. Their surprise followed by no action could indicate that while they may have been mildly astonished to realise that Germany's history was no longer as important, they also considered this development comprehensible. The relative paucity of references to Germany's history in the press refines the theses put forward by some academics that have placed Germany's trauma from the Second World War in the foreground when analysing the country's decision-making process to support a NATO-intervention.[148] Maull for example claims that three succinct slogans formed Germany's policy in Kosovo: 'never again', 'never alone' and 'politics before force.'[149] However, in the coverage leading up to the NATO-intervention in 1999, the 'never again' mantra seemed to pertain to never allowing another 'genocide' to unfold rather than never again engaging in war. Previously the two had been inextricably linked, but this was no longer the case here.

146 Richard Meng: Generation Normalo. In: *FR*, 27.02.1999, p. 3.

147 Ibid.; also in paa: Allianz ohne Strategie. In: *FR*, 27.01.1999, p. 3; me: Frappierend einfach. In: *FR*, 26.02.1999, p. 3; Rolf Paasch: Die zwei Gesichter Europas. In: *FR*, 12.03.1999, p. 3.

148 Maull: German Foreign Policy, Post-Kosovo; Hanns Maull (ed.): *Germany's Uncertain Power: Foreign Policy of the Berlin Republic.* Houndmills: Palgrave 2006; Beverly Crawford: *Power and German Foreign Policy: Embedded Hegemony in Europe*. Houndmills: Palgrave Macmillan 2007.

149 Maull: *Germany's Uncertain Power*, p. 6.

To understand this lacking historical debate over the German military intervention, one must turn to the progression of collective memory, which has been completely disregarded in the existing literature. As outlined in the introduction, the collective memory of the Holocaust had evolved during the post-war decades and by the 1980s had culminated to what historians termed *Betroffenheitsdiskurs* or 'discourse of dismay.' The public shame that marked this discourse resulted in a sense of collective guilt amongst the Germans. According to the literature this diluted to a more 'meta-physical' guilt which applied to everyone and not exclusively Germany by the early 1990s. While previous chapters argued that indeed the collective shame was more present in the 1990s than has been suggested, October 1998 marked a significant shift in the discourse on Germany's collective memory. Martin Walser, a prominent German author, proclaimed in a speech accepting the prestigious Peace Prize of the German book industry:

> Everybody knows our historical burden, the never ending shame, not a day on which the shame is not presented to us […] But when every day in the media this past is presented to me, I notice, that something inside me is opposing this permanent show of that shame.[150]

With this controversial speech, Walser publicly moved away from the shame-filled *Betroffenheitsdiskurs*. He expressed the diminishing enthusiasm amongst the German population to embrace collective shame. This well-publicised speech sparked a heated debate between Walser and Ignatz Bubis, President of the Central Council of Jews in Germany,[151] and has been seen as a sign for a movement away from the shame and guilt of the *Betroffenheitsdiskurs*.[152] The German press' near complete omission of discussing a potential German deployment in the context of the country's National-Socialist past manifests this. Moreover it suggests a desire to be an actor on equal terms in the Western alliance-structure.

150 Martin Walser: Erfahrungen beim Verfassen einer Sonntagsrede, 1998. http://www.friedenspreis-des-deutschen-buchhandels.de/sixcms/media.php/1290/1998_walser.pdf (accessed 02.09.2014).

151 Frank Schirrmacher: *Die Walser-Bubis-Debatte: eine Dokumentation*. Frankfurt am Main: Suhrkamp 1999.

152 Hans-Joachim Hahn: *Repräsentationen des Holocaust: Zur westdeutschen Erinnerungskultur seit 1979*. Heidelberg: Winter 2005, p. 23.

Chapter 8
March–May 1999: Reporting 'War' – The NATO-Intervention in Kosovo and Serbia

Dear Fellow Citizens, tonight NATO began its air strikes against military targets in Yugoslavia. In doing so, the alliance aims to prohibit further severe and systematic human rights violations and prevent a humanitarian catastrophe in Kosovo.[1]

(Chancellor Gerhard Schröder)

On the evening of 24 March 1999, NATO began its military strikes against Serbian forces in Kosovo, which was the first engagement of German soldiers in active combat since the Second World War. Though war was never officially declared, the alliance bombarded targets in Kosovo and later Serbia until 20 June 1999.[2] This was highly controversial, partly because it had not been legitimised by a UN-mandate. Out of fear that Russia and China would block such an endeavour in the Security Council, the NATO-states preferred to launch air-strikes without a mandate. Immediately, opponents termed it a 'war of aggression,' as they deemed this NATO-intervention a direct violation of international law. However, proponents labelled it a 'humanitarian intervention' and argued that NATO's actions were nonetheless justified

1 Gerhard Schröder: Erklärung von Bundeskanzler Gerhard Schröder zur Lage im Kosovo, 24.03.1999. http://www.glasnost.de/kosovo/990324schroeder.html (accessed 02.09.2014).

2 Although there was no official declaration of war, I will refer to the NATO-intervention as such, as the military engagement was *de facto* a war.

because their goal was to stop the undeniable refugee crisis unfolding in Kosovo.[3]

As some had feared, NATO's bombardment did not have the desired effect of immediately alleviating the humanitarian disaster. Rather the Serbian forces intensified their violence against Kosovo-Albanians as NATO began its air-strikes, and within mere days approximately 863,000 Kosovo-Albanian civilians were forced to find refuge from the violence in the neighbouring Albania and Macedonia. Further 590,000 civilians were internally displaced. Indeed, almost 90% of the Kosovo-Albanian population had to leave their homes during the conflict.[4] The long treks of Kosovo-Albanian refugees who had been forcefully displaced shocked the international community and dominated the German pictorial press-coverage.[5]

Figure 37: A long trek of Kosovar ethnic Albanian refugees walk on the road Priština-Podujevo, in what Yugoslav authorities say is a refugee trek coming back to their villages around Podujevo, Tuesday, 20 April 1999. AP; printed in *AJW*, 29 April 1999, p. 15.

Simultaneously however, these images reinforced the declaration by NATO-members including the German government that the 'humanitarian intervention,' as it had been declared, was fought for 'moral values' rather than 'traditional national interests.' Peter Rudolf argues that this distinction

3 Jones: *Genocide*, p. 575.

4 Webber: The Kosovo War: A Recapitulation, p. 451.

5 Images published in *BILD*, 31.03.1999, p. 1; *FR*, Ostern 1999 [02.04.–05.04.1999], p. 1.

fundamentally shaped the discourse of the war, leading to a 'hypermoralisation', particularly by Foreign Minister Joschka Fischer and Defence Minister Rudolf Scharping. This manifested itself in the use of "dubious historical parallels" to the Second World War and "rampantly emotional language," epitomised in the famous and frequently repeated phrase "*Nie wieder Auschwitz*."[6] In retrospect, the Minister of Defence has been criticised for consciously linking his word-choice to National-Socialism when describing Serbian politics.[7]

When taking public opinion into consideration, a clear majority of Germans polled were in favour of the NATO-intervention at the beginning, though their support dwindled after a few weeks. As a survey by Dimap Infratest produced in June 1999 indicates, German public opinion was quite volatile. Responding to the question: "Do you agree with NATO's air-strikes against Serbia and Kosovo?", the poll shows that even in the first week after the bombardments began, when support for the NATO-intervention was at its highest, 30% of the population – a significant minority – were against the air strikes.[8] After several weeks of bombardment, the opponents even overtook the supporters, which was primarily because the intervention had proceeded without any clear results.[9] These divergent opinions could be a reflection of the great diversity of viewpoints available in the German press at the time, which will be discussed in more detail in a moment.

Interestingly, the political debate in the *Bundestag* was much more unanimous. Indeed, the left-wing *Partei des Demokratischen Sozialismus* (PDS) – which held 36 of 669 seats – was the only faction which opposed the war.[10] With CDU/CSU, FDP, SPD and the Green Party – comprising 95% of the seats in parliament – in favour of the NATO-intervention, there was a noticeable accord of opinions voiced in the three debates held in the *Bundestag* during the period considered in this chapter.[11] The session on 25 March did not initially entail a debate on Kosovo and neither Chancellor Schröder nor Foreign Minister Fischer were present due to a simultaneous EU-summit they attended in

6 Rudolf: Germany and the Kosovo Conflict, pp. 134–136; also in Kundnani: Perpetrators and Victims, p. 279.

7 Friedrich: *Die deutsche Außenpolitik*, p. 94.

8 Dimap Infratest: Approval of Air-strikes?, June 1999. http://www.infratest-dimap.de/uploads/media/dt9906.pdf (accessed 02.09.2014) , p. 12.

9 In the week between 27.05. and 01.06.1999, 48% were agianst air-strikes against Serbia and Kosovo while 47% supported them.

10 Daniel Brunstetter / Scott Brunstetter: Shades of Green. In: *International Relations* 25,65 (2011), pp. 65–84, here p. 66.

11 Debates were held on 25 March, 26 March and 15 April 1999.

Berlin. The protocol from this parliamentary session reveals that after heavy protest from the left-wing PDS, the President of the *Bundestag*, Wolfgang Thierse, hesitantly altered the agenda, allowing all factions to speak on the situation in Kosovo.[12] Defence Minister Scharping (SPD) made an impromptu speech about the NATO-intervention, reminding his listeners of Germany's "responsibilities stemming from the experiences from the first half of this century." He argued that Milošević's government did not have "the right [...] to systematically murder" Kosovo-Albanians.[13] Angelika Beer, speaking for the Green faction, reiterated that there was no alternative but to stop the "war and murder in Kosovo."[14] Both representatives of the Red-Green coalition took an emotional approach, referring to normative arguments. Whether these were repeated or contradicted in the German publications will be analysed in this chapter.

The following day, on 26 March, members of the parliament engaged in a more in-depth debate on Kosovo, during which Chancellor Schröder and various other members of parliament voiced their opinion. As the first speaker, Schröder reminded the listeners of the political efforts of the preceding weeks, concluding that no option remained but to launch "air-strikes against military targets in Yugoslavia", carefully avoiding the term 'war' throughout his speech.[15] A particularly interesting occurrence arose while Joschka Fischer (Green Party) addressed the *Bundestag*. According to the transcript, Fischer responded to an interjection from the opposing PDS-faction, turning to them to address their comment. Dr. Helmut Haußmann (FDP) seemed to have criticised Fischer's addressing the PDS, though his comment was not audible. However, Fischer responded: "Why shouldn't I speak with the PDS? The PDS is articulating a position which is widespread in the German population and which is legitimate in light of war and peace."[16] This brief and seemingly insignificant exchange suggests that the overwhelming *Bundestag* majority in support of NATO's intervention encouraged a one-sided debate in which criticism of the intervention was more likely to be ignored than engaged with.

12 *Deutscher Bundestag*, Plenarprotokoll 14/30, Stenographischer Bericht, 30. Sitzung, 25.03.1999, pp. 2421–2429.

13 Ibid., p. 2424.

14 Ibid., p. 2426.

15 *Deutscher Bundestag*, Plenarprotokoll 14/31, Stenographischer Bericht, 31. Sitzung, 26.03.1999, p. 2571.

16 Ibid., p. 2585.

On 15 April, the debate on Kosovo covered 41 pages of the session's transcript, of which only 6 pages addressed reflections against the war, namely when the chairs of the PDS-parliamentary group Gregor Gysi and Heidi Lippmann spoke.[17] Their main arguments stated that NATO had engaged in a 'war of aggression' due to the missing UN-mandate;[18] that bombardments would not solve a humanitarian crisis;[19] and that the NATO-bombing was intensifying the refugee crisis.[20] The Green Party '*Fundi*', Hans-Christian Ströbele who insisted on his party's pacifist roots, reinforced this stance in an emotional speech. In it he proclaimed: "after 54 years, German soil is tainted by war again [...]" which was applauded by the PDS.[21] However, aside from these exceptions, the members of parliament were widely in favour of the NATO-intervention as well as Germany's contribution to it.

We now turn to the analysis of the German print media coverage at this time, which will shed light on the extent to which the German press mirrored the largely conform political debate and whether instances of this alleged media manipulation can be found. To answer these questions and others, this chapter analyses two intervals of the three-month NATO-intervention. The first period will cover 25 March to 17 April 1999, analysing the coverage of the first three weeks of the NATO-bombing and second timeframe will examine the coverage from 12 May to 17 May 1999, studying the days leading up to the Green Party Convention, which took place on the 14 May 1999, and the days following it. Here the domestic debate regarding the war climaxed, making this time particularly interesting.[22]

The chapter will begin with an analysis of several sub-themes which the publications used to underline their approval or disapproval of the war, such as: the portrayal of Milošević, how the term 'genocide' was used, and how Serbian civilians were covered. It will then turn to other themes which shaped the coverage, namely references to Račak and Srebrenica, the role of the

17 *Deutscher Bundestag*, Plenarprotokoll 14/32, Stenographischer Bericht, 32. Sitzung, 15.04.1999, pp. 2634–2638, 2641, 2648.

18 *Bundestag*, Plenarprotokoll 14/30, 25.03.1999, p. 2427; Plenarprotokoll 14/31, 26.03.1999, p. 2587; Plenarprotokoll 14/32, 15.04.1999, p. 2636.

19 *Bundestag*, Plenarprotokoll 14/30, 25.03.1999, p. 2428; Plenarprotokoll 14/31, 26.03.1999, p. 2588; Plenarprotokoll 14/32, 15.04.1999, p. 2635.

20 *Bundestag*, Plenarprotokoll, Plenarprotokoll 14/32, 15.04.1999, p. 2635.

21 *Bundestag*, Plenarprotokoll 14/30, 25.03.1999, p. 2423.

22 The analysis of two sections does not serve a methodological purpose, but was devised to make the exceedingly large quantity of articles more manageable. Thus any comparative conclusions made with previous chapters, for example the quantity of articles published, will treat this as one time-period.

Green Party and collective memory, as well as the publications' self-reflection of their delicate role as opinion-formers in time of war. The first point to make is that there was a significant surge of articles on Kosovo published as the NATO-intervention began. Even the tabloid *BILD* which had previously included very short and limited articles reflected the increased interest. A quantitative comparison of the five daily publications underscores this increase.

Publication	**Number of articles: NATO-Intervention (30 days in time-frame)**	**Number of articles: Račak (69 days in time-frame)**	**Number of articles: early Balkan violence (163 days in time-frame)**
Welt	422	159	191
FAZ	422	173	258
BILD	257	64	47
FR	485	147	217
taz	511	154	190

Table 9: Total number of articles published in three selected chapters.[23]

As the table shows, the total number of articles published in the five dailies was much greater than the quantity devoted to Račak, and even more so when measured against the coverage of the early stages of the Bosnian violence in 1991–92. However, as each of the three timeframes consisted of an unequal number of days, analysing the increased ratio of articles per day is even more revealing than the absolute numbers. This is demonstrated in the table below, which reveals that *Welt* published 6.1 times as many articles per day during the NATO-intervention than in the previous chapter on Račak and 11.8 times as many since the beginning of the violence in Bosnia between 1991/92.

Publication	**Increased ratio between NATO-Intervention and Račak-coverage**	**Increased ratio between NATO-Intervention and early Balkan violence**
Welt	6.1	11.8
FAZ	5.6	8.8
BILD	9.5	28.7
FR	7.7	12.5
taz	7.1	14.2

Table 10: Increased ratio of daily articles per day between three timeframes.

23 On Račak, see chapter 7; on early Balkan violence, see chapter 3.

By far the biggest change occurred in *BILD's* coverage, increasing 9.5 times since the Račak incident and 28.7 times since the beginning of the violence. The lowest alteration occurred in *FAZ's* coverage, which could stem from the fact that the broadsheet had always shown more interest in the Balkans than other publications.

The surge of articles could be explained with Germany's contribution to the NATO-intervention and thus deploying soldiers into active combat, which turned Kosovo into a domestic issue. This is underlined by the fact that *Welt*, *FR* and *BILD* devoted an entire sub-section of the paper to the intervention entitled for example 'The Kosovo-War' (*Welt)* or 'NATO at War' (*BILD*). However, it should be noted that one can trace a steadily increasing interest in the Balkans throughout the German press since the beginning of the violence in 1991/92. From this perspective, the increased coverage can also be seen as a gradual progression, demonstrating greater awareness and interest in the region and its violence.

The Media's Arguments for and against the War

All publications analysed in this chapter clearly expressed their support for, or opposition to, the NATO-intervention and this position can be categorised by their political affiliation. The conservative papers endorsed the NATO-intervention, arguing that military strikes against the Serbian forces were the only way to stop the violence in Kosovo since all previous diplomatic efforts had failed.[24] As a *Welt*-editorial articulated, the bombardment would only cease "[…] if the murder and torture in Kosovo stopped immediately and the Serbs retreated."[25] This view was emphasised in a *Welt*-interview with the Minister of Defence Rudolf Scharping, who had expressed "[…] that every plea with Milošević was futile and that there […was] no point talking to him about human dignity [and] human rights […]"[26] *AJW's* interpretation of the NATO-intervention was equally supportive of military action. Quoting Ignatz Bubis, President of the Central Council of Jews in Germany, one *AJW*-article argued that it was necessary to break the vicious circle of violence in Kosovo and that employing military force was better than to watch

24 For example: Einar Koch: Scharping – er wird ein echter ,Soldatenvater. In: *BILD*, 26.03.1999, p. 3; Herbert Kemp: Ist der Angriff gut überlegt? In: *Welt*, 25.03.1999, p. 10; Eckart Lohse: Der Außenminister muss sich nicht mehr um die verstaubte Programmatik scheren. In: *FAZ*, 26.03.1999, p. 1.

25 Martin Lambeck: Schröders Härtetest. In: *Welt*, 31.03.1999, p. 1.

26 Karl-Ludwig Günsche: Der Überzeugungstäter. In: *Welt*, 07.04.1999, p. 3.

'genocide' unfold.[27] The repeated use of the term 'genocide' in *AJW's* articles is worth noting and will be analysed in more detail later.
In contrast, the left-leaning and extreme publications generally opposed NATO's bombardment. *FR*, *taz* and *Spiegel* argued that since it was difficult to evaluate Milošević as a political opponent, a military intervention was too uncertain. If he refused to compromise and sustained the violence in spite of NATO's bombing, the alliance did not have an alternative strategy to counter this.[28] Secondly, articles in these publications argued that NATO's bombardment had intensified the refugee crisis rather than alleviating it,[29] drawing on similar arguments as those PDS had voiced in the *Bundestag*.[30] As one *FR*-article, entitled "This Vain Men's War Must Stop" underlined, the war was allegedly not motivated by human rights concerns, but by politicians eager to make a political mark.[31] This approach was even more noticeable in *taz's* articles, which declared that the intervention had failed almost immediately – an assessment which was constantly reiterated.[32] This is particularly striking in a *taz*-article published on 25 March – 24 hours after the NATO-bombardment had commenced – which asserted that there were "many indications that NATO had miscalculated and would not be able to stop the Serbian offensive against Kosovo-Albanians […]"[33] This critical stance is curious considering *taz's* Rüdiger Rossig's previous disappointment aired in two editorials when NATO decided not to bomb Serbia and attempt another diplomatic solution in February 1999.[34] The discrepancy can be explained by the fact that Rossig did not write any of the current pieces critical of the intervention. These were written by various other correspondents including Andreas Zumach, *taz's* UN-correspondent in Geneva who had specialised in human rights issues. This diversity underscores how prevalent the correspondents'

27 AJW: Hilfe in der Nato. In: *AJW*, 15.04.1999, p. 1.

28 For example: Jochen Siemens: Der Kampfeinsatz – eine Zäsur. In: *FR*, 26.03.1999, p. 3; Bettina Gaus: Vorkriegsstimmung. In: *taz*, 25.03.1999, p. 12; Anonymous: „Ich darf nicht wackeln". In: *Spiegel*, 05.04.1999, pp. 22–28.

29 Anonymous: „Ich darf nicht wackeln". In: *Spiegel*, 05.04.1999, pp. 22–28, here p. 23; Sergej Krylow: Die Nato will die Signale aus Belgrad nicht hören. In: *FR*, 08.04.1999, p. 5.

30 See chapter 8, fn. 17–21.

31 Snezana Bogavac: Dieser Krieg der eitlen Männer muss aufhören. In: *FR*, 01.04.1999, p. 5; also in Stefan Reinecke: Krieg macht dumm. In: *taz*, 07.04.1999, p. 1.

32 Bettina Gaus: Vorkriegsstimmung. In: *taz*, 25.03.1999, p. 12; rtr/dpa/AFP: Trotz Bomben: Kosovo leidet. In: *taz*, 26.03.1999, p. 1; Stefan Reinecke: Alternative statt Konsens. In: *taz*, 01.04.1999, p. 1; Andreas Zumach: Nach den Bomben Bodentruppen? In: *taz*, 01.04,1999, p. 2.

33 Andreas Zumach: Jetzt geht's ums Ganze. In: *taz*, 25.03.1999, p. 2.

34 See chapter 7, fn. 123–124.

opinions were in editorials and that they were not necessarily syndicated by the editor-in-chief.

Rudolf Augstein, who had founded *Spiegel* in 1947, strongly opposed the war, occasionally publishing his opinion in *Spiegel*-editorials.[35] One, entitled "What are we doing in the Balkans?" reminded the readers that Augstein himself had experienced the Second World War and knew what fighting in a war actually meant. Most actors in favour of the NATO-intervention had never experienced combat. If they had, he argued, they would not be as eager or at all enthusiastic about war. He also posited that it did not make sense to bomb the territory of the population [Kosovo] whom NATO was trying to help.[36] Augstein's editorials are especially noteworthy, as this was the first time he published his opinion about the violence in the Balkans. Moreover, they stood in contrast to the news-magazine's general stance on the war. As demonstrated in the previous chapter, various *Spiegel*-articles had argued that Milošević could only be stopped with clear military actions and not vague verbal threats. It is evident that *Spiegel's* founder and members of the magazine's editorial team were not synchronous with one another and that Augstein used his editorials to make known his contrary opinion.

JF also protested against the NATO-intervention in Kosovo, arguing that dropping bombs on Belgrade would not solve any of the region's problems. On the contrary, Milošević would just take advantage of the situation and persecute the Kosovo-Albanian population more vigorously.[37] It also condemned the strikes as a 'war of aggression,' as the alliance's territory had not been attacked.[38] This condemnation of the NATO-intervention was congruent with *JF's* general anti-international stance, which was sceptical of NATO-membership and preferred an isolationist German foreign policy. *Konkret* also clearly disagreed with the war, though its articles did not systematically elaborate on the reasons for their disapproval of what they repeatedly called a 'war of aggression.'[39]

Konkret's opposition was encapsulated by its articles' titles, for example "Surgical Strikes without Anaesthesia", which clearly emphasised the fact that in

35 Rudolf Augstein: Ein Krieg ohne Zufall? In: *Spiegel*, 29.03.1999, p. 24; Augstein: Was suchen wir auf dem Balkan? In: *Spiegel*, 05.04.1999, p. 24; Augstein: Rückfall in die Steinzeit. In: *Spiegel*, 12.04.1999, p. 26; Augstein: Von Trizonesien nach Kosovo. In: *Spiegel*, 17.05.1999, pp. 98–99.

36 Rudolf Augstein: Was suchen wir auf dem Balkan? In: *Spiegel*, 05.04.1999, p. 24.

37 Peter Lattas: Auf Krieg versessen. In: *JF*, 26.03.1999, p. 2.

38 Michael Wiesberg / Dieter Stein: Ein Krieg um Europa. In: *JF*, 02.04.1999, p. 1.

39 Heiner Möller: Salami am Ende. In: *Konkret*, May 1999, p. 33; Otto Köhler: Gelebte Tradition. In: *Konkret*, May 1999, p. 58.

spite of all modern-day precision in warfare, the NATO-bombardment still led to physical human suffering.[40] Other articles under headings such as "Never again Peace"[41] or "The German War"[42] were more general, but expressed bitter and strong criticism of a militarily active Germany. This, perhaps more than the issue of Kosovo, was central to *Konkret's* opposition. The monthly magazine published articles relevant to this chapter in two issues, May and June 1999, both of which proclaimed that they were a "war-edition" on the cover. Both expressed brutally direct and very powerful accusations against the German government, as well as other Western politicians. For example, the May cover, which portrayed Scharping, featured the headline "Clinton, Blair, Schröder: Politicians are Murderers." The headline of the second issue (June 1999) – "The First Victory in the Third War" – provocatively implied that Germany was engaged in a Third World War, which represents a scathing critique of the country's military involvement. Various articles included in these special issues dismissed NATO's claim that the bombardment was alleviating the civilian suffering, arguing that this was "government-propaganda." But they did not openly address the refugee crisis, nor offer insights into the suffering of the Serbian civilians under the NATO-bombardment.[43]

It is evident even from this brief review that while the press' coverage offered a wide range of interpretations, various individual publications focused on specific themes that allowed them to emphasise their distinctive opinions. The publication of views that contradicted previous interpretations in *FR*, *taz* and *Spiegel* partly stemmed from the missing UN-mandate, or resulted from changes in authorship. This underlines the varying opinions which sometimes existed within one editorial office, where the interpretation of events differed significantly. The editor-in-chief's willingness to publish contradicting views, thus presenting the reader with a balanced pool of opinions, is to be commended. However, it is also worth noting that although the left-leaning and far-left/far-right publications did not support the war, their reasoning did not include arguments trivialising Serbia's violence in Kosovo, nor did they directly address Germany's National-Socialist past as a reason to avoid a military intervention. Rather, a general scepticism towards war, which was typical in light of their political affiliation, marked their interpretation.

40 Oliver Tolmein: Kriegstreiberin aus Überzeugung. In: *Konkret*, May 1999, p. 46.

41 Hermann Gremliza: Nie wieder Frieden! In: *Konkret*, May 1999 p. 9.

42 Tjark Kunstreich: Der deutsche Krieg. In: *Konkret*, June 1999, p. 24.

43 Hermann Gremliza: Wessen Krieg ist der Krieg. In: *Konkret*, June 1999, p. 9; Georg Fülberth: Stammtisch-Zerlegung. In: *Konkret*, June 1999, p. 18.

'Genocide' and Concentration Camps in Kosovo

However, besides these general interpretations, various themes emerged in the reporting that were used by the different publications to underscore their particular viewpoints and thus manifest a rather unbalanced reporting style. The first was the question of whether 'genocide' was occurring in Kosovo which brings us back to the first pages of this book. The German Minister of Defence, Rudolf Scharping, had declared the situation was "incipient genocide," ("*Hier beginnt Völkermord*") a citation which appeared in various articles in *Welt*, *FAZ*, *BILD*, as well as *FR*, *Spiegel* and *taz*.[44] *FR* and *taz* merely reported Scharping's claim, though their articles did not contain judgement. The conservative papers on the other hand, explicitly agreed with Scharping's assessment, arguing that the international community was consequently compelled to act. Moreover, *Welt* and *FAZ* praised Sharping for being "the first politician to speak of genocide in Kosovo."[45] *Welt's* Wolfram Weimer continued in an editorial: "when the henchmen of the Serb-leader Milošević murder and displace, we cannot look away. Their atrocities are not singular deeds, but systematically planned [...]", continuing that the international community must put an end to "the genocide quickly and effectively."[46] *Welt's* liberal use of the term 'genocide' was epitomised in a striking advertisement published on 10 April, announcing its forthcoming Sunday edition. Entitled "*Der Genozid*", the advertisement promised to disclose details of "mass executions, mass rapes and mass displacement."[47] The picture of a skull which took up more than half of the advertisement underlined the sensational word choice. Even though *Welt am Sonntag* is not included in this study, a brief analysis of this issue revealed that contrary to its advertisement, there was no particular

44 DW: Russen starten Kosovo-Friedensmission. In: *Welt*, 29.03.1999, p. 1; F.A.Z.: Zweite Phase der Luftangriffe angeordnet: Massaker und Brandschatzungen im Kosovo. In: *FAZ*, 29.03.1999, pp. 1–2; fy: Scharping spricht von Völkermord. In: *FAZ*, 30.03.1999, p. 2; Anonymous: NATO-Phase II: Jetzt Bomben auf Bodentruppen. In: *BILD*, 29.03.1999, p. 2; Anonymous: Der Völkermord hat begonnen. In: *BILD*, 30.03.1999, p. 2; afp/ap/dpa/rtr: Nato nimmt Soldaten ins Visier. In: *FR*, 29.03.1999, p. 1; Richard Meng: Wer noch hoffen will, bleibt doch hilflos. In: *FR*, 31.03.1999, p. 3; Monika Kappus: Die leicht geneigte Haltung eines Lastenträgers. In: *FR*, 01.04.1999, p. 3; Rainer Pörtner / Alexander Szandar: „Alle hatten Skrupel". In: *Spiegel*, 29.03.1999, pp. 218–219; Anonymous: „Ich darf nicht wackeln". In: *Spiegel*, 05.04.1999, pp. 22–28; bs: Milošević treibt Albaner über die Grenzen. In. *taz*, 29.03.1999, p. 1; Andreas Zumach: Die Logik des Nato-Angriffsplans heißt Eskalation. In: *taz*, 29.03.1999, p. 2.

45 Carter Dougherty: Der niedergeschlagene Idealist. In: *Welt*, 07.04.1999, p. 11; also in Günter Bannas: Früher als andere sprach Scharping von einem Völkermord im Kosovo. In: *FAZ*, 10.04.1999, p. 3.

46 Wolfram Weimer: Frieden am Boden. In: *Welt*, 03.04.1999, p. 1.

47 Image published in *Welt*, 10.04.1999, p. 4.

mention of 'genocide' in any of the articles on 11 April.[48] This suggests that *Welt's* employment of the term was used as an unscrupulous marketing device to shock and evoke public interest.
BILD's most striking contribution was an editorial written by Elie Wiesel, a famous author and Auschwitz-survivor. He wrote on 14 April:

> 54 years later, many people feel reminded of the murder of the Jews by the National-Socialists during the Second World War, due to the violence in Kosovo. However this time the world was not silent. This time the world answered. This time we intervened![49]

Interestingly, Wiesel employed the term 'violence' instead of 'genocide.' However, the allusions to the Holocaust he generated were strong enough to create a sense of moral imperative. Moreover the echo of Auschwitz may have underlined the perception in the reader that 'this time' Germany was on the 'right side.' Wiesel, who had reached international acclaim for his memoirs, *Night* (1960), had been a vocal supporter of an international intervention in the Balkans from the early 1990s. For example, at the opening of the Holocaust Memorial Museum in Washington, D. C. in 1993, Wiesel addressed President Clinton who was also present in his speech:

> Mr. President, I cannot not tell you something […] I have been in the former Yugoslavia. I cannot sleep since for what [sic] I have seen. As a Jew I am saying that we must do something to stop the bloodshed in that country![50]

Wiesel's acclaim as a supporter for an interventionist foreign policy along with his experiences as a Holocaust-survivor were presumably the main reasons for *BILD's* choice to feature an article by him. Publishing such a call from a prominent Holocaust-survivor gave the NATO-intervention more authority.
In contrast, *Spiegel* cautioned that Scharping could be using strong terminology such as 'genocide' to persuade the population that NATO's cause was just; something it termed a "major rhetorical offensive."[51] *AJW* – which did not quote Scharping's evaluation – cautioned against misusing the term 'genocide' to label the events in Kosovo. One editorial alleged: "What is currently happening in Kosovo is ethnic cleansing; Auschwitz was no ordinary

48 *Welt am Sonntag*, 11.04.1999, pp. 1–6.

49 Elie Wiesel: Diesmal hat die Welt nicht geschwiegen! In: *BILD*, 14.04.1999, p. 2.

50 Anonymous: Bosnia: Clinton's Call. In: *Newsweek*, 02.05.1993. http://www.thedailybeast.com/newsweek/1993/05/02/bosnia-clinton-s-call.html (accessed 02.09.2014).

51 Claus Christian Malzahn / Jürgen Hogrefe / Paul Lersch / Rainer Pörtner / Alexander Szandar: „Zweimal total verkalkuliert“. In: *Spiegel*, 12.04.1999, p. 29.

war crime."[52] This stance was underscored in an interview with Aca Singer, President of the Union of Jewish Communities in Yugoslavia:

> Constantly we hear the comparison that this is genocide. This isn't genocide – genocide is what was done to the Jews. There have been crimes against Albanians and also against Serbians. But that has nothing to do with genocide.[53]

Singer's reiteration of the uniqueness of the Holocaust raises an important issue. There were no deliberations amongst the more widely-read German publications and politicians whether comparisons between the Holocaust and Kosovo impacted the historical-political as well as cultural perception of the Holocaust. Nor did any publications systematically compare the definition in the UN Genocide Convention with the violence in Kosovo to establish whether the label 'genocide' was applicable. Consequently, a legal term was turned into a political cause, in the coverage of the conservative papers, reiterating Peter Rudolf's previously mentioned theory of a 'hypermoralised' discourse.[54] Whether the press was merely searching for a fitting word to describe the catastrophic situation in Kosovo or if they consciously misused the term to generate support for NATO's intervention amongst their readers remains open.

To solidify his claims of 'genocide' unfolding, Scharping also stated that concentration camps existed in Kosovo, which was reported by *Welt*, *FAZ*, *BILD*, *taz* and *FR*.[55] However one week later, these claims could not be substantiated and indeed were disproven by photographic evidence of the alleged site taken by *Bundeswehr*-drones. Significantly, none of the papers that had quoted Scharping without hesitation rectified their error. *Spiegel* reported on the subject after it had been disproven, perhaps helped by its weekly editorial cycle.

The treatment of the alleged concentration camps in *BILD*-articles is worth noting. On 1 April, the first-page-article stated: "KZ. Concentration camp. A nightmare is revived again. Reports are accumulating that the Serbs are

52 Mjw: Auschwitz im Kosovo? In: *AJW*, 15.04.1999, p. 1.

53 Andreas Dietl: „Die Bomben fragen nicht, wer Jude oder Serbe ist". In: *AJW*, 29.04.1999, p. 2.

54 See chapter 8, fn. 7.

55 Martin S. Lambeck / Martina Fietz: Scharping: Starke Hinweise auf Existenz von Konzentrationslagern im Kosovo. In: *Welt*, 01.04.1999, p. 1; Alfred Dregger: Den Krieg beenden. In: *FAZ*, 06.04.1999, p. 16; Markus Franz: Fischer: „Jetzt nicht wackeln". In: *taz*, 01.04.1999, p. 1; Rolf Paasch: Nach Hamburg führt kein Weg. In: *FR*, 01.04.1999, p. 1; dpa/rtr/ap: Albanien prangert „barbarische" Gewalt an. In: *FR*, 29.03.1999, p. 1.

rounding up thousands of Albanians in huge camps[...]"[56] Though the article reported that Scharping had referred to "first indications" that such camps existed, this *BILD*-article and various others portrayed the camps as proven facts. The sensationalism was carried over into an editorial which stated that the "horror-institutions" in Kosovo meant that "Hitler and Stalin [...had] risen from the dead through Milošević."[57] Astonishingly, a further article published the same day stated that the German Ministry of Defence was in possession of videos showing concentration camps, although it did acknowledge that there were problems with this evidence: "However, it is not one-hundred-percent certain if these videos are current or if they were taken during the Bosnian War."[58] This admittance that the basis for the articles remained unproven was largely lost in the emotionally-laden content. The image showing a long refugee trek and headline on the first page of that edition arguably had much more impact than any article could have had, evoking, by now familiar images of Jews marching to concentration camps in the Second World War.[59] While it is fully comprehensible that the press would cite a statement made by the Minister of Defence, *BILD's* coverage clearly went beyond this.

Spiegel, *taz*, *Konkret* and *AJW* were much more sceptical of Scharping's claims, which *taz* deemed part of his "rhetorical repertoire", along with comparing Milošević to Hitler.[60] Several *Konkret*-articles reiterated that there was no proof to substantiate Scharping's claims and criticised the Minister for using unproven and false information. However, none analysed this issue any further.[61] *Spiegel's* articles also demonstrated a sense of indignation at Scharping's claims about concentration camps without producing the necessary proof.[62]

56 Anonymous: ...Sie treiben sie ins KZ. In: *BILD*, 01.04.1999, p. 1. *KZ* is the German abbreviation for "*Konzentrationslager*", or concentration camp.

57 Peter Bönisch: Wem gehört die Zukunft. In: *BILD*, 01.04.1999, p. 2.

58 Anonymous: Serben feuern auf schutzlose Flüchtlinge. In: *BILD*, 01.04.1999, p. 2.

59 Image published in *BILD*, 01.04.1999, p. 1.

60 Stefan Reinecke: Krieg macht dumm. In: *taz*, 07.04.1999, p. 1; Andreas Dietl: „Die Bomben fragen nicht, wer Jude oder Serbe ist". In: *AJW*, 29.04.1999, p. 2.

61 Karl Lorenz: Der Trottel als Kriegsgott. In: *Konkret*, May 1999, pp. 44, 46; Tjark Kunstreich: Der deutsche Krieg. In: *Konkret*, June 1999, p. 24.

62 Claus Christian Malzahn: Suche nach Quellen. In: *Spiegel*, 12.04.1999, p. 28; Jürgen Leinemann / Horand Knaup / Stefan Aust: „Ich bin kein Kriegskanzler". In: *Spiegel*, 12.04.1999, pp. 32–37; Anonymous: „Ich darf nicht wackeln". In: *Spiegel*, 05.04.1999, p. 25; Manfred Ertel / Rüdiger Falksohn / Renate Flottau / Olaf Ihlau / Siegesmund von Ilsemann / Dirk Koch / Helene Zuber: „Das Gespenst von Vietnam". In: *Spiegel*, 05.04.1999, pp. 150–164, here p. 152.

In an interview with Chancellor Schröder, *Spiegel* stated accusingly: "If the Defence Minister speaks of concentration camps, he needs proof." After an evasive answer from Schröder, the news-magazine pressed him further:

> two weeks ago, there was information that 10,000 or 20,000 people were being subjected to unbelievable brutality in Pristina's [football] stadium. When the *Bundeswehr* [...] sent drones over the stadium, the pictures proved that the stadium was empty.

To this repeated demand for an explanation Schröder simply replied: "those who want to see the misery of flight and expulsion don't need to wait for the proof from the aerial reconnaissance."[63] Schröder's admission regarding the careless treatment of proof or lack thereof is striking. Moreover, the news-magazine's insistence on a straight-forward comment from the Chancellor shows the indignation of the negligent misuse of claims as well as *Spiegel's* reluctance to simply regurgitate what politicians were telling the press. No other publication at this time underlined Scharping's mistake as emphatically as *Spiegel*.

It is worth noting that in spite of this distinctly unprofessional behaviour of disseminating unproven facts, Scharping never publicly justified himself. Gregor Gysi (PDS) reminded the *Bundestag* of Scharping's exaggerations during a speech he made on 15 April.[64] However, when the Minister of Defence spoke later in the debate, he did not address the issue, although he responded to various other matters Gysi had raised.[65] Furthermore, in Scharping's memoirs, he omitted the subject completely. This could underline the gravity of his error, which Scharping seemingly wanted to white-wash in his official record.[66]

Milošević – The Main Culprit?

The portrayal of Milošević was another important theme in all publications aside from *AJW* and *Konkret*. The conservative newspapers *Welt*, *FAZ* and *BILD* accused Milošević of having forced NATO's hand, leaving the alliance no choice but to put an end to the inhumane events in Kosovo.[67] "Milošević

63 Jürgen Leinemann / Horand Knaup / Stefan Aust: „Ich bin kein Kriegskanzler". In: *Spiegel*, 12.04.1999, pp. 35–36.

64 *Deutscher Bundestag*, Plenarprotokoll 14/32, 15.04.1999, p. 2636.

65 Ibid., pp. 2645–2648.

66 Scharping: *Wir dürfen nicht wegsehen.*

67 Torsten Krauel: Belgrad hilft der Nato. In: *Welt*, 29.03.1999, p. 1; Katja Ridderbusch: Milošević' Kalkül. In: *Welt*, 07.04.1999, p. 1; wie.: Luftschläge der Nato gegen Jugoslawien. In: *FAZ*, 25.03.1999, p. 1; Reinhard Müller: Das letzte Mittel. In: *FAZ*, 25.03.1999, p. 6; Günther

wanted this war [...]" one *Welt*-article stated bluntly.[68] A *FAZ*-editor, Berthold Kohler, expressed a similar assessment in his editorial: "this war was virtually forced upon the dithering NATO."[69] He reinforced this opposition of good NATO versus bad Milošević one month later in his description of the latter as a "dictator gone wild" who had forced NATO into this war and that "his murder-machine in Kosovo [must] be stopped".[70] Other *FAZ*-articles equally interpreted the Kosovo War through a clear-cut binary opposition, portraying NATO as good and Milošević as evil. For example on 27 March, Matthias Rüb contrasted the "comprehensive destruction of the Serbian-Yugoslav army in Vukovar, Sarajevo, Kosovo and other places in former Yugoslavia" to NATO's "surgical intervention aimed at weakening a military-apparatus."[71] This comparison was further underlined by the assessment that Milošević was pursuing 'ethnic cleansing' – an 'injustice' that NATO now needed to 'make right.'[72] This interpretation was also presented in a cartoon published in *FAZ*, which portrayed Milošević as a grinning politician who pursued his goal of constructing a Greater Serbia – symbolised through his hand-gesture, the Chetnik-salute – while destroying Vukovar, Dubrovnik, Sarajevo, Srebrenica and Kosovo to achieve his goal. Only with NATO's attacks on Belgrade, did Milošević finally alter his stance.[73]

Interestingly, this caricature equates the genocide in Srebrenica to other instances of Serbian violence such as the destruction of Dubrovnik, the siege of Sarajevo, or the events in Kosovo, none of which have been termed 'genocide'. While a reader at the time may not have noticed this detail, it emphasises the lack of discernment regarding the topic, even in abstract terms, found in other instances throughout *FAZ's* coverage.

BILD's treatment of Milošević can be summed up as an excessively populist depiction.[74] Mere days after the NATO-intervention had begun, *BILD*

Nonnenmacher: Der Ernstfall. In: *FAZ*, 26.03.1999, p. 1; fri: Solana nennt Angriffe erfolgreich. In: *FAZ*, 26.03.1999, p. 2; fy: „Vor allem das Massaker möglichst rasch beenden". In: *FAZ*, 31.03.1999, p. 2; Anonymous: Kommt heil nach Hause. In: *BILD*, 26.03.1999, p. 1.

68 Katja Ridderbusch: Slobodan Milošević, der Mann, der Europa verhöhnt. In: *Welt*, 26.03.1999, p. 11.

69 Berthold Kohler: Festbleiben. In: *FAZ*, 26.03.1999, p. 1.

70 Berthold Kohler: Ein Protektorat. In: *FAZ*, 07.04.1999, p. 1.

71 Matthias Rüb: Was kommt in Serbien nach Milošević. In: *FAZ*, 27.03.1999, p. 5.

72 Matthias Rüb: Die Teilung ist keine Lösung. In: *FAZ*, 01.04.1999, p. 12.

73 Cartoon by Fritz Behrendt, printed in *FAZ*, 27 March 1999, p. 5.

74 Anonymous: Milošević – ich ging mit dem Schlächter zu Schule. In: *BILD*, 27.03.1999, p. 3; Lothar Löwe: Das Dilemma. In: *BILD*, 25.03.1999, p. 2; Udo Roebel: Das Weinen des Krieges. In: *BILD*, 12.04.1999, p. 2.

published an article which reported that "they call him [Slobodan Milošević] the 'butcher of the Balkans'. His wife is simply called [...] 'the witch of Belgrade.'"[75] The article never detailed who specifically called Milošević and his wife these names and considering that there was no opposition worth mentioning in Serbia at the time,[76] this claim seems concocted. However, from this point onwards almost all *BILD*-articles referred to Milošević simply as '*der Schlächter*' or 'the butcher,'[77] which was epitomised by the tabloid's front cover on 27 March 1999. The headline proclaimed "*Der Schlächter: Slobodan Milošević immer wahnsinniger*" ("The Butcher: Slobodan Milošević increasingly insane"). This headline was accompanied by two pictures: one showed Milošević lighting a cigar; the other pictured a long refugee trek. The picture of Milošević was accompanied by the following caption: "Yugoslavia's President Slobodan Milošević: While civilians are dying gruesomely, he lights a cigar."[78] The pictorial juxtaposition of *BILD's* interpretation of perpetrator and victim along with the evocative headline clearly held Milošević personally responsible for the civilian suffering in Kosovo. In this context, one must remember that the tabloid, with a circulation of 4.45 million, was the most-read daily newspaper in Germany. Significantly, *BILD's* populist treatment of Milošević was strongly criticised by *JF*. As an editorial by Peter Lattas asserted provocatively, Hitler's Propaganda Minister "Joseph Goebbels would have been proud of *BILD* [...]"[79]

The left-leaning publications did not portray Milošević in the same manner as the conservative press, though they also allocated responsibility for the violence to him personally. The left-wing *taz* was the most explicit, describing Milošević as an "ego-maniacal dictator" who had thrust the Balkans into

75 Anonymous: Die Milosevics – eine schreckliche Familie. In: *BILD*, 26.03.1999, p. 4.

76 As reported in Matthias Rüb: Was kommt in Serbien nach Milošević. In: *FAZ*, 27.03.1999, p. 5; Nenad Stefanov: Das Elend der serbischen Opposition. In: *Welt*, 14.04.1999, p. 11.

77 Anonymous: Der Schlächter: Slobodan Milošević immer wahnsinniger. In: *BILD*, 27.03.1999, p. 1; Anonymous: Albanische Flüchtlinge berichten von Massakern. In: *BILD*, 27.03.1999, p. 2; Anonymous: Milošević – ich ging mit dem Schlächter zu Schule. In: *BILD*, 27.03.1999, p. 3; Anonymous: Das Leid der Flüchtlinge: Jede Stunde werden es 20 000 mehr. In: *BILD*, 29.03.1999, p. 5; Anonymous: Serben feuern auf schutzlose Flüchtlinge. In: *BILD*, 01.04.1999, p. 2; Anonymous: Die Kritik an NATO-Angriffen wächst. In: *BILD*, 06.04.1999, p. 2; Anonymous: Schau her, du Mörder! In: *BILD*, 07.04.1999, p. 1; Anonymous: Das leere Lager. In: *BILD*, 08.04.1999, p. 9; Anonymous: Kosovo-Krieg ... und Milosevics Sohn floh ins sonnige Griechenland. In: *BILD*, 12.04.1999, p. 2; Anonymous: NATO: Dieses Foto zeigt ein Massengrab. In: *BILD*, 13.04.1999, p. 3.

78 Anonymous: Der Schlächter: Slobodan Milošević immer wahnsinniger. In: *BILD*, 27.03.1999, p. 1.

79 Peter Lattas: Flüchtlings-Schach. In: *JF*, 16.04.1999, p. 2.

a decade of war.[80] A *FR*-article stated that "there is no [...option of] peace [when dealing with] more than an alleged war-criminal."[81] This slightly awkward description – in the original German: "*[...] mehr als [ein] mutmaßlicher Kriegsverbrecher*" – presumably aimed to express that even though Milošević had not been indicted by the ICTY, to the author, there was no doubt about the severity of his war crimes.

Spiegel's portrayal of Milošević was two-fold. On the one hand its articles made Milošević responsible for the war[82] and attributed derogative names to him, which hitherto only *BILD* had done. Terms such as 'Serb-tsar'[83] and 'Belgrade despot'[84], as well as the colloquial '*Über*-Serb'[85] were repeatedly used to describe Milošević while words such as 'butchers,'[86] and 'Milošević-killers'[87] described the Serbian forces. Simultaneously however, Rudolf Augstein argued in various editorials that Milošević's insistence on Kosovo's belonging to Serbia was comprehensible, as the region was an important element of the Serbian national conscience.[88] Moreover, Augstein reiterated that 'moralising' arguments such as declaring Milošević to be one of the worst criminals of the

80 Velten Schaefer / Karl Gersuny: Die Haupttäter. In: *taz*, 25.03.1999, p. 2; Paul Hockenos: Gesucht: ein ehrlicher Makler. In: *taz*, 30.03.1999, p. 13; Stefan Reinecke: Alte Feinde, neue Verhältnisse. In: *taz*, 06.04.1999, p. 1; Rüdiger Rossig: Lebensgeschichte eines Kriegstreibers. In: *taz*, 06.04.1999, p. 7.

81 Rolf Paasch: Dimensionen eines Krieges. In: *FR*, 06.04.1999, p. 3; also in Winrich Kühne: Unter dem Druck der Ereignisse in Kosovo. In: *FR*, 25.03.1999, p. 18; Rolf Paasch: Präzedenzfall Kosovo. In: *FR*, 25.03.1999, p. 3; Hans-Hagen Bremer: Bewährungsprobe für eine gemeinsame Sicherheitspolitik. In: *FR*, 25.03.1999, p. 7; Richard Meng: Alle spüren das – eine Zäsur in der deutschen Außenpolitik. In: *FR*, 27.03.1999, p. 6; Rolf Paasch: Dimensionen eines Krieges. In: *FR*, 06.04.1999, p. 3; Monika Kappus: Die leicht geneigte Haltung eines Lastenträgers. In: *FR*, Ostern 1999 [02.04.–05.04.1999], p. 3.

82 Renate Flottau / Olaf Ihlau / Siegesmund von Ilsemann / Dirk Koch / Jörg Mettke / Roland Schleicher: Alle Serben im Krieg. In: *Spiegel*, 29.03.1999, pp. 194–213; Roland Schleicher: Sehnsucht nach Tito. In: *Spiegel*, 05.04.1999, pp. 170–172.

83 Flottau / Ihlau / von Ilsemann / Koch / Mettke / Schleicher: Alle Serben im Krieg. In: *Spiegel*, 29.03.1999, pp. 194–213, here pp. 196, 203; Renate Flottau: „Hau ab, rette lieber deinen Kopf". In: *Spiegel*, 12.04.1999, p. 172.

84 Flottau / Ihlau / von Ilsemann / Koch / Mettke / Schleicher: Alle Serben im Krieg. In: *Spiegel*, 29.03.1999, pp. 194–213, here p. 210; Jürgen Hogrefe / Siegesmund von Ilsemann / Roland Schleicher: Letzter Ausweg zum Frieden. In: *Spiegel*, 10.05.1999, pp. 162–164.

85 Jürgen Hogrefe / Siegesmund von Ilsemann / Roland Schleicher: Letzter Ausweg zum Frieden. In: *Spiegel*, 10.05.1999, p. 164.

86 Manfred Ertel / Rüdiger Falksohn / Renate Flottau / Olaf Ihlau / Siegesmund von Ilsemann / Dirk Koch / Helene Zuber: „Das Gespenst von Vietnam". In: *Spiegel*, 05.04.1999, pp. 150–164, here p. 164.

87 Anonymous: „Ich darf nicht wackeln". In: *Spiegel*, 05.04.1999, p. 27.

88 Rudolf Augstein: Ein Krieg ohne Zufall? In: *Spiegel*, 29.03.1999, p. 24.

20th century were useless and did not contribute to finding a solution. Instead he focused his attention on what he described as the "war-trio Schröder-Scharping-Fischer," wondering why no one was accusing them for getting Germany involved in Kosovo.[89] This divergence of *Spiegel's* articles and the opinion of the news-magazine's founder offering different interpretations must be noted. Nonetheless, the articles that made Milošević responsible for the war outweighed Augstein's single editorial. Moreover, *Spiegel's* coverage emphasises that while the liberal/left-wing publications were fundamentally against the war, they nonetheless held Milošević personally responsible for the on-going violence, just as they had done before.
The manner in which these publications portrayed Milošević, substantiates two conclusions drawn in other media analyses of the Kosovo War. Reiner Grundmann argues that Germany's press tended to 'demonise' Milošević and concludes that the German press used direct analogies and comparisons to the Third Reich.[90] Moreover, Rossella Savarese postulated in her comparative European media analysis that Milošević was frequently likened to Hitler in various international publications including the French *Le Monde* and the Italian *Il Corriere della Sera.* This calls for a consideration of the German press' likening of the Yugoslav President to Hitler.

The only newspapers to utilise such comparisons were *BILD* and *FAZ*, though the tabloid did so in only one article.[91] However, the broadsheet featured them repeatedly, arguing that the harsh word-choice was justifiable considering Milošević's policies.[92] There was one exception in an editorial authored by Frank Schirrmacher, one of *FAZ's* editors-in-chief. "Milošević is not Hitler. And Kosovo is not Auschwitz", Schirrmacher wrote. When contrasting this evaluation with the previous eagerness of *FAZ*-authors and even Schirrmacher's co-editor-in-chief, Kohler, to use such analogies to underline the justification of NATO's intervention, it becomes all the more clear that editorials were personal opinions which at times stood in contrast to other

89 Augstein: Rückfall in die Steinzeit. In: *Spiegel*, 12.04.1999, p. 26.

90 Reiner Grundmann / Dennis Smith / Sue Wright: National Elites and Transnational Discourses in the Balkan War: A Comparison between the French, German and British Establishment Press. In: *European Journal of Communication* 15,3 (2000), pp. 299–320

91 Peter Bönisch: Wem gehört die Zukunft. In: *BILD*, 01.04.1999, p. 2.

92 Karl Feldmeyer: Ein hoher Preis. In: *FAZ*, 26.03.1999, p. 12; Berthold Kohler: Ein Protektorat. In: *FAZ*, 07.04.1999, p. 1; Eckhard Lohse: Frau Beers Brief und die Angst vor einem Himmelfahrtskommando. In: *FAZ*, 14.04.1999, p. 4; Richard Swartz: Serbischer Autismus. In: *FAZ*, 08.04.1999, p. 49.

members of the editorial team. Unfortunately this discerning article was easily lost in the majority of opposite interpretations found in *FAZ's* coverage.

All other publications also voiced their disapproval of such comparisons, though for different reasons.[93] *AJW* strongly disapproved of likening Milošević and Hitler, as well as Kosovo and the Holocaust, deeming them plainly incorrect.[94] Similarly, *Welt* argued, that such comparisons distorted the "Hitler-genocide" while simultaneously giving the reader a wrong sense of what was unfolding in Kosovo.[95] An editorial published in mid-May, entitled "The wrong Hitler", was even more explicit: "it is rude and politically stupid to stylise every military enemy as Hitler."[96] *taz* published various articles criticising such associations, as they "[…] trivialised the Hitler-crimes. The Jews may have been grateful if Hitler had merely lugged them to the border."[97]

This demonstrates that while comparisons to the Holocaust and Hitler could occasionally be found in the German press coverage, they were also perceived critically and limited to mostly one publication. Nonetheless, the treatment of Milošević in the German press was marked by what could be seen as an internal struggle. After nearly a decade of blaming Milošević for the Balkan-violence, it was perhaps gratifying to see NATO's attack against him. On the other hand, all publications except *BILD* – though to a differing degree – were weary of entangling themselves in unfitting historical comparisons. This dichotomy could explain the at times fluctuating treatment of Milošević. Moreover the bipartisan movement away from comparing Milošević to Hitler – again except in *BILD* as well as *FAZ* – manifests a sensitivity in the publications' editorial offices.

However, in this focus on Milošević in relation to the NATO-intervention all publications disregarded KLA as a significant contributor to the initial violence in Kosovo. A few months earlier, all had analysed KLA's activities and while there was a tendency to embellish their guerrilla warfare,[98] their contribution to the violence was at least acknowledged. This was no longer

93 For example: Gerhard Spörl / Jürgen Leinemann / Stefan Aust: „Es hat keinen Deal gegeben". In: *Spiegel*, 10.05.1999, pp. 52–56.

94 Micha Brumlik: Gerechter Krieg? Wann, wenn jetzt nicht? In: *AJW*, 29.04.1999, p. 1; also in ajw: Hilfe in der Nato. In: *AJW*, 15.04.1999, p. 1; Wolf Silberbach: Sorge, Solidarität und Streit. In: *AJW*, 15.04.1999, p. 2.

95 Herbert Kremp: Die Bahn der Eskalation. In: *Welt*, 09.04.1999, p. 10.

96 Thomas Schmid: Der falsche Hitler. In: *Welt*, 17.05.1999, p. 10.

97 Silke Mertins: Vom Nutzen des Pazifismus. In: *taz*, 10./11.04.1999, p. 5; also in Stefan Reinecke: Krieg macht dumm. In: *taz*, 07.04.1999, p. 1.

98 See pp. 176–182.

the case now that NATO was at war and needed a clear enemy. Even those publications, which did not approve of NATO's intervention, did not include KLA in their analyses. This is partially comprehensible considering the drastic humanitarian catastrophe caused by the Serbian forces at this time. In comparison, KLA's violence may have seemed like needle-pricks. Nonetheless, it must be noted that the German press completely disregarded an important actor who had been central to the coverage mere months earlier. This underscores a tendency to condense the conflict to a clear-cut black and white interpretation.

Serbian Civilians and the War

Amidst the coverage supporting and opposing the war, the treatment of Serbian civilians in the German press is very revealing. Serbian civilians, especially those living in Belgrade and other major Serbian cities, were strongly affected by the NATO-bombardment, particularly when power plants, media outlets, bridges and other targets NATO deemed tactically important were hit. Most nights were spent in air-raid shelters and many attempted to flee from Serbia. Similar to the secondary literature, *FAZ* and *Konkret* did not treat this subject-matter at all. *Konkret's* neglect is particularly surprising due to the magazine's avid opposition to the war. This would have made their coverage of the civilian suffering under NATO-bombardment particularly relevant.

Spiegel, *JF*, *Welt* and *BILD* gave it limited coverage.[99] The only *BILD*-article on this topic painted a vivid picture: "deafening sirens wailing, the crash of the explosions, blazing columns of fire […] the Yugoslav capital [has…] almost completely collapsed."[100] This reduced interest in the suffering of Serbian civilians under NATO-bombardment may have resulted from the difficult situation the German press was in. Even though some publications were critical of the intervention, none approved of the Serbian violence in Kosovo. Consequently Serbians primarily remained the perpetrators in a very condensed portrayal of the conflict. This was further underlined in various articles and editorials published by *FAZ* and *Welt*, which painted a very negative image

99 Karl P. Gerigk: „Wir lassen die Albaner ins Land". In: *JF*, 02.04.1999, p.3; Peter Lattas: Flüchtlings-Schach. In: *JF*, 16.04.1999, p.2; Anonymous Belgrade journalist: „Was habe ich verkehrt gemacht, dass ich hier geboren bin?" In: *Welt*, 15.04.1999, p.5; Karin Kneissel: Trommeln für Milosevic. In: *Welt*, 17.04.1999, p.3; Anonymous: Belgrad: Warten im Bunker, Rock-Konzert gegen Raketen. In: *BILD*, 29.03.1999, p.4; Oliver Santen: „Wir haben Angst vor einem langen Krieg". In: *BILD*, 31.03.1999, p.4; Alexander Szandar: Minenhund und Bodyguard. In: *Spiegel*, 29.03.1999, p.200.

100 Anonymous: Belgrad – die Stadt, in der Angst verboten ist. In: *BILD*, 07.04.1999, p.9.

of Serbian civilians. Some articles argued that the Serbian population had no sense of collective responsibility, let alone guilt for what was happening or what Milošević was doing in Kosovo.[101] One *FAZ*-editorial, entitled "Collective Blindness" stated that the Serbian people had a severe deficit in the "sense of wrong-doing", and that this was compounded by their "self-righteous not-wanting-to-look" attitude and their construction of a "victim-myth."[102] Clearly it was hard for them to be sympathetic for Serbians suffering from NATO violence.

FR and *taz* were the only publications that gave insight into the life of Serbian civilians at the time.[103] Many of these articles were written by their respective correspondents based in Belgrade: Stephan Israel for *FR* and Andrej Ivanji for *taz*. Israel reported that there was no sense of normalcy. "The people in Belgrade don't have a single quiet night anymore," since NATO-bombs were regularly hitting the city centre. When the Yugoslav Ministry of the Interior was destroyed by a NATO-bomb in the centre of Belgrade, Israel reported: "In the silent faces around the barrier in front of the ruins there is a mixture of anger and indignation. No one is speaking […]"[104]

taz's Ivanji also painted a sympathetic picture of Serbian civilians. He reminded his readers that the terror Belgrade's citizens were living through every single night reminded the population of the Nazi-attacks in 1941. Ivanji closed the article with an anecdote told by an older woman to a younger woman as both found shelter from the NATO-bombs in a cellar. The former reminded her listener that Sarajevo had been besieged for three whole years – a siege she said, Serbians had condoned. And Sarajevo's population had endured so much longer.[105] Ivanji's reminder that Serbians recognised their country's role as perpetrators stands in harsh contrast to the stance taken in the conservative

101 Richard Wagner: Slobodan Milošević muss endlich gestürzt werden. In: *Welt*, 12.04.1999, p. 11.

102 Matthias Rüb: Opferlamm in Feierlaune. In: *FAZ*, 06.04.1999, p. 49.

103 Andrej Ivanji: Belgrad ist vom Sieg völlig überzeugt. In: *taz*, 25.03.1999, p. 3; Ivanji: Patriotische Ermunterung durch Partisanenfilme. In: *taz*, 26.03.1999, p. 2; Ivanji: „Wo werden sie heute zuschlagen?" In: *taz*, 06.04.1999, p. 6; Ivanji: „Schießt doch, ihr Schweine!" In: *taz*, 09.04.1999, p. 4; Ivanji: Mit Rock 'n' Roll gegen die Nato. In: *taz*, 29.03.1999, p. 3; Ivanji: „Mama, werden wir jetzt alle sterben?" In: *taz*, Ostern 1999 [02.04.–05.04.1999], p. 8; Stephan Israel: Und die letzte freie Stimme schweigt. In: *FR*, 25.03.1999, p. 3; Israel: Bis gestern war Krieg ein fernes Geschehen. In: *FR*, 26.03.1999, p. 3; Israel: Die Theater spielen weiter. In: *FR*, 29.03.1999, p. 8.

104 Stephan Israel: Bisher gehört nur die Nacht der Nato. In: *FR*, 06.04.1999, p. 3.

105 Andrej Ivanji: „Mama, werden wir jetzt alle sterben?" In: *taz*, Ostern 1999 [02.04.–05.04.1999], p. 8.

papers which argued that Serbians had constructed a myth of victimhood and refused to acknowledge their country's part in the on-going violence. However, the author also reminded his reader that it was very difficult even in Belgrade to find out what was really happening in Kosovo and that most people in the capital were kept in the dark about these events.[106] This article is remarkable, as it merged 'normal' reporting of civilians in Belgrade with a commentary on their world-view. Rather than covering the many hostile anti-NATO protests in Belgrade, Ivanji chose to portray a quiet, reflective scene in an air-raid shelter. The result of this careful selection gave the *taz*-reader a rare, likable portrait of Serbians.

Images showing Serbian civilians in air-raid-bunkers[107] were printed alongside these articles, which gave the reader a more memorable impression of the Serbian civilians' fate. Other pictures published by *taz* and *Spiegel* presented Serbian civilian suffering more graphically, linking it directly to the NATO-bombing.[108] One, for example, showed a crumpled corpse amidst rubble; the caption specifies: "A NATO-strike in Pristina." *taz* pictured a close-up picture of an injured man standing in front of a bombed out house. The caption reads: "Serbian civilian after a NATO-bomb mistakenly struck a Serbian residential area in a town called Aleksinac."

We turn now to three side-issues which proved important in shaping the publications' reporting: the influence of Srebrenica and Račak; the Green party and collective memory of the Holocaust; and the media's self-reflection of its role in the war.

The Impact of Srebrenica and Račak

Srebrenica and Račak can be seen as milestones in the international understanding of the Bosnia and Kosovo War respectively. As discussed in the previous chapter, the incident in Račak – whether it was a 'massacre' or not – had sparked considerable interest in the German print media, but this quickly subsided. However, as the German press covered the NATO-intervention in Kosovo, Račak re-appeared in some publications. *AJW* understandably did not mention Račak in this context, as it had not covered the incident at the

106 Andrej Ivanji: Im großen dunklen Loch der Ungewissheit. In: *taz*, 30.03.1999, p. 4; Ivanji: Partisanenfilme statt Hollywood. In: *taz*, 09.04.1999, p. 4.

107 Images published in *BILD*, 29.03.1999, p. 4; *taz*, 29.03.1999, p. 3; *taz*, Ostern 1999 [02.04.–05.04.1999], p. 8; *FR*, 29.03.1999, p. 8.

108 Images published in *Spiegel*, 12.04.1999, p. 174; *taz*, 07.04.1999, p. 6; same image in *FR*, 07.04.1999, p. 5; *BILD*, 07.04.1999, p. 9.

time. *BILD*, *taz*, *Konkret* and *JF*, which had reported on the incident previously, did not refer to Račak now, though *Welt*, *FAZ*, *FR* and *Spiegel* did.[109] Mostly they reminded the readers of the conflict's length and the level of violence the Kosovo-Albanian population had been subjected to in the past. Significantly, the term 'massacre' was used indiscriminately in all four publications, in spite of the legal ambiguities surrounding the term.[110] Curiously *Spiegel* also published the by now familiar 'ditch-scene' from Račak twice – on 29 March and in mid-April.[111] While the caption in March clearly labelled the image as portraying a scene from Račak, the picture in the April edition was merely described with the following caption: "Massacred Albanians (1999): 'Brutal violence.'" This could indicate that the picture was deemed universally known, reiterating the prominence of the incident in the understanding of events in Kosovo. However, the condensed caption also underlined *Spiegel's* stubborn referral to Račak as a scene of 'massacred' Kosovo-Albanians without mentioning that 7–8 KLA-soldiers had been amongst the fatalities, nor that Serbia contested this version altogether, which the news-magazine had already disregarded in its initial coverage of the Račak incident.

Nonetheless it must be noted that although Račak re-appeared in some publications' articles, none of them argued that this was a particularly striking incident or that it justified the NATO-intervention. Indeed, the echo of the Srebrenica Massacre was much more prominent in the coverage of the NATO-intervention than Račak, although *BILD*, *Konkret* and *AJW* did not refer to it. All other papers referred to Srebrenica to underline the desperate fate of the Kosovo-Albanian civilians and remind the reader of the atrocities Milošević had already been involved with in the past.[112] Again *Spiegel*

109 Torsten Krauel: Belgrad hilft der Nato. In: *Welt*, 29.03.1999, p. 1; Nikolaus Blome: „Es gibt keine Planung für den Einsatz von Bodentruppen". In: *Welt*, 30.03.1999, p. 2; Lena Pawlovsky: Nur im Internet hat die Wahrheit eine Chance. In: *Welt*, 01.04.1999, p. 2; Matthias Rüb: Was geschieht in den Dörfern und Städten im Kosovo? In: *FAZ*, 29.03.1999, p. 3; Dunja Melcic: Kollektive Verblendung. In: *FAZ*, 08.04.1999, p. 52; Matthias Rüb: Trotz Satelliten und Videokameras keine Klarheit über die Ereignisse im Kosovo. In: *FAZ*, 17.04.1999, p. 3; Hans-Hagen Bremer: Bewährungsprobe für eine gemeinsame Sicherheitspolitik. In: *FR*, 25.03.1999, p. 7; Renate Flottau / Olaf Ihlau / Siegesmund von Ilsemann / Dirk Koch / Joerg Mettke / Roland Schleicher: „Alle Serben im Krieg". In: *Spiegel*, 29.03.1999, pp. 194–213.

110 See chapter 7, fn. 55–56.

111 Image published in *Spiegel*, 12.04.1999, p. 191; see figure 30.

112 Lord Weidenfeld: Das Dilemma der Demokratien. In: *Welt*, 03.04.1999, p. 10; Richard Wagner: Slobodan Milošević muss endlich gestürzt werden. In: *Welt*, 12.04.1999, p. 11; Richard Meng: Alle spüren das – eine Zäsur in der deutschen Außenpolitik. In: *FR*, 27.03.1999, p. 6; ap: Haager Tribunal führt Milošević auf Geheimliste. In: *FR*, 06.04.1999, p. 5; Manfred Ertel / Rüdiger Falksohn / Renate Flottau / Olaf Ihlau / Siegesmund von Ilsemann / Dirk

presented its reminder of Srebrenica with an image which strongly resembled the previously discussed image showing survivors from Srebrenica pushing elderly family members in wheel-barrows (see figure 10).[113]

The selection of this picture is telling, as it presents refugees fleeing from Srebrenica rather than the victims of the massacre itself. As elaborated in the previous chapter on Srebrenica, the enclave had been inaccessible to international journalists and observers as the genocide was unfolding. Consequently, the only sources of information at the time were the refugees who had fled to Tuzla. However, by the time this image was re-published in April 1999, forensic excavations of the mass graves in Srebrenica had been underway for several years and other images had become available. However, by choosing this picture of refugees, *Spiegel's* aim presumably was to remind the reader of known information rather than introduce new details. Moreover, this image of Srebrenica's displaced civilians draws a clear parallel to the current pictures of Kosovo-Albanian refugees, underlining the continuous destruction by 'the Serbs.' These underlying nuances which resonate with this image reveal how much Srebrenica influenced the interpretation of Kosovo.

This is further highlighted by two *FAZ*-articles reminding the reader that little had been known about Srebrenica as the massacre was unfolding in July 1995, but that four years later the public knowledge of the event was becoming more complete and the extent of the fatalities visible. With Srebrenica in mind, the articles argued, NATO's on-going intervention in Kosovo was legitimate. No one could be sure of knowing more than a fraction of what was really going on in Kosovo.[114] The message conveyed by these articles regarding the doubts of how reliable information was is very important, as it underlines the influence of the previous Bosnia War on the analysis of the on-going conflict in Kosovo.

taz, which had extensively reported on Srebrenica, used its references differently. One article argued that because Serbia had been the enemy during the Bosnia War, as well as the Kosovo War and was responsible for the Srebrenica Massacre, politicians were letting their trauma over the Srebrenica killings influence them, even though the on-going situation in Kosovo was very

Koch / Helene Zuber: „Das Gespenst von Vietnam". In: *Spiegel*, 05.04.1999, pp. 150–164; Andrzej Madela: Zwickmühlen der Moral. In: *JF*, 09.04.1999, p. 11; Michael Hanfeld: Von Separatisten und anderen. In: *FAZ*, 30.03.1999, p. 56; Richard Swartz: Serbischer Autismus. In: *FAZ*, 08.04.1999, p. 49.

113 Image published in *Spiegel*, 05.04.1999, p. 174: "Muslim refugees from Srebrenica, 1995."

114 Udo Ulfkotte: Die Nato ist im Bilde, doch gibt sie nur wenig preis. In: *FAZ*, 10.04.1999, p. 4; also in em.: Ein Einzelner. In: *FAZ*, 13.04.1999, p. 49.

different to that in Bosnia earlier.[115] Another *taz*-article criticised Scharping's statement that a second Srebrenica – where, according to the Defence Minister, 30,000 civilians had been murdered – was happening in Kosovo. The *taz*-editorial reminded its reader that UNHCR estimated the Srebrenica fatalities at 7,076. "But such details do not matter if you are on the 'right' side of a war […]" the author remarked sarcastically.[116] *taz's* critical editorial not only stressed that even four years later, the complete number of fatalities remained unknown.[117] It also drew attention to the occasional inflated cross-references made to Srebrenica, which exploited the massacre in a time of war.

The Green Party

As NATO's bombardment continued over several weeks without any signs of Milošević surrendering, the German public became increasingly sceptical of the war. Particularly the Green party base criticised 'their' politicians – mainly Fischer – for abandoning the most fundamental element of their ideology, namely pacifism. Consequently, on 14 May 1999, when almost as many people in Germany supported the war as opposed it,[118] a special Green Party convention was organised in Bielefeld, Germany, where this issue was debated. Here the delegates had to decide whether they would support Fischer and his policies, which meant a continuation of the war, or if Fischer should lose the backing of his party. This would mean that the Green Party was no longer *regierungsfähig*, or 'able to govern,' ending the Red-Green coalition. Facing this political crisis, Fischer gave a passionate speech to rally support for his policies, which was partially quoted or even printed in its entirety in all main-stream publications.[119] In it Fischer reiterated "Auschwitz is incomparable. But I stand for two principles: Never again war, never again Auschwitz;

115 Jonas Viering: Das Himmelfahrtskommando. In: *taz*, 07.04.1999, p. 8.

116 Stefan Reinecke: Krieg macht dumm. In: *taz*, 07.04.1999, p. 1.

117 According to current estimates made by Amnesty International in 2005, the Srebrenica Massacre cost more than 8,000 lives.

118 According to the Dimap Infratest poll, 48% supported the war and 47% opposed it. See Dimap Infratest: Approval of Air-strikes?, June 1999. http://www.infratest-dimap.de/uploads/media/dt9906.pdf (accessed 03.09.2014), p. 12.

119 V. Müller / G. Bauer: Fischer kämpfte – trotz stechender Schmerzen. In: *BILD*, 14.05.1999, p. 2; dpa: „Ich habe alles getan, was in meinen Kräften stand". In: *taz*, 14.05.1999, p. 2; Armin Fuhrer: Nach zähem Kampf Mehrheit für Fischer. In: *Welt*, 14.05.1999, p. 2; P. S.: Tritte und Schläge von den Kriegsgegnern. In: *FAZ*, 14.05.1999, p. 3; Vera Gärow: Zeitreise in die eigene Vergangenheit. In: *FR*, 14.05.1999, p. 3; Paul Lersch / Hartmut Palmer / Hajo Schumacher / Hans-Jörg Vehlewald: D-Day in Bielefeld. In: *Spiegel*, 17.05.1999, pp. 28–29;

never again genocide, never again Fascism: for me, both belong together […] and that's why I joined the Green Party."[120]

In the German press' coverage of this speech, readers learned that after several attacks of Fischer and his colleagues with paint bombs and butanoic acid, the convention ultimately voted in support of Fischer.[121] However, it is striking that none of the publications commented on the linkages Fischer made between Germany's past and the country's present foreign policy. Indeed, apart from the occasional reiteration that German soldiers were engaged in active combat for the first time since the Second World War[122] and allusions to the irony that a traditionally anti-war or even pacifist Red-Green coalition had made this decision,[123] there was no profound discourse on Germany's past and the role it played in the present. The German press' coverage of the Green Party convention corroborates a conclusion made in a different media analysis, namely that Germany's self-image had developed to the point that it was no longer defined primarily by the Second World War.[124] None of the publications considered the broader themes that resounded in this speech, for example how Germany would generally position itself in terms of foreign policy, having departed from its previous doctrine; and what the 'normalisation' of Germany and its past meant for the broader theme of Holocaust memory. This last theme highlights an interesting development in the German press coverage. While a debate on the collective memory of the Holocaust played a reduced role in the press, the Second World War and the

120 Joschka Fischer: Rede auf dem Außerordentlichen Parteitag in Bielefeld, 13.05.1999. http://staff-www.uni-marburg.de/~naeser/kos-fisc.htm (accessed 30.08.2014).

121 For example: Armin Fuhrer: Nach zähem Kampf Mehrheit für Fischer. In: *Welt*, 14.05.1999, p. 1; AP/dpa/Reuters: Belgrad: Mehr als hundert Zivilisten getötet: Opfer von Streubomben der Nato. In: *FAZ*, 15.05.1999, pp. 1–2; Vera Gärow: Zeitreise in die eigene Vergangenheit. In: *FR*, 14.05.1999, p. 3; Heike Haarhoff: Schlagstockeinsatz zum grünen Parteitag. In: *taz*, 14.05.199, p. 2, Georg Bauer: Bühne frei für Nackte & Randale. In: *BILD*, 14.05.1999, p. 1; Paul Lersch / Hartmut Palmer / Hajo Schumacher / Hans-Jörg Vehlewald: D-Day in Bielefeld. In: *Spiegel*, 17.05.1999, pp. 28–29.

122 Karl-Ludwig Günsche: Schröder entwaffnet seine Kritiker. In: *Welt*, 13.04.1999, p. 3; Michael Jeismann: Drei Reden. In: *FAZ*, 26.03.1999, p. 41; Helmut Lölhöffel: Parlamentarier in Gewissensnöten. In: *FR*, 26.03.1999, p. 6; Beate Seel: Bombenangriffe, solange „Milošević dies wünscht". In: *taz*, 26.03.1999, p. 2; Anonymous: Angst um unsere Soldaten. In: *BILD*, 25.03.1999, p. 2; Renate Flottau / Olaf Ihlau / Siegesmund von Ilsemann / Dirk Koch / Jörg Mettke / Roland Schleicher: „Alle Serben im Krieg". In: *Spiegel*, 29.03.1999, pp. 194–213.

123 Udo Röbel: Die Last der Geschichte. In: *BILD*, 25.03.1999, p. 2; Günther Jacob: 1968+1989=1999. In: *Konkret*, May 1999, p. 49.

124 Christiane Eilders/Albrecht Lüter: "Germany at War: Competing Framing Strategies in German Public Discourse", *European Journal of Communication,* 15,3 (2000), pp. 415–428, here p. 415 and 426.

Holocaust were omnipresent in the coverage, for example in the discussion about concentration camps.

German Expellees: No one knows it like us

Another example for the omnipresence of the Second World War is this last theme found in the coverage. Throughout the NATO-intervention *JF*, *Welt* and *BILD* introduced an interesting phenomenon to their coverage, creating a link between the plight of the Kosovo-Albanian refugees and Germans who had been forcefully expelled from Eastern Europe after 1945. To understand this cross-reference, a quick historical excursion is useful. During the 18th and early 19th century, Germans were settled along the Danube River in South-Eastern Europe, including modern-day Serbia. The Habsburg Empire had conquered this territory in wars against the Ottoman Empire between 1683–1699 and 1716–1718.[125] These settlers are often referred to as '*Donauschwaben*' or 'Danube-Swabians.'[126] According to a 1931 census 500,000 Germans lived in Yugoslavia. Most of them were peasants in the Vojvodina region north of Belgrade.[127] After the Second World War, these Germans were associated with Nazi-Germany and were thus dispossessed and forced to leave their homes. Long refugee treks formed, which headed towards Austria and Germany. The Germans living in Yugoslavia who refused to leave were subjected to mass-executions and some were confined in 'internment-camps.'[128] Their fate was interpreted in very different ways. Many refugees, their ancestors and sympathisers saw them as victims of history who were associated with the Nazis and the regime's policy of east-ward expansion using settlers, even though they had lived in these territories for approximately 200 years before the Third Reich. However, after 1945, this sense of victimhood did not find much sympathy in Germany's public discourse.

Returning to the links made to these German refugees in the reporting of the humanitarian catastrophe in Kosovo, *JF* published two articles about Kosovo which emphasised the German expellees who had been forced to leave the East-European territories – including the former Yugoslavia – after the Second World War. The far-right paper argued that these '*Vertriebene*' or

125 Immo Eberl: *Die Donauschwaben: Deutsche Siedlung in Südosteuropa*. Sigmaringen: Thorbecke 1989, p. 11.

126 Swabia is a region in south-western Germany, where these settlers originated from.

127 Zoran Janjetović: *Between Hitler and Tito: Disappearance of the Ethnic Germans from the Vojvodina*. Belgrade: Self-published 2000, p. 32.

128 Ibid., pp. 217–218; Eberl: *Die Donauschwaben*, p. 20.

expellees knew only too well what the Kosovo-Albanians were experiencing, as "the Kosovo-Albanian exodus" was being implemented with similar methods to those used in 1945 when the Germans were forced from their homes.[129] This was underscored with a cartoon.

Figure 38: "The century of displacement"; printed in *JF*, 9 April 1999, p. 2.

Welt's article voiced its incomprehension that there was so much solidarity for the Kosovo-Albanian refugees when the Germans who had been expelled "from the East" did not benefit from such understanding.[130] To underscore the similarities between the suffering of the Germans in 1945 and the Kosovo-Albanians in 1999, two sets of pictures accompanied this article. In both sets, a picture of the German refugees from 1945 (such as the image below) was printed alongside the present-day refugees in Kosovo.[131]

BILD's article featured graphic details of the atrocities the Germans had been subjected to in 1945: Serbians raping women and burning them with iron rods; men "[…] being chopped up in a corn husking machine or used as fuel in steam engines."[132] Along with these gruesome details, a memorable quote from Hans Sonnleiter, the chairman of a cultural foundation for

129 Dieter Stein: Blindflug auf Belgrad. In: *JF*, 09.04.1999, p. 1; also Anonymous: Vertriebene verurteilen Völkermord im Kosovo. In: *JF*, 02.04.1999, p. 7.

130 Anonymous: Die Heimatvertriebenen. In: *Welt*, 17.04.1999, p. 6.

131 Image published in *Welt*, 17.04.1999, p. 6: "The expellees"; *Welt*, 17.04.1999, p. 7.

132 Josef Nyary: Die Greueltaten gegen die Volksdeutschen. In: *BILD*, 07.04.1999, p. 8.

Figure 39: "Second World War – Flight in the East" ("*2. Weltkrieg – Flucht im Osten*"). Ullstein Bild – Arthur Grimm; printed in *Welt*, 17 April 1999, p. 6.

these German expellees, termed their fate 'genocide.' The *BILD*-article did not question this term, and the manner in which it was juxtaposed with the descriptions of atrocities, the author seemed to agree with this argument. Even though the article did not draw comparisons specifically to the fate of Kosovo-Albanians in 1999, the article was published under the page-heading "NATO at war", creating a direct link to the on-going war. It illustrates in particular the anti-Serbian undertone of most articles and their tendency to portray 'the Serbs' as historically cold-blooded murderers.

This connection was met with criticism in a *Konkret*-article published in June 1999. Entitled "Sudeten-Germans everywhere", it decidedly rejected the link made by other newspapers between German expellees and Kosovo-Albanian refugees. Andreas Spannbauer argued that it was only a matter of time before "[…] the Germans started speaking about their own refugees […]", which the author deemed a German effort to trivialise their own crimes by establishing themselves as victims. The article continued to remind the reader that the expulsion of the Germans in 1945 followed the Nazi's "racially-motivated policy of extermination", implying that the situation in Kosovo was very different and that the Germans were to blame for their own suffering.[133]

133 Andreas Spannbauer: Sudetendeutsche überall. In: *Konkret*, June 1999, p. 30.

These articles, while quantitatively insignificant, are very important qualitatively. They demonstrate a shift in self-perception in German public discourse and perhaps even in the self-perception of Germans and of Germany. In previous chapters – until roughly 1995 – the 'discourse of dismay' which dominated the collective memory of the Holocaust would not have allowed pity for German victims of the Second World War. However, by 1999, the reminder that Germans had also suffered under Serbians, even to the extent of terming this 'genocide,' indicates a major development in the stages of collective memory in Germany. Moreover these articles demonstrate that the assertion that the Second World War was no longer important to Germany's self-understanding is too simple.[134] In fact, it had become multi-dimensional and more complex, and could now also include the understanding of Germans as victims.

Media and War

We turn now to the role of the print media during the war and most importantly the press' self-perception of its delicate role as an opinion-maker. While international correspondents were allowed to stay in Belgrade or generally on Serbian territory during NATO's bombardment, they were quickly expelled from Kosovo. All main-stream publications drew attention to this inaccessibility and stated that the additional strict censorship in Belgrade made it very difficult to obtain trustworthy information on what events were unfolding in Kosovo.[135] *FR* was perhaps most adamant to reiterate this regularly, repeatedly printing a text, which informed the reader that "the war-coverage of Kosovo is subjected to difficult circumstances. Only few independent journalists are still active in the Yugoslav territory, amongst them *FR*-correspondent Stephan Israel in Belgrade." The text further cautioned that it was hard to verify facts and that all parties involved could be propelling their

134 See chapter 8, fn. 124.

135 Dh: Serbien weist ausländische Journalisten aus. In: *Welt*, 26.03.1999, p. 3; DW: Hohe TV-Quoten für den Krieg. In: *Welt*, 27.03.1999, p. 2; Herbert Kremp: Der Trümmerhaufen wächst. In: *Welt*, 27.03.1999, p. 10; Matthias Rüb: Was geschieht in den Dörfern und Städten im Kosovo? In: *FAZ*, 29.03.1999, p. 3; Michael Hanfeld: Blind in Belgrad. In: *FAZ*, 06.04.1999, p. 55; Jörg Quoos: Milošević: Sprache der Gewalt. In: *BILD*, 27.03.1999, p. 2; Sebastian von Bassewitz: Deutschlands mutigste Reporterin. In: *BILD*, 01.04.1999, p. 5; mk/dpa/afp/ap/rtr/FR: Nato setzt ihre Angriffe auf Serben fort. In: *FR*, 26.03.1999, p. 1; Stephan Israel: Bis gestern war Krieg ein fernes Geschehen. In: *FR*, 26.03.1999, p. 3; Anonymous: Hausmitteilung. In: *Spiegel*, 05.04.1999, p. 3; Claus Christian Malzahn: Suche nach Quellen. In: *Spiegel*, 12.04.1999, p. 28; Andreas Zumach: Belgrad unterstützt die Nato. In: *taz*, 27./28.03.1999, p. 12; Rüdiger Rossig: Der unheimliche Krieg der Zahlen. In: *taz*, 12.04.1999, p. 3.

own propagandistic interests.[136] But not all the problems came from Serbia's power. A *taz*-article entitled "NATO-Show: Talking a lot, Saying Nothing" starkly condemned NATO's inadequate information policy.[137] Other articles reported that NATO was publicising what they deemed unproven information without offering exact references regarding the sources.[138] This underlines that journalists felt both were compromising the quality of information available to the press.

FR's Stephan Israel, based in Belgrade, gave the reader further details regarding the painful process of gathering local information. Those who attempted to leave the city were quickly suspected of espionage. Journalists who wanted to know what was happening outside of Belgrade could only do so by joining a tour organised by the Serbian army. These trips focused on showing the destruction caused by NATO-bombing. Moreover "only those [...were] allowed to join who submit[ted] their reports to a kind of pre-censorship."[139] Israel further stated that no one could really know what was going on in Priština or Kosovo because all international journalists had been forced to leave shortly after the NATO-bombing had begun. Consequently the only sources of information available were the Kosovo-Albanian refugees who were arriving in Albania and Macedonia and the reliability of these sources was also deeply problematic. These examples indicate that the press was very aware of its extraordinary role in the war. Moreover, it communicated effectively to the readers that some of the information published at this time was fragmentary and difficult to verify. Arguably the images of Kosovo-Albanian refugee treks and especially *BILD's* loud and provocative headlines were more memorable than these quiet self-reflections. However, these would not have gone unnoticed to an attentive and critical reader.

Only *Spiegel* was able to avoid the news-blackout due to the fact that its reporter, Renate Flottau, had refused to leave Kosovo. In her compelling 'war-journal' published in the form of *Spiegel*-articles, she gave an extraordinarily close insight into the day-to-day life in Priština, as well as reporting

136 FR: In eigener Sache. In: *FR*, 10.04.1999, p. 5; also printed in FR: Kosovo-Berichterstattung. In: *FR*, 12.04.1999, p. 4; wn: Kosovo-Berichterstattung. In: *FR*, 13.04.1999, p. 7; wn: Kosovo-Berichterstattung. In: *FR*, 14.04.1999, p. 7; wn: Kosovo-Berichterstattung. In: *FR*, 16.04.1999, p. 5; wn: Kosovo-Berichterstattung. In: *FR*, 17.04.1999, p. 5.

137 Andreas Zumach: Nato-Show: Viel reden, nichts sagen. In: *taz*, 09.04.1999, p. 3.

138 Lutz Meier: „Die Nato muss auf Glaubwürdigkeit setzen". In: *taz*, 09.04.1999, p. 3; Andreas Zumach: Nato-Show: Viel reden, nichts sagen. In: *taz*, 09.04.1999, p. 3.

139 Stephan Israel: Schwarze Zielscheibe aus Karton. In: *FR*, 30.03.1999, p. 3; Israel: Ein gar zu williges Instrument. In: *FR*, 30.03.1999, p. 6.

on the perpetual danger she was in as an international journalist.[140] Through Flottau's journal, the reader learned about routine harassments by Serbian police, the long refugee treks lining the roads in Kosovo, and that the majority of Serbians had very little knowledge of the events unfolding in Kosovo or the extent of violence Serbian forces were perpetuating there.[141] Eventually she was forced to leave Priština and reported from Belgrade, where Serbian authorities harassed her. For example, in one entry she described the difficulties the Serbian authorities were imposing on her as a journalist. On the one hand they revoked her press pass, but on the other hand they did not expel her from the country, consequently leaving her in an uncomfortable limbo-situation.[142] It remains unclear whether this harassment also affected her articles in terms of censorship. In spite of Flottau's extraordinary proximity to the events, her articles did not report on the suffering of Serbian civilians. Especially once she was based in Belgrade and witnessed the heavy bombing, this must have been apparent to her. An explanation for this omission remains speculative. Perhaps she did include such details, which her editors in Germany cut from the article. Or one could speculate that having witnessed the disproportionate suffering in Kosovo may have narrowed her perception.

In light of the difficulties in obtaining reliable local information, the distribution of authorship in this time-frame is worth considering.

Newspaper	Percentage of articles authored by correspondents	Percentage of articles authored by press agencies	Percentage of articles amalgamated from various press releases, etc.
Welt	73%	15%	8%
FAZ	80%	15%	4%
FR	52%	45%	1%
taz	69%	24%	2%

Table 11: Percentages of articles according to authorship.[143]

140 Renate Flottau: „Hau ab, rette lieber deinen Kopf". In: *Spiegel*, 12.04.1999, pp. 170–175; Flottau: Lametta vom Himmel. In: *Spiegel*, 10.05.1999, pp. 166–167; Flottau: Die Teilung des Weinbergs. In: *Spiegel*, 17.05.1999, pp. 266–267.

141 Renate Flottau: „Hau ab, rette lieber deinen Kopf". In: *Spiegel*, 12.04.1999, pp. 174–175; Flottau: Die Teilung des Weinbergs. In: *Spiegel*, 17.05.1999, pp. 266–267.

142 Renate Flottau: Lametta vom Himmel. In: *Spiegel*, 10.05.1999, pp. 166–167.

143 All numbers short of 100% are anonymous articles which cannot be categorised.

Similar to the previous timeframes, all publications continued to prefer articles published by their own correspondents. For the first time, even *FR* published more articles in this category than derived from press agencies. Perhaps the desired result was that the correspondents – many of whom had covered the previous Bosnia War as well – could give the reader more insights and contextual analysis. Moreover, considering how careful the journalists were in alerting the reader to the limitations of their information, such articles were more nuanced than amalgamated press releases, which were barely published in this period.

The Press' Language

The level of self-awareness in the German press is further underlined by the reluctance to use official NATO-terminology such as 'collateral damage' rather than 'civilian fatalities' or 'military action' instead of 'war.' As one *FR*-article reported, the German Journalist Association had requested journalists to avoid such military jargon.[144] While this caution was undoubtedly relevant, especially considering some of the exaggerated terminology employed at times, the term 'collateral damage' was barely used. Indeed, it only appeared in *FAZ*, *taz*, *JF* and *Spiegel*, and in all cases it was used sceptically.[145] *FAZ's* Matthias Rüb referred to "so called 'collateral damage'" in his article reporting that a passenger train had been hit, killing Serbian civilians.[146] The *Spiegel*-article criticised 'the Serbs' on the one hand for positioning their radar equipment right next to kindergartens or hospitals so that any mistake made by NATO could be exploited by propaganda. In the next sentence, however, the article disapproved of the alliance's trivialising these deaths with terms such as 'collateral damage.'[147] This criticism of both NATO and the Serbian forces not only gave an interesting insight into how media coverage could be exploited by both sides, but also reiterates the news-magazine's critical stance towards NATO's military jargon. Furthermore it demonstrates that generally

144 Afp: Journalisten-Verband rügt „Hetzsprache" in Medien. In. *FR*, 30.03.1999, p. 7; see also Anonymous: Kosovo-Krieg: Presserat mahnt zu besonderer Sorgfalt. Press Release from the German Press Council, 04.06.1999. http://www.bdzv.de/aktuell/bdzv-branchendienste/bdzv-intern/artikel/detail/presserat_mahnt_zu_sorgfalt_bei_informationen_und_quellen_im_kosovo_krieg/ (accessed 27.11.2014).

145 Andreas Wild: Chirurgische Eingriffe. In: *JF*, 14.05.1999, p. 11; Barbara Örtel: Schuld ist immer nur Milošević. In: *taz*, 16.04.1999, p. 3.

146 Matthias Rüb: Trotz Satelliten und Videokameras keine Klarheit über die Ereignisse im Kosovo. In: *FAZ*, 17.04.1999, p. 3.

147 Alexander Szandar: Minenhund und Bodyguard. In: *Spiegel*, 29.03.1999, p. 203.

the German press did not merely regurgitate the information it received from NATO, as some existing media studies have alleged.[148] This is further underlined by some images printed in various publications which graphically presented this 'collateral damage.'

Equally the use of the term 'war' was used liberally in the press, even though the official political language avoided this word. Chancellor Schröder's speech on 24 March 1999, explaining to the German people that NATO, including Germany, had commenced air-strikes against Yugoslavia, had clearly avoided the term 'war,' opting instead for 'military action' or 'air-strikes.' Only when denying its existence did he utilise the term, reiterating that "we are not leading war"[149] – a statement quoted by *FAZ*, *FR* and *BILD*.[150] However, none of the publications analysed here mirrored such linguistic evasiveness in their coverage, repeatedly speaking of 'war' without using quotation marks or qualifying the assessment in any way.[151] Moreover, *FAZ*, *Welt*, *FR*, *taz* and *JF*, all reflected on why the official word-choice was shying away from such terminology, each offering an explanation that coincided with their interpretation of the war. The conservative *FAZ* and *Welt* attributed the politicians' avoidance to the "two world-wars" which they argued negatively coloured the label.[152] Conversely, articles in *JF*, *taz* and *FR* alleged that NATO was

148 See pp. 15–16..

149 Gerhard Schröder: Erklärung zur Lage im Kosovo, 24.03.1999. http://www.glasnost.de/kosovo/990324schroeder.html (accessed 02.09.2014).

150 Wie: Luftschläge der Nato gegen Jugoslawien. In: *FAZ*, 25.03.1999, p. 1; Die Erklärung von Bundeskanzler Gerhard Schröder zur aktuellen Lage. In: *BILD*, 25.03.1999, p. 2; dpa: „Nicht tatenlos zuschauen". In: *FR*, 26.03.1999, p. 6.

151 To list a few such articles: Mathias Zschaler: Der Krieg im globalen Dorf. In: *Welt*, 26.03.1999, p. 3; Wolfram Weimer: Demokraten und Zyniker. In: *Welt*, 16.04.1999, p. 1; Matthias Rüb: Was geschieht in den Dörfern und Städten im Kosovo? In: *FAZ*, 29.03.1999, p. 3; Stephan Israel: Bis gestern war Krieg ein fernes Geschehen. In: *FR*, 26.03.1999, p. 3; Rolf Paasch: Dimensionen eines Krieges. In: *FR*, 06.04.1999, p. 3; Bettina Gaus: Grüner Funktionswechsel auf der Regierungsbank. In: *taz*, 26.03.1999, p. 6; Stefan Reinecke: Krieg macht dumm. In: *taz*, 07.04.1999, p. 1 ; Peter Bönisch: Partner & Freunde. In: *BILD*, 26.03.1999, p. 2; Ute Brüssel: Streit um den Krieg: Erste Grüne fordern Fischers Rücktritt. In: *BILD*, 07.04.1999, p. 2; Manfred Ertel / Rüdiger Falksohn / Renate Flottau / Olaf Ihlau / Siegesmund von Ilsemann / Dirk Koch / Helene Zuber: „Das Gespenst von Vietnam". In: *Spiegel*, 05.04.1999, pp. 150–164; Sylvia Schreiber / Alexander Szandar / Thomas Tuma: Dr. Jekyll und Mister Hyde. In: *Spiegel*, 17.05.1999, pp. 78–81; AJW: Hilfe in der Nato. In: *AJW*, 15.04.1999, p. 1; Micha Brumlik: Gerechter Krieg? Wann, wenn nicht jetzt? In: *AJW*, 29.04.1999, p. 1; Peter Lattas: Auf Krieg versessen. In: *JF*, 26.03.1999, p. 2; Andrzej Madela: Zwickmühlen der Moral. In: *JF*, 09.04.1999, p. 11.

152 Dieter Blumenwitz: Krieg zwischen Bonn und Belgrad. In: *Welt*, 07.04.1999, p. 10; Michael Jeismann: Drei Reden. In: *FAZ*, 26.03.1999, p. 41.

aiming to manipulate public opinion with linguistic embellishments, reminding the readers of their view that the war was fundamentally illegal.[153] As the *FR*-article expanded, NATO's official language was euphemistic – using 'ethnic cleansing' instead of 'genocide'; 'bombardment' rather than 'war' – to avoid an 'international outcry.'[154] While the author makes a valid point, she presented 'ethnic cleansing' as a dilution of 'genocide' and disregards that these are two different matters – though the line between the two can be blurred – and indeed have vastly different legal implications for the international community.

As the publications did not simply absorb the official terminology offered by NATO and the German politicians, a degree of scepticism can be attributed to its coverage. They deliberated such issues carefully and indeed alerted and encouraged the reader to ask why politicians were using certain terms. This self-reflection was further underscored when *Welt*, *taz* and *Spiegel* remarked how manipulative the British media and politicians were. *Welt* criticised the "effect-seeking" pictures of tattered Kosovo-Albanian refugees, even British broadsheets such as *The Independent* published.[155] *taz* criticised the tabloid *Sun*, which had published an article entitled "Beat up Slobodan" and called him "Serbian butcher."[156] It is striking that *taz* did not apply the same criticism to *BILD*, which also routinely referred to Milošević as "the butcher", or that *Welt* acknowledged that the motif of desolate Kosovo-Albanian refugees was also present in the pictures published in German broadsheets.[157]

Welt and *Spiegel* directed their criticism towards the political process behind the media-coverage in Great Britain. Since the bombardments had started, not a day had gone by without either Prime Minister Tony Blair himself or one of his cabinet-members "[…] publicly hurling a forceful accusation at the Serbian dictator" – which *Welt* called "massaging the public conscience."[158] A *Spiegel*-article took a similar approach, portraying Alistair Campbell as Blair's 'spin doctor' who increasingly dominated NATO's media strategy to

153 Christian Semler: Welches Ziel? In: *taz*, 26.03.1999, p. 1; Astrid Höhler: Völkerrechtssubjekt Mensch. In: *FR*, 07.04.1999, p. 3; Dieter Stein: „Die Deutschen werden zu Vasallen der USA ohne Lohn". In: *JF*, 02.04.1999, pp. 4–5.

154 Astrid Höhler: Völkerrechtssubjekt Mensch. In: *FR*, 07.04.1999, p. 3.

155 Thomas Kielinger: Hat Ibrahim Rugova den Feind getroffen? In: *Welt*, 03.04.1999, p. 2.

156 Ralf Sotscheck: Der Kampf um Köpfe und ein ruhiges Hinterland. In: *taz*, 31.03.1999, p. 6.

157 See for example figure 23.

158 Ki: Beim Einsatz britischer Soldaten zankt die Nation nie. In: *Welt*, 08.04.1999, p. 2.

manipulate public opinion.[159] Such criticism implied that all three publications considered German media and politicians to be much better. Neither publication extrapolated the British example to the German case, deliberating how this affected the German press and whether the same mechanisms were also in place in Berlin. While a systematic and academic comparison to the British publications goes beyond the scope of this book, the critical and cautious coverage of the German press is worth noting.

Contrary to the conclusions of a homogenous German press coverage made by other media analyses, this chapter demonstrates that the articles covering the NATO-intervention were very diverse in the nine publications considered. Unlike the previous coverage analysed in earlier chapters, the publications were clearly divided along political lines. Broadly speaking, the conservative papers (*Welt*, *FAZ* and *BILD*) supported the NATO-intervention, which the liberal/left-wing papers (*Spiegel*, *FR* and *taz*) did not. Both far-left and far-right publications also opposed the war, though for different reasons, while *AJW* endorsed the NATO-intervention, but disapproved of comparisons between Kosovo and the Holocaust. This division along political lines also ensured that various views and interpretations were available to the German readers throughout NATO's bombardment of Serbia and Kosovo. This balance arguably compensated for the at times biased reporting in some – usually conservative – publications. Moreover, the press' coverage was more diverse than the parliamentary debates at the time.

From the beginning of the intervention, arguments for and against NATO's military strikes were available to the German public. Nonetheless, as the analysis of the larger themes – 'genocide' and concentration camps, the portrayal of Milošević and the treatment of Serbian civilians – showed, the conflict was at times marked by biased reporting, which compromised the information offered to the public. This bias was marked by articles which lacked deliberation, instead featuring blunt categorisations of good and bad. Simultaneously however, in each of these cases, a more balanced coverage could be found by reading other main-stream publications which qualified the partial coverage. *AJW*, *JF* and *Konkret* will not be considered here, as they catered to a very particular and narrow readership and did not treat all the themes explored above.

159 Sylvia Schreiber / Alexander Szandar / Thomas Tuma: Dr. Jekyll und Mister Hyde. In: *Spiegel*, 17.05.1999, pp. 78–81.

Theme	Issue	One-sided coverage	Balanced coverage
'Genocide'	Unreflected and unqualified use of the term 'genocide'	*Welt, FAZ, BILD*	FR, *Spiegel*
Concentration Camps	Reporting of alleged camps without proof	*BILD*	*taz, Spiegel*
Portrayal of Milošević	Excessive populism NATO good / Milošević bad	*BILD, Spiegel* *FAZ*	None
Milošević = Hitler	Comparisons / analogies	*FAZ, BILD*	*Welt, taz*
Coverage of Serbian civilians	No consideration of Serbian civilian suffering	*Welt, FAZ, BILD*	FR, *taz*

Table 12: Themes of main-stream media coverage.

The table allows us to see at a glance that the section of 'one-sided coverage' is dominated by the conservative newspapers, particularly the tabloid *BILD* and the broadsheet *FAZ*. Only in one instance the liberal *Spiegel* joined the category, namely when in the section pertaining to the excessively populist portrayal of Milošević. The balancing role frequently taken by the left-leaning media could arguably result from their scepticism of war and their inclination to question NATO's endeavours. However, when considering how Milošević was portrayed, none of the publications balanced out the excessive populism and black/white categorisation presented by *BILD*, *Spiegel* and *FAZ*. In conclusion, when considering the coverage in the condensed format offered by the above table, one can discern that while there were incidences in which some publications revealed biased reporting, the broader press coverage available in Germany at the time was more balanced than has been suggested in the existing academic literature. The only exception here is the portrayal of Milošević, who was held responsible for the violence by all publications.

Conclusion

This media analysis of the wars in Bosnia and Kosovo has emphasised how many varied interpretations were presented by the German press as the complex conflicts were unfolding. Moreover, the recurring influence of different historical events on the reporting of Bosnia or Kosovo underlines that a conflict or war is frequently interpreted through the prism of preceding events. The ever-present Second World War and the re-examination of the Srebrenica Massacre during the Kosovo coverage are two prime examples for this interplay.

The structure of two parallel parts in this book offers interesting comparative conclusions and allows a more nuanced interpretation of larger themes linked to both case studies. For example, the sole focus on – and in some cases excessively populist depiction of – the Serbian President Slobodan Milošević in the German press coverage of the 1999 NATO-intervention cannot be fully understood without studying the press' portrayal of him during the Srebrenica Massacre, the Dayton negations and the early violence in Kosovo. Moreover, comparing the German press coverage of Bosnia and Kosovo reveals an increasing readiness of the international community to intervene militarily, as well as the press' support for this, which started in Bosnia (especially after the Srebrenica Massacre) and culminated in the 1999 NATO-intervention in Kosovo and Serbia. Lastly, Germany's transformation to contribute to such a military intervention was a separate process which was closely linked to the developed conception of collective memory of the Holocaust in Germany and how important the national press deemed the country's past in analysing its contemporary foreign policy.

In addition, a number of quantitative comparisons are very telling. It must be noted that all of them will only evaluate the five daily newspapers, namely *Welt*, *FAZ*, *BILD*, *FR* and *taz*. The remaining publications were weekly, bi-weekly or monthly editions and are therefore not measurable with the daily press for this purpose. First, we consider the quantity of articles published in the German daily press throughout the studied timeframes.

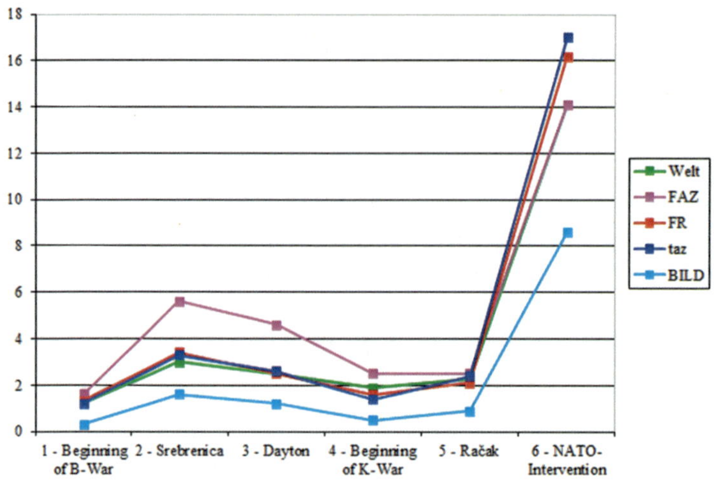

Figure 40: Ratio of articles published per day in daily newspapers.

Due to the varying number of days in the six timeframes, the ratio of articles published per day is more significant than the absolute numbers. As the above graph indicates, there were two peaks of interest. The Srebrenica Massacre (timeframe two, July–August 1995) resulted in a significant spike in reporting during the Bosnia War, while the coverage climaxed due to the NATO-intervention in timeframe six during the Kosovo War. The explosion of interest marked by the NATO-intervention in 1999 can be ascribed to the deployment of German soldiers into active combat for the first time since the Second World War, which transformed a foreign conflict into one with domestic relevance. It is remarkable that, apart from *FAZ*, the press' initial interest in the outbreak of violence in Kosovo (timeframe four), was only marginally higher than it had been at the beginning of the conflict in Bosnia (timeframe one). This underlines that the press' attention was not devoted to long-term systemic problems in the Balkans, but rather that its interest was sparked by imminent violence. Lastly, it is significant that the Račak incident

did not attract a disproportionate interest in the German press compared to the other five periods.
A second quantitative comparison pertains to the ratio of images published per article, which adds to the qualitative image analyses in the preceding chapters.

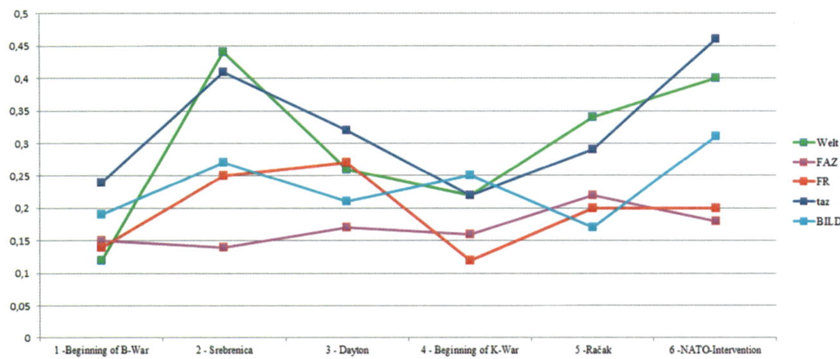

Figure 41: Ratio of images[1] to articles in daily newspapers throughout all chapters.

Significantly, the distribution of images (figure 41) was not as linear as the ratio of articles per day (figure 40). Generally one can see in the above graph that *FAZ* was comparably reluctant to publish images alongside its articles, while *taz* was more inclined to do so. Surprisingly, *BILD's* ratio was average and during the Račak coverage even lower than all other newspapers. While a common preconception of the tabloid's coverage could have been that it published more images than other publications, this was not the case in its coverage of the violence in Bosnia and Kosovo. Similar to the preceding graph, there were peaks during the Srebrenica coverage and in most cases during the reporting of the NATO-intervention, which indicates an increased interest in both in the visual coverage, along with the high numbers of articles published in this timeframe. Clearly, all publications except *FAZ* were more inclined to portray the horror resulting from the Srebrenica Massacre pictorially, than from Račak, even through Srebrenica itself was inaccessible. This is an important observation considering the alleged 'media-spectacle' surrounding the Račak incident.
One last quantitative comparison addresses authorship, which has been mentioned throughout this media analysis.

1 All data excludes maps and graphics and pertains only to caricatures and photographs.

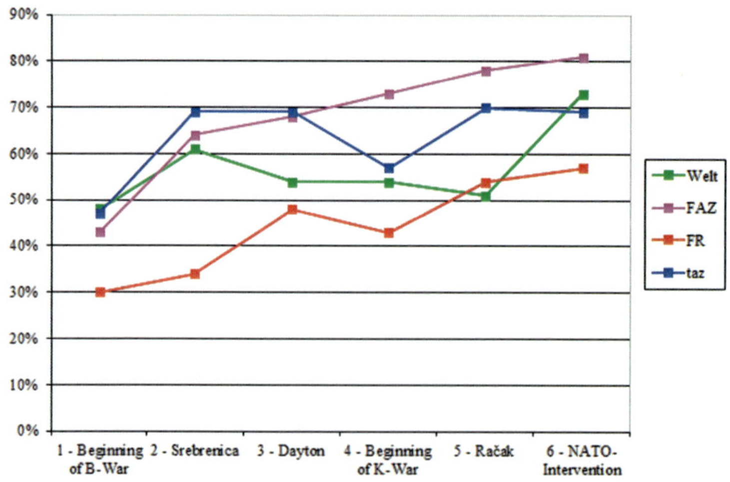

Figure 42: Percentage of articles authored by newspapers' correspondents.

As the above graph depicts, most newspapers relied more on the reporting of their own correspondents rather than amalgamated press agency reports or press releases. Only in the case of *Welt* did the proportion of articles authored by the paper's correspondents gradually decrease, though it surged again during the NATO-intervention. This demonstrates that the publications preferred articles based on their correspondents' research, representing their selection and interpretation of events. A remarkable conclusion that can be drawn from figure 42 is that all newspapers published more correspondent-articles during the Dayton negotiations – which were heavily censored – than at the beginning of the conflict in Bosnia. This peculiarity is striking, but explicable with qualitative considerations. Here the content of the articles must be discerned: not all articles published in the third timeframe were about the Dayton negotiations themselves; many also addressed the on-going violence in Bosnia or NATO's preparations for the deployment of the International Peace Force. This underscores how limiting and at times misleading a purely quantitative study can be without considering qualitative nuances.

Generally, the centrality of a journalist in forming the news presents itself in this book. In many instances, a particularly partisan piece or a significant word-choice could be attributed to a particular correspondent rather than a press agency article or press release. Moreover, many journalists covered both the Bosnia and the Kosovo wars for the same publication. Consequently, after a decade of reporting on the violence in the Balkans, it can be presumed that correspondents had experienced a deep engagement with and had profound knowledge of the region, its history and perhaps languages, as well as a wide network to the political and cultural elites. Perhaps it was this individual experience and knowledge that formed the distinctive opinions found in the editorials, which expressed at times contrary voices in the publications.

With this in mind we turn to the qualitative conclusions which can be drawn from the press analysis. Most importantly, in many cases the publications' basic political affiliations did not prescribe the interpretations published about themes related to the wars in Bosnia and Kosovo. The selection of primary sources has allowed a broad comparison of discourses ranging from far-left to far-right. While a multitude of interpretations and perspectives was indeed present, in numerous cases, the clustering of publications was not confined by political orientation. To demonstrate this, some key examples have been taken from the analysis: the right-leaning newspapers are marked blue, the left leaning ones red. The first example stems from the Srebrenica coverage in chapter 4. Here the fate of the refugees was covered with

reduced interest by: *Welt*, *FAZ* and *FR*	prolonged interest by: *taz*, *Spiegel* and *BILD*

Similarly, the quick dismissal of the Serbian version of events regarding the Račak incident was not defined by the publications' political affiliation. The Serbian perspective was

dismissed by: *FAZ*, *FR*, *taz* and *Spiegel*	considered by: *Welt* and *Konkret*

It is noteworthy that *FAZ* never published an interpretation which could have been categorised as traditionally 'left-leaning.' Rather, *taz* occasionally featured content which could be deemed generally conservative. Germany's diverse press landscape in turn emphasises that when analysing the German print media's coverage of the wars in Bosnia and Kosovo, one cannot speak of 'the conservative newspapers' or 'the left-leaning publications,' let alone of 'the media.'

Nonetheless, there were some exceptions to this non-partisan reporting. One such example is Scharping's use of the term 'genocide' to describe the violence in Kosovo, as discussed in chapter 8. His careless employment of such a loaded term was

supported by: *Welt*, *FAZ* and *BILD*	rejected by: *FR*, *taz* and *Spiegel*

This alignment was mirrored in the coverage of the NATO-intervention in 1999, which was

supported by: *Welt*, *FAZ* and *BILD*	rejected by: *taz*, *FR*, *Spiegel* and *Konkret*

At times a convergence occurred along the lines of the publications' political affiliations, especially during the coverage of the NATO-intervention. However these remained exceptions and the analysis of each publication's individual, nuanced and multi-faceted interpretations offered much more valuable insights.

Further qualitative conclusions can be drawn with regard to the four larger themes which have been traced throughout the entire book. Firstly, the changing perceptions of the German press regarding the Serbian President Slobodan Milošević and who was to blame for the conflicts; secondly, how the armed forces, including the Yugoslav Peoples' Army and the Kosovo Liberation Army were presented in the German press; thirdly, the persistent presence of the Second World War in the press' reporting, as well as the Holocaust and how they shaped the press' interpretation of the violence; and lastly, how Germany's role in the region was evaluated by the national press – both in the realms of diplomacy and military intervention.

Starting with the first theme, most German publications initially explained the outbreak of violence in Bosnia and Kosovo with references to long-standing antagonism in the region. This mirrored the general stance found in the secondary literature available at the time. Such congruence suggests that as violence erupted in this largely unknown region, most journalists informed themselves by turning to the secondary literature. However, throughout the coverage of the Bosnia War, the German press increasingly focused on the role of Milošević, seeing him as the primary cause of the violence by 1995. In spite of this progression, there was no excessively populist portrayal of Milošević or 'name-calling' in the press' coverage at this time. By 1998, when the violence in Kosovo intensified, there was an exclusive focus on Milošević's policies and the concept of ancient hatreds was no longer important. This progression reveals the evolving perception regarding the causes of violence in the German press, which gradually made the journalists' own interpretations more prevalent. The near exclusive spotlight on Milošević during the Kosovo conflict partially stemmed from his role in the preceding war in Bosnia and especially the Srebrenica Massacre. This underlines the influence of the Bosnian War on the journalists' interpretation of the violence in Kosovo. Moreover, the gradually increasing importance of Milošević in explaining the violence suggests a certain learning curve on behalf of the journalists. With violence erupting in former Yugoslavia somewhat unexpectedly in the early 1990s, the observers inevitably had to construct research-based interpretations in a volatile and unknown political situation. However, as the correspondents spent more time on-site and perhaps understood the complex conflict, the more they could communicate their own insights and interpretations.

This growing focus on Milošević in most publications analysed here introduces a second theme that re-appeared throughout this book: the portrayal of the parties involved in both conflicts. Throughout the Bosnian War, the German publications presented the JNA and later the Bosnian-Serb army as the only combatants. Sarajevo's armed forces were not mentioned at all, which was epitomised by the negligent reporting of a UN-soldier's death in Srebrenica in the third chapter. This one-sided focus on the Serbian forces was mirrored in the coverage of the initial violence in Kosovo, which embellished KLA's belligerence. Indeed, as analysed in chapter six, some publications displayed a tendency to 'spare' the KLA by explaining their actions with the Kosovo-Albanian civilian suffering. However, a few months later, in early 1999, the KLA was portrayed perhaps more realistically as an organised, heavily-armed force, especially in pictures.

The third theme traced throughout this book, namely the presence of the Second World War in the German press coverage revealed an interesting interplay between the war itself and the collective memory of the Holocaust as well as its influence on the foreign political debate. On the one hand, the Second World War continuously influenced the German press' word-choice in reporting on the wars in Bosnia and Kosovo. In the Bosnia coverage, terms such as '*Lebensraum*', the Serbian '*Herrenvolk*' and 'pogroms' were used, while in the reporting on Kosovo, 'concentration camps' and 'genocide' were used regularly, even when the terms were inaccurate or blatantly wrong in some cases. On the other hand, the collective memory of the Holocaust and its influence on the discourse led in the German press decreased. During the Bosnian War, the debates published in various German publications were strongly shaped by the Holocaust. Consequently, many considerations about Germany's foreign political involvement were contextualised with deliberations about the country's National-Socialist past and whether this permitted a diplomatic or military involvement. This interpretation matched the secondary literature on Germany's collective memory explored in the introduction, which saw the *Betroffenheitsdiskurs* of the 1980s and early 1990s as the climax of collective memory and shame. This confined Germany to being the 'country of perpetrators' and hindered any active foreign policy by Germany, let alone a military engagement. Academics found that by the early-1990s, the *Betroffenheitsdiskurs* was gradually replaced by the concept of the 'universality of guilt' which meant recognition by the international community for its partial responsibility with regard to the Holocaust. This transformation could also be traced in the German press coverage, though at a different pace than suggested by the literature. Judging from the German press coverage on Bosnia, the Second World War continued to play a central role in the press' coverage until 1995. Only from the Kosovo coverage in 1998 onwards did the German publications analysed here nearly completely omit any interpretation of Germany's foreign policy and potential military involvement with regard to the country's past.

This decreasing focus on the foreign political restraints resulting from the Second World War went so far that some conservative papers likened the Germans who were expelled from various territories in Eastern Europe after 1945 – including Serbia – to the Kosovo-Albanian refugees of 1999. These German expellees, some of whom continue to fight collectively for the reappropriation of their lost property after the Second World War, were often dismissed as basking in Germany's National-Socialist past. Consequently this likening to the Kosovo-Albanian refugees in the late 1990s indicates a desire in the *Welt*, *BILD* and *JF* to recognise the German refugees' victimhood and thus suggests a movement away from the pure absorption of guilt and shame.

This gradual 'normalisation' of the country's self-perception can be traced throughout all chapters with regard to the German press' evaluation of Germany's role in Bosnia and Kosovo. Surprisingly, the national press attributed progressively less importance to Germany throughout its Bosnia-coverage. After the pioneering position Germany took in Balkan politics in the early 1990s by recognising Croatia's and Slovenia's independence before its European partners, the country took a back-seat. This was particularly emphasised in the reporting from November–December 1995, during which the German publications barely acknowledged the presence of a German delegation in their reporting on the Dayton negotiations. It was further manifested in the coverage of the violence in Kosovo, where the term '*Bündnissolidarität*', or 'alliance-solidarity' was drawn on persistently. This progression to blend in with the Western alliance-structures and 'normalise' its foreign policy within these supranational institutions can also be linked with the politics of Holocaust memory, which has permeated the print media analysis throughout.

In addition to these large themes, other conclusions are worth noting. The German press coverage of the two watershed-examples of atrocities – the Srebrenica Massacre and Račak incident – is very interesting. The inaccessibility of the Srebrenica enclave strongly influenced the press coverage of the massacre at the time. Analysing the press' articles produced in 1995 revealed that the number of fatalities and the dimension of what would later be termed 'genocide' were not available until much later. With this in mind, the reaction regarding Račak becomes more comprehensible. While some observers deemed the immediate presence of journalists in Račak part of the 'media spectacle' which was allegedly being staged by KLA and the OSCE, perhaps this seemingly hasty reaction was simply an instance where the international community had learned from the past. As discussed in chapter seven, the Srebrenica Massacre continued to play a significant role in the press' interpretation of events, especially as the extent of the fatalities was uncovered. Consequently, one could conclude that with Srebrenica in mind, journalists and international observers attempted to visit Račak as quickly as possible before it could be closed off and remain inaccessible for years to come.

A further development that can be traced throughout the Bosnian War is the consistently decreasing importance of Russia in the German press-coverage. While the reporting in the early 1990s still featured a lot of anti-Russian language, reminiscent of the Cold War, this had vanished almost completely by the mid-1990s. While Russia's pro-Serbian position in the UN-Security Council during the Kosovo Conflict was covered in the German print media, the antagonism which still dominated the German press' interpretation of the early violence in Bosnia did not return. Considering the progression of international relations at this time, this is understandable. As the Bosnian War unfolded in 1991/92, the Cold War had just ended and the Soviet Union had recently collapsed. Consequently post-Soviet Russia was still perceived as an unreckonable force which was distrusted by almost all German publications analysed here. However, by December 1995 Russia had become a relatively trusted partner which included itself in international endeavours, such as the post-Dayton peace implementation force headed by NATO. This gained Moscow enough trust amongst international observers and may account for omission of anti-Russian word-choices in the German publications and indicates a more nuanced review of relations with Russia.

AJW's coverage of the wars in Bosnia and Kosovo – albeit non-existent in most timeframes – allows another interesting conclusion. Some secondary literature postulates that the "Jewish Lobby" in America was very influential in the country's policy towards Bosnia, which was an interesting point of departure to analyse *AJW*.[2] However, the newspaper's publisher, the Central

2 Mira Beham: *Kriegstrommeln: Medien, Krieg und Politik.* Munich: dtv 1996, p. 8; Jörg Becker / Mira Beham: *Operation Balkan: Werbung für Krieg und Tod.* Baden-Baden: Nomos 2006.

Council for Jews in Germany, did not use *AJW* to disseminate its viewpoints regarding the wars in Bosnia and Kosovo or Germany's foreign policy in this respect. While *AJW* categorises itself as a weekly cultural publication, it did address political debates, ranging from the legitimacy of Palestinian territories to the assassination of Yitzhak Rabin in November 1995. However, the violence in Bosnia and Kosovo, the controversial comparisons made between the Holocaust and Kosovo, or the genocidal dimension of the Srebrenica Massacre never found their way into *AJW's* coverage. This in turn indicates that disseminating its core values and conveying important messages to the public, for which the Central Council for Jews in Germany would likely have used its organ *AJW*, was not of central importance until the NATO-intervention of 1999.

The reporting of the two publications, *JF* and *Konkret* must also be considered separately. Surprisingly, both frequently offered comparable interpretations throughout their coverage of Bosnia and Kosovo. Brought together by their anti-American and anti-multilateral stance, articles in *JF* and *Konkret* often called for abstinence from military involvement in the Balkans. However, in spite of some parallels in their coverage, both were strongly entrenched in their far-right or far-left positions. *Konkret* in particular was simply contrary to almost all viewpoints expressed in the mainstream press rather than substantively contributing to their readers' understanding of the subject matters.

Lastly, the visual analysis of both pictures and cartoons has proven to be a valuable facet of the German press' reporting. The memorable pictures of long refugee treks, heavily armed soldiers and destroyed homes produced an immediacy that was difficult to produce in the day-to-day articles. Moreover, pictures and cartoons expressed viewpoints or issues that were left unsaid in the articles. This was particularly relevant in the reporting of Srebrenica, during which most publications' articles shied away from blaming the international community for not intervening, perhaps due to the limited information available at the time. However, the cartoons published in almost all newspapers expressed a scathing criticism of the international community's inaction. Additionally, the image analysis in various chapters revealed that some pictures were reprinted after several days or weeks. This underlined that the pictures viewed by the reader did not necessarily stem from a recent event, but may simply have been in the publications' image catalogue. Lastly, the close examination of the pictures printed in *Spiegel* as the violence unfolded in Kosovo (analysed in chapter 6) underlined that a seemingly spontaneous snapshot may have been more choreographed than suspected. These considerations underline the power of images in war-journalism and emphasise the importance of incorporating them in a press analysis.

This book has offered a comprehensive analysis of the German press coverage of the wars in Bosnia and Kosovo, taking into account many themes, currents and interpretations which have thus far been under-researched. The plurality of perceptions and viewpoints offered by the various publications at different stages of the wars has underlined that no unanimous opinion dominated the German press' understanding. Indeed, the German war-journalism of Bosnia and Kosovo was diverse and at times even contrary to the argumentation of leading politicians. Thus, a careful analysis of the German print media contributes to a more nuanced understanding of the complexities surrounding the wars in Bosnia and Kosovo.

Since the end of violence in the Balkans, there has been continuous change and development in the region. Milošević was ousted from power in 2001 after domestic upheaval and was indicted for war crimes by the ICTY in The Hague, where he died of a heart failure in 2006. Slovenia became a member of the EU and NATO in 2004 and introduced the Euro currency in 2007. Croatia became an EU-member in 2013. Serbia has been an EU- candidate country since 2012 while Bosnia has been a potential EU-candidate country since 2003. However tensions between Croats, Serbs and Muslims living in Bosnia prevail. Kosovo declared independence in 2008, though Serbia amongst other countries refuses to recognise this status.

Figure 43: Ministry of the Interior, Belgrade. Personal photograph, taken August 2012.

However, amidst all these developments towards a more stable and peaceful region, the ghosts of the past remain. Belgrade's city centre remains marked by NATO's 1999 bombardment.
For example, the Yugoslav Ministry of the Interior (figure 43) has been left as a sign of what many Serbians still consider an unjust NATO attack. Simultaneously, graffiti highlighting the 1389 Battle of Kosovo is a common sight.

Figure 44: "We are not giving up Kosovo 1389". Personal photograph, taken August 2012.

These examples underline how omnipresent the recent past remains in the region and the long path that lies ahead.

Appendix

Brief Chronology of Conflict and War in the Balkans

(primarily Bosnia and Kosovo)

8 May 1989	Slobodan Milošević becomes Serbian President and introduces constitutional reforms.
22 April and 2 May 1990	Elections in Croatia; Franjo Tudjman becomes President of Croatia.
20 December 1990	Alija Izetbegović becomes President of Bosnia.
25 June 1991	Declaration of Independence by Croatia and Slovenia.
27 June – 7 July 1991	Ten-Day War between Slovenian territorial defence forces and Yugoslav Peoples' Army.
19 December 1991	Bosnian-Serbs proclaim a Serbian Republic (*Republika Srpska*).
23 December 1991	Germany's recognition of Croatia's and Slovenia's independence.
15 January 1992	Remaining EC-members recognised Croatia's and Slovenia's independence.
January 1992	Deployment of UN-soldiers (UNPROFOR) to Croatia.
29 February – 1 March 1992	Bosnian referendum on independence.
3 March 1992	Bosnia's Declaration of Independence.
5 April 1992	Bosnian-Serb military begins siege of Sarajevo.
6 April 1992	Open fighting in Bosnia between Bosnian Muslim, Serbian and Croatian forces, as well as the Yugoslav Peoples' Army.
25 May 1992	Unilaterally proclaimed elections by Kosovo-Albanians; Ibrahim Rugova elected President of Kosovo.
June 1992	UN-troops (UNPROFOR) deployed to Bosnia, initially to protect Sarajevo's airport.
May–August 1992	Bosnian-Serb concentration camps were set up in the East-Bosnian towns Omarska, Keraterm, Trnoplje and other locations.
Summer 1992	Discovery and coverage of concentration camps in international media.

January 1993	UN-Special Envoy Cyrus Vance and EC-representative Lord Owen began negotiating a peace treaty with the warring parties, known as the Vance-Owen Plan.
April 1993	Following a UN-Resolution, NATO implemented a no-fly-zone (Operation Deny Flight) over Bosnia.
6 May 1993	UN declared 'safe areas' in Sarajevo, Srebrenica, Goražde, Tuzla, Žepa and Bihać.
4 June 1993	UNPROFOR-troops are authorised to protect these 'safe areas'.
18 June 1993	Vance-Owen Plan pronounced officially failed after a Bosnian-Serb referendum refused its terms.
July 1993	UN-Special Envoy Thorvald Stoltenberg and EU-representative Lord Owen began negotiations for Owen-Stoltenberg Plan.
29 August 1993	Rejection of Owen-Stoltenberg Plan by Bosnian Muslims.
9 November 1993	Destruction of Mostar's landmark bridge by Croatian forces following several years of war.
5 February 1994	Bombing of Sarajevo's Merkale Market.
9 February 1994	NATO authorised air-strikes requested by UN of Bosnian-Serb army in Sarajevo.
February 1994	Negotiation of Contact Group Plan began, attempting to construct a peace treaty.
28 August 1994	Referendum in Bosnian-Serb Assembly rejected the plan.
December 1994	UN-troops used by Bosnian-Serb army as 'human shields' against NATO-attacks.
June 1995	EU and NATO establish "Rapid Reaction Force" for Bosnia.
2 June 1995	An American aircraft is shot down by Bosnian-Serb artillery.
6 July 1995	Bosnian-Serb attack of UN-'safe area' Srebrenica.
30 August – 20 September 1995	Operation Deliberate Force: NATO-bombardment of Bosnian-Serb forces.
1–21 November 1995	Negotiations of Dayton Agreement in Ohio.
14 December 1995	Dayton Agreement formally signed in Paris.
February 1996	First declared action by Kosovo Liberation Army (KLA).
March 1998	Intensified violence in Kosovo, especially in the Drenica region.

13 October 1998	Holbrooke-Milošević-Agreement negotiated: cease-fire and deployment of OSCE-observers.
15 January 1999	Račak Incident, killing 45 people.
6–23 February 1999	Negotiations to find a peace agreement in Rambouillet.
18 March 1999	Publication of EU-autopsy report on Račak fatalities. Kosovo-Albanian delegation signed Rambouillet Agreement; Serbia refused.
22 March 1999	OSCE-observers withdrawn from Kosovo.
24 March 1999	NATO-bombardment of Serbian targets in Kosovo and Serbia began.
3 June 1999	Milošević signed agreement to allow peacekeeping-troops to be stationed in Kosovo.
20 June 1999	Termination of NATO-bombardment.

List of Tables

List of Figures

List of Abbreviations

Newspapers

AJW	Allgemeine Jüdische Wochenzeitung
FAZ	Frankfurter Allgemeine Zeitung
FR	Frankfurter Rundschau
JF	Junge Freiheit
taz	die tageszeitung

Other

CDU	Christian Democratic Union of Germany (*Christlich Demokratische Union Deutschlands*)
CSU	Christian Social Union of Bavaria (*Christilich-Soziale Union in Bayern*)
dpa	Deutsche Presse Agentur
DUTCHBAT	Dutch Battalion
EC	European Community
EU	European Union
EU-FET	European Union Forensic Expert Team
FDP	Free Democratic Party (*Freie Demokratische Partei*)
ICRC	International Committee of the Red Cross
ICTY	International Criminal Tribunal for Former Yugoslavia
IFOR	Implementation Force
IVW	Informationsgemeinschaft zur Feststellung der Verbreitung von Werbeträgern
JNA	Yugoslav Peoples' Army (*Jugoslovenska Narodna Armija*)
KLA	Kosovo Liberation Army
KZ	Concentration Camp (*Konzentrationslager*)
LDK	Democratic League of Kosovo (*Lidhja Demokratike e Kosovës*)
MSF	Doctors Without Borders (*Médecins Sans Frontières*)
NATO	North Atlantic Treaty Organisation
NDH	Independent State of Croatia (*Nezavisna Država Hrvatska*)
NGO	Non-Governmental Organisation
OSCE	Organisation for Security and Co-operation in Europe
PDS	Party of Democratic Socialism (*Partei des Demokratischen Sozialismus*)
PR	Public Relations
RS	Republika Srpska
SDA	Party of Democratic Action (*Stranka Demokratske Akcije*)
SPD	Social Democratic Party of Germany (*Sozialdemokratische Partei Deutschlands*)
UÇK	Kosovo Liberation Army (*Ushtria Çlirimtare e Kosovës*)
UK	United Kingdom
UN	United Nations
UNHCR	United Nations High Commissioner for Refugees
USA	United States of America
UNSC	United Nations Security Council
WEU	Western European Union

Bibliography

Print Publications

Allgemeine Jüdische Wochenzeitung, Zeitungsabteilung der Staatsbibliothek zu Berlin, Signatur 2°Ztg 10240.

BILD, Zeitungsabteilung der Staatsbibliothek zu Berlin, Signatur 2°Ztg 10139.

Der Spiegel, Online-Archive: http://www.spiegel.de/spiegel/print (last accessed 18.09.2012).

die tageszeitung, Zeitungsabteilung der Staatsbibliothek zu Berlin, Signatur Ztg 10123.

Die Welt, Zeitungsabteilung der Staatsbibliothek zu Berlin, Signatur Ztg 10103.

Frankfurter Allgemeine Zeitung, Zeitungsabteilung der Staatsbibliothek zu Berlin, Signatur Zsn 2668 MR.

Frankfurter Rundschau, Zeitungsabteilung der Staatsbibliothek zu Berlin, Signatur 2°Ztg 10096 MR.

Junge Freiheit, Zeitungsabteilung der Staatsbibliothek zu Berlin, Signatur 2°Ztg 10078.

Konkret, Die Jahrgänge 1974–2009: Lesen, Recherchieren, Drucken [CD-Rom].

Literature

Alexander, Jeffrey: *Cultural Trauma and Collective Identity*. Berkeley: University of California Press 2004.

Amnesty International: *Kosovo: The Evidence*. London: Amnesty International 1998.

Anonymous: Report of the EU Forensic Expert Team on the Račak Incident, 17.03.1999. http://www.ess.uwe.ac.uk/Kosovo/Kosovo-Massacres2.htm (accessed 07.06.2012).

Anonymous: Bosnia: Clinton's Call. In: *Newsweek*, 02.05.1993. http://www.thedailybeast.com/newsweek/1993/05/02/bosnia-clinton-s-call.html (accessed 28.08.2014).

Anonymous: Kosovo-Krieg: Presserat mahnt zu besonderer Sorgfalt. Press Release from the German Press Council, 04.06.1999. http://www.bdzv.de/aktuell/bdzv-branchendienste/bdzv-intern/artikel/detail/presserat_mahnt_zu_sorgfalt_bei_informationen_und_quellen_im_kosovo_krieg/(accessed 27.11.2014).

Anonymous; Obituary. Alija Izetbegovic. In: *BBC*, 19.10.2003. http://news.bbc.co.uk/2/hi/europe/3133038.stm (accessed 27.08.2014).

Asmus, Ronald: *German Strategy and Opinion after the Wall. 1990–1992*. Santa Monica: RAND 1994.

Auswärtiges Amt (ed.): *Deutsche Außenpolitik 1995: Auf dem Weg zu einer Friedensregelung für Bosnien und Herzegowina: 53 Telegramme aus Dayton*. Bonn: Auswärtiges Amt, Referat Öffentlichkeitsarbeit 1998.

Bach, Jonathan: *Between Sovereignty and Integration. German Foreign Policy and National Identity after 1989*. Hamburg: LIT 1999.

Banac, Ivo: *The National Questions in Yugoslavia. Origins, History, Politics*. Ithaca: Cornell University Press 1984.

— : Bosnian Muslims: From Religious Community to Socialist Nationhood and Post-Communist Statehood, 1918–1992. In: Mark Pinson (ed.): *The Muslims of Bosnia-Herzegovina: Their Historic Development from the Middle Ages to the Dissolution of Yugoslavia* .Cambridge, Mass.: Harvard CMES 1996, pp. 129–154.

—: Sorting out the Balkans: Three New Looks at a Troubled Region. In: *Foreign Affairs* 79,3 (2000), pp. 152–157.

Banchoff, Thomas: *The German Problem Transformed. Institutions, Politics, and Foreign Policy, 1945–1995.* Ann Arbor: The University of Michigan Press 1999.

Baring, Arnulf: *Germany's New Position in Europe. Problems and Perspectives.* Oxford: Berg 1994.

Bassiouni, M. Cherif: The Policy of Ethnic Cleansing: Final Report of the United Nations Commission of Experts Established Pursuant to Security Resolution 780 (1992), 28.12.1994. http://ess.uwe.ac.uk/comexpert/ANX/IV.htm (accessed 27.10.2012).

Bauer, Yehuda: *Rethinking the Holocaust.* New Haven: Yale University Press 2001.

Becher, Klaus: Nationalitätenkonflikte auf dem Balkan. In: Karl Kaiser / Hanns Maull (eds): *Deutschlands neue Außenpolitik*, vol. 2: Herausforderungen. Oldenburg: Forschungsinstitut der Deutschen Gesellschaft für Auswärtige Politik, pp. 137–155.

Becker, Jörg / Mira Beham: *Operation Balkan. Werbung für Krieg und Tod.* Baden-Baden: Nomos 2006.

Beham, Mira: *Kriegstrommeln: Medien, Krieg und Politik.* Munich: dtv 1996.

Beker, Avi: Building up a Memory: Austria, Switzerland, and Europe Face the Holocaust. In: Eric Langenbacher / Yossi Shain (eds): *Power and the Past: Collective Memory and International Relations.* Washington, D. C.: Georgetown University Press 2010, pp. 97–120.

Bell-Fialkoff, Andrew: A Brief History of Ethnic Cleansing. In: *Foreign Affairs* 72,3 (1993), pp. 110–122.

Bellou, Fotini: Srebrenica – The War Crimes Legacy: International Arguments, Intervention and Memory. In: *Southeast European and Black Sea Studies* 7,3 (2007), pp. 387–398.

Bennett, Christopher: *Yugoslavia's Bloody Collapse. Causes, Courses and Consequences.* London: Hurst 1995.

Bennett, Matthew: The Kosovo Liberation Army. In: Matthew Bennett / Paul Latawski (eds): *Exile Armies.* Houndmills: Routledge 2005, pp. 159–168.

Bergem, Wolfgang (ed.): *Die NS-Diktatur im deutschen Erinnerungsdiskurs.* Opladen: VS Verlag für Sozialwissenschaften 2003.

—: Barbarei als Sinnstiftung? Das NS-Regime in Vergangenheitspolitik und Erinnerungskultur der Bundesrepublik. In: Id. (ed.): *Die NS-Diktatur im deutschen Erinnerungsdiskurs.* Opladen: VS Verlag für Sozialwissenschaften 2003, pp. 81–104.

Bieber, Florian: After Dayton, Dayton? The Evolution of an Unpopular Peace. In: *Ethnopolitics* 5,1 (2006), pp. 15–31.

Bildt, Carl: *Peace Journey. The Struggle for Peace in Bosnia.* London: Orion 1998.

Biondich, Mark: *The Balkans. Revolution, War & Political Violence since 1878.* Oxford: Oxford University Press 2011.

Bird, Chris: Kosovo Slides Back into War. In: *The Guardian*, 17.01.2001. http://www.guardian.co.uk/world/2001/jan/17/warcrimes.balkans (accessed 28.11.2014).

Bode, Sabine: *Die deutsche Krankheit – German Angst.* Stuttgart: Klett-Cotta 2006.

Böhm, Andrea: Srebrenica-Moment. In: *Die Zeit*, 26.03.2012. http://www.zeit.de/2012/13/Eliasson (accessed 28.11.2014).

Bose, Sumantra: *Bosnia after Dayton: Nationalist Partition and International Intervention.* London: Oxford University Press 2002.

Brunborg, Helge / Torkild Hovede Lynstad / Henrik Urdal: Accounting for Genocide: How Many Were Killed in Srebrenica? In: *European Journal of Population* 19,3 (2003), pp. 229–248.

Brunstetter, Daniel / Scott Brunstetter: Shades of Green. In: *International Relations* 25,65 (2011), pp. 65–84.

Bundeswehr: Friedensschaffende Einsätze. http://www.einsatz.bundeswehr.de/portal/a/einsatzbw/!ut/p/c4/04_SB8K8xLLM9MSSzPy8xBz9CP3I5EyrpHK9pPKU1PjU-zLzixJIqIDcxKT21ODkjJ7-4ODUPKpFaUpWql1aUmZqC4OsXZDsqAgBQaGH7/ (accessed 05.08.2012).

Byford, Jovan: When I Say 'the Holocaust', I Mean 'Jasenovac': Remembrance of the Holocaust in Contemporary Serbia. In: *East European Jewish Affairs* 37,1 (2007), pp. 51–74.

Calic, Marie-Janine: German Perspectives. In: Alex Danchev / Thomas Halverson (eds): *International Perspectives on the Yugoslav Conflict*. Houndmills: Palgrave Macmillan 1996, pp. 52–75.

—: *Geschichte Jugoslawiens im 20. Jahrhundert*. Munich: C. H. Beck 2010.

Čekić, Smail / Muharem Kreso/ Bećir Macić: *Genocide in Srebrenica, United Nations 'Safe Area', in July 1995*. Sarajevo: Institute for the Research of Crimes against Humanity and International Law 2001.

Cigar, Norman: *Genocide in Bosnia. The Policy of 'Ethnic Cleansing'*. College Station: Texas A&M University Press 1995.

Chirot, Daniel / Clark McCauley: *Why Not Kill Them All. The Logic and Prevention of Mass Political Murder*. Princeton: Princeton University Press 2006.

Cohen, Lenard: The Balkans Ten Years After: From Dayton to the Edge of Democracy. In: *Current History* 104,685 (2005), pp. 365–373.

Cohen, Roger: C.I.A. Report on Bosnia Blames Serbs for 90% of the War Crimes. In: *New York Times*, 09.031995. http://www.nytimes.com/1995/03/09/world/cia-report-on-bosnia-blames-serbs-for-90-of-the-war-crimes.html (accessed 28.11.2014).

Collon, Michel: *Media Lies and the Conquest of Kosovo. NATO's Prototype for the Next Wars of Globalization*. New York: Unwritten History 2007.

Commission on Security and Cooperation in Europe: The Referendum on Independence in Bosnia-Herzegovina February 29 – March 1, 1992. www.csce.gov/index.cfm?FuseAction=Files.Download…id=331 (accessed 30.08.2014).

Conversi, Daniele: German-Bashing and the Breakup of Yugoslavia. In: Sabrina Ramet (ed.): *The Donald W. Treadgold Papers*. Seattle: University of Washington 1998.

Cottin, Heather / Alvin Dorman: War Propaganda Aimed at Jewish Opinion. In: Ramsey Clark (ed.): *NATO in the Balkans: Voices of Opposition*. New York: International Action Center 1998, pp. 210–219.

Cousens, Elizabeth / Charles Cater: *Toward Peace in Bosnia: Implementing the Dayton Accords*. Boulder: Lynne Rienner 2001.

Crawford, Beverly: *Power and German Foreign Policy: Embedded Hegemony in Europe*. Houndmills: Palgrave Macmillan 2007.

Daalder, Ivo: *Getting to Dayton: The Making of American's Bosnia Policy*. Washington, D. C.: Brookings Institution Press 2000.

Daalder, Ivo / Michael E. O'Hanlon: *Winning Ugly. NATO's War to Save Kosovo*. Washington, D. C.: Brookings Institution Press 2000.

Dalgaard-Nielsen, Anja: *Germany, Pacifism and Peace Enforcement*. Manchester: Manchester University Press 2006.

Dannatt, Richard: *Leading from the Front. The Autobiography*. London: Corgin 2010.

Dauphinee, Elizabeth Allen: Rambouillet: A Critical (Re)Assessment. In: Florian Bieber / Židas Daskalovski (eds): *Understanding the War in Kosovo*. London: Routledge 2003, pp. 101–121.

De Graaff, Bob: The Difference between Legal Proof and Historical Evidence. The Trial of Slobodan Milošević and the Case of Srebrenica. In: *European Review* 14,4 (2006), pp. 499–512.

Dedijer, Vladimir / Ivan Bozic / Sima Cirkovic / Milorad Ekmecic: *History of Yugoslavia.* New York: McGraw Hill 1974.

Dedijer, Vladimir: *Jasenovac. das jugoslawische Auschwitz und der Vatikan.* Freiburg: Ahriman 2011.

Deichmann, Thomas: From 'Never Again War' to 'Never Again Auschwitz': Dilemmas of German Media Policy in the War against Yugoslavia. In: Philip Hammond / Edward Herman (eds): *Degraded Capability: The Media and the Kosovo Crisis.* New York: Pluto 2000, pp. 153–163.

Dervišbegovic, Nedim: Revised Death Toll for Bosnian War. In: *Bosnian Institute*, 23.12.2004. http://www.bosnia.org.uk/news/news_body.cfm?newsid=1985 (accessed 28.11.2014).

Deutscher Bundestag, Plenarprotokoll 13/49, Stenographischer Bericht, 49. Sitzung, 13.07.1995, pp. 4045–4094.

Deutscher Bundestag, Plenarprotokoll 13/76, Stenographischer Bericht, 76. Sitzung, 06.12.1995, pp. 6631–6673.

Deutscher Bundestag, Plenarprotokoll 14/22, Stenographischer Bericht, 22. Sitzung, 25.02.1999, pp. 1607–1631.

Deutscher Bundestag, Plenarprotokoll 14/30, Stenographischer Bericht, 30. Sitzung, 25.03.1999, pp. 2421–2429.

Deutscher Bundestag, Plenarprotokoll 14/31, Stenographischer Bericht, 31. Sitzung, 26.03.1999, pp. 2571–2631.

Deutscher Bundestag, Plenarprotokoll 14/32, Stenographischer Bericht, 32. Sitzung, 15.04.1999, pp. 2620–2658.

DiCaprio, Lisa: The Betrayal of Srebrenica: The Ten-year Commemoration. In: *The Public Historian* 31,3 (2009), pp. 73–95.

Dimap Infratest: Approval of Air-strikes? June 1999. http://www.infratest-dimap.de/uploads/media/dt9906.pdf (accessed 28.11.2014), p. 12.

Eberl, Immo: *Die Donauschwaben. Deutsche Siedlung in Südosteuropa.* Sigmaringen: Jan Thorbecke 1989.

Eilders, Christiane / Albrecht Lüter: Germany at War: Competing Framing Strategies in German Public Discourse. In: *European Journal of Communication* 15,3 (2000), pp. 415–428.

Eilders, Christiane: Media as Political Actors? Issue Focusing and Selective Emphasis in the German Quality Press. In: *German Politics* 9,3 (2000), pp. 181–206.

Elsässer, Jürgen: *Nie wieder Krieg ohne uns. Das Kosovo und die neue deutsche Geopolitik.* Hamburg: Konkret 1999.

Erb, Scott: *German Foreign Policy. Navigating a New Era.* Boulder: Lynne Rienner 2003.

Eyal, Jonathan: *Europe and Yugoslavia. Lessons from a Failure.* London: Royal United Services Institute for Defence Studies 1993.

Fac: Ein Herz für kleine Nationen. In: *Welt,* 18.04.2004. http://www.welt.de/print-welt/article314465/Ein-Herz-fuer-die-kleinen-Nationen-Zum-Tode-von-Carl-Gustaf-Stroehm.html (accessed 28.11.2014).

Feuchtwanger, E. J.: *Bismarck.* London: Psychology Press 2002.

Fine, John: The Various Faiths in the History of Bosnia: Middle Ages to the Present. In: Maya Shatzmiller (ed.): *Islam and Bosnia. Conflict Resolution and Foreign Policy in Multi-Ethnic States.* Montreal: McGill-Queen's University Press 2002, pp. 3–23.

Fischer, Joschka: Die Katastrophe in Bosnien und die Konsequenzen für unsere Partei Bündnis 90/Die Grünen, 30.07.1995. http://www.gruene.de/fileadmin/user_upload/Dokumente/Gr%C3%BCne_Geschichte/JoschkaFischer_Die_Katastrophe_in_Bosnien_und_die_Konsequenzen_fuer_unsere_Partei_1995.pdf (accessed 30.08.2014).

—: Rede auf dem Außerordentlichen Parteitag in Bielefeld, 13.05.1999. http://staff-www.uni-marburg.de/~naeser/kos-fisc.htm (accessed 30.08.2014).

Forbes, Nevill / Arnold J. Toynbee / D. Mitrany / D. G. Hogarth: *The Balkans. A History of Bulgaria, Serbia, Greece, Rumania, Turkey.* Oxford: Clarendon 1915.

Freedman, Lawrence: Why the West Failed. In: *Foreign Policy* 97 (Winter 1994/1995), pp. 53–69.

Friedman, Francine: *Bosnia and Herzegovina. A Polity on the Brink.* London: Routledge 2004.

Friedrich, Roland: *Die deutsche Außenpolitik im Kosovo-Konflikt.* Wiesbaden: VS Verlag für Sozialwissenschaften 2005.

Giesen, Bernhard: The Trauma of Perpetrators: The Holocaust as the Traumatic Reference of German National Identity. In: Jeffrey Alexander (ed.): *Cultural Trauma and Collective Identity.* Berkeley: University of California Press 2004, pp. 112–154.

Glaurdić, Josip: *The Hour of Europe. Western Powers and the Breakup of Yugoslavia.* New Haven: Yale University Press 2011.

Glees, Anthony: *Reinventing Germany. German Political Development since 1945.* Oxford: Bloomsbury Academic 1996.

Glenny, Misha: *The Fall of Yugoslavia. The Third Balkan War.* London: Penguin 1996.

Goldhagen, Daniel Jonah: If You Rebuild It… A New Serbia. In: *The New Republic* 220,20 (17.05.1999), p. 16.

Gow, James: *Triumph of the Lack of Will. International Diplomacy and the Yugoslav War.* London: Hurst 1997.

Grundmann, Reiner / Dennis Smith / Sue Wright: National Elites and Transnational Discourses in the Balkan War: A Comparison between the French, German and British Establishment Press. In: *European Journal of Communication* 15,3 (2000), pp. 299–320.

Gutman, Roy: *A Witness to Genocide. The First Inside Account of the Horrors of 'Ethnic Cleansing' in Bosnia.* Shaftesbury: Element 1993.

Hahn, Hans-Joachim: *Repräsentationen des Holocaust. Zur westdeutschen Erinnerungskultur seit 1979.* Heidelberg: Winter 2005.

Hedges, Chris: In Yugoslavia, the Consequences of Not Reporting the Truth. In: *Nieman Reports,* Summer 1999, pp. 15–16.

Herf, Jeffrey: Remembering the Holocaust in Germany. In: Dan Michman (ed.): *Remembering the Holocaust in Germany, 1945–2000.* New York: Peter Lang 2002, pp. 9–30.

Herman, Edward / David Peterson: CNN: Selling NATO's War Globally. In: Philip Hammond / Edward Herman (eds): *Degraded Capability: The Media and the Kosovo Crisis.* London: Pluto 2000, pp. 111–122.

Hils, Jochen: *Manipuliertes Volk? Mediendemokratie und die militärische Interventionspolitik der USA am Beispiel der Kosovokriege.* Baden-Baden: Nomos 2007.

Hofmann, Günter: Wie Deutschland in den Krieg geriet. In: *Die Zeit,* 12.05.1999. http://www.zeit.de/1999/20/199920.krieg_.xml, p. 2 (accessed 30.08.2014).

Holbrooke, Richard: *To End a War.* New York: Modern Library 1998.

Honig, Jan Willem: Strategy and Genocide: Srebrenica as an Analytical Challenge. In: *Southeast European and Black Sea Studies* 7,3 (2007), pp. 399–416.

Honig, Jan Willem / Nobert Both: *Srebrenica: Record of a War Crime.* London: Penguin 1996.

Hyde-Price, Adrian: Germany and the Kosovo War: Still a Civilian Power? In: Douglas Webber (ed.): *New Europe, New Germany, Old Foreign Policy? German Foreign Policy since Unification.* London: Routledge 2001, pp. 19–34.

ICTY: The Prosecutor of the Tribunal against Radovan Karadžić [and] Ratko Mladić: Indictment, Case No. IT-95-18-I. http://www.icty.org/x/cases/karadzic/ind/en/kar-ii951116e.pdf (accessed 30.08.2014).

Ignatieff, Michael: *Virtual War. Kosovo and Beyond.* London: Picador 2000.

Independent International Commission on Kosovo: *The Kosovo Report: Conflict, International Response, Lessons Learned.* Oxford: Oxford University Press 2000.

Jackson, Jennifer Kimberly / Margit Viola Wunsch: Introduction: The Armenian and Bosnian Genocides in Comparative Perspective. In: *Studies in Ethnicity and Nationalism* 14,3 (2014), pp. 481–483.

Jacobsen, Carl: War Crimes in the Balkans: Media Manipulation, Historical Amnesia and Subjective Morality. In: *Coexistence* 4 (1993), pp. 313–325.

Janjetović, Zoran: *Between Hitler and Tito. Disappearance of the Ethnic Germans from the Vojvodina.* Belgrade: Self-published 2000.

Janning, Josef: A German Europe – a European Germany? On the Debate over Germany's Foreign Policy. In: *International Affairs* 72,1 (1996), pp. 33–41.

Jones, Adam: *Genocide. A Comprehensive Introduction.* London: Routledge 2011.

Judah, Tim: *Kosovo. War and Revenge.* New Haven: Yale University Press 2002.

—: *The Serbs. History, Myth and the Destruction of Yugoslavia.* New Haven: Yale University Press 1997.

—: Growing Pains of the Kosovo Liberation Army. In: Michael Waller / Kyril Drezov / Bülent Gökay (eds): *Kosovo. The Politics of Delusion.* New York: Frank Cass 2001, pp. 20–29.

Jungclaussen, John: Liberal bis in die letzte Zeile. In: *Die Zeit*, 26.02.2004. http://www.zeit.de/2004/10/Economist (accessed 28.11.2014).

Junge Freiheit: Nachrufe auf Carl Gustaf Ströhm. In: *Junge Freiheit,* 21.05.2004. http://www.jf-archiv.de/archiv04/224yy29.htm (accessed 28.11.2014).

Kaiser, Karl / Joachim Krause: Deutsche Politik gegenüber dem Balkan. In: Iid. (eds): *Deutschlands neue Außenpolitik*, vol. 3: Interessen und Strategien. Oldenburg: Forschungsinstitut der Deutschen Gesellschaft für Auswärtige Politik 1996, pp. 175–188.

Katzenstein, Peter J. (ed.): *Tamed Power. Germany in Europe.* Ithaca: Cornell University Press 1997.

Kaplan, Robert: *Balkan Ghosts. A Journey through History.* New York: Picador 2005.

Knightley, Phillip: *The First Casualty. The War Correspondent as Hero and Myth-Maker from the Crimea to Kosovo.* Baltimore: Johns Hopkins University Press 2002.

Kölsch, Julia: Politik und Gedächtnis: Die Gegenwart der NS-Vergangenheit als politisches Sinnstiftungspotenzial. In: Wolfgang Bergem (ed.): *Die NS-Diktatur im deutschen Erinnerungsdiskurs.* Opladen: VS Verlag für Sozialwissenschaften 2003, pp. 137–150.

Kundnani, Hans: *Utopia or Auschwitz. Germany's Generation and the Holocaust.* London: Hurst 2009.

—: Perpetrators and Victims: Germany's 1968 Generation and Collective Memory. In: *German Life and Letters* 64,2 (2011), pp. 65–84.

LeBor, Adam: *Milošević. A Biography.* London: A&C Black 2003.

Lemkin, Raphael: *Axis Rule in Occupied Europe.* Clark: The Lawbook Exchange 2005.

Lepsius, Rainer: Das Erbe des Nationalsozialismus und die politische Kultur der Nachfolgestaaten des 'Großdeutschen Reiches'. In: Max Haller / Hans-Jürgen Hoffmann-Nowottny / Wolfgang Zapf (eds): *Kultur und Gesellschaft: Verhandlungen des 24. deutschen Soziologentages, des 11. österreichischen Soziologentags und des 8. Kongresses der schweizerischen Gesellschaft für Soziologie in Zürich 1988*. Frankfurt am Main: Campus 1989.

Leydesdorff, Selma: Stories from No Land: The Women of Srebrenica Speak out. In: *Human Rights Review* 8,3 (April–June 2007), pp. 187–198.

Libal, Michael: *Germany and the Yugoslav Crisis, 1991–1992*. Westport: Praenger 1997.

Little, Allan / Laura Silber: *The Death of Yugoslavia*. London: Penguin 1996.

Lituchy, Barry: Media Deception and the Yugoslav Civil War. In: Ramsey Clark (ed.): *NATO in the Balkans: Voices of Opposition*. New York: International Action Center 1998.

Loquai, Heinz: *Der Kosovo-Konflikt*. Baden-Baden: Nomos 2000.

Macdonald, David Bruce: *Balkan Holocausts? Serbian and Croatian Victim-Centred Propaganda and the War in Yugoslavia*. Manchester: Manchester University Press 2002.

Maier, Charles: *The Unmasterable Past. History, Holocaust and German National Identity*. Cambridge, Mass: Harvard University Press 1997.

Malcolm, Noel: *Bosnia: A Short History*. London: Macmillan 1994.

— : *Kosovo: A Short History*. London: Harper Perenniel 1998.

Maull, Hanns (ed.): *Germany's Uncertain Power: Foreign Policy of the Berlin Republic*. Houndmills: Palgrave 2006.

— : Germany in the Yugoslav Crisis. In: *Survival* 37,4, (1995/96), pp. 99–130.

— : Germany and the Use of Force. Still a 'Civilian Power'? In: *Survival* 42,2 (2000), pp. 56–80.

— : German Foreign Policy, Post-Kosovo: Still a 'Civilian Power?' In: *German Politics* 9,2 (2007), pp. 1–24.

Mazower, Mark: *The Balkans*. London: Modern Library 2000.

McMahon, Patrice / Jon Western: The Death of Dayton. In: *Foreign Affairs* 88,5 (2009), pp. 69–83.

Mertus, Julie: *Kosovo. How Myths and Truths Started a War*. Berkeley: University of California Press 1999.

Michman, Dan: *Remembering the Holocaust in Germany, 1945–2000. German Strategies and Jewish Responses*. New York: Peter Lang 2002.

Milošević's 1989 Speech in Gazimestan, the Field of Black Birds (or Kosovo Polje). http://www.hirhome.com/yugo/bbc_milosevic.htm (accessed 25.08.2014).

Moran, Michael: Terrorist Groups and Political Legitimacy. In: *Council on Foreign Relations*, 16.03.2006. http://www.cfr.org/terrorism/terrorist-groups-political-legitimacy/p10159#p4 (accessed 28.11.2014).

Mulaj, Klejda: Resisting an Oppressive Regime: The Case of the Kosovo Liberation Army. In: *Studies in Conflict and Terrorism* 31,12 (2008), pp. 1103–1119.

Naimark, Norman: Ethnic Cleansing. In: *Online Encyclopedia of Mass Violence*. http://www.massviolence.org/IMG/article_PDF/Ethnic-Cleansing.pdf (accessed 28.11.2014).

Naimark, Norman / Holly Case (eds): *Yugoslavia and Its Historians. Understanding the Balkan Wars of the 1990s*. Stanford: Stanford University Press 2003.

NATO: Peace Support Operations in Bosnia and Herzegovina. http://www.nato.int/cps/en/natolive/topics_52122.htm (accessed 28.11.2014).

Neu, Alexander: *Die Jugoslawien-Kriegsberichterstattung der Times und der Frankfurter Allgemeinen Zeitung*. Baden-Baden: Nomos 2004.

Obradovic-Wochnik, Jelena: Knowledge, Acknowledgement and Denial in Serbia's Responses to the Srebrenica Massacre. In: *Journal of Contemporary European Studies* 17,1 (2009), pp. 61–74.

OSCE: Kosovo/Kosova: As Seen, As Told: An Analysis of the Human Rights Findings of the OSCE Kosovo Verification Mission October 1998 to June 1999. http://www.osce.org/odihr/17774 (accessed 27.08.2014).

Petritsch, Wolfgang / Robert Pichler: *Kosovo-Kosova. Der lange Weg zum Frieden*. Klagenfurt: Wieser 2004.

Pettifer, James: The Kosovo Liberation Army: The Myth of Origin. In: Michael Waller / Kyril Drezov / Bülent Gökay (eds): *The Politics of Delusion*. New York: Frank Cass 2001, pp. 25–29.

Philippi, Nina: *Bundeswehr-Auslandseinsätze als außen- und sicherheitspolitisches Problem des geeinten Deutschlands*. Frankfurt am Main: Peter Lang 1997.

Pohl, Scott / Naveed Hussain: Jolie Highlights the Continuing Suffering of the Displaced in Bosnia. In: *UNHCR*, 06.04.2010. http://www.unhcr.org/4bbb422512.html (accessed 28.11.2014).

Prantl, Heribert: Ikone mit löchrigem Mantel. In: *Süddeutsche Zeitung*, 26.09.2012. http://www.sueddeutsche.de/politik/altkanzler-helmut-kohl-ikone-mit-loechrigem-mantel-1.1478853 (accessed 28.11.2014).

Probst, Lothar: Der Holocaust – eine neue Zivilreligion für Europa? In: Wolfgang Bergem (ed.): *Die NS-Diktatur im deutschen Erinnerungsdiskurs*. Opladen: VS Verlag für Sozialwissenschaften 2003, pp. 227–238.

Rainio, J. / K. Lalu / A. Pentillä: Independent Forensic Autopsies in an Armed Conflict: Investigation of the Victims from Racak, Kosovo. In: *Forensic Science International* 116,3 (2001), pp. 171–185.

Rathfelder, Erich: *Sarajevo und danach. Sechs Jahre Reporter im ehemaligen Jugoslawien*. Munich: C. H. Beck 1998.

—: *Kosovo*. Berlin: Suhrkamp 2010.

Reißmüller, Johan Georg: *Der Krieg vor unserer Haustür*. Stuttgart: DVA 1992.

Ristelhüber, Rene: *A History of the Balkan Peoples*. Boston: Twayne 1971.

Rohde, David: *Endgame: The Betrayal and Fall of Srebrenica, Europe's Worst Massacre since World War II*. Boulder: Westview 1998.

Rudolf, Peter: Germany and the Kosovo Conflict. In: Pierre Martin / Mark R. Brawley (eds): *Alliance Politics, Kosovo, and NATO's War*. New York: Palgrave Macmillan 2000, pp. 134–136.

Ruigrok, Nel / Jan A. de Ridder / Otto Scholten: News Coverage of the Bosnian War in Dutch Newspapers: Impact and Implication. In: Philip Seib (ed.): *Media and Conflict in the Twenty-First Century*. New York: Palgrave Macmillan 2005, pp. 157–184.

Rusinow, Dennison: *Yugoslavia. Oblique Insights and Observations*. Pittsburgh: University of Pittsburgh Press 2008.

Savarese, Rossella: 'Infosuasion' in European Newspapers: A Case Study on the War in Kosovo. In: *European Journal of Communication* 15,3 (2000), pp. 363–381.

Scharping, Rudolf: *Wir dürfen nicht wegsehen. Der Kosovo-Krieg und Europa*. Munich: Ullstein 2001.

Scheufele, Dietram: Framing as a Theory of Media Effects. In: *Journal of Communication* 49,1 (1999), pp. 102–122.

Schirrmacher, Frank: *Die Walser-Bubis-Debatte: eine Dokumentation.* Frankfurt am Main: Suhrkamp 1999.

Schöllgen, Gregor: *Die Außenpolitik der Bundesrepublik Deutschland: Von den Anfängen bis zur Gegenwart.* Munich: C. H. Beck 2004.

Schröder, Gerhard: Erklärung von Bundeskanzler Gerhard Schröder zur Lage im Kosovo, 24.03.1999. http://www.glasnost.de/kosovo/990324schroeder.html (accessed 02.09.2014).

Schwab-Trapp, Michael: *Kriegsdiskurse. Die politische Kultur des Krieges im Wandel 1991–1999.* Opladen: VS Verlag für Sozialwissenschaften 2002.

—: Der Nationalsozialismus im öffentlichen Diskurs über militärische Gewalt: Überlegungen zum Bedeutungswandel der deutschen Vergangenheit. In: Wolfgang Bergem (ed.): *Die NS-Diktatur im deutschen Erinnerungsdiskurs.* Opladen: VS Verlag für Sozialwissenschaften 2003, pp. 171–185.

Sebak, Nened: The KLA – Terrorists or Freedom Fighters? In: *BBC*, 28.06.1998. http://news.bbc.co.uk/2/hi/europe/121818.stm (accessed 28.11.2014).

Sells, Michael: *The Bridge Betrayed.* Berkeley: University of California Press 1996.

Sells, Michael: The Construction of Islam in Serbian Religious Mythology and Its Consequences. In: Maya Shatzmiller (ed.): *Islam and Bosnia: Conflict Resolution and Foreign Policy in Multi-Ethnic States.* Montreal: McGill-Queen's University Press 2002, pp. 56–85.

Shatzmiller, Maya: Introduction. In: Ead. (ed.): *Islam and Bosnia: Conflict Resolution and Foreign Policy in Multi-Ethnic States.* Montreal: McGill-Queen's University Press 2002, pp. xi–xxiv.

Siedschlag, Alexander: *Die aktive Beteiligung Deutschlands an militärischen Aktionen zur Verwirklichung kollektiver Sicherheit.* Frankfurt am Main: Peter Lang 1995.

Simms, Brendan: *Unfinest Hour. Britain and the Destruction of Bosnia.* London: Penguin 2002.

—: From the Kohl to the Fischer Doctrine. In: *German History* 21,3 (2003), pp. 393–414.

—: Road to Libya Runs through Srebrenica. In: *The Independent*, 29.05.2011. http://www.independent.co.uk/opinion/commentators/brendan-simms-road-to-libya-runs-through-srebrenica-2290326.html (accessed 28.11.2014).

Singleton, Fred: *A Short History of the Yugoslav Peoples.* Cambridge: Cambridge University Press 1985.

Spohr, Kristina: German Unification: Between Official History, Academic Scholarship, and Political Memoirs. In: *The Historical Journal* 43,3 (2000), pp. 869–888.

Stankovic, Slobodan: *Titos Erbe.* Munich: R. Oldenbourg 1981.

Suljagic, Emir / Reuf Bajrovic: Keine Schutzzone ohne Schutz. In: *Die Zeit*, 02.03.2012. http://www.zeit.de/2012/10/P-oped-Suljagic (accessed 28.11.2014).

Tabeau, Ewa / Jakub Bijak: War-related Deaths in the 1992–1995 Armed Conflicts in Bosnia and Herzegovina. A Critique of Previous Estimates and Recent Results. In: *European Journal of Population* 21,2 (2005), pp. 187–215.

Toal, Gerard / Carl T. Dahlman: *Bosnia Remade. Ethnic Cleansing and Its Reversal.* Oxford: Oxford University Press 2011.

Traynor, Ian: Yugoslav Army 'Guilty of Atrocity Campaign'. In: *The Guardian*, 17.01.1992.

United Nations: Convention on the Prevention and Punishment of the Crime of Genocide. Adopted by the General Assembly of the United Nations on 9 December 1948. http://treaties.un.org/doc/Publication/UNTS/Volume%2078/volume-78-I-1021-English.pdf (accessed 25.08.2014).

—: The Fall of Srebrenica. In: *Report of the Secretary-General Pursuant to General Assembly Resolution 53/35*, vol. A/54/549. New York: United Nations General Assembly, 1999.

—: The Policy of Ethnic cleansing, 28.12.1994. http://ess.uwe.ac.uk/comexpert/ANX/IV.htm (accessed 25.09.2012).

United Nations Security Council: Security Council Authorizes Secretary-General to Use 'All Resources Available' to Restore Srebrenica's Status as Safe Area. Press Release Security Council, SC/6066, 12.07.1995.

—: Security Council Demands Bosnian Serbs Allow Humanitarian Agencies Access to Civilians in Srebrenica. Press Release Security Council, SC/6067, 14.07.1995.

—: At London Meeting, Secretary General Stresses Need for UNPROFOR to Remain in Bosnia with Clearer Mandate. Press Release Secretary General, SG/SM/5689, 21.07.1995.

—: Security Council Demands Access to Detainees in Areas under Serb Control in Bosnia. Press Release Security Council, SC/6082, 10.08.1995.

Vickers, Miranda: *Between Serb and Albanian. A History of Kosovo.* London: Hurst 1998.

Volmer, Ludger: *Die Grünen und die Außenpolitik – ein schwieriges Verhältnis. Eine Ideen- Programm- und Ereignisgeschichte grüner Außenpolitik.* Münster: Westfälisches Dampfboot 1998.

Wahl zum 13. Deutschen Bundestag am 16. Oktober 1994. http://www.bundeswahlleiter.de/de/bundestagswahlen/fruehere_bundestagswahlen/btw1994.html (accessed 28.11.2014).

Walser, Martin: Erfahrungen beim Verfassen einer Sonntagsrede. http://www.friedenspreis-des-deutschen-buchhandels.de/sixcms/media.php/1290/1998_walser.pdf (accessed 28.11.2014).

Watson, Fiona / Tom Dodd: The Dayton Agreement: Progress in Implementation. In: *International Affairs and Defence Section, House of Commons Library.* London, Resarch Paper 96/80 (09.07.1996).

Webber, Mark: The Kosovo War: A Recapitulation. In: *International Affairs* 85,3 (2009), pp. 447–450.

Weine, Stevan: *When History Is a Nightmare. Lives and Memories of Ethnic Cleansing in Bosnia-Herzegovina.* New Brunswick: Rutgers University Press 1999.

Weller, Marc: The International Response to the Dissolution of the Socialist Federal Republic of Yugoslavia. In: *The American Journal of International Law* 86,3 (1992), pp. 569–607.

Weller, Marc / Stefan Wolff: Bosnia and Herzegovina Ten Years after Dayton: Lessons for Internationalized State Building. In: *Ethnopolitics* 5,1 (2006), pp. 1–13.

Wolfgram, Mark: Democracy and Propaganda: NATO's War in Kosovo. In: *European Journal of Communication* 23,153 (2008), pp. 153–171.

World Press Photo Website. http://www.archive.worldpressphoto.org/search/layout/result/indeling/detailwpp/form/wpp/q/ishoofdafbeelding/true/trefwoord/year/1998 (accessed 28.11.2014).

Zifonun, Darius: *Gedenken und Identität. Der deutsche Erinnerungsdiskurs.* Frankfurt am Main: Campus 2004.

Zveržhanovski, Ivan: Watching War Crimes: The Srebrenica Video and the Serbian Attitudes to the 1995 Srebrenica Massacre. In: *Southeast European and Black Sea Studies* 7,3 (2007), pp. 417–430.